Foreword

People call me crazy all the time. They think hiking, biking, or paddling as much as I have is crazy. Even with as much long-distance hiking and traveling as I've done, I've never thought about hiking a Calendar Year Triple Crown. That is crazy. Hiking a Calendar Year Triple Crown while never thru-hiking a long-distance trail isn't just crazy, it's certifiably insane.

Brandon's journey is not only impressive, but it is hard for most people to even comprehend. Even for a well-traveled thru-hiker, it is difficult to imagine the level of commitment and ambition that a trip of over 8,000 miles requires. In all my many years of hiking, I have never hiked that many miles in a single year, nor even considered doing so.

Brandon's journey is inspiring, beautiful, and can be either hilarious or harrowing depending on the day. His story is unbelievable. His writing is great. And his book is hard to put down.

This book maintains a wonderful balance of describing the hardships of the trail, painting a vivid picture of the beautiful scenery that is always around, and expressing the complex internal dialogue of a person spending that many days alone while chasing an all-encompassing goal.

Whether someone is a seasoned thru-hiker or has never stepped foot on a hiking trail, this book will inspire you, make you laugh, make you think, make you want to get outside, and above all else, make you realize that you are capable of so much more than you think.

— Bill Nedderman a.k.a. "One Gallon" who was the first person to complete the iconic Triple Crown trails four times each in a lifetime, has camped outside over 8,000 nights of his life while traveling by human power, has thru-hiked 54,000 miles, bicycle toured 88,000 miles, and paddled 45,000 miles, and is believed by many to have covered the most human-powered miles on Earth

THIS IS GONNA HURT

Written By:

Brandon Weis

a.k.a. "Horsepower"

Printed by:
Brandon Weis

Printed in the United States of America
First Printing Edition, 2023
ISBN: 9798866802500

Website: https://naturalhorsepower.wixsite.com/naturalhorsepower

Instagram: @naturalhorsepower

Preface

Thru-hiking is simply the activity of a person hiking a long-distance trail from end to end. While there are numerous long-distance trails in America, the iconic Triple Crown is comprised of the Appalachian Trail, Pacific Crest Trail, and Continental Divide Trail. The Appalachian Trail is ~2,193 miles and goes from Georgia to Maine. The Pacific Crest Trail is ~2,653 miles and stretches from Mexico to Canada through California, Oregon, and Washington. The Continental Divide Trail is ~2,600–3,100 miles, depending on route choices, and runs from Mexico to Canada along the divide of the country in the Rockies. It normally takes thru-hikers 5–6 months to complete one of these trails during the ideal hiking season.

It is a monumental accomplishment for someone to complete one of these 2,000+ mile hikes. To do all three in a lifetime is an achievement not shared by many. Those that do, earn the title of "Triple Crowners," and are considered to be some of the most experienced long-distance hikers in the world. To do all three of the Triple Crown trails in a calendar year was never even thought of as possible until "Flyin" Brian Robinson impressively became the first person to complete all three within the year of 2001.

Between 2001 and when I left in 2021, nine others completed the endeavor, bringing the total to ten finishers. Many people would consider the "Calendar Year Triple Crown" to be the pinnacle of thru-hiking due to the sheer distance, tight timeline, and weather considerations necessary to be successful across America's most iconic trails through the mountains.

My original plan was to hike one of the trails each summer after graduating college, starting in 2020 with the Pacific Crest Trail. I ended up canceling that hike due to the coronavirus pandemic, but I still wanted to fit all three hikes into the timeline I had set aside for it, so I could then begin law school after three summers as I had planned.

I began to work on my plan. *Maybe I could hike the Pacific Crest Trail and Continental Divide Trail in one year and then do the Appalachian Trail early the next year to finish early and still go back to school in August.*

That was my new plan … for about an hour. *Well, if I'm already doing two of them in a year, why not throw another one in there? I wonder if that's been done before.* In the back of my mind, I felt like I had heard about it. I did some research and found out that ten people had done it. *So it wasn't impossible.*

That was all I needed to know.

This book is dedicated to all those who walked before me.

Table of Contents

Phase I:

Appalachian Trail

Springer Mountain, GA to Clarendon Gorge, VT

January 13th-March 19th

Winter at Springer

What the hell did I get myself into? I thought to myself as my parents pulled away from the parking lot of Springer Mountain in Georgia. I was less than 50 yards into the Appalachian Trail when I began to feel my eyes water. Alone in the wilderness, I held back the tears. I would not show weakness — even to just myself.

My mind had plenty of negative thoughts to focus on. *There is no way I can hike 8,000 miles in a year. Only ten people have ever done this, and they were much more experienced than me. I have never even thru-hiked a long trail before. How do I know if my body will hold up? My plan for success is to average 24 miles per day on the Appalachian Trail and 30 miles per day on the Pacific Crest and Continental Divide Trails, but those are just estimates. My longest backpacking trip previously was averaging 18 miles per day for two weeks, and I was exhausted after it.*

I haven't backpacked in winter conditions before and would now be doing the whole Appalachian Trail in winter. This is crazy. Every logical indicator is pointing towards me failing. Why did I think this was a good idea?

I told everyone I knew I was going to do this, and now I'm going to have to tell them I failed.

These thoughts screamed over my every conscious thought for hours, like a horde of locusts constantly buzzing with reaffirming negativity as I passed barren tree after barren tree, all seeming to scowl at me, telling me to go home. There was no one else around, and worse, no sound — no wind, no rushing water, no creaking trees. The silence was deafening. It had snowed a few days prior, so the ground was still damp, and none of the fallen leaves covering the dead landscape could offer so much as a crinkle to break the silent echoes of my overwhelming thoughts.

The only sound in the lonesome woods was the haunting repetitiveness of my footsteps. With no other sounds in the woods and nothing else to focus on, these footsteps became not a sign of progress, but yet another testimony of my insecurity.

I have to hear this sound of my feet hitting the ground over 16 million more times if I miraculously somehow finish this "impossible" endeavor.

The weather was as conducive as it could be on the Appalachian Trail: sunny with a slight breeze, warm for winter, and above all else, no rain or snow was falling However, the rainclouds of my ambition seemed to hover overhead all day.

The melting pot of insecurity, fear, and anxious self-doubt continued boiling the remainder of the first day until I got to camp. It was around 20 degrees when I arrived at the shelter for the night. My singular focus was to get everything taken care of as quickly as possible, so I could get inside my warm sleeping bag.

Once comfortable, I had a little powwow with myself. I accepted that, yes — this was an insane goal. I had known that going into it. But like anything else, as long as I continued to put in the work, I could get there. Consistency was the key to success in most things in life, but especially in this endeavor. All I had to do was wake up, walk, see beautiful places, eat, sleep, and repeat. It was a simple life.

I woke up the next morning with a newfound sense of peace with what I was doing. My mind went from racing with negative thoughts to focusing on one thing only: my next food resupply. Starting today, my only concern was the next footstep in front of me.

Although I felt better mentally, physically was a different story. The wind was biting in the morning with already cold temperatures. Normally, the dense forest of the Appalachian Trail provided adequate protection from the wind, but not this morning. I glimpsed a beautiful sunrise through a break in the trees before seeking refuge from the cold in a pit toilet at a road crossing, where I could warm my hands from the chilling breeze outside.

Despite countless hours of research and preparation for the trip, it wasn't until shortly before I began the trip that I realized I needed some heavy-duty winter mittens for the temperatures in which I would be living. Every gear store I went to was sold out of what I was looking for, so I had to order them online and wouldn't have them for a couple of weeks. I was frustrated at my unpreparedness because it could've easily been avoided, but especially after this morning on trail, I was anxiously counting down the days until I got my winter mittens.

It was my first basic hiking lesson learned the hard way.

It's easier to send gear home if you bring too much rather than to get more gear when you're already out hiking, especially in the frigid brutality of winter backpacking.

Feeling more comfortable after the sun elevated the temperature a few degrees, I summited Blood Mountain on a beautiful day. There were dozens of day hikers out because of the rare sunny weather. Many of them were surprised to see a thru-hiker out already on January 14th when most begin their journey in March or April.

As I explained what I was doing, I could see their wheels turning, until it finally clicked. I could see the moment they realized how ridiculous my goal was. They would react in one of two ways: They would be genuinely excited for me, or they would look at me side-eyed and wonder what my deal was. The moment of realization was amusing. I never grew tired of it.

After the descent from the summit, I arrived at Mountain Crossings, a store and hostel around Mile 30, and my first resupply stop. Resupply is a general term used by hikers for a place to get food or anything else they would need. Mountain Crossings is a landmark on the Appalachian Trail because it's the first resupply for most hikers, and the tree out front is ominously littered with hanging footwear. Allegedly, 25% of thru-hikers on the AT (Appalachian Trail) quit at that very spot. Many that do, toss their boots or shoes in the tree as an homage to the trail.

Fortunately, the thought of quitting on Mile 30 of an 8,000-mile trip seemed like a bad joke, so I went inside.

The worker was friendly and gave me basic thru-hiking advice while I checked out with my food. He was mainly telling me to drink plenty of water. Little did he know that on the AT in winter, I would drink less than two liters most days, and even less than one liter a decent number of days. I hardly sweated; the water was too cold to want to drink, and it was so cold I never wanted to stop to get water. Funnily enough, not drinking enough water was never a problem.

After my resupply, I moved considerably slower. I was surprised at how fast I was moving before that, but soon realized it was because I was hardly carrying any food previously. After adding nearly four days' worth of food at the store, my pack gained considerable weight, but I still made it to the next shelter around 7:30 p.m. It was my first full day on trail and I covered 27 miles. I felt pretty good about myself, but knew that with the weather and terrain, I wouldn't be able to keep that pace every day.

I had another pleasantly dry night sleeping inside a shelter. The AT is unlike most other trails in that it has "shelters" every 5–15 miles typically.

These weren't exactly five-star hotels, but they were three walls and a roof in the middle of the woods. They had one open side, so they weren't wind-protected like a cabin, but they would keep me out of the rain or snow for the night. Snow covered most of the ground along the whole trail, so I always tried to end my day at a shelter to avoid camping on snow and having to pitch my tent. Being able to just lay my sleeping bag out and sleep inside a shelter was much simpler and more time-efficient than having to find a campsite and set up a tent.

On the morning of Day Three, I started in a haze of mist and fog. However, I would happily take it since it was supposed to rain all day. Many days would feel just like this on the Appalachian Trail. Although it wasn't raining, it still felt damp and dreary.

Even in the somber conditions, the day passed by quickly, and I had covered 23 miles. Upon my arrival at a shelter, I was annoyingly greeted by a gang of mice. This was the beginning of a long and hateful relationship between me and the little, furry, wretched creatures that seemed as inescapable as achy bones to an old man.

At this point, I was carrying a stove and cooking at the end of each day. While doing so at this shelter, a family of mice fearlessly ran around my stove, or up my leg to try to jump into the pot, because of the smell emanating from my food. It was as if they were on kamikaze missions to boil themselves alive. I got frustrated by constantly brushing them away, only to have them scurry back, and wondered how many shelters would be like this along the way.

The next morning was cold and windy with fresh snow falling. I put on my microspikes which were supposed to help with traction. With it being my first time hiking in winter, I'd never used them before. I quickly learned of their uselessness in fresh, wet snow. All they did was clump mud, leaves, and snow to the bottom of my shoes. I crossed my first state line into North Carolina in the early afternoon with massive snowflakes falling and chuckled internally on how just a few years earlier I would've thought it was crazy to be walking in snow like this in these southern coastal states. I got to a shelter around 5 p.m. and took off my shoes.

Yikes! My feet were soaking wet all day from walking in snow, and my skin looked sickening. There were white calluses and cracks already forming, skin flaking off, and they were so pruned that it looked like I had been in a bathtub for hours. After seeing that, my day ended there.

My paramount concern for the whole trip was the health of my feet. I'd had numerous stress fractures in the past, and I'd done enough research to know that trench foot and other grave ailments were real dangers out here with as much hiking in wet conditions as I would be doing. With needing to walk 30 miles every day, the well-being of my feet was as important to me as the health of Steph Curry's right hand was to him. This was my version of load management to be able to cover more ground in the long run.

One of my principles for the year-long hike was to not let my choices today ruin tomorrow. This was a slight modification of a former principle I had regarding drinking too much alcohol on Friday nights before a noon Ohio State football game.

My feet were slightly improved the next morning after drying out, but my shoes were frozen rock solid. With no way to force them on my feet, I sat on them for ten minutes. This warmed them just enough to where, if I undid all the stiff frozen laces, I could shove them on my feet. At first, it felt like I had cement blocks for shoes, but with my feet inside, they quickly warmed up. This shoe-sitting routine became another daily theme of hiking the AT in winter, along with cohabitating with starving mice.

I got to the summit of Albert Mountain where I was greeted by my first fire tower, and better yet, two other young hikers taking a break. I chatted with them for a bit and learned that they were in college and were thinking about taking off their next spring semester and hiking the AT. They asked for advice, but other than saying "Go for it," I didn't feel like I could offer much since I was only on Day Five. People who give advice are often just reassuring their own self-doubts, so I usually try to avoid giving advice unless I know I'm an expert on the matter.

They said goodbye, and I climbed the fire tower. I couldn't access the top enclosure since it was locked, so I enjoyed the view from the top of the stairs before continuing on. While doing so, I was actually pleased it snowed. There was an interesting contrast in the landscape based on elevation. The lowlands were still a brown mass of dead trees, but the higher mountains were covered in all white with trees coated in snow and ice.

After descending from the summit, I turned a corner and saw an open view of the mountains ahead. They were covered in dead trees with little snow, so they were a reddish-brown, and looked a little hazy off in the distance. It looked like a shot from an old western. Seeing this landscape, and taking it in, timed out perfectly with "My Way" by Frank Sinatra beginning to play in my headphones.

Sometimes it takes this perfect synchronization of visual and audio stimuli to wake us up to the true beauty that is always around us. It felt like a special cinematic moment. But the truth is we all experience what could be beautiful cinematic moments constantly. We just usually glide through life without noticing them. A person tiredly slumped in a seat on a city bus, with their head leaning against the window as rain is cascading down the barrier between them and the outside world, or somebody mindlessly driving a car on an empty country road with unending fields in every direction, might not feel special in the moment. Yet, in movies, these can be some of the most beautiful shots the viewer will see. We live life every day with beauty all around us whether it be mountains, trees, skyscrapers, oceans, fields, cars, animals, rivers, or the community of mankind. Beauty is actually all around. Sometimes we just need a wake-up call to remind us.

When "My Way" came on in unity with the epic view, it was an empowering reminder that I was alive. Even if I felt miserable at times in the wet and wintry conditions, I was still surrounded in constant beauty. I could choose to glide through it without appreciating it, or I could consciously cherish it with all its splendor and all its brutality, not experiencing one without the other.

At the next road crossing, I had to get into Franklin, NC to buy my food resupply. There was one car in the parking lot, so I was not hopeful about easily getting a ride. It was a busy highway, but I had my thumb out for 15 minutes with no luck. Then, the car owners finished their day hike and walked into the parking lot.

I pushed aside normal reluctances to ask for help and walked up to the two young ladies and said, "I'm thru-hiking. Would you possibly be able to bring me into town to get food?"

They were happy to help! On the ride, we bonded over our disdain for wet feet. They were complaining about how bad theirs were on a single day hike and said they didn't know how I would deal with soggy feet every day as I would trudge on northward toward Maine. *I didn't know either.* They dropped me off at Walmart and wished me luck.

On the way into the store, I noticed the road by Walmart had a busy intersection, so it would be tough to get a hitch in that much congestion. It was also getting dark which made hitchhiking nearly impossible. I bought my food resupply and downed two footlongs at Subway while trying to figure out how to get back to the trail.

I pulled out Uber but had no luck. Looking on Guthook — my GPS, mapping, and information app — I learned that a local resident shuttled hikers and gave him a call. After he brought me back to the trail, I hustled the last five miles to try to beat the snow, arriving at the shelter just after it started. There were three other guys and one dog there for the night. I was happy to see them and enjoy a little community, but it did surprise me since I figured I'd be alone basically every night on the AT.

It was fun to be able to talk to people, but even more importantly, they had a fire roaring. I had my feet airing out while having most of my body in my sleeping bag and eating dinner in the shelter. This was one of the few nights where mice were nowhere to be found because the dog was running around the shelter constantly. I feared he was going to tear my heavy-duty, zero-degree, sleeping bag because he was recklessly stepping on it, but it held strong against the fiery spirit of the dog.

It was my best night yet. I was surrounded by great company. Mice weren't a problem. It was warm. And one of the guys put my shoes by the fire to dry out, so I could start the morning with dry feet for once. It was as perfect a night as a solo thru-hiker in winter could get. Life was good.

I even got a sneak peek at the mittens I would soon get. One of the guys had a pair, and after a barrage of questions, his only complaint was that they were too warm. It was music to my ears!

But my ears weren't my only sense registering activity. My nose began to smell something burning. I looked over, and my shoes were on fire! I couldn't move, not from shock, but because I had just put Vermont Bag Balm on my feet. It was originally made to soothe cow udders, but it does wonders for preserving human feet in wet conditions.

With this thick goop covering my bare feet, I calmly asked one of the guys to run over to the fire and grab my shoes. My newfound friends felt horrible about it — probably worse than me. But after assessing the damage, I thought it was hilarious. I had prepared for rain, snow, and extreme cold, but fire damage was one danger I had not considered during my preparation for a winter thru-hike. Laughing off bad situations rather than getting upset is one of my better skills, and this proved to be an invaluable trait in the world of thru-hiking.

The next morning, I laced up my shoes, or at least what was left of them. There were a few holes burnt through them, the largest being near my left pinkie toe. The fire also singed two laces on my left shoe, so I couldn't tighten it. As soon as I stepped outside the shelter, I learned there were five fresh inches of snow covering everything. It looked serene, but it wasn't exactly how I wanted to start my first day with holes in my shoes.

Nevertheless, it was a marvelous day. I climbed up to Wayah Bald, Wesser Bald, and then descended the narrow ridge down to Nantahala Outdoor Center. It was a healthy dose of nostalgia; on my three previous section hikes on the AT, these were some of my favorite spots, and they were just as memorable this time.

I trudged through snow above my ankles in the morning, but later in the day, I came across tracks from other hikers, which at least made less snow go directly into my shoes. I soon caught up to the other hikers, and they turned out to be thru-hikers! It was invigorating to see three other crazy idiots out this early in the year. I introduced myself as Horsepower, and we talked for a while. They said they were doing around ten miles a day, so I never expected to see them again And after we separated, I didn't. After I passed them, it was back to trailblazing in deep snow. I considered it my training for the upcoming, daunting Smoky Mountains.

The next day was filled with a combination of stress, excitement, and fear. After getting little sleep due to rambunctious mice running across my sleeping bag all night, I hiked a few miles down to the road to get into Fontana Village, NC, the last stop before heading into the Smoky Mountains. There was no grocery store in town, so I had a package of food sent to the post office to get me through the next stretch.

Before I left to begin the journey, I organized a bunch of food in my parents' basement for them to send to me. Since my mom still couldn't believe my thru-hiking diet, I left detailed instructions so all she had to do was throw a pile of food in a priority mailing box and bring it to the post office. I didn't want her to have to do it often, but it was necessary for towns like this with only a post office and no grocery store.

When I arrived in Fontana Village too early to pick up my food box because the post office hadn't opened yet, I killed time in a heated bathroom. It was paradise. It had heat, running water, and power outlets so I could charge my phone and power bank before the Smokies. I cooked up a ramen bomb (ramen noodles, mashed potatoes, and tuna) which I had hardly been doing. The mice at the shelters were so irritating that I didn't want to cook most nights. I usually just forced down 2,000 calories of peanut butter, spoonful after spoonful, and went to bed.

After getting my food box and permit for Great Smoky Mountains National Park, I walked across the Fontana Dam and began the 3,000-foot climb into the Smokies. My mind alternated between excitement that it was going to be a wild couple of days and fear that shit might hit the fan — either way, I needed to be ready for it.

The Smokies were at a high elevation for the East and frequently got extreme weather, especially this early in the year. Hikers that would start the trail three months later would be worried about the potential spring weather challenges posed by the Smokies. However, this was still the heart of winter in the middle of January. With my schedule for the year, I had no time to worry about that.

The only way was thru. I had to move on; prepare for the worst and pray for the best.

I spent a lot of time each day thinking, reflecting, generating new ideas, or thinking about absolutely nothing. On the climb into the Smokies, I had the realization that I was planning on hiking the Pacific Crest Trail last year, and my goal was to average 18 miles per day. Now I was hiking the Appalachian Trail, where the terrain was more difficult, meaning you naturally move slower, and I was doing over 20 miles almost every day from the start. And it was winter! I was vastly more capable than what I gave myself credit for, and maybe I was ready for this crazy adventure after all.

We are all capable of so much more.

Sleep eluded me my first night in the Smokies because I was under the same roof as the craziest and most daring mouse to date. I kept feeling some rustling on my sleeping bag, but I assumed it was just the wind until I turned on my headlamp and realized it was a mouse. The little bastard had just chewed three holes in my sleeping bag!

To say I was furious would be an understatement. Hell hath no fury like a winter thru-hiker who had a sleeping bag chewed through by a mouse.

There was no food inside my sleeping bag, so my best guess was that the tiny demon was attracted to the Vermont Bag Balm I put on my feet every night to help them recover. I hastily threw some Leukotape over the three holes. It certainly was not the best solution, but it would have to do.

I spent the next few hours half trying to sleep, and half trying to bash the mouse with my shoe whenever it came near. But it was a quick little bugger. I was never able to exact my revenge.

Not well-rested, I left around 10:30 a.m. I waited until the downpour softened to a light rain. I was hoping it would continue to weaken, but it rained the whole day.

This was my worst day yet. I found myself trudging through deep snow, sinking into it up to my shins, or navigating through slushy, ice-cold water that numbed my feet. Frustration overwhelmed me, and I couldn't help but release random bursts of exasperated yelling.

Strangely, part of me found solace in the terrible conditions, believing that the following day could only be better.

While my feet remained wet and numb from walking in icy water all day, my body faced a different predicament. Layered with Under Armour leggings, hiking pants, and rain pants, I realized that I had unnecessarily bundled up. Despite the cold rain, I found myself sweating profusely, creating an entirely new set of challenges. My heightened emotions were further tested when I encountered another mouse in the shelter that night.

However, my main concern shifted to the incessant itching that consumed my lower half. I tried with all my might to resist the temptation, but it felt like my entire lower half was covered by the world's worst mosquito bites. Unable to stop itching, it was impossible to get any sleep.

As predicted, the following day brought relief, if only because it couldn't be worse than the previous one. Waking up to a bone-chilling temperature of ten degrees below zero, I waited for the sun to emerge before venturing out of my warm sleeping bag. I layered-up my upper body with a synthetic base layer, merino wool midlayer, synthetic jacket, and even a fleece which I only used a handful of times. I had learned my lesson with too many lower body layers and wore only my Under Armour leggings and shorts. The itching sensation subsided once I began hiking.

The air was cold, but the views were crisp. Not a trace of haze tainted the sky. Perched above 6,000 feet, I observed puffy clouds rolling over the valleys below. Embracing the sun on my face and the undercast beneath me, I trekked a few miles to reach Clingman's Dome, the highest point on the AT, standing at 6,643 feet. Capturing a few quick pictures, I hurriedly moved on, as the frigid temperature made it unbearable to linger. In winter, beauty often demands a quick consumption.

During my solitary journey, influenced by the forces of nature and solitude, my emotions were heightened. Many songs, memories, or thoughts had a much stronger impact on me while out in the wilderness, and few more so than the song "7 Years" by Lukas Graham. I was listening to it as I was descending from Clingman's Dome, and the song was hitting me in such a way that I felt it in my core. I had only been on the journey for ten days, but I was already feeling a new level of introspection that I would never feel in my normal day-to-day life.

The rawness of my emotions and the vulnerability I felt became a testament to the transformative power of the trail. With a line like, "I only see my goals, I don't believe in failure," the song felt like it was speaking directly to me and to this journey. Then there was a line where he was talking about being an unhappy old man and said, "I hope my children come and visit once or twice a month."

I wept. The only times in my life that I could remember crying were at funerals. With crying being such an irregularity for me, this was strange. I just thought it was so sad that a person would be so discontented with life that the only thing he looked forward to was the possibility of his kids visiting him once a month. How could I be so upset about this when I was on trail? I couldn't help but think how depressing a life like that would be.

It made me thankful to be out there — miserable and cold. It made me appreciate the sub-zero temperatures, the snow, the wet feet, the isolation. While it was extremely challenging and every day was a grind, I loved what I was doing! I loved each new day and the adventure it would bring along with it. I wasn't sure if my tears were sad tears from the song, or tears of joy from realizing how happy I was. It was confusing, but it felt good to feel something so all-encompassing break through my normal reluctance to show tears.

I felt alive.

Shortly after this unexpected emotional exploration, I arrived at Newfound Gap, the sole road crossing on the AT in Smoky Mountains National Park. It was a circus. I hadn't seen a person since I left Fontana Village two days prior, but because this was the main road through the park, there were dozens of people stopping for the view. Since the temperature was a little warmer now, I moved a pair of waterlogged socks from inside my pack to hang on the outside to air out. Out of the corner of my eye, I saw an old man looking at me with disgust. I smiled to myself and continued on.

Heading north from the parking lot, there was a sign that read "Katahdin Maine 1,972 miles." I laughed. Rather than get overwhelmed, like I did on my first day, now I could laugh at the absurdity of 1,972 more miles through the snow and cold, in addition to the 5,000+ miles thereafter.

On the hike to the scenic point of Charlie's Bunion, I came across a group of girls turning around. They said it was too icy and were wondering how I was able to hike in it. I showed them my microspikes, and they joked that I was cheating. All of the day hikers must have followed in their footsteps because when I got to the Bunion, I had it all to myself. In summer months, it would be nearly impossible to be alone somewhere as beautiful and popular as this. The previous time I had been here, there were over 50 people crowded at the viewpoint. I was rewarded with complete solitude at most viewpoints along the AT in the winter.

For the rest of the day, I enjoyed views of the Smoky Mountains through the dead trees along the ridge I was hiking on. Around 5:30 p.m., the sky began to turn a fiery orange during the sunset. It was stunning.

My instincts wanted me to stop and enjoy it, but I knew I couldn't. I knew with my goal for the year, I would not be able to waste time sitting down and enjoying a view for too long. If I took the time to stop moving and properly appreciate every spectacle I saw, I would never cover the miles I needed to. I accepted that sacrifice before I left. My tradeoff was seeing more remarkable places, just for a shorter time. This was the first time on the hike where I felt that tradeoff and had to push on and keep hiking, when all I wanted to do was take a seat and enjoy God's creation. It was also always freezing cold during winter, so I couldn't stop moving for long.

Pulling up to a shelter after dark, I saw another hiker. He was a southbound thru-hiker and said I would see more southbounders in the coming days. I pulled out Guthook before bed and worked on my plan.

I wanted to make it to Hot Springs, NC by Sunday afternoon to watch the NFL playoffs. This was a Friday night, and I was over 50 miles away, so it was not going to be easy. I was hoping to do 34 miles today to put me in a better position, but only ended up doing 26 because my hip slowed me with a ceaseless stabbing pain. Walking in deep snow and ice all day didn't help either.

Eager for football, I was up and hiking before the sun came out the next day. I crested a ridge with an open view of the surrounding mountains just as the sun was creeping over the ridgeline and "Roar" by Katy Perry was playing in my headphones. It felt like a monumental moment in a late 2000s feel-good movie. *It was going to be a good day.*

Moving fast all morning, I tried to get down and out of the Smokies as soon as possible. I wanted to lose elevation and have slightly warmer temperatures, but even more so, I wanted to start hiking in some better conditions. In the Smokies, the trail was either shin-deep snow with no tracks, or a sheet of ice after other people packed down the snow and it froze over. I was excited to get back to some dirt, or at least less snow, and to take off my microspikes for seemingly the first time in days after descending below 3,500 feet.

Needing sustenance, I went to Standing Bear Hostel along the trail and had to look around for a while before I could find anyone to help me. They didn't expect any fool to be thru-hiking this early. I bought a few snacks to get me to Hot Springs the next day. After leaving, there was little to no snow at the lower elevations, and I was loving it!

I went up and over the popular Max Patch after dark and rolled into a shelter around 9:30 p.m. There was a crowd of people sleeping there because it was close to a parking lot and easy to get to. Luckily, when I arrived, one guy woke up and moved over to make room. I was trying to be as quiet as possible to be polite, but it didn't matter. One of the guys in the shelter was groaning and making other noises so loudly that I initially feared he might be dying. He would go from "Ohhhh my gosh, it hurts!" to

"Ahhhh the pain!" Nobody else in the shelter seemed concerned, so I assumed he'd be alright.

Already feeling tired, I rushed to get to bed, knowing it would be a short night. It turned out to be much tougher to fall asleep to a man yelling in anguish rather than a bubbling brook or rustling wind.

Involuntarily, I woke up at 4:58 a.m., two minutes before my alarm, because my body knew I was a man on a mission: a mission for football. I started hiking well before sunrise around 6 a.m.

In the early cold months of the journey, it would take me about an hour to get moving in the morning. I would eat, pack up, and usually go to the bathroom, all while trying to enjoy the last bits of rest and warmth before I began traversing snow-covered mountains. Then, I'd do the same thing the next morning. Later in the trip, it would take 10–30 minutes from wake-up to walking, depending on my motivation level.

Soaring down the trail, I covered the 18 miles to Hot Springs by 1:30 p.m. with a few hours to spare before the NFL games started. I made my way to Laughing Heart Hostel to get a bed for the night and was surprised to find that there were a few other hikers staying there. They were late southbounders nearing the end of their journey.

Immediately upon arriving, I asked to get a shower and to get my laundry started. When I went into the bathroom and disrobed, I was appalled. My butt and legs were covered in quarter-sized hives. Now the insatiable itching made more sense.

In addition to wearing the leggings with two layers on top of them, I realized that in the Smokies I had worn the leggings for a few days straight without changing or even taking them off. I'm no dermatologist, but I assumed that was what led to the hives and itching that kept me up at night. From then on, I vowed to alternate my lower body layers every day.

It was only Day 12, but the shower felt soul-cleansing; more from the hot water than actually getting clean. Out in the frozen wilderness, I would forget what true warmth felt like.

After the shower, I put on a radical set of loaner clothes from the hostel which resembled John Travolta in *Pulp Fiction*. I started my laundry and headed down to the sports bar in town to watch the NFL games with a southbound hiker named Mayo who was also staying at the hostel.

While Mayo wasn't a common trail name, it wasn't the strangest either. I met people named everything from Captain Jackass, to Pocket Guac, to Felony Dan, and everything in between. Trail names are a fun aspect of thru-hiking culture where someone can take on a new name or identity for their trail self. They are likely not the same person they are in normal society, so why not take on a new identity better fitting to this new lifestyle? Most people have their trail names bestowed on them by others, usually from an embarrassing or funny story. I hardly saw any other hikers until I got to Southern California, so thankfully I had earned one before I left, even though I hadn't thru-hiked before. I earned the trail name "Horsepower" on my first backpacking trip in 2018 from continually hauling a 70-pound pack overflowing with a lot of the group's gear. I didn't know a nickname from that trip would evolve to be my new identity while trying to hike 8,000 miles just a few years later.

I spent the next six hours watching football with Mayo while stuffing my face full of greasy bar food and sucking down Dr. Pepper like it was my first sip of water after walking across the Sahara. This was my first time drinking soda pop in ten years, and I dove back in like I was trying to catch up in one day. I don't know how many refills I got over the six hours, but I was charged for multiple soft drinks, so I hit some sort of limit. After maybe seven refills, I started to feel jittery and wasn't sure why, until I later discovered that there was caffeine in Dr. Pepper. I don't drink coffee, energy drinks, or any caffeine, so I wasn't used to it. I even feared I might be having a heart attack as a 23-year-old man.

While we were eating, Mayo mentioned he would be living in Massachusetts after he finished and that I could crash at his house when I passed through. I was thankful and filed that away in the back of my brain. That seemed so far away, and I didn't want to get ahead of myself.

This kind of generosity and hospitality was not uncommon in the thru-hiking world however. When two thru-hikers meet, there is an instant connection. It's like when two kids meet on the playground, have the same pair of shoes, and decide they're instantly friends. This instant bond just has a little more depth. We know the struggles each other has gone through, the indescribable euphoria of living outside, the beauty and simplicity of traveling by foot through the natural landscape, and the strong character that is needed to succeed at this challenging endeavor.

This kindness and respect even extends to people that haven't thru-hiked. People are so amazed that someone can achieve something so seemingly monumental and implausible that they're eager to help in any way they can. I received aid from countless kind souls along the journey. Whether they had thru-hiked, lived near the trail, or only knew about it because of our conversation, people were genuinely happy to help.

We got back to the hostel, and the others were trying to get me to stay one more night since it was supposed to rain the next day, but I held firm that unnecessary rest days were not in the cards for me. After downing several spoonfuls of peanut butter, I headed to bed in my own private bunkhouse since so few people were in the hostel.

Once the post office opened, I picked up protein powder I had sent to myself before leaving home. Trying to force protein powder into a Smart water bottle was a task in itself, so this was a practice I would soon abandon.

It rained all day, and after crossing the French Broad River, the trail was a mess. I should've been miserable with the conditions, but a smile graced my face all day, nonetheless. It didn't matter that visibility was ten feet, or that I was constantly walking in inches of water. All I felt was joy.

After covering the 52 miles to Hot Springs on a timeframe, I finally felt like I belonged. This didn't really make sense, considering there was hardly anyone out there, and I was usually alone. But I now felt confident in my ability to cover big miles when I needed to. Before that, I was hiking at a strong pace, but that was the first time I truly pushed myself, and it made it seem real. The insane goal was now more plausible.

After hiking all day with a stomachache and sudden attacks of diarrhea, I ended the day after struggling to do 20 miles. I wasn't exactly sure what caused these ailments, but I bet the combination of greasy bar food and drinking enough pop to kill a large child after ten years of abstinence were both factors.

The hives on my lower body were itching all day again, so when I got to the shelter, I let my lower half air out. That was a benefit of hiking in winter when nobody else was out — nearly always having shelters to myself. After withstanding the cold on my bare skin for as long as I could, I crawled into my sleeping bag for the night.

In the morning, I changed into shorts after the temperature rose overnight. Letting my legs breath felt liberating. It was my first day with a high of 50 degrees and things looked to be going my way, until I began hiking on the Appalachian River — formerly the Appalachian Trail, which was now under inches of water from continuous rainfall.

The whole day consisted of walking in, or trying to avoid walking in, several inches of water. Every day on the AT, I would come to accept the fact that I would have wet feet, but there was something about flat-out stepping in water that was always unappealing.

While hopping between puddles, I passed some of my favorite views on my previous section hikes: Whiterock Cliffs, Blackstaff Cliffs, and Big Firescape Bald. Even though it wasn't raining, it was so foggy that I couldn't see ten feet in front of me. Passing by beautiful views in bad weather was just one of the things that came with hiking the AT. I went up and over Big Butt Mountain, before capping off the day at 23 miles after surpassing 300 miles on the trail.

Throughout the day, I still had bouts of diarrhea, but the real kicker was that I ran out of toilet paper. Fortunately, there was a plethora of rhododendron leaves around, and I went all natural. I much preferred toilet paper, but at least I ran out of toilet paper in the woods of Appalachia rather than the prickly desert of New Mexico.

I woke up the next morning eager to get moving. There was a winter storm that was supposed to start that evening, so I wanted to be hunkered down inside a shelter before that rolled in. I started the day with a steady climb up to Big Bald. The sky was mostly cloudy, but there were a few "God Rays" shining through, which looked incredible over the mountains. Up near the summit, my nose started to bleed. I attributed it to doing more than ten farmer sneezes every day because my nose was always running in the cold. I wiped most of the blood with a few leaves, told myself, "I ain't got time to bleed," and kept on trucking.

Unrelated to my bloody nose, I was dehydrated, but scarfed down five Fudge Rounds to tide me over for five miles before I could rehydrate. My water intake had been lower than it should've been. I never wanted to drink any before bed because I didn't want to have to leave my sleeping bag during the night. I also learned that I couldn't keep any before I went to bed because it would freeze overnight. I tried putting it in my sleeping bag to keep it warm, but the water was far too cold and uncomfortable to sleep with. While I was moving during the day, I usually didn't want to stop to deal with it in the cold or carry the weight. This led to little water consumption, but most of the time, it was so cold that I didn't need much.

I finished my 21 miles by 3 p.m. I could've done a few more miles to stay at a hostel, but I opted to end earlier since I had just stayed at one. I didn't want to get too accustomed to nicer living or spend the money to do so. Frugality, accompanied with a low standard of living, were necessary attributes I needed to remain loyal to in order to sustain this journey.

I started the next day by breaking trail on a thick layer of fresh snow. Everything looked tranquil, as if the snow was perfectly laid for a movie shoot. I hiked down to Uncle Johnny's, a hostel right on the trail, to resupply. They didn't have much food this time of the year, but it was enough to get me 50 miles to the next town, and I was able to get some toilet paper, pledging to always carry too much rather than too little.

After I left, the serenity of the beautiful snow began to be matched by my annoyance with it. I was constantly battling rhododendron and other plants that were covered in snow and sagging over the trail like roadblocks. I would have to try to beat the snow off of it, so it might shift back away from the trail; or I would have to try to crawl under it; or I would just barge my way through like a bull in a China shop. None of the methods worked effectively. Snow was constantly sliding down the back of my shirt, which never ceased to illicit a shockingly cold sensation.

When I arrived at "Beauty Spot," an aptly named bald summit, it was all worth it. I wasn't even concerned with the surrounding view because the bald was astonishing itself. With the recent snow and freezing temperatures, there was a thick layer of crystalized ice coating the tall grass and surrounding trees. The whole place looked pristine, covered in gleaming white ice, a beautiful reminder of the barbarity of winter.

I had to quickly take in the scene because the wind was howling, and my hands were numb and aching. I continued climbing in elevation after Beauty Spot. The trail was engulfed by large pine trees, which lessened the impact of the wind, but there was more snow up on Unaka Mountain. I went from walking in snow above my ankles to snow above my knees because it was drifting, but I was alright with it. The slower moving was worth its minor frustration to witness the wintry splendor.

When I awoke the next morning in Cherry Gap Shelter, the frigid air slapped my face like the world's most cruel but effective alarm clock. It was cold every morning on the AT in winter, but this one felt extraordinarily cold. I had no cell reception, so I couldn't check the actual temperature.

Regardless, I began trudging through the snow before the sun came out. My hands started to hurt shortly after I left the shelter, but I told myself that they would feel better if I kept moving and warmed up. I made it a half-mile before I couldn't take it anymore. My hands hurt so badly, they felt like they were going to explode. The pain was so overpowering that I became dizzy and nauseous. All I wanted to do was lay down and throw up, but everything was covered in snow.

I rushed back to the shelter as fast as I could, which was not fast. The whole way, I was just trying to ignore the excruciating pain in my hands, while trying to stay upright with the world spinning around me, and also trying to hold down the food in my stomach. The last thing I wanted out there was to waste calories. When I made it back to the shelter, I managed to open my pack with my teeth since my hands had been rendered useless. I somehow got out hand warmers and tried shaking them for a bit to get the heating mechanism started, but I quickly gave up.

The pain was unbearable.

I couldn't think straight. My brain couldn't form a single coherent thought. All it could do was repeatedly shout "PAIN!" — seeming to only get louder and more excruciating with each passing second as I could feel the fear continuing to mount in my chest. I went through every possible action to take in my foggy and impaired head but fell to my last resort: I shoved my hands into my crotch and started to roll around in a ball inside the shelter while yelling at the top of my lungs in pure animalistic agony.

This is where it got a little fuzzy. I remembered rolling around for a few minutes, but I think I passed out from the overwhelming pain. There was no way I could have fallen asleep in that much torment, but the next thing I remembered was waking up with the sun shining on me. After laying there for a few seconds, my hands feeling better but still hurting, I thought to myself, "Well, I think I just got frostbite."

I laid there for a few minutes, trying to comprehend what had just happened, and then chuckled to myself as the brutal reality of thru-hiking kicked in. *I need to keep moving.* There was no time for self-pity. I had already wasted enough time getting frostbite — I couldn't waste anymore. I had to get moving and get to the next town.

I loved the absurdity of some poor situation happening, and the only option being to keep moving. If I wanted to stop hiking, that was fine, but I only had a limited amount of food, water, and time to get to the next resupply. *This traumatic morning doesn't affect my ability to walk at all, and I've still got 1,832 miles to finish the AT. I might as well keep moving.*

The only way is thru.

With frostbitten hands, wet feet, and a stubborn attitude, I got moving, wondering what other crazy things would happen to me this year if this already happened, and I wasn't even 5% done with the journey yet.

Hours later, I had cell reception, and the nearest town's weather report said it was currently two degrees, which felt significantly warmer than the negative ten degrees it recorded earlier in the day. I was up higher at 4,000 feet, so it was likely somewhere between 15 and 20 degrees below zero. Now the unusually cold morning and frostbite made more sense. I had never wanted my heavy-duty mittens so badly. Before this journey, I never would have imagined in my wildest dreams that it could get so atrociously cold in North Carolina, but now I was exposed to the cruel reality of winter in the mountains, whether I knew of its brutality or not.

My water filter was frozen solid all day. This was bad for multiple reasons, the first being that I couldn't use it. My water consumption for the day consisted of eating snow off of plants along the trail. It was fun at first, but it quickly became undesirable to continuously make my mouth an ice box. The second reason it was bad was because water filters were not supposed to freeze. I'd heard that you shouldn't let your water filter freeze, but I thought that was just for the sake of using it. At the time, I didn't know that if it freezes it may no longer be effective at treating water. I learned that after I had let it freeze over 20 times. Luckily, the water was clean along the AT in winter, and I never got sick from it.

After blazing trail all day through deep snow, I passed by Roan High Knob Shelter and onto the Carver Gap parking lot. That shelter was the highest one along the AT, standing at 6,270 feet. Knowing that, I knew it would be cold up there, and after this morning, I wanted to be as warm as possible and sleep at a lower elevation.

I was hoping the pit toilet in the parking lot would be unlocked so I could sleep in it to escape the wind and cold. I had a bad feeling in my gut as I was walking up to it, and it was confirmed when I grabbed the handle and it was locked. I was enraged but didn't want to go any farther, so I camped in the vestibule area immediately outside the bathroom door to have a slight shelter from the wind. This was my first night using my tent instead of sleeping inside the protection of a shelter.

The reason I didn't want to hike any further that night was because the Roan Highlands were immediately ahead, and I wasn't going to pass through that special area after dark and miss its beauty. When I saw the sky the next morning, I knew I had made the right decision.

The sky was one of the most picturesque displays of majesty I had ever seen. The sky was orange but covered with pink altocumulus clouds as far as the eye could see. They looked as if they had been chopped by God to create a staccato symphony in the sky. Mornings like this made it all okay. The pain, the snow, the cold — it was all worth it.

It was good that I had such a profound start to the day. It distracted me from the fact that I was nearly out of food since I had been moving slower than expected through the deep snow. Around 9 a.m., I ate three tuna packets and a Honey Bun, the last of my food, and had 12 miles to go before I made it to the next road crossing and resupply. Hunger could wait.

Filled with open ridge walking, the day was exceptionally beautiful. It was a welcomed change to be out of the dense forest and enjoying constant views of the rolling mountains covered in snow with the backdrop of hazy gray skies and the occasional hint of blue peeking through.

The beauty helped me overcome the tough hiking. The snow was still shin-deep, with tracks only near the eventual road crossing. It was exhausting breaking trail as much as I had been lately in deep snow, but I knew that wasn't going to change any time soon.

Along with the obvious energy expenditure of my lower body, the laborious movement also sapped the strength out of my shoulders and arms as I tried to use my trekking poles through the snow. They would frequently get caught in deep snow or ice, and be difficult to remove, although they did save me from falling countless times. Just before the road crossing, I tried to use them again to stop a fall, but it was too much this time. The bottom part of one pole snapped, and I ended up face down in the snow. Until I could get a replacement part sent, I would be rocking one full trekking pole and one that was over a foot too short for someone my height.

When I made it to the road, I was beat. While slogging through deep snow the past few days, I was also dealing with nagging ankle pain. I didn't roll it, but it was aching constantly. On the approach to the road, I was strongly considering calling it a day and staying at a hostel after I got my resupply. With the combination of my fatigue, ankle pain, and another winter storm coming that night, a hostel sounded growingly enticing.

While internally debating this, I got a text from a friend reminding me that all this hardship now was so that I could earn the big miles in the summer. It won't be immediate, but the payoff will come. I needed that. I didn't need a hostel. I vowed to push nine more miles to the next shelter thanks to the encouragement from my friend.

Before I left home, I asked a few friends to write me a personal note, motivational speech, or funny story from our past. I wanted to have something I could look to when I was at my lowest, feeling terrible, or wanting to take it easy. However, I was so stingy with saving them, always expecting I would face a worse situation down the line where I would need the encouragement more, that I never actually used them. But I liked always knowing that I had a shot of mental epinephrine ready if I needed it. Whenever someone would randomly reach out like this friend did, it blasted new wind into my sails. I had to stay perpetually motivated.

With that decision made, it didn't make getting a hitch into town any easier. I was waiting for a while alongside the road before some day-hikers came back to their car and gave me a ride after I asked.

I resupplied at my favorite store for hikers: Dollar General. They have everything you need and nothing more. Getting a ride back to the trail was less enjoyable than my lovely in-store experience. I asked a woman outside the store if she was heading back past the trail. After some deliberation, I found out that she was, and she said she would give me a ride.

After I hopped in the backseat of the jam-packed truck, she began to close the door but then stopped. She looked at me and earnestly said, "Oh, and I forgot to ask — you're not gonna pull a gun on me or anything, are you?" She wasn't smiling, laughing, or giving any indication it was a joke.

This caught me off guard, so I wasn't sure what to say. I half-smiled and said, "Um, no, I don't have a gun on me or anything like that."

It was a cringey, awkward exchange, and the conversation on the ride continued to be so. Once she dropped me off at the trail, I was relieved to be spared the oddities of that scatterbrained conversation. Being a 6'2" and 200-pound man afforded me the privilege of never feeling the danger associated with hitchhiking, but that privilege did not shield me from weird conversations or uncomfortable rides with the occasional oddball.

Within the first half mile, the snow began to fall. There was no easing in or warm up period. It came down like it was on a deadline. It dropped a few inches before I even made it to the shelter and continued to snow through the night. Even with the heavy snow, I was glad that I didn't end the day early and stay at a hostel. I was tired, and my body was aching, but choosing to hike on through a winter storm reassured my confidence that I was tough enough to succeed on this journey. I could push on when the lazy part of my brain was telling me to slow down and take a break. I could refuse to take the easy way out. *I could achieve the insane.*

I was having an excellent night of sleep in the storm until the mice came out to play around 4 a.m. I took all the food I had lazily strewn around in the shelter and hung it on mice lines. I tried bashing the critters with a shoe, but they were too quick. I was unable to fall back asleep with the enemy openly invading my quarters. I was so scarred by getting three holes chewed into my sleeping bag in the Smokies that I was now paranoid.

After laying there for a few hours in a state of semi-rest, I got moving. It stopped snowing for a time, but in the early morning the ominous sky decided to start dropping rain instead. I was getting wet from the rain, but I was getting even more soaked from the snow-covered tree branches and rhododendron sagging over the trail. There was no avoiding getting covered in snow while trying to go through them and gasping every time a clump of snow shot down my back, chilling my body.

With fresh rain falling on top of fresh snow, the trail was a slosh pit all day. I was falling left and right like someone had littered the trail with banana peels. The only thing keeping me moving through the rain, snow, and ankle pain was the thought of staying indoors that night.

When I was doing a section hike in this area in 2019, I was crossing a road when a car stopped me. A gentleman gave me some food and his phone number to call if I needed any help. At the time, I didn't want to bother him, so I didn't plan on calling. The day I was approaching Hampton, TN, where he lived, it was a downpour. I ended up calling him so I could do laundry and dry out. He let me stay the night and offered the same if I was ever back in the area.

I remembered his offer a few days prior and figured I might as well ask him again to hopefully hide from winter for a night. I began to look for his number in my phone, but there were two problems. The first problem was that I couldn't remember his name. How terrible! A person is incredibly kind to me, allows me to stay in his home with his family, and I couldn't remember his name. The second, and more important problem, was that his phone number wasn't in my phone. I didn't have his contact information, and my call log didn't go back that far. My hopes of an indoor night seemed doomed. I ended up getting ahold of Verizon and learned that their call logs only went back a certain number of months — not a good sign.

But the trail provides! The month that I called him ended up being the farthest back their call logs would go. Perfect. Now I was back to the first problem. I didn't know his name! I wasn't sure if he'd remember me and didn't want to call without knowing his name.

For the days leading up to Hampton, I would think about it for hours. I could picture him, remember our conversations, remember meeting his young grandson and trying to convince him that the Lakers were only good because of Anthony Davis, not Lebron. But I could not remember his name. Then, on the final day going into Hampton, it hit me like a lightning bolt from above. I shouted, "RAY! HIS NAME IS RAY!"

Everything worked out perfectly. I called him, and he was happy to let me stay again, especially because there was another winter storm coming. He picked me up and took me to Dollar General before heading back to his house. My first order of business was a hot shower. It had only been a week since my last, but that week was filled with so much snow, ice, rain, and a touch of frostbite, that this was one of the best showers of my life.

He and his wife were so accommodating it was unbelievable. If I had any slight inconvenience, it was a personal affront to their character. We caught up while I was downing food and Cokes like it was my last supper. They offered to let me stay a few more nights since there was a nasty winter storm coming in. The expected snowfall in town was 5–7 inches, and it would be much worse up in the mountains.

The trail from Hampton, TN to the next town of Damascus, VA predominantly rides the ridge all the way there, so I knew the conditions would be rough with the storm. Regardless, I thanked them for the offer, but stated I needed to stay on schedule, so I couldn't be spending too much time in towns. Winter storm or not, I had to keep moving.

I said goodnight to my hosts and retired to the cozy guest room to catch up with some phone calls to my parents and friends. I awoke the next morning to discover the weather forecast had been updated. The expected snowfall for the town and lower elevations was now 8–12 inches, but what I really cared about — the expected snowfall for the surrounding ridgelines was now 18–24 inches. When I read that, part of me felt fear, but part of me felt excitement. This was going to be truly wild.

My wonderful hosts reiterated that I was welcome to stay, but I told them I was excited to get out there and weather the storm. I scarfed down an unhealthy amount of breakfast and weighed myself before I left. When I got to their house the day before, I was 197 pounds, after starting the trail at 215 pounds. Leaving their house, I was 206. I wasn't sure how sustainable it would be to gain ten pounds in every town, but I was happy to see it.

We made a quick trip to the post office, where I picked up my heavy-duty winter mittens and a new pair of shoes to finally replace the burnt ones. I was thrilled to get my hands on both. I would have sufficient warmth for my hands, and I would have shoes without open slots for snow and water to slide in unencumbered. Life would be better.

As Ray dropped me off back at the trailhead, he gave me one final look of, "Are you sure you want to do this?"

After I saw the trail and heavy snow already falling, I wasn't so sure. Nonetheless, I thanked him and headed back out to embrace the storm.

Snowstorm to Super Bowl

As I felt the snow falling on me, while I was already walking in several inches of untouched snow, I began to smile and laugh. Oh, how I laughed! All I could think about was how dumb this was, and I loved it. We need a word in the English language to describe the feeling of pure joy due to the realization of how absurd a situation is. Whatever that word would be, I felt that frequently, but rarely more than this day.

I was walking through an area, mostly on a ridge with no tracks, no people, two unpopular road crossings, and deep snow during a winter storm. I felt like Joaquin Phoenix's Joker as I would just start laughing without a real reason. It's times like these that unless someone has thru-hiked and had similar experiences, they will never be able to understand.

It was snowing before I started hiking and continued to snow all day. It was snowing when I got to my shelter that night. When I woke up the next day, it was snowing. It was snowing when I began hiking again. It snowed for 30 hours straight. I didn't know how much snow fell in total, but when I left the shelter the next morning, my eight-inch-deep footprints were already covered over and blended in with the new white forest floor.

Before reaching Damascus, I crossed the border from Tennessee to Virginia. I was and wasn't looking forward to Virginia. I had heard that it could drag on and get a little boring, but I had also heard that it flattened out more and was easier to do big miles.

I had walked from Springer to Damascus over a few former section hikes, but after Damascus, the rest of the year would be unchartered territory for me. I was excited to see a plethora of new places, but worried as I reached the end of my familiar territory. Most of the people that do the Calendar Year Triple Crown have already hiked all three trails before they do them again in a single year. Knowledge of the trail is a huge help in having proper expectations.

It didn't take long for a surprise to hit in this "new" territory. I rolled into Damascus at 5:15 p.m., and the grocery store was already closed! They were working limited hours because of a labor shortage. I didn't expect to end my day in Damascus, but continuing on without food wasn't an option. The store also didn't open until 9 a.m., so I would get a late start out of town. It wasn't an ideal situation, but I accepted it and found a hostel.

After I had already paid, and unpacked everything to dry out, one of my friends from college texted me and told me that her mom lived in Damascus and would love to help. She ended up driving me to an out-of-town grocery store at 7 a.m. and paying for my food. It was an incredible kindness for a person she had never met.

When I got back to town, I made a quick trip to the post office to mail home my camping stove. This marked three weeks on trail, and I had only used it a handful of times. With the combination of the consistent mice and my lack of energy at the end of every day, cooking never seemed appealing. I'd heard from other hikers before I left that I would need a hot meal every day, but that ended up not being the case for me. I would much rather just quickly down 2,000 calories of peanut butter and go to bed.

Before I left town, I laid down for a 15-minute nap. This ended up lasting over two hours, and I didn't start hiking until after noon. My early start didn't pan out. Feeling more rested, I exited Damascus with clear skies above. It didn't rain at all, but it was another day of getting wet from the snow-covered tree branches and rhododendron hanging low over the trail.

The temperature rose above freezing for the first time in several days. It was a welcomed change, but the cold had been much more tolerable lately. I always had plenty of bodily layers to combat it if I planned right, but now that I had good protection for my hands with the new mittens, the cold was a less formidable foe than it once was.

One of the most surprising things was that my feet never felt cold. I couldn't insulate my feet much, and my feet were wet every day of winter hiking in the snow. Yet, they never felt cold enough to where I was worried. As long as I was moving, they always kept warm. My mindset in the winter was simple: I either wanted to be moving or bundled up in my sleeping bag. If I was doing either of those, I felt adequately warm.

When I made it up around 5,000 feet, the snow was much more intense. There were no tracks from anyone else, so I was breaking trail, and my kneecaps would sink below the surface with every step. The snow looked firm on top, but just when I put the last of my weight into each step, it would sink below the surface. This is called postholing, and it was a nasty and frequent enemy. It was comical though. Sinking far above my knees with every step was ridiculous. I was moving slowly and wasn't even sure if I was moving in the right direction.

After expending a lot of extra energy weaving off-route frequently, I made it to Thomas Knob Shelter, where I saw more people than I had seen the entire trail so far. I went up to the two-story shelter to air my feet out and grab a snack. I started talking with the campers and it turned out it was the Virginia Beach Fire Department, and they did an annual trip like this.

I found it funny that these beach boys that work with fire took a vacation out to the frigid mountains every winter, but unsurprisingly, they did have an exceptional fire blazing. We talked for a while, and they found it amusing that I was doing over 20 miles a day in these conditions while wearing shorts and trail running shoes. They were extremely kind and tried to talk me into staying there. It was a tempting offer because I knew a group of guys like this would have a lot of good booze and a lot of good stories, but I had to keep trucking.

Right after I left, I hit the 500 mile-marker, and it began to dump heavy snow. I was infuriated because it wasn't supposed to snow today. I asked myself if I should've just stayed at the shelter but threw that notion to the side and kept moving forward, refusing to go back on my decision. I rejoiced when the snow only lasted 15 minutes.

After dark, I ended up getting a mile off trail. Guthook's maps and GPS feature had been glitching lately, so it was not an ideal situation. I slowly began to bushwhack my way through trees and knee-deep snow to head back towards trail using my partially accurate mapping app.

On the way, I stumbled into a small grove which was different from what I had been seeing. Instead of deep snow, there were large circular areas on the ground where it was all melted. *That was strange.* Then I saw bear scat and thought, *I better get the hell out of here.* I didn't want to be there when they returned. They might be upset someone was walking through their home, and I didn't want to see how they'd defend their residence.

After a lot of stress and knee-to-chest walking, I made it back to the trail and found an unoccupied shelter for the night. With the combination of the snow, it being after dark, and me getting far off trail, I didn't get to witness any of the ponies in Grayson Highlands. Seeing them was usually a staple for hikers passing through — another sacrifice for the greater journey.

It rained off and on throughout the night, which would occasionally wake me up when it started pounding on the metal roof. As usual, there were mice in the shelter. They didn't chew through my sleeping bag this time, but they did eat a whole bag of Rolos.

When I was wrapped up in my sleeping bag, I remembered I had some leftover snacks in my pocket. I was already warm and didn't want to get out of my cocoon, so I flung the bag of Rolos as far as I could outside the shelter. When I awoke the next morning, the only remnants of my pocket snacks were the wrappers, which I sadly picked up as I thought about how much I liked Rolos.

Due to the falling rain, the snow was sloppy, and it was slow moving through the woods. I was drained after 24 miles. In decent winter conditions on the AT, 24 miles would be the perfect ratio of getting good mileage, but not tiring myself out too much. However, with the current snow, 24 miles was exhausting. I spent the night at a shelter and had more battles with fearless mice. The war raged eternal.

The next morning was acutely painful. I was still in deep snow, but the trail was almost exclusively on ridges, so it had been blasted with wind and hardened into ice. It didn't harden enough to be able to walk on, just enough to step on and have my feet break through at the last second. This hurt. Instead of just sinking in snow up to my shins or knees, the surrounding snow that had metamorphized into ice sliced into my ankles and legs with the cutting edge of a samurai sword. I winced with every step, but I couldn't do anything about it unless I learned how to levitate. I could usually tell a day wasn't going to be great if I was randomly yelling out in anger, which was happening every time a chunk of ice cut into my leg.

After I dropped off the crest of the ridge, the ice gave way to snow later in the day. I continued to drop in elevation, and the snow depth changed from over a foot to just several inches as I passed the quarter-way marker for the Appalachian Trail that afternoon.

Even though I'd been trying to avoid big-picture thinking since day one, I allowed myself to think about how far I had come. It felt good to be 25% done with the AT, but my brain focused on the 75% more to go, knowing it would only get more difficult the further north I went. I quickly dispelled that idea from my mind, and hiked late into the night, doing the only thing I knew I could do for certain without becoming overwhelmed or looking ahead too much: keep moving forward.

I made sure to make it into town for the Super Bowl. Watching football is one of my favorite aspects of being a human, so I wasn't going to miss the last game of the season. I arrived in Bland, VA with time to resupply and grab a couple of 2-liters of Dr. Pepper before the game started.

Even though I was wired like a 12-year-old that had been mainlining sugar the last time I drank it in Hot Springs, I was going to stick with my plan to drink pop on this journey. I knew that losing weight was inevitable when hiking 25–30 miles every day, so I had to try to consume as many calories as possible to fuel myself and try to maintain weight. I knew I would still lose weight, but I had to try my best to hammer calories, and liquid calories are the easiest ones to get down. I also thoroughly enjoyed the taste and had to capitalize on the small luxuries I could get.

It turned out to be a terrible game, but it was pleasant to get a little rest in town and watch Tom Brady cement his legacy earning his seventh Super Bowl win. I'm not a fan, but I am a fan of people that strive to be the best they can be at all costs and undeniably excel at their craft. Seeing other people's success and understanding the work they had to put in to get there can be the best source of motivation.

With some downtime in town, I began to reflect on the first 26 days on trail. Every time I stayed indoors for a night felt like a personal reset. It was usually about a week in between indoor nights because I didn't want to get too used to them, but they were *much appreciated* — and sometimes *needed* — in the winter months. Rather than thinking of it as a 2,193-mile hike through the constant snow in the winter, I could think of it as a week-long trip until the next hot shower and cozy bed — and repeat.

But this town stop and personal reset felt a little different since I had recently finished the first 25% of the trail. I was averaging nearly exactly the miles I predicted, but I wasn't satisfied. I had the feeling that I should be doing more, even with getting barraged by storm after storm and hiking through constant deep snow which had been slowing me down drastically.

I realized that this feeling was based on emotion rather than logic. It came from the innate sense of always wanting to do better in everything I had ever done — from school, to lifting weights, to now walking as much as possible. I set my goals for the sky, and get disappointed when I don't surpass them and end up in the stratosphere.

Dissatisfaction is a symptom of ambition.

I also realized that I wasn't enjoying it as much lately. In the beginning, everything was novel and exciting. Lately, it felt more like a continual struggle to just make it to the next town. I attributed this partially to the trail being less scenic lately, but more so to the increase in difficulty due to the deep snow and ice. I accepted that the struggle from town to town might just have to be what the AT was in winter and that all this extreme adversity now was to ready myself for the bigger and easier miles in the summer months. I was at peace with that.

I'm the kind of person that will always take more suffering now in the hope, futile or not, that there is a promise of a better future, and this better future was summer. That dedication to delayed gratification was necessary for the Calendar Year Triple Crown.

Alone in a Dark Wood

I was raring to get moving the morning after the Super Bowl because the weather was supposed to be accommodating for several consecutive days, something I hadn't seen in a while. I got a ride back to the trail before dawn, and with the sun shining and warm temperatures, I put in a championship performance of my own and crushed 42 miles. Surprising myself, I actually got to walk on dirt for almost half of the day! Between doing that, and walking in ankle deep snow, rather than knee deep snow, I was able to move much faster.

Late in the day, I saw mountain lion tracks, which was strange because I thought those weren't in the East, excluding Florida. I remained alert but pushed the thought to the back of my mind. Paranoia wouldn't do me any good. When I arrived at the shelter that night, there were signs warning of a mountain lion in the area. *At least it confirmed I wasn't crazy.*

I was slogging through deep snow again the next morning, making my way down to Narrows, VA to pick up a package with a trekking pole replacement part and food. Before I got to town, the trail was beautiful ridge walking with views of the surrounding snow-covered mountains. It took me a half hour to get a hitch into town, but it evened out. As I was walking out of the post office, a car slowed and asked if I needed a ride back to the trail. There are few things in the world that I love more than maximum efficiency.

On the north side of town, there were no tracks, and I was breaking trail in over a foot of snow. There was no inkling of where the trail was supposed to be under the snow, so I had to find my own way through the woods, looking for white blazes and cut logs, among other things. It didn't help that the trees were covered in snow, hiding the white blazes, and there weren't many white blazes in this area to begin with. I later heard from some locals that this section of trail was notorious for being a little more rugged.

The real stress began as twilight was approaching. There were seemingly two paths that looked legitimate — a fork in the road. I chose one, and it turned out to be correct... for a time.

Shortly after, and for the rest of the night, it was impossible to find any indication of where the trail was supposed to be. The fact that it was dark made everything significantly more difficult. I could've been walking in circles for all I knew. I know I ended up walking miles of extra steps, weaving over the alleged "trail" constantly. After walking for a while, I'd look at my GPS app, which still wasn't accurate, and I'd be a quarter mile to the east, walk for a while, and then be a tenth of a mile west. I repeated this for seven hours. It never got any less frustrating as I was constantly looking in all directions, but found no help in deciding where I was supposed to go.

In addition to wandering through the woods with no trail to follow, two things made the experience even worse. The first was around 9 p.m., when a heavy fog rolled in, and it began to rain. I already couldn't see because my headlamp was dying, but now I couldn't see five feet ahead.

The second annoyance actually seemed like a good thing at first. I started to see some animal tracks, and they seemed to follow the trail fairly well according to my GPS. *That will help.* But once I looked closer, I realized that they were mountain lion tracks again. In this deep of snow, and with how windy it had been, these had to be fairly fresh.

To compound the distress of seeing mountain lion tracks, they appeared to double back on themselves — not good. Mountain lions do that when they are hunting or feel threatened, two things I did not want. I had to keep my head on a swivel, especially since the tracks were in the same general direction as the trail, and I saw them frequently for hours.

After hours of extreme frustration, stress, and fear, I made it to a shelter around 1 a.m. and passed out an hour later after unpacking everything and eating. I walked an extra 5–7 miles from weaving and wandering far off trail because of the deep snow.

During the trek, I journaled every night before bed. I would do a full recap if I had the time and energy, or I'd just jot down some quick notes to expound upon the next day if I was overly tired. I was exhausted after this night, but it's my favorite short journal entry of the year:

> *Fuck this bullshit. Fuck this motherfucking trail, this motherfucking snow, the motherfucking dark where I can't see anything, the motherfucking lack of blazes on trees, the motherfucking animal tracks going in every direction, the motherfucking lack of any human tracks, and motherfucking Guthook for not working and having me go the wrong way at least 50 times tonight. FUCK THIS!*

Like I said before, the harsh beauty of thru-hiking was that I had no option but to keep going. The only way was thru.

It was a horrible night and a horrible situation, but the thought of quitting never crossed my mind. I knew the next day couldn't possibly be that bad. I told myself, *Tomorrow will be better, because it has to be.* It couldn't possibly be worse. This foolhardy and optimistic mindset is what drove me on when I had my most difficult days.

I awoke the next morning after sleeping until 8 a.m., giving myself a full six hours of sleep to recover. It rained the entire day, nature seemingly trying to foil my optimistic mantra. The positive side of my brain was happy that the rain was helping melt the snow a bit, but it certainly didn't feel good, especially on my feet. They were wet every day, but extraordinarily wet when walking in rain that was also turning the snow into a sloshy mess.

In the middle of the day, I took off my dreadfully wet shoes and socks. I wrung out a disturbing amount of water from my socks before putting them back on and screaming internally while doing so because they were still saturated and cold. It ended up being a 19-mile day full of misery, but with a few moments of that psychotic joy as I laughed at how ridiculously miserable the situation was.

The rain continued the next day, except it came down harder. *What happened to that nice weather that was supposed to come?*

I started off the day by making my water filter defective. As I was leaning over a stream to fill up, a plastic ring fell out of my water filter into the stream. I immediately plunged my hand into the icy water but didn't pull out anything other than a numb hand. Until I could get a replacement piece, I would be using a faulty water filter.

Later walking through a pasture, two farm dogs began to follow me. They didn't seem aggressive, so I wasn't worried. But later in the day, I was up on a ridge and saw another dog. *Am I losing it? Am I hallucinating?*

I actually thought it might have been from a lack of water. In addition to the filter breaking, I hadn't been drinking much water lately because of the constant rain making me not want to stop moving to collect it. But I noticed the dog was leaving footprints, so I figured it was probably real. I just found it particularly odd for a stray dog to be up on a ridge in the middle of the forest in winter. I also saw an aerial battle between a couple of large birds in the misty sky. It was an odd day for animal sightings, but more relaxing than following mountain lion tracks after dark.

A lot of the day was ridge walking, but there were no views with the lack of visibility. Missing good views was a sacrifice I knew I had to accept, but it still hurt a little. I saw a sign for the Eastern Continental Divide, which didn't matter much to me, but it reminded me how excited I was to get to the real Continental Divide Trail. The struggles now would be worth it later.

I nearly called it a day in the afternoon after a sorry 13 miles. I took off my shoes and socks to air out and started chowing down on some food. I felt miserable slogging through another day of rain and wanted to stop.

While snacking, I turned on a podcast with David Goggins, an inspirational figure one of my friends told me to check out. While listening to this podcast, I couldn't believe I hadn't heard of this guy before. If he could do all these unbelievable things: be the only member of the U.S. Armed Forces to complete SEAL training, Army Ranger School, and Air Force Tactical Air Controller training; run 100 miles with no training and nearly die; become an elite ultra-endurance athlete; break the world-record for pull-ups; and much more — all after being a self-described "fat piece of shit" — there was no way I was going to take the easy way out and call it a day after a pathetic 13 miles! It was the first time I'd heard his story, and it was so inspirational that it made me fly down the trail to make it a respectable 23-mile day.

At the end of the day, I hiked three-tenths of a mile off trail to get to a shelter. I hated walking any extra distance off trail, but I had to stop to resupply the next day when the gas station was open. Gas stations weren't the ideal resupply location because of their higher prices and limited selection, but I would take their ease of convenience if they were near the trail rather than heading into a town miles away for a grocery store.

When I started unpacking at the shelter, everything was soaked through. My rain gear felt as if it had been sitting in a washer after three days of unrelenting rain. The clothes underneath were all wet, my socks being the most affected. My sleeping bag, the most important thing, fortunately remained dry because it was at the bottom of my pack and double protected with a garbage bag for water protection.

However, that smart move by me was soon diminished by an idiotic one. I knew that if I hung up my clothes, they'd freeze by morning because it was too wet and the temperature was now below freezing. I had previously laid out clothes to "dry out" overnight, only to have them freeze and be awfully uncomfortable to put on in the morning. I wanted to stop repeating that mistake, so I put some of my soaked clothes in my sleeping bag with me to help it dry out from my body heat.

I shouldn't have done that.

It was too wet to do so. I woke up in the middle of the night shivering, which I never did in this winter sleeping bag. The down insulation started to get soggy from the clothes, so I tossed them outside the bag and just hoped they didn't freeze. I caught it early enough where the down in the sleeping bag wasn't useless, just slightly less warm. I'd have to choose frozen clothes over a damp sleeping bag in the future.

When I woke up the next morning and looked outside the shelter, I saw a score of coyote tracks going right up to the shelter and turning around. I'd heard them howling the night before, but definitely didn't think they were that close. They must've smelled food and came to inspect until they saw a human. Wild animals came within a few feet of me, but turned around, thanks to millennia of instinct telling them that I was a predator they shouldn't mess with. *Thank you ancestors.*

My clothes didn't freeze solid overnight, but they were stiff and uncomfortable to put on. It took me over two hours to get packed up and moving for the day because everything was so wet and cold that my motivation level was near zero. The temperature dropped, turning the rain to snow overnight and making the trail slippery and tough to manage.

My pace stayed slow, especially around Dragon's Tooth. I was walking over massive boulders covered in sheets of ice. I had a slight meltdown when I was navigating across one. A trekking pole slipped out of my hand and slid 50 feet down a wall of ice. My heart sank for a second. I took a deep sigh, and then the anger set in. I yelled about every cuss word I knew and cursed my pole. Then, I began working my way down to get to it. It was a 15-minute endeavor to move 50 feet through the playground of ice.

Soon after, I was able to laugh about it. Several miles after my trekking pole recovery mission, I resupplied at a gas station in Catawba, VA and got Hunt Brothers' gas station pizza for the first time in my life. It was better than I expected. I also got a Mountain Dew Voltage for the first time in a decade. It was incredible how much joy these two things brought me in the midst of the unending soggy misery that was my life on the AT in winter. The acceptance of misery was so regular that happiness was easy to come by.

I made my way to McAfee Knob, one of the most iconic spots along the entire trail — but not for me. There was no visibility from the jutting-out cliff over the sprawling valley below, but I wasn't surprised. I hadn't seen the sun in four days. I carefully skimmed across the ice near the edge and set up my mini tripod to take a picture of me sitting on the edge over a vast sky of gray — an action that later upset my grandmother because I was too close to the edge.

The rest of the day remained dull and gloomy. As I was walking along a cliff, two massive ravens leapt, took flight, and faded into the gray mist that covered the entire sky. It looked like a bad omen in a horror movie, but nothing extraordinarily bad seemed to happen. This day officially marked one month on trail, and I was at mile 720, exactly where I estimated to be. One month going pretty much as planned might seem like a monumental feat, but I knew it was only the first of ten or eleven — no reason to get too excited yet. I acknowledged the progress but kept my mind on the overall objective. There was still much work to be done.

I woke up at 4:30 a.m. the next morning, something I had attempted and failed numerous times so far. One thing made it possible today: the thought of staying in town and getting dry. It would be a quick nine miles into Daleville, and I wanted to get there early and rest for most of the day. It was raining the whole way into town and looked like it wouldn't stop all day.

When I rolled into Daleville around 10 a.m., the cheapest motel was less than a tenth of a mile off trail — perfect.

They gave me a thru-hiker discount and let me check in early — amazing.

A shady guy in the hallway asked what I was doing with a backpack. When I told him, he started pedaling some camera equipment — annoying.

I told him I was content with my phone and walked away. With the way I looked and felt, I didn't want to buy anything. All I wanted to do was get dry, but I had one last chore to do first: resupply. I wanted to get it over with since it was going to be raining the rest of the day.

There was a Kroger .6 miles away, so I headed back out in the rain. I loaded up for a normal resupply: bars and candy for energy while walking; trail mix, Oreos, Pop Tarts, chips, and a block of cheese to eat in the morning or at short breaks for sugar and sodium to keep moving during the day; and peanut butter and tuna to load up on calories and protein before bed. For me, there was no such thing as meals. I would eat most of my calories in the morning when I woke up and right before I went to bed. I would eat snacks anytime I stopped moving during the day and never stopped for "lunch." I would eat roughly 5,000 calories per day, 2,000 of which were me inhaling peanut butter before I went to bed. Every hiker's system is different, but this seemed to work for me.

In addition to my normal resupply, I also bought rest day treats, which consisted of a 12-pack of Dr. Pepper, Hot Pockets, and other pleasures that needed a microwave or would spoil quickly out on the trail. By the time I was walking back, carrying nearly a dozen grocery bags of goodies, my arms were ready to fall off. I was hoping a car would see how miserable I was and stop to take me a few tenths of a mile, but none did. I struggled the whole way back to the motel, but eventually made it, saturated and arms inflamed. That was the most fatigued my arms had been in a while.

When I got ready to shower, I took a look in the mirror and noticed my body had changed quite a bit. I wasn't yet at the malnourished-looking level. So far, I had just lost a lot of body fat, and I looked good.

After my shower, I started to do my laundry with detergent I bought from the motel. Normally I would wear my rain gear while doing laundry because it didn't need to be washed, but it was all soaking wet and muddy. I was in a bind, but I needed to get dry. I threw on a towel for my quick trips to the laundry room, and thankfully nobody saw me. I just wanted to get my laundry done and get some dry clothes on as soon as possible to escape my perpetual sodden state.

The rest of the day was relaxing and much needed. It continued to rain all day and was supposed to continue for the next few days. It felt great to have one day's respite from the rain. Other than waking up every hour during the night from a crying baby in the room above me, it was perfect. I'd still take a crying baby over the ceaseless, pestering mice.

When I left the next morning, a motel worker came running after me in the parking lot. I had dropped one of my mittens in the lobby, and she chased after me to return it. If I had been a few miles out of town, and then realized I didn't have it, I would've been furious, but thanks to the kindness of a stranger, my day was saved.

It wasn't raining most of the day, even though the sky looked bleak. Yet even without the rain, I returned to my perpetual state of sogginess. I was constantly getting pelted by melting ice from the trees overhead. *I should've brought a helmet.*

Like the whole day, and most days lately, visibility was nonexistent as a bleak fog plagued the area. Through the haze, I spotted a parking area with a single car along the trail. I figured nobody else would be out hiking since the weather was poor. I rarely saw other people while hiking the AT in winter, but I would never see people out on the trail on gloomy days. The only time I might see hikers was with a rare combination of a nice day and a scenic overlook. And of course, that scenic overlook had to be only a few miles from a parking lot.

Checking all the boxes of those variables wasn't too common. For most of the winter, I would only see other humans when I went into town to buy food. Then I wouldn't see another person until I got to the next town. There were frequent "town stops" along the AT due to the population density of the East compared to the West, but I still didn't see another human over half of my days on the AT in winter. I was alone, but the feeling of existential loneliness never struck me.

As I walked by the car on this dismally dreary day, I saw two teenagers just sitting in the car: not on their phones, not talking, just sitting. I got a good laugh out of it, and even though I didn't sneak out of the house to go get high, I imagined it would be pretty fun as a teenager.

Two hours before I made it to my shelter for the night, it started to pour and didn't let up. I was already wet from the falling ice all day, but this was the point where I went from uncomfortably wet, to soaked to the bone. This shelter had shingles for a roof instead of sheet metal like most, so the rain was actually pleasant to fall asleep to. It ended up raining through the night and turned into a light rain when I left the next morning.

Immediately upon leaving, I realized the trail was in bad shape. With the ice melting off of trees yesterday in small chunks, there were ice cubes covering the whole trail. They were small enough that my steps would go under them, and the ice cubes would engulf my feet up to my ankles. In addition to that, there was water lurking underneath the ice cubes from all the rain last night, and it was frigidly cold. With nearly every step all day, my foot would sink up to my ankle in ice water. It was like I was putting my feet in an ice bath with every step, and I never seemed to adapt to it, constantly gasping and wincing from the cold shock.

Normally my feet felt fine, no matter the temperature, but this was the first day that they actually felt cold while walking. Part of that was attributed to a discovery I made during a break. If I took my shoes off, but not socks, my feet felt colder than if I had taken my shoes and socks off. The socks were full of ice water that got chilled by the wind quickly, which then in turn, chilled me into a state of discomfort no one should experience.

I was moving slowly because of the ice water. It was exhausting trudging through the cumbersome ice cubes covering the trail all day. I swallowed my pride and called it a day around 5 p.m.

Before that, I didn't realize how slowly I was moving, but when I got to a shelter, and it was only 11 miles of hiking, it hit me hard. It was tough accepting that poor of a day, even though it wasn't from lack of effort. I had to remind myself that days like this were the reason I started so early. I started on January 13th, earlier than most others that had completed the Calendar Year Triple Crown, in order to give myself extra flex time in case I had days like this or an injury that sidelined me for a time. I still wasn't happy, but I had to accept it.

I was in bed by 6:30 p.m. and woke up a few times throughout the night because of the wind but didn't think much of it. When I got moving the next morning before dawn, I realized it was a little more serious. There had been a big windstorm overnight that left downed trees scattered everywhere. In hindsight, it was a good thing I stopped early, otherwise I would've been hiking until midnight to get to the next shelter, and I would've been out in the storm. *Maybe this was the danger that the ravens were trying to warn me of several days prior.*

Even though I was still walking on the ice cube-littered trail, and things were still tough, once the clock hit 7:06 a.m., it didn't matter. The sun was rising in the sky. It was the first time I saw the big fiery ball in a week.

Exhilaration coursed through my body, but the excitement was short-lived as I hit an area of trail that was terribly wrecked by the wind. I couldn't go more than five steps without having to walk through some broken branches or climb over fallen trees. By the measure of how much I yelled and cussed out loud, this was the angriest I had been to date on the trip. I couldn't even single out one thing that was the worst. It wasn't just branches constantly hitting me in the face, or a branch catapulting one of my trekking poles 20 feet down a ledge, or a tree beginning to slide downhill as I was straddling it on my way over. I was just in a constant state of anger all day. I finally had a beautiful day of weather and wanted to enjoy it, but with the many trees slowing me down, it was hard to remain joyful.

Once I was able to walk on dirt without the downed tree obstacle course, it felt like I was flying. It had been days since I was able to get up to a decent pace. With all the recent rain and melting ice, one of the streams I had to cross was much higher than normal. Where one would normally hop across on a few rocks, the water was higher than all the rocks. I moved upstream and found a log I could use to cross the waterway. I was always a little nervous doing this because all it took was one slippery step to fall into ice-cold water and completely ruin my day. This could be dangerous on larger streams, but on the AT, the streams were small and posed no threat.

After shuffling across the log with the rapidity of a geriatric on their way up a flight of stairs, I got a hitch into Glasgow. I was glad to resupply but overjoyed to get a replacement part for my water filter. After a week without it, I could confidently drink clean water again.

Back on trail after my ride out of town, I realized I left my earbuds in one of the cars — big mistake. I ordered new ones to be delivered to a post office ahead, but I knew it would be a less enjoyable experience until I could get them.

Some people would say, "You shouldn't listen to anything while you're hiking. You should just enjoy the sounds of nature."

To that person I'd say, "You're a loser. Don't tell me what to do."

I needed my music. There were times when it was pleasant to walk in silence and be totally engulfed in the surroundings, but certainly not always. On a normal thru-hike, a hiker would see other hikers multiple times per day, but that was not the case for me in winter. Going days without seeing people gives you a lot of time to think to yourself, sometimes too much. You definitely have to be comfortable with yourself, which I was. If you're the kind of person who isn't comfortable spending extended periods of time alone, the Calendar Year Triple Crown is not for you.

I am an ambivert. Every time I take an extrovert vs. introvert quiz, it always seems to come back in the middle. I love huge parties. I love meeting new people. I love putting myself out there to experience new things. But I like my alone time too. I'm perfectly content with sitting on the couch for a full-day, solo movie marathon. I am most productive working on something, like this very book, when there is no one else around. And I don't mind being alone for long periods of time. Being in the middle seemed to be valuable for thru-hiking; I could deal with the obvious extended times of isolation, and I was also able to do things like hitchhike, chat up anyone I met, or party a full night with strangers with no difficulty.

Even with my versatile personality type, if I didn't listen to any music, my mind would've gotten bored or gone to bad places simply due to the sheer amount of silence. If I had never listened to music or podcasts while hiking the AT in winter, I would've just thought about how miserable I was all the time. Music and podcasts did a good job of distracting me from the fact that I was perpetually cold and wet, and that the physical misery wasn't going to end anytime soon. In the first stretch of the year on the AT, I would listen to music or podcasts for a few hours a day. As the year went on, my listening time increased, until, by the end, I was always listening to something while hiking unless it was a long stretch between towns when I really needed to conserve battery.

Even aside from the distraction of boredom, music enhanced my hiking experience. It made me feel more in touch with my natural surroundings. It made me feel happy, sad, poetic, powerful, wistful, nostalgic, or rageful based on the song I was listening to. It made me feel like I was the most important thing in the world and that what I was doing right now was the pinnacle of human existence. It made me feel good.

A Secluded Shenandoah

The day passed in total silence. After capping off a 40-mile day around 1 a.m., I was dead tired. A winter storm was fast-approaching, and I had a friend of a friend that said he'd let me crash at his place near Waynesboro, VA. I wanted to get there before the storm and avoid the worst of it. With that motivation of a hot shower and bed, I only slept two hours before I was up and moving again. A strong yearning to be indoors seemed to be the most effective alarm clock.

The snow had already started, and I was losing the trail frequently. I started to just climb up the steep slope of the mountain whenever I got lost, and it would keep reconnecting with the trail. When in doubt, just go up.

I made it into Waynesboro in the afternoon. In true hikertrash fashion, it was below 30 degrees, snowing, and I was sitting on a curb outside of Little Caesar's devouring a large pizza and a 2-liter of Dr. Pepper. I got a multitude of stares from strangers, but I didn't care. I would be warm soon, and that was all that mattered. Just as I finished my pizza, Pat — the friend of a friend who soon became my friend — pulled up in his pickup truck, which gloriously had the heat pumping.

He said he lived in a cabin in the woods without running water, so we'd be staying at his girlfriend's house. That was a good sign. I didn't know the guy, but even if he wasn't a thru-hiker, he was a not-so-distant cousin to hikertrash if he lived in the woods with no running water. I was also glad that his girlfriend was okay with hosting a crazy guy hiking in winter that her boyfriend didn't even know. Again, I was amazed at the kindness people showed to strangers because they were attempting something extraordinary.

They were amazing hosts. I got a shower, a hefty meal, and laundry done — everything a thru-hiker would ever need.

As we were lounging around and getting to know each other over a few beers, Pat mentioned that he had a friend near the trail in New Jersey. Pat asked him about me staying there when I got to New Jersey, and his friend was cool with it. So, when I got up to New Jersey, I would be staying with a friend of a friend of a friend. People are remarkable.

The next morning, Pat dropped me off at the trailhead and gave me $50 for my next resupply, truly benevolent. Once I started hiking again, I realized a few things. The storm wasn't a joke. I was relieved I was indoors and missed the brunt of it. The more important note was that my pack was heavy as hell. I had brought four days of food for this stretch, which was on the extremely conservative side. In addition to buying four days of food, I also had leftovers from my hosts. It was enough food to last me six days, more than I had carried the whole time up to date, and my back strained under the burden of that weight.

As I started hiking, I immediately entered Shenandoah National Park. The weather was nasty. It was foggy and looked like it would start raining or snowing any time. I expected the poor weather I had been experiencing in Virginia to continue — constant fog with rain. I assumed I wouldn't see any views in Shenandoah, but I was wrong. In the afternoon, it cleared up, and was an astoundingly beautiful day.

Arriving at Blackrock just before sunset, it was the first breathtaking beauty I had seen in over two weeks. The summit was a pile of rocks covered in untouched snow with frost-coated trees in every direction 30 feet below, overlooking rolling mountains of dead trees and a sharp blue sky as a background with the sun dropping in the west.

Basking in this stunning and pristine scene, the cold chased me away quickly. I hiked another couple of miles to a picnic area and got ready for my first ever "privy bivy," — I would be sleeping in a bathroom. The next shelter wasn't for 11 miles, and I had mailed home my tent a while back to save weight since I never used it. The pit toilet at Dundo Picnic Area would be home for the night.

I couldn't help but worry it would be locked. My heart was racing as I walked up to the door, but when I turned the handle and it rotated, I breathed a sigh of major relief. Going in, I expected that I would sleep in the women's bathroom because I know what disgusting creatures men are.

However, I was surprised. I ended up sleeping in the men's because somebody seemed to have had an explosion in the women's. In the past, I'd always had a pretty low standard of living, but this was a new level... and I loved it. I didn't know how much I would love sleeping on the floor of a bathroom, but it was so warm in there! I was enclosed in four walls to protect me from the wind, and it was at least 5–10 degrees warmer in a pit toilet than outside. This was the beginning of a constant search to sleep in a bathroom whenever it was available while hiking.

I didn't notice how cold it was throughout the night since I was cozy in the bathroom, but it was three degrees when I got moving for the day. There was a water spigot at the picnic area. When I filled my bottle, some water splashed onto my gloves and froze almost instantly. The water in my bottle began to freeze within ten minutes, but I had my big boy winter mittens, so I wasn't worried about another bout with frostbite.

That being said, the mittens were so thick and bulky that they were a hassle to take off. On days like this, I hardly took any pictures, checked my map, or used my phone. I dreamed of a day later in the year, where I would be able to just pull out my phone and take a picture instantly. I also dreamed of a day when every time I looked down at my phone, there wouldn't be snot running down from my nose onto it. A man can dream.

But the optimistic side of me couldn't be held down. I was joyous it wasn't precipitating anymore. Cold wasn't too bad. Cold and wet was deadly.

The skies were clear again, so I was able to enjoy the beauty of Shenandoah. I also had the place to myself because of the recent snow and ice. Park officials closed Skyline Drive — the main road through the park. So the only way into the park was on foot. With it being winter, that wasn't a popular thing to do. I essentially had a 200,000-acre national park to myself.

It ended up being a 32-mile day even though I didn't plan on that. My plan was to hike to another picnic area 26 miles away but plans frequently go awry when thru-hiking.

When I got to the picnic area with the bathroom to sleep in, my fear became reality. It was locked. My stomach dropped, and I hurriedly hiked another six miles to a shelter, trying to get there as early as possible to take cover from the imminent midnight chill. However, it wasn't an easy six miles because I had broken my headlamp a few days prior. After dark I had to hold the light in my hand like a flashlight to illuminate my path.

I knew it would be an interesting night. The forecasted temperature in the nearest town was negative eight degrees. I was up in the mountains where it would be colder. I'd hoped to stay in another bathroom because it was going to be even colder than the previous night where I slept inside of a bathroom because of the dangerously low temperature. However, this night, I would have to make do in a shelter since it the bathroom was locked.

As soon as I arrived, I unpacked and got inside my sleeping bag. I downed gobs of peanut butter and appreciated the fact that the extreme cold would keep mice from being a problem. The forest was actually so quiet it was eerie. There was nothing moving: no wind blowing, no trees creaking, no sound at all. It was like everything knew it was too cold to be doing anything. I journaled before bed but couldn't write too much. My hands were going painfully numb from being outside my sleeping bag.

Wanting to avoid the worst of the cold, I slept in the next morning. I was plenty warm consumed by my sleeping bag, so I didn't notice the cold much at first. Then I realized my cheese was a solid brick, and a lot of the water sources were frozen. But none of that mattered. It was a magical day.

To kick it off, over 100 deer stood in a frosty meadow under clear blue skies and curiously gazed at me as I passed. I made it to Crescent Rock in the early afternoon, and there was a small ledge jutting out with a vast view over the valley below. I made it my personal McAfee Knob and enjoyed my time sitting on an exposed ledge over a valley with far-reaching views — again upsetting my grandmother.

While feeling blissful three miles later, I opted to do something I don't always do — hike off trail miles to see a view. I made the side trip to a scenic overlook. It was gorgeous, but on the way, I had a little wake-up call. The trail was a diagonal sheet of ice, and the ice continued on an angle on the side of the trail heading down the mountain. I thought I could get across it quickly without having to put on my microspikes.

I thought wrong.

I slipped and fell. I started to slide down the mountain at a tenderly slow pace, but that was how it always started out. I knew I would start picking up speed soon. I could not get any grip or grab onto anything.

Instinctually, I grabbed one of my trekking poles, several inches from the bottom, and stabbed it into the ice. It stuck. I stopped sliding and started to slowly swing side to side like a pendulum from my trekking pole. I grabbed the other one and started to gradually make my way back to the trail by stabbing them into the ice and moving at a glacial pace. When I got back up to the trail, I had a little breather and realized that I had just self-arrested for the first time. The best way to train was by doing, I guess.

That night, I got to a highway crossing where there was a restroom facility. It was better than I could have ever imagined for a shelter. First, there were multiple singular bathrooms, so I didn't have to worry about somebody needing to use the one I was in. Second, there were electrical outlets and running water, although it was scalding hot and did taste a bit like paint — or I should say, what I think paint tastes like. I haven't drunk paint. Lastly, the bathrooms were heated! I was going to hydrate, charge up my electronics, and get a good night's sleep. *It was going to be a perfect night.*

Then I learned that there were two downsides. The lights couldn't turn off, and there was a loud beeping every 15 minutes from an air freshener. With these two complications, I didn't sleep soundly. When I occasionally dozed off, I would be jerked awake by the beeping. My body would tense up every time, like Dwayne Wade waking up in a Gatorade commercial. I would never complain about sleeping in a heated facility, but it did feel like some sort of torturous sleep deprivation experiment.

After being up most of the night, I started packing up in the morning when somebody knocked on the door. I packed up quickly because I was hoping they weren't waiting on me. When I stepped outside, I was relieved to see nobody. I was unrelieved, however, to see the weather.

It was alternating between freezing rain and snow. I wasn't surprised. After three days of sunshine, I was due for some normal AT weather. In the afternoon, the skies cleared, and there were some splashes of blue between patches of fog. When I was in the fog, the temperature seemed to be about five degrees colder, making me want blue skies even more.

I exited Shenandoah National Park and stayed at a shelter right outside the park. I previously had little knowledge of the park but loved my time there. It might've helped that, excluding a major highway crossing perpendicular to Skyline Drive in the park, I had the whole place to myself.

That solitude ended immediately outside the park at the next shelter. Another person showed up! This was my third time camping with another person. We chatted for a while. It turned out he was road tripping across the country and elected to camp in an AT shelter instead of getting a hotel room. He also mentioned that his car was at the next road crossing, and he could give me a ride into town. This was perfect because the road crossing wasn't too far away. I would've gotten there before sunrise, and it would've been tough to hitchhike in the dark, but now that didn't matter.

We woke up early and began hiking. I tried to MacGyver my broken headlamp to a trekking pole with Leukotape. That lasted all of five minutes before breaking. I continued on, clumsily holding it in my mitten. Before long, we arrived at his car, and he brought me to a gas station. I didn't need much, just some warm food for a change, which he volunteered to pay for. With kind souls like this, I sometimes felt like a broken record because I was saying thank you so much. I ended up downing four liters of water in the ten minutes we were there since I had been drinking so little lately in the cold.

He dropped me back off at the trail just before daybreak. I was fueled up, hydrated, and back on trail before I would've even started the day if he hadn't shown up the previous night. It was a lovely day of clear skies and pretty uneventful …

Until I hit the 1,000-mile marker. I didn't often look at the overall mileage from the start of the trail, but that afternoon, I did accidentally. I had just started the "Roller Coaster," a notorious section of trail that repeatedly goes up and down to short peaks and valleys unnecessarily, and I wanted to see how long it was. When I did so, I realized I was around Mile 997 of the trail and would hit Mile 1,000 shortly.

When I got there, there was no marker of any kind. That was alright. I made my own. I drew out a big "1,000" in the snow to mark my humble achievement. It was a gratifying feeling. Soon after, I passed a group of day hikers going in the opposite direction. I wondered if they would know when they saw it or wonder why this guy just randomly wrote out "1,000" in the snow. I was riding high. I tried to ignore most milestones because of how incomprehensibly long the journey was, but some I just couldn't.

"The journey of 1,000 miles begins with a single step."

The journey of 8,000 miles begins with a thousand miles.

Capping off the day at 33 miles, I had one more day before reaching Harper's Ferry. I had family in Maryland, near Harper's Ferry, that was going to pick me up to spend a night at their house. The motivation to get indoors was strong once again.

I woke up at 5 a.m., raring to go, and a couple of hours later, I hit the West Virginia state line after spending three weeks in Virginia. Finally! It was a totally arbitrary distinction on a map made by humans that made no actual difference to the hiking conditions, but it felt tremendously satisfying. I was so sick and tired of Virginia. For so much of the state, I had bad weather and bad trail. I was ready for something new, *or at least the idea of something new*. Maybe that's all we need sometimes.

The truth was that I expected the weather and the trail to only get continually worse heading north, but I was delighted to put the cruel bastard that was Virginia behind me.

It was a hot day by winter standards, which had some positives and some negatives. On the plus side, it was warm. I didn't have to worry about my hands going numb or not being able to stop during the day. I could finally shed some layers. I was down to just my shorts and long sleeve shirt, an outfit that was never before possible with how cold it had been. The combination of the heat and sun also provided the first day that seemed like it could start to melt some of the winter snowpack. On the flip side, because so much snow was melting, I was walking in puddles and slosh all day with soaked feet. With the clear skies and bright sun, I was getting fried by the UV rays reflecting off the snow. I could feel myself getting progressively more sunburnt throughout the day.

In the late morning, I was feeling a little self-pity. I was sweating like a nervous teenager, which I wasn't used to after being in a perpetual state of cold all winter. I had no protection from the sun. I could feel myself getting scorched. And I was just tired and wanted to be resting indoors already.

Then I saw two hikers coming my way. It was a father and his young daughter with a full backpacking setup, not day hiking. This 12-year-old girl was exuding confidence and joy, the likes of which I hadn't seen in ages. Her dad said she didn't say one negative word the whole overnight trip. She didn't care about hiking in the snow, or the cold at night, or blistering sun during the day. She was just happy to be out there.

Several things crossed my mind. First, this little girl was on track to be the next Wonder Woman if she was backpacking in February at this age. Second, it was the cutest thing I had seen in a long time. Lastly, and most importantly, if this little girl was hiking in this and not complaining, I better toughen up and deal with it.

Positive attitudes and positive people are contagious. They remind us that we are okay. There is no need to fret. We can handle this. Seeing this little girl enjoying the brutality reminded me that I'm perfectly capable to do the same. I might as well stop feeling sorry for myself and instead appreciate the journey for what it is, whether it be freezing cold, or now the blistering sun. I would've begged for the latter while in most of Virginia.

Life was good! I cruised the rest of the day, riding high on my renewed sense of appreciation, and made it into Harper's Ferry just before sunset. I witnessed the sky change to vibrant shades of pink and orange over the Potomac River and then got picked up by my relatives in front of John Brown's armory.

Before I stayed with Todd and Jill in Maryland, we had never met. They were part of a big extended family on my mother's side.

On the ride back to their house, Todd said, "We better stop and get some beer." *That was a good sign. These people are going to be cool.* Then, when he walked out of the carry-out with a 30-pack of Natural Light for me, my thoughts were confirmed. They really were my family.

When I got back to the house, I met the rest of the family. I met my second cousin, Jill, and her three young kids. One was a baby, but the other two were little bundles of energy. I wanted to try to figure out how to bottle up that energy and take it with me on the trail. They would go back and forth between marveling at me like I was a zoo exhibit and wanting to show me everything in their house. It was fun being around some kids again after being isolated with my own thoughts for so long.

After showering, consuming more food than their whole family combined, and knocking back a few beers, I went to bed with the freedom of not setting an alarm — such a liberating feeling after being so regimented on the hike. When I woke up in the morning, I decided to take my first rest day. I was debating taking one, and when I woke up in the morning and didn't want to move, I committed to it. My relatives were pleased to have me stay an extra night, and I was ecstatic to have another day indoors with real food — simple pleasures.

We went to a grocery store so I could buy food for the next stretch. While there, I also picked up a half gallon of ice cream for a little challenge I would be doing later. While standing in the checkout line, I had a thought cross my mind that would stick with me not only the rest of the year, but the rest of my life:

There are no shadows in the storm.

We are alone in this world. We try to fool ourselves into always thinking everything will be okay, no matter what happens. "If I get in a car crash, an EMT can save me." "If my marriage is falling apart, a marriage counselor can save it." "If some tragedy were to happen when I'm hiking out in the wilderness, Search and Rescue can save me." "No matter what happens, God will save me."

But maybe traffic is bad, so the EMT can't get to you in time, and you die because your cardiovascular system is weak after years of poor diet and exercise. Maybe it's too late to save your marriage because you've been overly selfish for years, and there's no possible retribution or change that can alter the way your spouse now sees you. Maybe Search and Rescue can't get to you because there's a hellacious storm preventing them from leaving. Maybe God has better things to do.

There are no shadows in the storm. When things are at their absolute worst — when the wind is howling, the trail is disappearing, the temperature is dropping, ice is coating your eyelids, snow is smacking you from every which way, and black clouds are blocking out the sun — you can only depend on yourself. You can't even turn to your own shadow for support. No one else is there. It's just you, and you've got to be ready to face anything — alone. You are the only person in the world that you can fully, completely, and undoubtedly rely on. Maybe you'll get lucky and a rare fortune of fate or an unlikely passing stranger will help you, but it is foolhardy to rely on anyone else to save you.

After forming this meta thought in a grocery store checkout line, I tried to push it out of my head and enjoy relaxing the rest of the day. But after supper, there was no time for relaxation — it was game time.

I got the half gallon of ice cream out of the freezer and was ready to go. Normally, the halfway point on the AT is near a store where hikers can buy ice cream and try to eat a half gallon in honor of being halfway done with the trail. In winter, that store was closed, so I had to make do. I would pass the halfway point in a few days and thought this night, where I was warm and indoors, was the perfect time to attempt the "challenge."

Although, I hesitate to even call it that because it was so unchallenging. I wasn't even thinking about it. I was just casually eating it while talking, and before I knew it, it was gone. After having already eaten a full supper, I devoured the half gallon and legitimately thought I could've easily eaten ¾ of a gallon, maybe even a full gallon. After a few more Natural Lights, I went to bed, thankful for the kindness of family and comfort of indoors.

My cousin dropped me off in Harper's Ferry the next morning. Sad to see me go, her daughter said, "Maybe, when you get to Maine, you can turn around and come back to visit."

I smiled and told her, "I'll think about it." I said one last goodbye to the kids and strolled over the bridge into Maryland.

It seemed like I blinked, and I was already leaving Maryland. The trail was so generous, I was covering ground quickly. When it came to the views, Maryland wasn't anything special, but it was a cool historical state. There were a lot of markings from the Civil War, and I also visited the original Washington Monument right on trail. The remake is certainly more visually appealing than the original.

For my one night in Maryland, I camped at a shelter right by Interstate 70. I crossed a bridge over the interstate right before getting to the shelter and it was a cathartic moment. It was a good reminder of how blessed I was to be out here, rather than being stuck in traffic, on my way home from an unsatisfying job. While I counted my blessings often, traffic seemed to be one of the most visual reminders of how different and blessed of a life I was currently living compared to most people.

Immediately before starting this hike, I was working a job I despised to save up money for the adventure. I truly hated my life for eight hours every day. But I knew it was all for something. It was for this. This adventure was the light at the end of the tunnel that gave me hope in the weird year of 2020. The best part of my day that whole year was when I got off work and immediately started working out. The next three hours weren't easy, but they were for something. They were for this trip to be successful. And I knew it would be successful because I visualized success constantly, even when I wasn't conscious. From the day I committed to this endeavor until I left, I would dream about being on the trail every night. I was so singularly focused that my mind wouldn't wander to anything else in my life. I would grind away at a horrible job during the day, train all evening, and dream about the adventure all night.

Now I was living my dream.

Even after this moment of grateful clarity, my rage became untethered and knew no bounds that night in the shelter with an aggressive mouse. He kept running up on me, even after me repeatedly shooing him away in annoyance.

He made a mistake. This fool was slower than the mice I had been dealing with all year. This was my first chance to actually get a victory — and I did. I sat still, with my shoe in my hand, ready to strike. The pestering nuisance flew a little too close to the sun, and I got my first kill of the year.

I'm not a killer, but don't push me.

It was a peaceful night of sleep thereafter. It had snowed and sleeted throughout the night but turned to rain in the morning. After 20 more miles, I crossed the Mason-Dixon Line and returned home to the Union.

The following day was a trial on the extent of my patience. I came to a road crossing where I needed to hitchhike into town to resupply. It was pouring rain, and I stood there for 40 minutes with no luck. It was a busy road, and I was becoming more furious with every car passing by in the rain.

Eventually, I started to walk the three miles into Fayetteville, PA. Within five minutes of me walking alongside the road, a car stopped and brought me into town. This person was an angel. He brought me to Dollar General, waited for me to check out, and then brought me back to the trail. He also gave me his phone number if I needed any more help while in the area. My opinion of other people had gone from rock bottom, when every car was passing me in the rain for 40 minutes, to unbelievably generous.

The rain was unrelenting. It was raining when I woke up. It rained all day. And it was raining when I went to bed. Hiking wasn't very enjoyable. I spent the entire day trying to navigate the canal that was the trail. There was 2–6 inches of water lying on the trail, depending on the area, and melting snow embankments on the sides. I would try to walk on the snow embankments but would slide down into the water. I would try walking wide-legged with one foot on each side of the trail. Aside from it being terribly inefficient, it only worked for a short time, until I took a step in a puddle of water hiding underneath some snow. The trail was just absurd. Everything on me was soaked through.

In the afternoon, I came across a bathroom with a hand dryer. I was ecstatic. I began to laugh at myself as I was holding my socks under the hand dryer and repeatedly hitting the button so it ran constantly. *This is ridiculous. I'm holding my socks under a dryer in the hopes that they'll get to the point where they're almost bearable, just to go back outside and again walk in puddles and wet snow in the pouring rain.* But I loved it in a dumb way and could appreciate the goofiness of the situation — just another day in the paradise that is thru-hiking.

I passed three markers for the halfway point on the trail. The first one, which was actually the correct distance, was just a wooden board with graffiti on it. The second one was the halfway point in 2018, but the trail had been extended since then. The trail I hiked was 2.1 miles longer than in 2018, so it was about .001% more difficult in my estimation. The 3rd marker was the most robust and would've been a decent photo op, but my hands were too wet to operate my phone.

When I arrived at my shelter for the night, I reminded myself of the main benefit of thru-hiking in the winter. Nobody was around, certainly not in this weather. I took off all my waterlogged clothes and hung up the sodden rags around the shelter. I didn't expect them to be dry by morning, but I was at least foolishly hopeful they would be slightly improved. In my birthday suit, I ate and journaled while standing up and walking around in the shelter. I wanted my sopping and wrinkled skin to dry out before I curled up in my sleeping bag. It was bitterly cold and unenjoyable, but it felt good to be dry by the time I was in my warm sleeping bag.

After walking a mile and a half in the depressing rain the next morning, I realized I left my glove liners back at camp. I stood in place for a minute and contemplated how much monetary value I put on walking back 1.5 miles. When I decided it was less than the cost of the gloves, I yelled out of frustration and went back for them. I then angrily walked the 1.5 miles back to where I made the unpleasant revelation and did a small resupply at a general store, before hiking 11 more miles into Boiling Springs, PA, where I met my familiar shuttle driver.

I was excited to get to this point where I could bypass 160 miles and move up the trail. My original plan was to start the Calendar Year Triple Crown on January 4th. That changed when my Ohio State Buckeyes made it to the National Championship in football.

As an Ohio State graduate, football lover, and enthusiastic partier, I was not going to miss being in Columbus for that. I ended up hiking 160 miles of the AT in Pennsylvania that first week in January before the championship. I went back to Ohio for the championship game, which had a less-than-desirable outcome. Still hungover, I hit the road the following day to head to Georgia to start at Springer Mountain on January 13th.

Now I had made it back to Boiling Springs, one end of the section I had hiked, and met up with my shuttle driver, Mike. We were friends by this point. He shuttled me over three hours when I did the Mid State Trail in Pennsylvania during the month of December as my final training. He shuttled me in January when I did that section in Pennsylvania. And this would be our 3rd time spending an hours-long car ride together. He was an interesting guy and charged a fair price — nothing else I could've asked for.

After he dropped me off, it was a quiet day. I battened down the hatches at the shelter for the night. It was going to be 15 degrees with wind gusts up to 50 mph, so it would be five or ten below zero with the wind chill. I hardly noticed. I was cozy inside my sleeping bag, and only woke up to the sound of the wind a few times. It was also a peaceful night because it was the first night on trail where I didn't set an alarm. Tomorrow was going to be a short day, so my start time didn't matter.

I awoke the next morning feeling uninhibited by the dependency on an alarm clock. It was liberating. I hiked seven miles into Delaware Water Gap while calling a few friends since I knew I would be indoors tonight and could charge my phone. I would be staying with Nick — the friend of the friend who I stayed with in Virginia. He got off work in the early afternoon, so I loitered at a pizza place in town until he came. They had a little bit of indoor dining available, which was always an uncertainty with the pandemic. Like bathrooms being unlocked, I was never sure going into a place if they would allow indoor dining or not. With the weather being nasty most of the time, takeout wasn't really an option for me.

After downing a 16-inch meat lover's pizza and a couple of 2-liters of Dr. Pepper, Nick came and picked me up. We went back to his place, and I had a peaceful night indoors. I was grateful to get my things dried out for the first time in a while.

New States in New England

Crossing the Delaware River, I began the next day by leaving Pennsylvania and entering New Jersey. Instead of a serene natural boundary, I found myself walking across a bustling road bridge, but it served as another vivid reminder of how fortunate I was to be here, living my dreams.

When I arrived at a trailhead to head back into the woods, I was overjoyed to see that there were track marks from other hikers, so I wouldn't be breaking trail all day. It was now March 3rd and temperatures were fairly warm at times.

I liked the warmer temperatures, but they intensified the postholing. I was reminded of this later in the day when the tracks over the trail disappeared and the sun was beating down. I found myself sinking above my knees, hoping each step wouldn't plunge me into an unexpected void. By day's end, the endless high-knees movement had drained me completely.

After slogging through several miles the next morning, I made it down to a road crossing where I needed to hitch into town to do a resupply. This was my longest wait yet. I waited 45 minutes before a kind-hearted lady stopped. This was my first time — and one of only a handful of times all year — in which I was picked up by a single woman for a hitch. I was always a little surprised and particularly grateful at their willingness to put themselves at a perceived risk. Some of them knew about the trails, so they knew it was safe. But some didn't, and they picked me up anyways.

This woman did know about the trail, and we had a lively conversation about the AT. She gave me the best compliment I had heard in weeks. She said she was surprised that I didn't smell unbearable like normal hikers. That was one of the few benefits of hiking in winter since I didn't usually sweat. She was also the third local recently that told me that they hadn't seen a winter like this in ten years. In addition to the snow, she said that normally the lakes only froze for two weeks in January, but they were still frozen solid now in March. This was my first intense winter hiking, so I didn't have anything to compare it to, but I just found it funny that it had to be this year. This driver was such a wonderful person that she waited in the car while I shopped and then dropped me back off at the trail. After the initial wait for a hitch, her selflessness meant the world to me.

After getting back on trail, my appreciation for human kindness was overtaken by aggression at compacted solid water molecules. The snow was killing me. It was exhausting — continuously sliding, lunging, and falling with each step. Water was sitting on top of the snow from the melting. My feet got exceptionally wet from sinking in snow all day. They stayed dry for a short time because I used a little pro trick. I put Walmart bags between my socks and shoes as an extra layer of water protection. I did this often while traveling in the snow, but the protection usually doesn't last. It depends on the terrain, but the bags will tear and then water gets through. With as much sliding around as I was doing that day, they didn't last 20 minutes.

Later in the day, I wandered off trail and was walking on some snow when it collapsed. My feet plummeted into black, murky water up to my knees. *Anger. Yelling. Grimace. Sigh. Release.*

After dreadfully struggling through most of the day, I got a sudden surge of energy in the last two hours. Needing fuel, I downed ¾ of a family size bag of Peanut Butter M&M's while taking a short break because I was hungry, and none of my other food was easily accessible. I started to feel sick. I felt bloated and gaseous. I just couldn't let out a perfect belch to relieve the pressure I felt. While listening to an EDM playlist, I felt strange and was in a hypnotic state. My head felt hot. My stomach was churning. I felt dizzy, and my vision was wavy. I sat down for a minute and then kept moving without much relief. Repeatedly burping, I tried to push out the bad feeling until, right on a beat drop, I let out the most satisfying belch that I felt surge through my nose and ears. It cleansed my soul. *I think I just survived a sugar overdose.* My head felt decompressed and it was go time.

I reached the high point in New Jersey after dark, making it hard to appreciate the view. However, the intense winds gusting at 70–80 mph added a touch of wildness to the experience. As I attempted to capture a photo of the high point, I had to tightly grip my gloves, fearing they might be swept away. The relentless wind made it challenging to hold onto my phone. Even my pack cover flailed about, threatening to detach and take flight. After getting numb hands from only being up there a couple of minutes, I rushed back down below tree line as fast as I could.

When I made it to High Point Shelter, I was surprised to see another hiker there. He was doing a section hike for a few days. While I didn't understand why he was voluntarily out in these conditions, I respected him for doing so, and questioned if I sounded equally crazy when I told people I was out voluntarily thru-hiking in these conditions. There were not many people like him doing section hikes in the winter. This was my fourth time out of 58 days not having the shelter to myself in the solitude of winter.

I had a later-than-expected start the next morning. My kryptonite was always getting up and moving when it was still so damn cold. I'd put it off for as long as I could, until I finally accepted that waiting wasn't going to make it any better. When I started an hour later, it was still one degree with the wind chill. But with the frigid temperature, the snow was firm, and I wasn't postholing much. That helped with my speed and level of enjoyment.

After seven miles, I took a short detour to do a quick resupply at a general store. After my purchases, I sat on the porch in the freezing cold and tried to eat as much as possible, so I could carry less weight on my back. My ability to binge eat was one of my best assets of the year.

Later in the day, I reached Pinwheels Vista, a popular day hiking area. The trail had turned into a treacherous sheet of ice from the heavy foot traffic. Some hikers I encountered dared to tackle it without microspikes or any traction, and I couldn't help but feel sorry for them. Realistically, I doubted whether I could navigate it safely without my microspikes. As I reached the summit, I gazed in awe at the distant high point tower where I had spent the previous night — 20 miles away. It was rare that I could see so evidently the progress I had made.

I crossed over into New York the following morning but nearly missed the state line because the painting on the rocks was partially covered with snow. Shortly after entering New York, I realized that I could see the city off in the distance. It was an interesting contrast — America's most densely populated city within sight of this "wild" trail.

Taking a detour into Greenwood Lake, I did a small resupply at a deli. I got a couple of sandwiches, but other than that, the selection at the store wasn't catered to hikers. The owner said it surprised him to see anyone up that far north this early, but that he normally carried more hiker-specific food in the summer. He was generous enough to let me use the "Employee's Only" restroom. Little generosities like that made me so grateful.

While checking the weather in town, I learned it was going to significantly warm up soon. I was torn. Obviously, I liked warmer temperatures, but I had grown fond of the cold temperatures as of late. They weren't unbearable, but they did a good job of keeping the snow firm. Excluding a couple of warm days and cold nights as outliers, it had been 10–15 degrees at night and mid-to-high 20s during the day, seemingly perfect.

After leaving town, I learned that the terrain in New York wasn't particularly enjoyable. The climbs seemed to only be rewarded with nothing except an immediate steep descent because trees were blocking any potential views. Some climbs were so steep that I had to ditch my poles and scramble on all fours to keep moving up on snow and ice. It would've been much less cumbersome if snow and ice weren't everywhere, but this was my journey.

After doing a steep descent of what locals call "Agony Grind," I made it down to a road crossing. A trail angel had agreed to pick me up there and treat me to some pizza in town. In retrospect, I shouldn't have wasted time resupplying earlier in the day. However, I was hesitant to continue on without food and count 100% on a stranger to pick me up on a road where I didn't know how busy it would be. I also didn't know if there would be cell signal if he didn't show up, so I played it safe and resupplied earlier in the day, just in case. I only wanted to 100% count on myself.

There are no shadows in the storm.

But a different sort of storm began raging the following day. It wasn't a storm of snow, ice, wind, or rain, and it wasn't a storm dealt with in solitude like my mantra evokes. It was a storm of congestion, a pressurized buildup of too many human bodies in a single space resulting in shorter tempers, shorter strides, and shorter distances covered in a given time.

On the Appalachian Trail in winter, it was rare that I would come across a person, exceptionally rare that it would be more than a couple. However, when I reached Bear Mountain in New York, I saw more people than I had seen the whole time on trail.

It was a popular spot close to New York City, and I was there on a Sunday. It was far too busy to be enjoyable. I was constantly coming up behind people hoping they would allow me to pass because I felt rude asking to pass, even though, in reality, I was much faster and perpetually in a hurry. The other side of the mountain, on the descent, was even worse because that's where the parking lot was. The trail was so congested, going in two lanes, that it was impossible to pass. I gritted my teeth and moved at a pace slow enough to please a tortoise.

Amidst the bustling crowd, I stood out like a bodybuilder at the beach. Some of the people had daypacks, but most had nothing. Meanwhile, I had a fully stocked backpack with a giant bag of Lays potato chips strapped on the outside, as if on display because it was the only size the little store had. I heard a lot of people laughing at it, and someone even remarked, "That's the best ad for Lays chips I've ever seen." I liked to imagine that they thought Lays hired a disheveled-looking man to go out and wander in the mountains with a visible Lays bag to get people to buy more chips. It was these little jokes to myself that kept me sane.

Toward the end of the day, I stopped at a gas station to get a burger and a small resupply. Primarily, my intention was to hang out and charge my phone while working on my plan. In this section of trail, there was a nearly 50-mile stretch without a shelter, and since I wasn't carrying a tent anymore, that didn't leave a lot of options. This was the first night that the shelters were so spread out that not having a tent was actually an issue. If I was out west, I would just cowboy camp, but with the wet weather in Appalachia, I would never count on that. My original plan was to just hike all through the night and be miserable. I could have done it, but I just really wasn't feeling it, and it would mess up my sleep schedule.

I learned that Graymoor Spiritual Life Center, a church nearby, would let hikers camp on their property. Arriving there around dusk, I found a spot to cowboy camp under a pavilion that was under construction. It had a roof and looked safe enough, which met my low standard of living. I made sure to be out of there by the time the construction workers got there in the morning to avoid questions.

With the added pressure of being scolded by the workers, I actually woke up on time — an unusual feat for me. It was a perfectly mediocre day, capped off with a perfectly mediocre pizza at a deli slightly off trail. The owner was gracious enough to let me dine in, even though it was closed.

After a restless night of sleeping alongside three energetic mice, I walked through swamps via boardwalks and got a hitch into Pawling, NY to do a quick resupply. The cashier was puzzled at what I was doing at first, but after I explained it to her, she was fascinated. She began telling everyone in the store. I was their hottest new attraction for the next few minutes until I got out of there. The circus-like attention did get me a ride out of town before I even had to ask. Securing a ride while in the store was a skill I would try to master as time went on.

The weather had been beautiful for several consecutive days, an uncommon occurrence in Appalachia. I even broke out my short shorts and relished in the liberating sensation of UV rays toasting my legs. It was such a freeing feeling, rather than wearing long pants or tight leggings every day.

I hardly needed food in the next town of Kent, CT. This area of trail was littered with frequent potential resupply locations, resulting in me often only carrying one day of food. It was nice to have the lighter pack weight and frequent town luxuries of real food and Dr. Pepper. While lounging in Kent and charging my phone, I downed a 2-liter of Dr. Pepper and 3,000 calories of food from my resupply. I always wanted to eat as much as possible in town to then carry the least amount of weight possible in my pack. I didn't believe in meals, or spacing out calories, or anything like that. Calories go in. Energy comes out. It's that simple.

My main task while in town was to begin trying to set up my summit for Katahdin, the end point of the Appalachian Trail, and a highly restricted area. Previously, I had sent an application, and been granted permission to summit the mountain on March 31st, the last day it is open for winter summits. After March 31st, it is closed until the park opens it up in late May or early June. If I was to continue northward, I would get there around mid-April. Since it would be illegal to summit then, my working plan was to get a ride up there to summit on March 31st, and then head south to wherever I flipped from.

While in Kent, I began to work on a ride to the park. I knew it wouldn't be easy to get a seven-hour shuttle, which is why I started asking around three weeks ahead of time. I contacted every possible shuttle in Maine that I could find online, mostly with no luck, but there were a few that said they might be able to do it. I began to work on the logistics with them over the coming days.

The logistics of this ride were one more thing I would now constantly be thinking about, along with: *Are my average miles on pace? How is the weather looking? How is the snowpack in the Sierra? Do I need any gear changes mailed to me? How is my budget looking? Am I pushing myself too hard? Do I have enough food? Am I eating enough? Am I drinking enough? Where will I end the day? Are my feet just in pain or seriously injured? Am I going to be able to make it?*

A million more thoughts just like these bounced around in my head at all times, like a never-ending lottery ball machine of worries. I was so focused on this singular goal; my mind was always thinking about the next step to set myself up for success.

While sitting, engrossed in my planning, two older women stopped by the community center where I was sitting. We were talking for a while, and eventually, I explained what I was doing, not just with the AT, but with the whole year. They couldn't believe it. I never got tired of seeing people's reactions when I told them. In my past, I would've been just like them. I had first heard about the Appalachian Trail and Pacific Crest Trail in 2018. When

I learned there was a trail from Georgia to Maine and another from Mexico to Canada, I thought it was preposterous. I couldn't believe that every year, humans were walking these trails for over 2,000 miles. *They had to be lying.*

I thought the same the first time I'd heard of the Calendar Year Triple Crown. I was listening to a podcast with a guest that completed the feat. When he first explained what it was — hiking all three Triple Crown trails in a single calendar year — I figured he had to be lying. At that point, my knowledge of thru-hiking was limited. I hadn't done it, but I knew that to do a single one of the Triple Crown trails typically took hikers 5–6 months each. And people were so tired after a single trail! *There's no way he did all three in one year. That's impossible!*

And now, here I was, doing the impossible, and inspiring others the same way I was inspired just a few years earlier — from awe and disbelief.

As I began to walk back to the trail, a truck stopped, and the driver asked if I needed a ride. I happily hopped into the truck bed since the cab was full. He had a cooler full of beer in the cab, which might not have been the safest thing, but I was gracious when he offered me one. Sitting in the bed of a pickup truck, with a Budweiser in hand and the wind blowing through my greasy hair on a beautiful day, was one of the coolest feelings I'd had in a while. I felt alive.

Once I got back on trail, the hiking proved to be effortless. The trail ran along a serene river and most of the snow was gone. With all the warm weather recently, there were only occasional patches of snow at these low elevations, but nothing like the wintry conditions I'd encountered previously.

The weather was so splendid that when I got to Pine Swamp Brook Shelter, it was the first time all year that I ate my end-of-the-day food at a picnic table outside the shelter. Ideally, it was better to keep the smell of food outside of shelters to not attract mice and bears, but the weather was usually too cold and nasty to do so.

Little did I know, I wouldn't be alone at the shelter. I had to contend with mice nearly every night on the AT. It was not ideal. They were annoying. They were disgusting. They kept me awake. I would try to fight back, but other than one, they were always too quick. Over time, I had become accustomed to sharing my living space with them.

This night was different, however. As I settled down, I heard something running around in the shelter, but it was louder. Instead of hearing a little scurrying across the floorboards, I heard a deep scratching into the wood as this creature moved about. This wasn't a mouse, but a rat that must've joined in the exodus from New York and took up residence in this shelter. Despite its substantial size, it was astonishingly agile. I only caught glimpses of it when I turned on my headlamp, before it darted out of sight like a monster in a horror movie. It continued running around all night like a second-grader after four Mountain Dews. Needless to say, I probably only slept for an hour amidst the ruckus.

I tiredly hiked through a marshy area in the morning. I knew it was risky, but I threw my worries to the side and kept moving. Unsurprisingly, the snow below me collapsed and I sunk into black putrid swamp water up to my thighs. I frantically got onto solid ground, hyperventilating from the shock, and then proceeded to yell some expletives. Thankfully, my "Good Vibes Only" mindset kicked in quickly. I was happy it didn't ruin my phone, and I would be getting new shoes in a couple of hours and throwing these now disgusting ones away. Unfortunately, in the fiasco, I broke off over half of my trekking pole in the marsh, so I was down to one pole.

After I began a short road walk into Falls Village, I was assaulted by two dogs. They were barking and snapping at my legs for over five minutes before the owner obliviously emerged. It then took the owner more than five minutes before he could even control them enough where I could pass the house. Most of my animal encounters where I genuinely felt threatened were not bears, but uncontrolled dogs. Man's best friend isn't so friendly when another man is walking by his master's property.

Upon arriving at the post office, I picked up a package of essentials. Especially, because of how my morning went, I was grateful to get new shoes and socks. I also had my tent sent to me. When I was in New York with infrequent shelters, I panicked and had it mailed out. Although it seemed that shelters were now more frequent, I held onto the tent as a precautionary measure. I also had food sent to me for a resupply since this was a small town with limited options.

It was a sight to behold as I spread out my supplies across the grass beside the post office, attracting curious gazes from locals. Some regarded me as if I were a madman, while others displayed a genuine interest and enthusiasm. Before departing, the kind folks at the post office generously filled my water bottles and wished me luck on my journey.

With newfound provisions in hand, I resumed my journey and soon passed the 1,500-mile marker. It had been a while since reaching a big milestone, so I hadn't been thinking about the mileage. Gradual progress adds up, whether you're thinking about it or not.

When I arrived at the shelter that evening, I was surprised to see another person there. He was talking on his phone when I arrived, which I didn't mind … at first. He then continued to talk loudly and indecorously for over 20 minutes, complaining about his ex-wife and other things I didn't want to hear. Once he got off the phone, I brushed that aside and let it go. We talked, and he then started to ask a lot of questions about what I was doing, and I made the mistake of telling him.

He soon became the most annoying person I encountered all year. He essentially told me I would die in the White Mountains. He treated me like I was an imbecile, even though I had just walked there from Georgia in the winter, and he did some hiking in the White Mountains on the weekends. My favorite remark revolved around the fact that if I hiked in the White Mountains with trail runners in the winter, my shoes would come off when my feet postholed, and then I would be stranded barefoot in the snow.

This guy was painfully annoying. All I wanted to do was to tell him to shut the hell up and leave me alone, but the Midwesterner in me wouldn't allow that. Instead, I just tried to respond as little as possible and give the clear indication I didn't want to talk. I don't think he picked up on it. When I wouldn't respond, he would continue blabbering as if I had answered him. This continued on for a while in the shelter, without me responding, before he finally stopped talking so I could sleep. He was a perfect representation of what I thought of for a stereotypical northeastern asshole.

Eager to distance myself from that insufferable individual, I anxiously set off the next morning, fully aware that I needed to push for a long day of hiking, as I planned to rest the following day.

I aggressively and therapeutically climbed up to Bear Mountain for the sunrise. Although the sky was shrouded in clouds, the colors that seeped through were vivid and captivating. The descent from Bear Mountain proved to be arduous. There were frozen waterfalls cascading down where the trail was supposed to be, with nowhere safe to descend. I had to go painstakingly slow to find a viable path, and it was still dangerous. It took me 20 minutes to descend one frozen waterfall that was 40 feet tall, and then there were only more after that. I somehow made it down several seemingly-impossible waterfalls before getting back down to semi-normal terrain.

After that morning challenge, I crossed the state-boundary into Massachusetts and commenced the ascent up Mount Race. Right at the border sign was my first true ford of the Appalachian Trail. Normally, hikers would be able to rock-hop across the stream, but with all of the melt that was going on, the water was high and I had to get my feet wet, which was much more mentally painful than physically. I just kept telling myself everything would be dry tomorrow when I was indoors.

The climb up Mount Race was nothing short of breathtaking. The trail was on a side of the mountain with open ledges and graceful birds gliding nearby the whole time. There were a few more beautiful summits and scenic vistas before the day mellowed out. I even got a free beer before capping off a 37-mile day and getting picked up by a familiar face.

Cold Hell

I enjoyed a relaxing rest day with Mayo, a southbound hiker I met in Hot Springs, NC. His house had everything I could've asked for: running water and heat. But it also had a sauna and a hot tub with a view overlooking the surrounding mountains. I really enjoyed a day in the high life.

In the middle of the day, we ventured out to the grocery store and McDonald's. I got a relatively small order by my standards: five double cheeseburgers and two large fries. I guess other people didn't think it was small. The worker couldn't help but laugh as he was reading it back to me because he knew it was only for one person. When I picked it up from the counter, I turned around and saw two girls with their mouths ajar in disbelief. I smiled and walked out to the car. Mayo said that after I left, they kept talking about it for the next five minutes. "Like damn! Where does he put that?! I know he's tall but where??"

My eating skills may have impressed people even more than my multi-thousand-mile hiking endeavor.

After lounging around Mayo's house and gratefully enjoying a warm night indoors, I got back on trail the next morning. It was daylight savings time, so the clocks even had the same desire as me — move forward.

The temperature had dropped back down below freezing from its recent highs, making the snow hard-packed again. In addition to the lower temperatures, it was windy. When I got to camp for the night, the wind was around 30 mph, and its effect was annoyingly noticeable.

Rather than end my day early at a shelter, I decided to hike an extra few miles to a campsite. I was just off a rest day, and I was feeling good, so I opted to push farther, even if it meant not sleeping in a shelter.

That was a mistake.

I set up my tent on top of the snow and laid down for the night. The temperature began to drop quickly and before I knew it, it was 20 degrees below zero. This was certainly not a night to have stayed in my tent instead of a shelter. Really, I shouldn't have even been outdoors with as lethally cold as it was, but my tent was definitely the worst option. All night, I felt the wind ripping through the nylon material, blasting me with another wave of cold misery. I had on every layer of clothing that I had, and I was still worryingly cold.

All I could think about was how the main noticeable symptom of hypothermia was wanting to fall asleep. But how would I notice that if I got it while trying to go to sleep? *If I fall asleep, is that good because I'm resting, or bad because I'm dying?* The paranoia of this paradox kept me awake, and I probably slept a total of 15 minutes throughout the night. All of the other hours were spent shivering with a cramped and strained back while wondering if I might not make it through the night.

The next morning, I waited to get out of my tent until after 9 a.m., so it was a little warmer with the sun shining. It was still -11 when I got moving. After the misery of taking down my tent with throbbing, numb, and painful fingers, I began hiking as fast as my body allowed. I ran when I could, trying to heat myself up. Every single thing on me was cold.

After four miles of struggling to move because of exhaustion and a lack of rest, but needing to move for warmth and survival, my cold night in hell ended. I made it into Cheshire, MA and triumphantly retreated into the post office for shelter. I sat down inside, enjoying the modern marvel of heat, while also wondering how close I really was to hypothermia.

After recovering for an hour and getting back to baseline, I picked up a new trekking pole and some food. I had what I needed, and I was warm enough — it was time to get moving again. The only way is thru.

Climbing 2,500 feet up to Mount Greylock, the tallest peak in Massachusetts, wasn't overly challenging on the south side. There were tracks from two people that snowshoed the route, but it must've been on a warm day because the imprints from their snowshoes were over two feet deep. I mentally thanked them because without those, it would've been much more difficult. I was already doing high knees and hopscotch all day to avoid downed tree branches, but at least I wasn't postholing.

Near the summit, there was a little shed that held firewood, I and hid out there for a bit to escape the cold. While in there, I called a trail angel in the area. This woman contacted me recently and said she'd like to help. I wasn't going to ask her for help unless I really needed it. Now I needed it! The ensuing night was supposed to be nearly as cold as the previous night. I didn't want to go through hypothermia paranoia again.

Calling the trail angel, I asked if I would be able to stay at her house. She said she lived far away from where I was but volunteered to pay for a motel for me for the night. It was so generous. Because if she didn't offer, I would have stubbornly slept outside again. I had stayed indoors two nights ago and I didn't want to pay for a night indoors again so soon.

Joyful now that I knew I would be indoors tonight, I began the descent down the mountain. Before I knew it, it was dark and I was walking in Williamstown. It was impossible to get a hitch after dark, so I had to walk a few extra miles to get to the motel. On the way, I did a small resupply and got four footlongs from Subway. With as cold as it had been lately, I had hardly been eating or drinking anything.

I checked into the motel that the lovely trail angel paid for, savoring a steaming hot shower after two days of bone-chilling cold. I ate two of the footlongs before retiring to bed, and the other two in the morning.

It was a little warmer when I left the room to get back out on trail. I waited near the road for 15 minutes for a hitch with no luck. Then I started walking back to the trail. I made it about a mile before a car stopped and brought me the rest of the way. The driver was on his way to drop his kids off at school. I loved how he was doing something so normal and opted to take a little detour to bring a hiker back to the trail.

Shortly thereafter, I crossed the boundary into Vermont — my 12th state of the journey. I was now also on the Long Trail, a hiking trail spanning the state of Vermont. After crossing into Vermont, I would not see the ground again. Previous states at least had patches of dirt, but in The Green Mountain State, every square inch was snow-covered.

It was a tough day of hiking to make it 20 miles. There were at least faint remnants of tracks from other people. They must have hiked on the nice days because, although the tracks were starting to drift over, they appeared to be made from some deep postholes. I didn't drink much water because I told myself I'd make up for it at camp, but when I got to the shelter, the water source was frozen over with several inches of ice.

When I awoke the next morning, I had no idea what was in store for me. I didn't know that it would be one of the most frustrating days of the year, and that doing 17 miles would feel like a 45-mile day. I expected more people would get out and hike the Long Trail in the winter, but that was not the case. There were no footprints to follow, and there were no blazes on trees that were visible. Having white blazes on trees that were covered in white snow wasn't the best situation. Following the alleged "trail" was impossible because the pristine snow covering the forest floor all looked the same. The trail could feasibly be anywhere under the four feet of snow I was walking on, and sinking through, all day.

I postholed constantly. I would be walking and jarringly fall down three feet. The only thing that stopped me from falling farther was my other leg jamming into the snow. I did this at least 20 times that day. I even managed to hit myself in the face with a trekking pole that was stuck in the snow and recoiled when I fell. Another time, I accidentally performed a version of seppuku as I collapsed forward with a trekking pole immovably entrenched in the snow ahead of me. As gravity carried me down towards the earth, the pole pierced into my gut with a blunt pain from the rounded form of the handle. Laying on the ground, gasping for breath, I questioned why I was still on the Appalachian Trail.

At times on this day, when I knew I was supposed to be going uphill, I would just climb as vertically as possible. I had no idea where the trail was supposed to go. I hoped this would save some time rather than checking my GPS every five seconds, which was the case most of the day. I could deal with postholing even though it frustrated me, but this lack of a trail to follow was not sustainable for the mileage I needed to maintain.

This day was so miserable and slow-going that I knew it was time to start thinking about switching trails. I could continue heading north for ten more days, summit Katahdin on March 31st, and then head south like I planned. But if I did that, the whole trail would likely be like this. There was no reason it would improve at all heading north. It would only get worse. There was just too much snow remaining to be able to read where the trail was or to make decent miles.

In addition to the tough hiking of the day, I also ran out of food because I was moving so unexpectedly slow. I didn't want it to become a bigger problem. Even though I got to camp late and was exhausted after my day of misery, I started the next day early, after only a couple of hours of sleep. I wanted to get to town before the real hunger started to set in. I took an alternate route around Stratton Mountain to try to stay at a lower elevation and get into town faster. Missing the summit was a bummer, but I would rather not starve than see a pretty view.

It was preposterously tough hiking again, but I ended up making it into Manchester Center, VT before the real hunger set in. The snow was less extreme at the lower elevations, but I was still set in my decision to get off of the Appalachian Trail for the time being. Once I got into town and booked a motel room, I began working on my plan to get to the Continental Divide Trail to start the southern section in New Mexico. I ended up buying a plane ticket for three days later. I decided I would do one more day of hiking, but it would be a road walking alternate, and then I would be done with the AT … for now.

Going into this endeavor, I knew it would be difficult to go straight through on the AT, but I remained naively hopeful I would do it. Reaching Vermont wasn't easy, but the big mile days just weren't sustainable when I got there with the harsh winter the state was having. With the perpetual postholing and lack of any trail, it was difficult to move even close to 1 mph. That was not compatible with completing the Calendar Year Triple Crown.

Travel and Tribulations

It was quite the enterprise getting from one trail to another. After my last day on the AT, I went into Rutland, VT. I stayed at the Yellow Deli — a commune, which could be better described as a cult. They allow hikers to stay with them, and I had heard other hikers say that they loved it there. That wasn't the case for me. It was much cheaper than a hotel, which was the only reason I stayed there, but it was unnervingly strange. It's probably less awkward during normal hiker season with many hikers there, but in winter, I was the only non-cult member — whoops, I meant hiker — there. I was the talk of the night, and everyone singled in on me.

After sitting in their sandwich shop for several hours, seeing if I passed their vibe check, they granted me permission to stay with them and brought me back to their compound. They gave me a quick tour of the places they wanted to show me. Then we went to their religious service. They said that was the one requirement of staying with them — attend their religious service. "You don't have to participate, but we'd like you to be there." I didn't mind. I'm a religious man, and we all praise the same God.

I was not prepared for how different their religious service was compared to the Catholic ones that I was used to. People sing at the masses I go to, but they don't sing and dance like that. This group sang a medley of songs for over an hour, all while continuously dancing in a circle like they were drunk at a Bar Mitzvah. Even after my repeated protestations, they grabbed my hands every three minutes and tried to get me to join, looking disappointed every time I declined. I don't even have the confidence to sing at my regular church. I wasn't about to start there.

After the hour of song and frequent peer pressure, they moved onto a reading segment of the service. I sympathetically, but awkwardly, listened to a man with a third-grade reading level stumble his way through a passage that seemed to lose all meaning in the broken-up language. After the reading portion, it was time to mingle. This was when the most bothersome part of the night began. I quickly noticed that some of the women had to be on lithium or some other psychotropic drug because they acted unnaturally airy and weren't all there mentally. The group must've had a game plan for me because it was wave after wave of people talking to me and soft-recruiting me to join. Some were much less-skilled than others, but there was a common theme among many of the conversations. Aside from talking about my hiking and general questions, I got repeated questions you would never ask somebody while making small talk. *Are your parents divorced or together? Are they alive? Are your grandparents alive? Did any of your siblings die? Do you have friends? Have you ever lost a close friend? Have you ever been in a car accident? Do you have depression? Are you scared you'll die alone?*

It was painfully odd, but hard not to audibly laugh at the absurdity of some of the questions. They were looking for some sort of trauma that they could dig their claws into and tell me how joining their cult — whoops, I meant commune — could help.

After the mandatory awkward mingling, it was time for dinner. I could hardly enjoy my food or get a word in edgewise because I was constantly told I *had* to try their tea. All I could think was, "I am extremely uncomfortable. I am not going to take the risk of drinking your cult-tea and waking up to a hypnotic video in a sensory deprivation chamber to slowly be brainwashed for days-on-end." But verbally, I just reiterated over a dozen times that I don't like tea, which is the truth.

I couldn't wait to get out of there the next morning. Grateful to be alive, free, and on my way to New Mexico. I went to the post office to send home most of my winter gear since I was heading to the desert. I then got picked up by Jeanne, a family friend. She drove me several hours to Burlington and gave me a tour of the town before dropping me off, and paying for my stay at a hotel. I passed out in less than 45 minutes.

Up by 3:30 a.m., I was ready to go, but the day started slow. My taxi was over 30 minutes late. It was getting to the point where I was about to walk the three miles to the airport when the taxi finally arrived.

At the airport, they announced that our plane was small and normal carry-on bags wouldn't fit in the overhead compartment. I'd heard horror stories of hikers' backpacks being ruined if they checked them below the plane. I was emphatic on not letting that happen. One way or another, this bag was getting on that plane with me. I was already upset because security had confiscated an unopened jar of peanut butter and my microscopic pocketknife. I thought peanut butter would be okay if it was sealed and a knife that small would be okay, but I was wrong on both accounts.

I went to the bathroom and threw out anything I could replace, water bottles, baggies, etc., but the pack was still large. Once I got onto the plane, I shoved it under the seat in front of me and put my legs on top of it. Since it was so early, the plane was dim, and none of the flight attendants noticed my knees at my chin. I rode the whole flight with my legs on top of my pack, pressed up against my chest. It was extremely uncomfortable, but I didn't have to worry about something tragic happening to my pack.

Before landing in Phoenix, I had a layover in Detroit and realized this would be the closest I would be to my home in Ohio the whole year.

One of my biggest flaws as a human is not having the patience to navigate public transportation. In Phoenix, there was a bus from the airport to the Greyhound station, but after trying to figure it out for three minutes, I just walked the two miles to the station instead. As I was boarding the bus, the driver looked at my ticket and smilingly asked why the hell I was going to Lordsburg, NM. I guess it wasn't a popular stop on the route.

I had been in contact with a person named Jeff who lived near the start of the Continental Divide Trail. He shuttled hikers to the terminus regularly, and he even picked me up in Lordsburg after midnight and let me crash at his house. He was a real sport about the timing. The bus was delayed because the driver kept stopping every 20 minutes to kick people off for smoking. Greyhounds are always an experience.

The next morning, I slept in after being up for 23 straight hours. I shaved my beard which had been growing for 80 days. It felt refreshing to be clean-shaven again. In the early afternoon, we drove around and cached water for me in the six designated locations. The boot-heel of New Mexico is so dry that the trail agency has six locations where people can cache water for themselves so they have something to drink while hiking. It's a scary thing to have to depend on it, but it's the way things are in the arid desert.

Once we were finished caching the water, we started the drive to the terminus. After a few miles of driving on extremely rugged dirt roads, I was standing at the Mexican border, ready to start the next leg of my journey.

Phase II:

Continental Divide Trail

Mexico to Monarch Pass, CO

March 22nd–April 22nd

Discovering the Desert

My first day hiking in the desert proved to be an eye-opening experience to say the least. The contrast between hiking in snow-covered Appalachia and the arid desert was striking, as if engaging in two completely different activities. Although I found myself leaning towards favoring the desert, it presented its own unique challenges. Besides the ever-present concern for water, navigating the trail proved to be a great challenge right from the start. Rather than frequent blazes on trees, or even a clearly defined path, there were only scattered, tall, metal signs faintly marking the route. Upon reaching a marker after weaving through prickly plants, the next sign would appear, barely visible off in the distance.

The initial day in the desert was rough yet rewarding. Strong winds whipped up dust, gradually coating my throat as the day went on, leaving it dry and chalky. Despite not starting at the border until 5 o'clock, I managed to cover an impressive 13 miles by 9 p.m. The ease with which I accomplished this, in comparison to the demanding Appalachian Trail, filled me with a sense of exhilaration. I had a feeling I was going to like this trail.

One of the most captivating aspects I cherished about the bootheel of New Mexico was its complete and utter barrenness. The inhospitable landscape held a certain allure. On the Guthook mapping app, I noticed a marker for a tree because it was such an anomaly in the area. Originally planning to camp beneath it, I was disappointed to find a cougar hunter sleeping in his car, occupying all the flat ground. Continuing on, I settled for cowboy camping in the dry wash I had been hiking along.

The night was chilly after mailing my winter sleeping bag home and relying on my lighter summer bag, but waking up under clear shimmering skies as the sunrise began made everything alright. It was a cathartic feeling after waking up every day on the AT inside a shelter with gray skies outside.

I was ready to have a memorable day.

I was hiking without trekking poles because my ones from the AT were all bent to hell, and I couldn't fly with them. Before I left Vermont, I ordered new ones on Amazon. They were supposed to be delivered in New Mexico so that I could have them before I started. Suffice it to say, Amazon was late, and I started without them.

Not having poles for walking didn't bother me. That was only a minor nuisance. My main concern was my tent. Now, I had a lighter tent for the drier, western climate, where dew and condensation weren't as much of a concern as in the East. The tent was lighter because it didn't have tent poles. It was designed to use normal hiking poles to set it up. Normally, it's a great innovation that cuts down on weight — as long as you have trekking poles. Without them, I had no feasible shelter at the time. I looked at the weather, and it was a 1% chance of rain for the next ten days. That sounded good. This was the desert. It doesn't rain.

Arriving at the first water cache in the morning, I soon discovered that the trail went from faint to non-existent. Instead of tall metal signs marking the route, this section used small wooden posts. In addition to them not being visible, hidden among plants of the same height, the recent winds had knocked many of them over. Even if they were upright, it still would've been difficult to navigate. Essentially, I had to bushwhack ten miles across the desert, occasionally checking my map to ensure I wasn't veering too far off route. It was slow going and put me behind pace for the day. I started to worry that if every day was like this, I wasn't going to be able to do the consistent 30+ mile days that I needed to do. The overwhelming, loud, and negative voices in my head from my first day of the Appalachian Trail resurfaced. I tried to remember my training — push those negative thoughts out of my head and focus solely on the footsteps in front of me.

This fear compounded with another — drinking too much water. I was so overly concerned about being dehydrated and running out of water that I overcompensated. I drank a gallon at every water cache and carried out multiple liters, which led to me drinking over four gallons of water per day. The temperature was warm, but not yet hot. My stomach felt unsettled all day, leading to diarrhea and loss of appetite.

Even while flirting with water intoxication I was thankful for the water caches as I passed one cow pond that had a skunk crawling out of the water. On a more pleasant animal note, I saw my first jackrabbit shortly thereafter. It was a real hoot to watch. It was there, and then faster than I could open a can of Dr. Pepper, it was gone — unbelievably quickly.

The winds picked up again in the afternoon, and by 6 p.m., the clouds started to roll in. As the sky grew more ominous by the minute, I grew more uneasy. After not expecting to use it, I got out my rain gear from the bottom of my pack to have it at the ready.

Calling it quits at 8:30 p.m., it still hadn't rained. I laid out all my belongings to cowboy camp again. As soon as I finished, I laid my head on my pillow, and within five seconds, it started raining. *Okay, I guess we're doing this*, I thought to myself while promptly packing up my gear. If it was raining, I wanted to be hiking with all my gear inside my pack, so it could stay dry.

Frustration began to build. I was already exhausted from hiking all day and getting lost repeatedly. After I walked a few steps, I realized I only had my underwear on the lower half of my body. But it was too late. I already had my pack on and was walking. In the chilling temperature of 35 degrees, with rain pouring down and ferocious 40 mph winds tearing across the exposed desert, I trudged forward, shivering with each step.

After an additional hour of hiking, I couldn't take it anymore. I was miserable and freezing. Through my chattering teeth, I started to shout to the sky and plead with God.

"Please make it stop! Please show some mercy!" I fervently cried out, the sound of my prayers quickly dissipating in the ferocity of the wind for 30 minutes until they were answered, and the rain ceased at last.

Relief washed over me. I continued hiking until I could find some semblance of shelter from the wind in the open desert. I stumbled upon a small crevice that was the beginning of a tributary to a wash. It was flat and had walls just high enough to protect me from the wind while laying down.

Once again, I arranged my cowboy camp and laid down. Within five minutes, the rain returned. *Nope. I'm not doing this again. It's not going to rain that long. It's the desert.*

It proceeded to pour relentlessly for the next six hours, and I had the worst night of my life.

I had no protection from the rain. I draped my tent over me like a blanket, as if that would help. It was quickly soaked through, and I could feel every raindrop hitting the tent on top of me. It seemed to intensify the chill. All night long, every cold raindrop that hit the tent transferred a cold droplet through the tent fabric, and then gently glided over my skin, as if it was personally sent on a mission to chill me to the bone. The threat of hypothermia consumed my mind. With the temperature being around 35 degrees, accompanied by high winds, and me being soaked, it was a real possibility.

Amidst extreme discomfort, mentally and physically, I might've gotten 45 minutes of sleep that night. All I did was lay there and think about how miserable I was. Even if I did fall asleep, I would wake to the feeling of freezing cold water falling on my forehead. The sleep never lasted long. In hindsight, I don't know why I didn't get up and keep hiking. I was exhausted, but it's hard to imagine it would've been worse than lying there in the cold rain while everything was getting exceedingly saturated.

When the sun finally graced the morning sky, it was as if God had to remind me He existed. It felt divinely wonderful to have some sense of warmth again. Packing up all my gear was a most dreadful task. It was all soaking wet and significantly heavier. With each step, I endured the abrasive sensation of wet clothes harshly rubbing against my body like soggy sandpaper — an utterly unpleasant experience. After 15 minutes of walking, it started to rain again. I didn't yell at the sky or pray nonstop like last night. Instead, I truly accepted the validity of Murphy's Law and kept moving.

Seven sodden miles later, I stood on Highway 9 where I made a decision. When Jeff dropped me off at the terminus, he mentioned that if I needed any help while in the area, I shouldn't hesitate to reach out. I just figured that was something nice people said, and that I wouldn't take him up on his offer. But after the hellish night I had, I changed my mind. I knew I had to dry out my gear, and I knew he lived somewhere on this road. There was no cell phone signal, so I started walking in hopes that somebody would stop to offer me a ride until I spotted his house.

After a couple of miles on the desolate road, a truck stopped. It was a border patrol agent, of which I had been seeing a lot. Once they saw I was White, they would go on their way. I imagined it would be a different experience for a Hispanic hiker. I explained my situation and how I needed to get a few miles up the road to dry out my gear, in hopes that he would give me a ride. Instead, he said "Good luck," and drove away.

I was upset but kept walking because that was the only option. It wasn't too much longer before Jeff cruised by and saw me! He stopped and gladly drove me back to his house, enjoying a hearty laugh when I told him my story from the previous night.

Upon arrival, I promptly began doing laundry, determined to dry everything, particularly my sleeping bag. Unexpectedly, snow began to fall in the late morning. Never in my preparations for the trip had I anticipated encountering snow within 50 miles of the Mexican border. I learned a lot about the "desert" in less than 48 hours. It wasn't just this wasteland of blazing sun, infinite sand, and void of precipitation that I was always led to believe. In my first three days in the desert of New Mexico, I dealt with scorching sun, high winds, rain, snow, and temperatures well below freezing, all while not seeing a single other person. *This was a wild place.*

I spent most of the day catching up on sleep. It was a terrible situation, but I took solace in the fact that this chaos happened close to Jeff's house, where I had a place I could retreat to and dry out. Nearly anywhere else in New Mexico, I would've been out of luck. Jeff mentioned they hadn't gotten rain like that in months, so I was happy for the area. I just wished I wasn't sleeping out in the open during it. But I was looking on the bright side. Statistically speaking, it was extremely unlikely that I would deal with rain again while in New Mexico.

Moving Past a Rough Start

Jeff dropped me of at the trail crossing on the highway the following morning. It now felt like I was actually going to start the Continental Divide Trail after getting off on the wrong foot. The previous three days were so strange that they didn't feel like part of the hike. I was ready to correct course.

Things went exactly as I expected in the desert for the first time since starting this trail. The hiking was easy, and the navigation was straightforward. There were still the worries about water, but easy hiking was my main concern. Every day on the AT, when I was struggling, I would remind myself how much easier things would be when I went west. It would be warmer; there wouldn't be constant snow; and the trails would be less demanding because they were graded for pack-animals unlike the AT. Now was the time those reassurances were supposed to come into existence, and this fourth day in the desert was when I began to feel justified in that belief.

It ended up being a nearly 40-mile day, and I made it into Lordsburg but had to stop because I needed to visit the post office in the morning. I had packed so much food that I could've kept hiking through if it wasn't for the post office. My extra food was a combination of two factors. I brought a little extra food as a precaution since this was my first time in the desert. But the bigger mistake was that I was drinking so much water that I didn't want to eat anything. Despite being in the desert, I had never been more hydrated. Even under the blazing sun all day with no reprieve, my urine was as clear as water every time. I was so scared of dehydration that I went overboard. Now I was harming my body, wrecking my digestive system, and eroding my appetite. I was also wasting time having to dig a cat-hole ten times a day.

When I got into town, I grabbed some snacks from Dollar General and camped in a memorial park in town. I wasn't sure if I was allowed to or not, but I figured the worst thing that could happen would be that a cop would ask me to leave. Maybe I'd get a ticket, but probably not. I slept there and nobody bothered me, but it wasn't a calm night. I repeatedly woke up from dogs barking or jerks revving the engine on their tricked-out cars.

Arriving at the post office the minute they opened, I learned Amazon had still not delivered my trekking poles or my water filter. I urgently needed my trekking poles to set up my tent, and I desperately needed that water filter. I had one that I used on the AT, but I let it freeze frequently, and it didn't work anymore. On the AT, it didn't matter because it was winter, so there was nobody else out there to contaminate the water. However, the water on this trail was disgusting. There were hardly any natural water sources. The only sources were cattle tanks and ponds, both of which usually had something growing in them. Occasionally, they were hooked up to a solar panel, so the water would be running rather than stagnant, but that often wasn't the case. I knew drinking water from these kinds of sources would be unavoidable, but I knew a trusted water filter would be necessary to do so. I had been able to avoid bad sources so far and only drank at the water caches, so I didn't need to use my filter. But I knew soon enough, I would be counting on that filter for my well-being.

I couldn't fathom how the biggest logistics company in the world could take over a week to deliver two things that were supposed to take two days. The post office was willing to redirect my deliveries to Silver City, but it was Friday and now I wouldn't get them until Monday at the earliest.

My day wasn't off to a great start. I then left town, taking an alternate route rather than the official CDT. Alternate routes were everywhere along the trail and allows hikers to make their own adventure along the way, rather than always following a designated line. Alternates are used much more on the CDT compared to other trails. They are preferential to hikers for a few reasons. They can either be more scenic, cut off a few miles, reroute around a boring road walk, or avoid an exposed ridge during a storm. This particular alternate was going to save me two miles.

I had already walked five miles on it when a truck stopped alongside the road. Initially, I thought the driver might offer water. Instead, he asked what I was doing, already knowing the answer. He said that if I continued, I would eventually trespass on his neighbor's property. He insisted that I get in his truck and he would bring me back to the official trail.

Outwardly, I remained composed, but internally, I seethed with anger. It would be one thing if it was his property, or if I actually reached the boundary, or was already walking on it. But making me stop because it was his neighbor's property aggravated me. I'm guessing it would've been a small area in which I was trespassing, and I would've been off of it before the property owner even noticed. Otherwise, it wouldn't have been on my map. I wasn't entirely in the right, but I was mad I wasted so much time.

The driver dropped me off right back where I had started two hours earlier. The sole bright spot was that I met two other CDT thru-hikers! He had done the same thing to them earlier. We commiserated about what a dork he was while I dined on some M&M's and animal crackers. While we were talking, I ended up spilling the beans about the Calendar Year Triple Crown, and they were visibly thrilled for me. I said goodbye, and they said they'd probably never see me again. It turned out they were right.

I hadn't even been thinking about other thru-hikers lately. It was the first time that I saw any since my first week on the AT. I had become accustomed to either seeing nobody, or at most, a day hiker out for a couple of miles if it was a nice day. I was asked constantly, both during and after the trip, if I felt lonely. I never really did. I felt alone, in the factual sense that I was by myself 99.9% of the time, but never a deep longing to just be in the presence of another human being. I was at peace with who I was, so I never really minded being alone.

There are few better defenses to loneliness than a healthy love and understanding of one's self. I was also so singularly focused on my goal that I didn't have time to feel sorry for myself. I'd forged my entire year to be successful at one thing. I wasn't going to let something like loneliness get in the way of that. A goal that consumes your entire being does a good job of combatting loneliness, self-pity, and other internal negative dialogues, simply because your mind is constantly focused on how to be successful. Everything else is secondary. I made the best of what I could. I cherished the people I did meet, no matter how short our time together was. Whether it was a person giving me a ride into town, or a hiker I stopped to talk with for a few minutes, they felt like a friend — and trail angels felt like family.

Nobody is alone in this world. The only thing keeping someone from being happy is the belief that they are alone.

After that tumultuous start to the day, things lightened up. For a while, the trail was just a line on a map over barren pastures. I set my bearing and walked straight over completely flat earth with not so much as a rock as an obstruction. After that wasteland, I was in an area greener than I had seen in a while. It was strange to see bountiful trees. One of my favorite parts about the southernmost part of the CDT were markers on my map, or comments left from other hikers, in regard to a tree. It was a funny concept to celebrate a single tree after traversing an endless forest on the AT.

With the threat of rain looming, I decided to call it a day before sunset — a rare occurrence. I sought refuge beneath a grand tree in a serene wash, finding solace in the slight shelter it provided. Though the impending rain dampened my spirits, I was grateful for my foresight. I awoke to raindrops falling on my forehead at 3 a.m. but felt refreshed as I had already had a full night of sleep before the gentle shower.

As morning arrived, I ascended into the Burro Mountains. The rain transformed into heavy snow, descending purposefully from the heavens. Visibility diminished, and I couldn't help but feel foolish. I left the AT to escape such wintry conditions, only to encounter precipitation on more than half the days of my first week in the desert.

While taking an alternate route because of a controlled burn, I wandered off the edge of my map. The dirt road on my map that I planned to use to reconnect to the trail, didn't exist in reality. I had to hope and pray that if I continued on the current one, it would somehow bring me back to the trail. Several miles later, I was pounding my feet on pavement, graciously heading back to the trail and the comfort of my map. I was less than a week in, and I was already depending on the edges of my maps to be able to find a route to reconnect with the trail.

After a lot of road walking, I made it to the Walmart in Silver City. The guy that gave me a ride across town said I could camp behind the store. As I was walking out after my resupply, I heard a man trying to get my attention. His name was Shad, and he turned out to be embarking on his CDT thru-hike the following week. He immediately helped me out by telling me this Walmart sells Sawyer Squeeze water filters. I wasn't aware, so the two of us marched back inside, and I got a working filter. He also told me that the back of Walmart is filled with a lot of drug users. Since I had a bunch of delicate and expensive hiking gear, I thought it would be better to camp away from people on meth.

He kindly dropped me off at a local campground where I could stay for the night. Paying for a spot to set up my tent felt ridiculous after sleeping for free so much, but I got a shower out of the deal. I felt undeserving after a mere three days of hiking since my last one. After setting up, I looked at the comments from other hikers on this place, and they said it was great, until the sprinklers turned on at 3 a.m. Fortunately, I had a dry night, which I couldn't take for granted in this desert.

Shad picked me up the next morning to drop me off at the trail. I mentioned how I couldn't set up my tent because I didn't have trekking poles, so we went back to his house to look for some. He was able to find a pair and gave them to me. I was beyond thankful. If it wasn't for that, I was going to have to take a rest day in Silver City, wait for one of the small gear stores to open the next day, and just hope they had a pair, which they probably wouldn't. I didn't want to waste a day, so the kindness of a stranger saved me again. Finally, I had the means to have shelter. Previously, I wouldn't have cared about that in the desert, but with as bad as the weather was my first week, I felt like a new man. The trail provides!

I started the Gila Alternate, a scenic route off of the official CDT that follows the breathtaking Gila River through a captivating canyon in the wilderness. Ninety-five percent of thru-hikers take this alternate because it's a must-see. It's also a nice change of pace to have water constantly available rather than once a day from a cow tank.

However, navigating this section posed a challenge right from the start. I was lost before even beginning the alternate. The route commenced at a four-way intersection, and I inadvertently took the wrong path. Realizing my mistake after 20 minutes, I bushwhacked through dense brush to reconnect with the correct route and get back on track.

Later in the day, I stumbled upon an area that was ravaged by a wildfire, leaving the landscape completely charred and devoid of any trace of the trail. The latter part of the day was spent traversing up and down the mountainside, battling through thick vegetation in an attempt to find a path of least resistance — without much luck. I was constantly running through sharp tree branches. It felt like I time traveled back to football practice as a kid, running through tires, except this was more painful because these desert plants were sharper than tires. My body was covered in ash from involuntarily rubbing against burnt trees all day.

I strayed significantly off course at times, necessitating scaling steep mountainsides. I was so adept in getting lost, I was confident there were numerous times that day that nobody else had ever taken the exact route I did. At least, I hoped they didn't because it felt dangerous.

As dusk settled, I lost the trail yet again as the side of the mountain was blanketed in deep snow. Descending a steep snow-covered slope after dark, with no trail to follow, relying solely on a vague sense of direction, was another exercise in my patience for the desert. For the second half of the day, I was moving less than 1 mph, reminiscent of my time in Vermont.

It was a cold night, so I didn't get moving until sunrise the next day. Although the sleeping bag I was using was rated for 15 degrees, it was a few years old and a lot of the insulation had leaked out of it. I think it was more like a 30- or 40-degree sleeping bag now. But I sleep warm, so I made do with it, even though it got down into the 20s most nights in New Mexico.

I hiked five more miles of dirt roads and bushwhacks before I finally made it down to the Gila River, the real point of this alternate. It was a harsh greeting. I knew I would have to ford the river over 100 times in the upcoming days, but the initial crossing was an eye opener. The water was cold and deep. I couldn't find any shallow place to cross, so I had to cross in water up to my belly button. Although the current wasn't swift enough to pose a significant threat, I didn't want to get that wet. Fortunately, all the subsequent fords were mild. Most were only shin-deep fords with absolutely no danger. While only ankle-deep in one, I ran into a javelina hunter that told me the current flow in the Gila was unusually low — a rare piece of good news I received from a local.

Hiking through this area proved arduous. For the first three-quarters of the day, there was no trail to follow. I would walk along one side of the river until I hit a wall, then I'd cross to the other side and repeat. I knew I had to follow the river, so it was impossible to get lost. However, the lack of a well-defined path made it difficult to maintain an efficient pace. Late in the day, I came across a faint trail, occasionally marked by cairns, that allowed me to pick up speed.

It turned out to be an eventful day for wildlife encounters. I saw my first javelina, which is basically an uglier pig. I saw a coyote, looking as sly as ever, and the river was teeming with ducks. Unfortunately, I also came across dead fish floating in the water, serving as a sobering reminder that I didn't know what was in the water I was drinking. But my new water filter gave me peace of mind.

My aim for the day was to reach Doc Campbell's Outpost, a general store where I had sent a resupply box to stock up on food for this remote section. However, due to the fading daylight, I decided to call it an early day. I didn't want to tackle river crossings in the cold of night or try to navigate without a real trail after dark.

When I made camp, it was the first time I set up my tent since the previous summer. It was like riding a bike. I also realized that I lost my phone tripod, so I wouldn't get any pictures of me in this beautiful section of trail. If it wasn't for that tripod, I would hardly have any pictures of myself in all the amazing places I visited. I could still take landscape pictures, but I seem to remember places better and have fonder memories if I'm in the frame. Seeing myself in a beautiful place helps to ground me back to the moment I experienced there and reminisce.

Once I took off my shoes, I discovered that my feet were in bad shape — unsurprising, since they were submerged underwater most of the day. Wet feet were unavoidable on this alternate. There was also a lot of debris in my shoes from the constant fords that I couldn't fully get out. In a perfect world, I would've liked to have sandals for this section, but that was logistically too much work while on a thru-hike.

I slept in the next day because it was freezing cold in the canyon, and I didn't want to start fording the river that early. Leaving at 9:30 a.m., it was still shockingly cold on the crossings. That water quickly dispelled any grogginess I had. It was ten degrees colder in the shaded part of the canyons where the sun had not yet hit, only chilling me more than I already was. The late start turned out to be okay because when I got to Doc Campbell's for my resupply, they weren't even open. When they did, they were extremely friendly. The only negative was that the Wi-Fi didn't work, so I wasn't able to order a new tripod and pack cover since I lost both.

I ended up staying there until 1 p.m. when I dropped back down to the river in a gorgeous canyon. The water was higher today, and I even spotted some decent-sized fish. I had to stop early again, around 6:30 p.m. I was at a fantastic campsite, and it looked like a narrow canyon for the next few miles, so I wasn't sure if there would be any suitable camping spots. The Gila was a unique and beautiful experience, but it really limited my hiking time with the cold in the morning and reluctance to do river crossings or hike at night. On the bright side, I was catching up on sleep.

For dinner, I had one of the most disgusting things I've had on trail. I had cold-soaked ramen noodles, which I had been doing the whole time in the desert. Cold-soaking means you put food, like ramen noodles, in a jar and put in a little water and let it soak for a time, rather than cook it. The result doesn't taste good, but it's edible, and is a different way to get calories other than consuming the same dried foods all the time. The problem this time, however, was that I put in far too much water. The noodles had become a mushy mess and had the consistency of eating puke. It was so repulsive that I considered digging a hole and burying it, but I forced it all down. From that day on, I would not make the mistake of adding excessive water again, although I often erred on the side of using too little water, making the noodles hard to eat. It was a learning process throughout the year, and while I improved, I never achieved perfection.

The next morning, I slept in again and didn't start hiking until 9 a.m. While in the frigid shade of the canyon, I bent over and filled a water bottle in the river, and my hand quickly went numb. After several river crossings with numb feet as well, I stepped into the sunlight. I was overcome with a warm, cozy feeling — like someone turned on the furnace for the first time in autumn in the Midwest.

As I crossed the river over 30 times, the trail got progressively more challenging the farther I got away from Doc Campbell's. There was a significant amount of bushwhacking, and the sharp plants mercilessly shredded my skin. It was a combination of getting cut by those and getting sunburnt that made my calves feel like I was getting tattoos inked on them all day long. I hadn't been putting sunscreen on my legs because they were constantly caked in mud, but I guess that didn't have a strong SPF.

I made it to the final junction with the Gila High Route, an alternate path I planned to take the next day to avoid getting my feet wet yet again. My feet were in rough shape and were searching for any respite. I avoided the high route prior to that because I wanted to fully experience the low route. I loved this area and knew I'd come back someday. I could explore the high route then. However, plans change. The tail-end of high route would spare me one more day with waterlogged feet along the low route.

Stumbling upon a cave, the opportunity to camp there seemed too enticing to pass up, but it wasn't ideal. It was too rocky for me to feel comfortable enough to blow up my inflatable sleeping pad, fearing it would puncture, so I slept on the hard ground. *This was real cowboy camping.*

After a subpar night of sleep, I was ready to enjoy some dry hiking again. As I sat up to start the day, a large chunk of rock from the cave's ceiling fell exactly where my head had been just moments before. I sat there in awe for a few seconds starting at the spot, thankful to have woken up punctually today, unlike most days. It wouldn't have killed me, but it would've cut my head open and hurt. A bleeding head wound was not something I wanted to deal with in the backcountry.

Trying to avoid more of the ceiling collapsing on me, I attempted to hurriedly pack up, but without much success. It was the coldest night I had dealt with in the desert. My water was frozen solid, along with my shoes. I had to sit on my shoes to thaw them before forcing them on my feet and leaving the cave. I hadn't dealt with these problems since leaving the AT, but at least I was accustomed to them and knew what to do.

Taking the high route, I ascended and traversed Aeroplane Mesa, a massive plateau adorned with waist-high, golden grass flowing in the breeze with the rhythm of the ocean. It was a charming sight, and a good indicator for what the rest of the day would be — golden grass stretching as far as the eye could see in every direction.

While still on the alternate, but after I had left the river, I had to drink from my first vile water source on the CDT. It was a large, brown, and stagnant pond. There was a solar panel nearby, so I was hopeful water would be running somewhere, but it wasn't set up properly and nothing was flowing. I filled up one bottle with the murky, brown liquid and tried not to look at it as I filtered the water into my clean bottle, where it turned a cloudy gray. It didn't taste exceptionally terrible as I tried to chug as much as I could at one time, attempting to avoid tasting it as much as possible..

Later in the day, I began to see a large cloud of smoke from a fire ahead. Without any cell signal, I couldn't determine if it was a controlled burn or a wildfire. I manifested that it was a controlled burn and carried on.

After a few hours of walking a dirt road, a car finally drove by, and I stopped the driver to ask. They confirmed it was controlled, and a wave of relief flooded over me. I kept hiking on the dirt road until dusk and passed by a bunch of the wildland firefighters in trucks heading out for their shift change. As I openly laid on the ground to sleep, thirty yards off the road, I heard wolves howling off in the distance. Maybe they were out hunting the numerous elk I had seen earlier in the day — better them than me.

I woke up freezing cold the next morning but got moving in hopes that it would warm me. Soon after, I saw the same firefighters back on the road in the opposite direction to head back to the fire. The first time I saw them, they were going the same direction as me, so I didn't see their faces. But this time, they all looked either confused or intrigued as to why I was walking alongside this dirt road in New Mexico.

After a few more miles on that road, I rejoined the official CDT and arrived at my sole water source for the day around 9 a.m. I chugged as much as I could and carried three liters for the rest of the day. I felt a little dehydrated by the end of the day, but not horrendously so. I was gradually improving at drinking a more appropriate amount of water rather than testing the limits of water intoxication.

It was an unusual day of hiking as I found myself getting winded much faster than usual. Despite the ease of the terrain, with just a few small climbs and generally straightforward trail conditions, I needed frequent breaks. It puzzled me as to why a seemingly easy 28-mile day was proving to be such a challenge. I didn't feel like myself. I didn't feel like Horsepower.

As the sun began to set, I found myself trekking through a dense, wooded area. The thick foliage obstructed my view, but I could hear sounds all around me. Coyotes howled in close proximity, their calls echoing from every direction — no more than 50 yards away. While I wasn't particularly afraid of coyotes, I wasn't keen on being surrounded by a pack either.

To ward them off, I started loudly singing "6 Foot 7 Foot" by Lil Wayne, hoping to make my presence known, and so we could avoid each other. I continued this for ten minutes before they respected the lyrical creativity, and the howls grew distant enough to alleviate my concerns.

Upon reaching my stopping point for the day, I had to move some cow patties out of the way to set up my tent. I didn't mind though. I felt invincible now that I had the ability to set up my tent, and I didn't have to worry about overnight rain like earlier.

Throughout the night, I was repeatedly awoken by the howls of nearby coyotes. Consequently, I slept in and started my hike later than usual the following morning. I made it to my sole water source for the day shortly after I left camp. Grateful to see the solar panel working, I could collect clear, running water from a pipe, rather than stagnant, brown water from a nearby tank with a fish living in it. I left with only three liters, realizing the foolishness of my decision several hours later when the day was heating up.

But the trail provides! I came upon a couple at a road crossing who were preparing for a day hike. They kindly replenished my water supply, saving me from a potentially dangerous situation. It was pure luck since they were the only day hikers I encountered throughout the entire state.

My uncharacteristic fatigue persisted throughout the day, and by day's end, I was utterly exhausted — yearning to rest and recover. Likely from being dehydrated, my body felt disproportionately out-of-sorts.

I arrived at Davila Ranch after dark, which was a metal shelter put up by a ranching family who allowed thru-hikers to camp there. It was a cool spot, furnished with a cot, fridge full of Cokes, food for hikers, and even a shower. However, given the freezing nighttime temperatures in April, the water supply was still shut off. A shower would've been too good to be true.

Camping there that night, I had a relaxing next day, lounging around until 4 p.m. It was a Sunday, and I had a food package waiting for me at the post office in Pie Town, NM, a mere 14 miles away. There was no rush to get there since I would have to wait for the post office to open. So I stayed at the Davila Ranch, while downing some Cokes, devouring as much of my food as I could, and reveling in the rare luxury of having a few bars of cell phone signal. I even watched *There Will Be Blood,* a movie that perfectly complimented the desolate but beautiful New Mexico landscape.

I made it into Pie Town after dark, and before I blinked, I was in the middle of town and knew I had arrived at my destination when I saw the peculiar decorations. It was the Toaster House: a hiker hostel that is evident because the whole house is covered in toasters, among other odd relics. Why? The same reason the sky is blue — I don't know.

After a knock on the door, I was greeted by Jefferson, the caretaker of the place. While there, I got to shower again without feeling like I really earned it. I viewed showers on trail much differently than showers in my day-to-day life. The biggest difference was that you *have* to shower in day-to-day life, otherwise you'll stink, and it's not acceptable to stink in society. But while out on trail, everybody stinks, and if they don't, they should. There can be no judgement when you're outside, moving and sweating all day.

Aside from the general acceptance of body odor, I also viewed showers differently in that they should be earned for a few reasons. The first reason was that I was on such a time crunch to succeed at hiking all three trails in one year, I simply couldn't afford to waste time showering on my quick town trips. For most of the towns I went into, I would buy my resupply, go to a restaurant to eat, charge my phone, rest, and head back to the trail — all in less than a few hours.

Moreover, I viewed showers as a symbol of my dedication to delayed gratification, which was practiced frequently on the trip, with everything from pushing miles to saving a candy bar. Obviously, I liked taking showers, but the longer I went without them, I felt harder, stronger, more feral. I felt more wild. The more wild I felt, the more I felt like I was up-to-par with finishing this insane challenge. And lastly, frequent showers were futile. I'd immediately head back out into the woods, mountains, or desert after showering, and I would be grimy again the same day, grungy within two days, and within three days, it was like I hadn't even showered.

Showering for hygiene reasons was never on my mind. Sunlight was my soap, and the fresh air was my deodorant. I only showered because it felt pleasant, most notably in the cold depths of winter. But once I went west, and the temperatures rose, showers became an infrequent reward I savored when I had them — similar to dessert in normal life. You don't want too much of a good thing. With dessert, you might get fat. With showers while on trail, you might get soft.

I was anxious to keep moving forward after a short previous day, but I ended up leaving later than I had hoped. When I retrieved my food package from the post office, it was more food that needed cooked or cold-soaked than I was expecting.

Still haunted from my sickening cold-soaked food a few days prior, I cooked four packs of ramen noodles at the Toaster House so I wouldn't have to cold-soak as much. It wasn't easy to eat four packs of ramen at once, and it was probably enough sodium to kill the average man, but I got it down and started hiking around 11 a.m., just as the day was heating up.

This was my first day of hiking that was a road walk the entire day. Most of the time, I didn't mind road walking because it was a dirt road in the middle of nowhere. It was easy hiking, yet still felt wild.

Today was different. It was a dirt road, but that wasn't because it was wild. That was just the type of roads that were in this remote area of New Mexico. It was also busy, which was good and bad. It was annoying having cars pass frequently and kick up dust, but many cars stopped throughout the day to offer me water. I also met one interesting driver that confidently told me aliens were active out here.

I gave an answer any normal person does when they don't want to be rude but want to disengage in the conversation quickly. "Oh, really?"

He took that as my consent to fully fly off the handle. He quickly started spewing information. "Oh, yeah. Big time! You don't need to be worried, though. You look like an alright feller. And as long as you stay positive, they'll leave you alone. They read our thoughts you know — every single one of us. No one in your family has been abducted, have they?"

"Nope, can't say they have."

"Okay, that's good. They only take people from the same family tree, so you'll be fine. You got nothing to worry about. See, I had two uncles and a grandpa that been taken. The two uncles come back, but they kept ol' grandpa. Thing is, they like my family's blood. Last fall, my son and I were building a teepee in our yard — they got a special relationship with Indians — and their machine came right over us. My son started to get worried, but I told him, we just keep doing what we're doing and pretending they're not there, and they'll go away. Sure enough, they did. They was just hoverin' there for three hours, but we paid them no mind."

Unprompted, he then showed me the bottom side of his arm, which had a large scar on it, and said, "Did you know one out of every ten people — you cut their arm open, they bleed black? That's what they really like. They like that cause that DNA is easy to replicate. They take that DNA, and then they go and sell it on the backside of the sun. That's the people they're looking for. And just my luck, my family's blood runs black."

I was looking for any out in the conversation, but I didn't have a good excuse. I would spend the rest of the day walking this very same dirt road. With nowhere to escape off to, excuse-wise or in reality, I continued responding with vague acknowledgments of "Hmm" and "Wow" before he finally ran out of steam and his presentation ended. He drove off, probably heading to Roswell, and I walked on, heading towards Colorado with a deep newfound understanding of human anatomy, space, and so much more.

My enlightened state was interrupted when I encountered a large, black steer standing in the middle of the road. The surrounding area was fenced-off with barbed wire, leaving me puzzled as to how the animal ended up there. It must have been quite a journey for him, but it quickly turned into a desperate retreat.

Upon spotting me, he panicked and attempted to leap over the barbed wire fence, only to fall short. His body was split between the two sides, with his undercarriage getting entangled in the sharp wires. Frantically, he made several more failed attempts, injuring his stomach in the process, before finally managing to clear the fence. I stood there, grimacing in empathetic pain and a sense of helplessness. Although I carried on, that disturbing image haunted my thoughts for the remainder of the day.

I had to find a place to camp alongside the road after dark. This area was not surrounded in barbed wire fence, so I didn't have to jump one. I found a flat spot 50 yards off the road devoid of sharp plants — a rarity.

Lying under the stars, sleep didn't come easily. My mind was racing about the aliens from the lunatic earlier in the day, while the nearby howls of coyotes further disrupted my rest. I dreamt that I woke up, and they were chewing on my nearby food. And then I actually woke up. Alarmingly jerking awake is not a calming experience, especially after you just had a dream about animals eating your food within an arm's length of you.

A sense of paranoia also gripped me with every pair of headlights illuminating my area from the road nearby. I feared that each of them would peripherally see me and come to investigate. I wasn't sure if this land was private or belonged to the Bureau of Land Management. Nobody ever talks about it, but there seems to be a gentleman's agreement that if you hike the CDT, you will have to illegally camp sometimes. Perhaps illegally is too strong a word, but I certainly found myself setting up camp in places where I wasn't entirely sure of the land's ownership. I had a permit to camp on BLM land in New Mexico, but the BLM land was rarely labeled on my maps, so most nights, I wasn't sure if I was on public land or not.

I started late the following morning in the hope that waiting until the sun was up would give the solar panel time to get the water flowing at the cattle tank that was a few miles ahead.

Upon arrival, I was unpleasantly surprised. Not only was the water not flowing, but the tank was completely dry. Nearby, a secondary tank stood frozen solid, and was filled with more nauseating, icy algae than water. I kept hiking, trusting that things would work out. The whole day would be a road walk, so I figured I might get lucky with passing cars offering water. Within five minutes of stepping back on the dirt road, a truck stopped and gave me a liter of water. That was enough to tide me over.

Several miles later, I connected with a paved road that I'd walk on the rest of the day. The narrow shoulders and heavy traffic made the journey challenging. Yet, the bustling nature of the road eased my concerns about water supply, even with the blistering sun beating down on the asphalt.

When I got thirsty, I held out my water bottle while walking alongside the road, and within five minutes, a truck stopped and offered me a jug of the numerous gallons he had in his truck bed. It was interesting seeing what people in different parts of the country carried as necessities in their car. In Vermont, I learned it was sleeping bags and microspikes. In New Mexico, it was water. I talked with this nice guy that had stopped for a few minutes while gulping down as much water as I could. He was an interesting fellow, and he even offered to drive me into Grants, NM — the town that I was walking this paved road to get to. It was hard to turn down, but I came out here to hike the CDT, so I declined his kind offer.

Continuing on, the wind raged fiercely, blowing at 30 mph according to The Weather Channel app, but it was gusting much higher. It was at my side most of the day, so it was a nuisance. In the afternoon, the road turned, and I was going straight into the wind, making progress considerably more difficult. One entertaining part of it was watching birds flap their wings with all their might and just stay perfectly in place — like a bird treadmill. Occasionally, they would be caught off guard by gusts, and my heart skipped a beat as one narrowly avoided colliding with a nearby barbed-wire fence, a disturbing reminder of the steer's plight the day before.

As the sun began its descent in the sky, I took a brief respite in a small parking lot by the roadside. To my surprise, the familiar truck from earlier in the day pulled in. He said he figured he'd see me again along the road. When he was leaving town, he bought a gallon of water for me and a 12-pack of donuts, encouraging me to eat as many as I could. The road was full of trail magic from water to donuts! I took him up on his offer and wolfed down four donuts before saying goodbye to him and his family.

As the sun dipped below the horizon, I arrived at a campground and was ecstatic to reach it because I seriously had to use the bathroom. Hiking alongside a busy road all day makes that a challenge. I realized I would also have to camp there for the night. Finding a camping spot along this busy road that was always enclosed on both sides by fencing would have been a challenge. And hiking on this busy road at night would have been the most dangerous thing I did all year. The dangers of hiking are minimal, but when you start to add in dependence on drivers to not be distracted, it becomes actually dangerous.

I was content though. I relished in the warmth of a privy bivy in a pit toilet at the campground. People occupied all of the campsites, but I didn't mind. I was perfectly satisfied with the pit toilet. After so many cold nights, I was happy to be cozy and enclosed on four sides.

An easy 11-mile road walk the next morning brought me to the homeplace of the most mediocre fast food: Subway. I got two footlongs but had to eat them outside like a vagrant because indoor dining was closed. I felt odd eating them outside the gas station with every person pitifully gazing at me as they went in. One guy's curiosity got the best of him and he politely asked what I was doing — overjoyed that he did when I explained my journey. He repeatedly wished me good luck and offered to give me some money for the adventure. I don't know why, but I didn't accept any. In hindsight, I should've taken it and donated it to my charity fundraiser.

Onward to Grants, NM, I saw a flip phone with the battery and sim card taken out and smashed along the side of the road. I was in New Mexico, and I've seen enough drug running movies and shows to think I had a pretty good idea of what went down there.

In Grants, I picked up a package at the post office that contained my new tripod and then resupplied at a grocery store. I loitered in the family bathroom for 30 minutes because I didn't want to leave the comfort of climate control. After mustering the resolve to leave my oasis, I hiked the four last miles of road walking before rejoining actual dirt trail heading up to Mount Taylor — a majestic 11,000-foot peak and one of the highest in the region. I hiked a few miles on the dirt path before finding a spot to camp where I prepared for the next day, grateful to be back in the wilderness.

When I left Grants, I wasn't sure if I was going to take the alternate to summit Mount Taylor or not. As I studied the route, it appeared that if I took the official CDT and avoided the peak, there was a guarantee of no water along the way. Conversely, the alternate route held the promise of a water trough and a potential water cache, not to mention the chance to conquer the summit. Fueled by these possibilities, I opted for the alternate.

The next morning, I reached the anticipated water cache, only to find disappointment awaiting me. It held a meager, single liter of water, which was far less than I had hoped for. Concerned for future hikers, I left half a liter, foolishly assuming that others would pass by soon. In reality, I was so far ahead that it would likely be weeks before another hiker got there.

When I arrived at the subsequent cattle trough, I began to worry. It was frozen, and even if it wasn't, there was so much algae that it was hard to even see the ice. It just looked like a tank of solid green. There wasn't water for another 15 miles; it was a warm day; and I was at the highest elevation I had dealt with up to this time. At higher elevations, your body needs more water to function properly. I was worried. Just as panic began to grip me, a forest service worker drove by on the road and I flagged him down, garnering another half-liter to sustain me.

Hiking up to the peak only posed a minimal challenge. I was getting tired quicker than usual because of the higher altitude, and it was by far the biggest climb I had done in a while. But the snow wasn't bad. There were occasional patches where I had to be careful and move slower, but nothing was noticeably dangerous.

However, upon descending from the summit, I faced a stark reality. The north side of the mountain was still blanketed in four feet of snow. With the warmth of the day, every step I took sank deep into the delicate snow until my waist stopped the fall. I was doing this in shorts, so my legs were getting cut up by the icy snow and leaving traces of red. It felt like

Vermont again, but worse because I was falling even faster since the snow was so delicate with the heat. Each step I took left a deep four-foot imprint where I was, not to mention that I fell down frequently and left a whole-body imprint. Yet, there weren't imprints from anybody else. *Nobody else was stupid enough to go down the north side of the mountain this early in the year.*

I exacerbated the agony of constant pain and postholing by taking the wrong route and descending to the wrong valley. Realizing it after an extra mile of hiking, I elected to climb 500 feet straight up the mountain rather than retrace my steps through the insufferable snow. I felt like I was developing vertigo as I relentlessly ascended the treacherously steep mountainside, but I made it back to the correct route.

It took me far longer to descend from the summit than it should have, of which the impact was amplified because I was fighting dehydration. Later when I reconnected with the official CDT, I had to look for a cattle tank in the area. I knew there was one around but finding it would be a challenge. The location on the map for it was incorrect, so I was reliant on instructions from past hikers to find it. After a few incorrect locations, I was overcome with immense relief upon discovering the much-needed water source. I didn't even mind that there was a mud pit to get to the water or that both of the tanks were filled with algae. Water is life in the desert.

My exhaustion overcame me as I was holding a bottle under a pipe to collect water. My fatigue made it increasingly difficult to maintain balance. My whole body shuddered with tiredness; my hand trembled; and the bottle went into the pipe and collected a bunch of the nasty algae that was growing inside the pipe. I was furious. The water was trickling out of the pipe agonizingly slowly, taking me ten minutes to fill a single bottle. Now I had to empty this one and try to clean out the algae, wasting more time. I chanted "Woosah" a few times to calm me down and got back to collecting and filtering water, which ended up being an hour-long endeavor. This was also the first time I double purified it with aqua tabs out of pure disgust.

The next morning gifted me with the warmest temperatures I'd seen in a while — hovering around 35 degrees. It was delightful to feel warm while packing up. While hiking in the morning, I unexpectedly encountered a wolf just 50 yards ahead on the trail. Surprisingly, it was alone. I first saw it in the right periphery of my vision. It walked directly perpendicular to the trail, then stopped when it stepped on the trail. It rotated its head left, looked at me with total indifference, and then continued its stride until it vanished from my line of sight. Although it was largely anticlimactic, it was remarkable, and one of my most cherished wildlife sightings of the year.

The relentless onslaught of 30+ mph winds persisted for the fourth consecutive day, gradually blending into my daily routine. The ceaseless battering drained my energy reserves, with the wind seemingly always assaulting me from the sides or, more often than not, head-on. It's funny how the wind never seemed to offer any respite by blowing at my back during the entire thru-hike.

Because I didn't pass by a puddle of water all day, I had to ration the three liters I had from filling up the night prior and take more breaks than usual. By the end of the day, my urine signaled exceptional dehydration. It ended up being a 28-mile day even though I stopped early to set up camp before entering a burn area. I didn't want to have trouble finding a campsite after dark, and even if I did, there would be no shelter from the high winds among the sparse and blackened, narrow tree trunks.

Even with the slight refuge from the wind, the night proved bitterly cold. In turn, I slept in and started later. I was waiting for it to warm up a bit, and it sure did — hitting 90 degrees in the afternoon.

After initially traversing a burn area devoid of protection, I soon returned to the barren openness of the scorching desert. Despite the sweltering conditions, the day bestowed breathtaking beauty upon me. The hiking was tough relative to what I had been doing. There were frequent short climbs and descents on mesas in the desert. The slight challenge was worth it however. The views from standing atop them, over the vast and dry desert, were always entrancing. But it had been 35 miles since I had last seen water. *Were the views truly spectacular, or am I beginning to hallucinate?*

While hiking along, I stumbled upon a half gallon of water lying in the dirt in the middle of nowhere. There were no roads nearby or anything close where somebody would have brought it and dropped it off. I held it for 30 seconds while thinking to myself, *I wonder what the chances are that this is spiked with acid or some other drug?*

I decided I was down for the ride if it was and started to chug. The water tasted strange, but I didn't care. Before this random half gallon, I took a prolonged break under a meager shade bush and was starting to question if I would make it to the next water source in the heat of the day. This abandoned half gallon of weird-tasting water, that had probably been cooking in the desert sun for weeks, saved me.

Later on, I came across a real water source — a cattle trough that proved surprisingly refreshing, despite all the dead bugs on the surface. It even had a sheet metal cover on top of it, so the water was cold, which felt sensational during a scorching day in the blistering sun. The only problem was that there was no shade above ground, so I sat filtering water and drinking as much as I could while still frying in the blazing sun.

I made it to another water source later in the day, which pleasantly turned out to be a cache — the best kind of water for a thru-hiker. There's no need to filter; you know it won't be disgusting; and there's a thrill and a fear of wondering if the cache will be stocked or not. Taking shelter underneath a small shade tree, I eagerly downed a gallon, still feeling out-of-sorts from my earlier dehydration.

That evening, I passed a ranch where I saw people gathered outside, so I went up and asked if I could camp on their property for the night. They said yes, so I went away from the party to set up my tent on the back of the property. After I was done, I heard them calling for me to join them.

They started with all the basic questions thru-hikers encounter. "What are you doing? WHY are you doing it? Do you get lonely? Do you have a gun? What about animals?" Thru-hikers are used to answering all these questions, so I didn't mind. It also helped that they were gladly sharing their alcohol with me. While they were learning about me, I was learning about them. I picked up on who the jokesters in the group were, who the moms were, who the instigators were, and who the wise elders were. The last was easy to tell because they mainly complained about how old they were and joked about how they wanted to go to bed.

With open arms and an open bar, they embraced me as part of their tribe for the evening. It was a fun night filled with laughter until dusk had long passed. I didn't know these people before this night, but I knew these kinds of people, and they were easy to get along with.

For the socially adept individual, there's really only a limited number of common types of people in the world. There are outliers, of course, but chances are, most people you meet will remind you of someone else. And you can use that person as a baseline of how you'll get along with the new person. Being socially intelligent can make getting along with new people come as second nature, but if that skill is lacking, simply being friendly is much easier and yields similar rewards.

It had been quite some time since I had that much fun. Other than all the tequila they made me drink, it was a perfect night. I hate tequila.

The following morning was far less pleasant. I woke up at 7 a.m. with a pounding headache and a dog relentlessly barking right outside my tent. Needless to say, it was a rough day of hiking, plagued by a persistent hangover, throbbing head, and aching muscles that made every step a struggle on the way to Cuba, NM.

When I got there, I wanted to get a motel room to rest up. The first place I called had no vacancies because of a group of contractors in town. The second one I called was the Cuban Lodge. They said the same thing, but once I mentioned I was hiking the CDT, everything changed. The owner, who was on the phone, was instantly fervent about getting me a room. She urged me to come by, assuring that she would have a room ready by then.

Upon reaching the hotel, I found her rushing her son and his fiancé out of the room they were occupying to clear it for me to stay in. I couldn't help but laugh! The owner's sheer joy at encountering an early-season hiker, coupled with the comical sight of her rushing her son out of the room, made it impossible for me to feel guilty or remorseful.

The remainder of the day unfolded in a blissfully relaxing manner. I indulged in a refreshing shower, followed by my customary order of seven double cheeseburgers and two large fries from McDonald's. Accompanied by copious amounts of Dr. Pepper, I kicked back and enjoyed both *Bad Boys* movies playing on cable.

I loved days like this. All I needed was some fast food, Dr. Pepper, a cheap motel room, and a few hours of resting instead of walking, and I was the happiest man on earth. As much as I loved hiking, I loved not hiking even more at times.

Pain in San Pedro Parks Wilderness

I allowed myself to sleep in the next day and felt much better leaving town than entering it. *That feeling would fade in time.*

Other than getting chased by a feisty dog, everything was fine as I cruised at a 3 mph pace and climbed 3,000 feet up to 9,500 feet, entering San Pedro Parks Wilderness in northern New Mexico.

As I reached higher elevations, the challenges escalated dramatically. Above 9,500 feet, there were layers upon layers of snow, causing my speed to plummet to less than half a mile per hour. The entire forest was blanketed in snow over four feet deep, but that wasn't even the worst part.

It was so warm that the snow was a false floor. With every step I took, I immediately sank down four feet, just hoping that there wouldn't be a rock or log below to roll my ankle or hurt my foot. Progressing through the snow became a grueling task, as I constantly found myself sinking up to my mid-thigh and, at times, even above my waist. Climbing out of these deep holes proved to be a protracted challenge. Every attempt to climb out would result in the surrounding snow collapsing, resembling a cruel form of quicksand where the more I struggled, the worse it became.

The snow cut up my legs so badly that I was leaving streaks of red in my path. In addition to the bleeding cuts, my legs were riddled with countless micro-cuts, making my legs constantly burn. The only thing that stopped me from sinking down further into the snow was my other leg ramming hard into the snow, and this aggressive jolting shot pain into my hips on every step. This experience surpassed the miseries of both Vermont and Mount Taylor, pushing the boundaries of my tolerance.

Unsurprisingly, there were no tracks from anyone else, which meant I was the first idiot to tackle this terrain in a long time. The imprints I left behind, four to five feet deep, ravaged the snowscape, serving as a visible testament to the difficulty of this unexplored area. The sheer difficulty was mind-boggling, but it also made perfect sense why others had chosen to steer clear of this unforgiving wilderness this early in the year.

There were at least five times throughout the day where I was walking along, completely unsure of where the actual trail was, and fell through the snow into a stream below my feet. As if I wasn't furious enough already, sinking into a creek of freezing cold water and soaking my feet was an easy way to put me over the edge. I yelled at the top of my lungs in frustration, but really couldn't do anything about it other than continue on. The only way is thru.

At one point in the day, it looked like the snow had melted at a higher elevation on a ridge near me from sun exposure. Filled with hope, I scaled the side of the snow-covered mountain, anticipating a semblance of normal walking conditions along the ridge that would lead me back to the trail. However, upon reaching the crest of the ridge, I discovered only a small area where the snow had indeed melted. My attempt to find an alternate route only resulted in veering off course and wasting over 20 minutes, leaving me more fatigued than before.

The day ended early when I was fortunate enough to find a flat spot where snow had melted for me to set up my tent. It was the first dry patch for camping I had seen since climbing above the snow line, so I didn't want to press my luck. I spent the rest of the day lying in my tent, questioning how I was going to do nine more miles of this hell before I dropped back down in elevation and the snow would lessen.

The following day was an agonizing continuation of the same wretched conditions, only seeming to intensify along with my frustration. I covered a mere six miles. Having a day with that low of mileage decimated my confidence. My journal entry from that day serves as a poignant reminder of the sheer misery that enveloped me:

Words can't really describe how miserable the last 2 days have been. On the surface, my legs are cut up and burn. My feet are constantly chilled because I will be walking in snow which looks normal, but then collapses and beneath it is a running stream. That's not to mention trying to cross streams and having the snow or ice break beneath me. My shoulders hurt from constantly trying to put all my weight on my trekking poles to avoid postholing. My hands are blistered up from gripping so tight.

Today it took me over 7 hours to cover 6 miles and I called it a day around 3 p.m. because the postholing just gets worse as the day goes on. I actually found a semi flat spot, out of snow, and wasn't sure when I'd see that again so I ended the day early. I've got about 3 more miles to go until the snow should hopefully disappear.

I thought there would be snow up here at this elevation, but I did not think it would be this bad. I'll probably have to find an alternate route to finish New Mexico because a lot of it is at this elevation or higher.

Wisely, I attempted to start early the following day to do the last three miles, but it was so bitterly cold that I couldn't.

Fearfully, I worried about my hands since I had gotten frostbite on the AT and now only had light gloves.

Paradoxically, I waited for the sun to emerge, which then in turn made the postholing worse.

It was three more excruciatingly cruel miles of postholing until I finally exited San Pedro Parks Wilderness and descended in elevation. I had never been so happy to see dirt again and gave the last chunks of snow the middle finger on my way out.

When I was finally back down on good old-fashioned earth, I was flying. I was immeasurably more appreciative of everything around me, since I had spent two days seeing how things could be at their absolute worst. For the rest of the day, the trail remained difficult compared to most of New Mexico. But I didn't care. As long as I wasn't sinking four feet with every step in a postholing nightmare, everything seemed like a walk in the park.

It was a scenic day with its own special moments. As I climbed a mesa and glanced behind me, I noticed an intimidating cloud of smoke approaching. I pulled out my phone to check if it was a controlled burn, but there was no cell service. I continued on in hopes that it was a controlled burn, instead of a wildfire.

Throughout the day, I found myself in an optimistic but vulnerable mood, my emotions running high from the looming fire danger, the trauma of the past few days, and the sheer vitality of a thru-hike.

I had previously downloaded some podcasts that were recorded speeches in history. This afternoon, I was listening to the renowned "I Have a Dream" speech. I couldn't remember if I had heard the whole speech before or not, but if I did, it didn't matter. It felt remarkably powerful. A few minutes into the speech, I started bawling because it was so beautiful. My eyes were already watering earlier in the speech but hearing Martin Luther King declare "Let freedom ring" from mountaintops nationwide was so moving, it overtook me. I hiked for 20 minutes with blurry vision, my tears flowing more abundantly than any water source in the state of New Mexico. Nobody else was around, and it felt unbelievably liberating. I hadn't had something overtake me like that since a song in the Smokies. Rarely have I ever felt more human than in these moments.

As evening approached, the scenery around me turned cinematic. I walked through a canyon as the sun began to set, and the world came alive with vibrant colors. The green desert brush seemed more animated than ever, while the red sandstone walls of the canyon glowed with fiery intensity in the fading light, reflecting the desert's resilience. The white clouds above transformed into a cotton candy pink, contrasting against the diminishing blue sky. Even the dirt beneath my feet appeared richer and more alluring, painted in shades of red. The day ended with more beauty than a hundred days in San Pedro Parks Wilderness could have misery. In this wasteland of sparse life and abundant hardship, I felt undeniably alive.

After dark, I began the Ghost Ranch alternate and found shelter in a pit toilet at a campground. It was the dingiest bathroom I had slept in yet, but it was still warmer and more enjoyable than outside. Waking up with spiders crawling on me was a small price to pay.

The next morning, I realized I had been hiking for 100 days. Yet, it didn't feel any different. It didn't make anything easier, so I got up and started hiking just like any other day. The first six miles were brutal on my feet as I traveled a dirt road scattered with big rocks that were impossible to avoid. I was relieved to reach the pavement that would lead me into Chama.

This road walk was an alternate I decided to take because the actual trail to the east was mostly above 10,000 feet, and I didn't want to deal with the same treacherous snow that I just hiked through in the San Pedro Parks Wilderness. From the road, I could see the high mountains where the trail would have taken me. Considering the amount of snow I saw off in the distance, I was happy that I chose to remain at the lower elevation. Nestled in some trees near a creek bed, I made camp a few dozen feet off the road.

It was a quick next day on the road. I made it into Chama, NM, secured a room at a motel, and was met with surprise and genuine happiness from the staff. It was rare for them to see a hiker arriving so early.

The clerk told me that a few years prior, the people in the town didn't like the hikers coming through since they smelled and looked like vagabonds. To open their minds, she wrote an article in the local paper describing how difficult it was to hike the trail, and what kind of person it takes to do so. With that single article, she changed the mindset of the people in town. She was a kind and caring woman, who made a true impact.

I ventured across the street to a market to grab my resupply and a 12-pack of Dr. Pepper as my treat for the day. The remainder of the day was dedicated to meticulous planning. With the snow I had been dealing with, I knew the official trail in Colorado would be too challenging to hike this early in the year. I even called a few local places around the trail to get some input, and they all said the snow was at least five feet deep around them and even more so at the higher elevations.

Still having about ten days before I was going to start the Pacific Crest Trail, I wasn't going to waste time sitting around. I devised an alternate plan to hike in Colorado, and an alternate plan off of that alternate plan. I was fairly certain I would have to go with the alternate-alternate plan, and I was okay with that. Although 180 miles of paved road walking wouldn't be the most wild or enjoyable experience, it would be easy to do in six days, which is the time I had before my plane to California. I felt good about it and went to bed, excited to get going the next morning.

I woke up to nearly a half-foot of fresh snow on the ground, and it looked like it was going to continue all day. Reluctantly, I made the decision to take a rest day and avoid the worst of the snow.

After inhaling five Hot Pockets and a pack of ramen noodles to fuel up, I set out in the morning to brave the elements when it was still ten degrees. I didn't have the adequate gear for that temperature, but I hoped the day would warm up quickly with the sun shining. I had to get moving: I now had to do 180 miles in five days instead of six.

A few miles later, I crossed into Colorado after 27 days in New Mexico. The land of enchantment had certainly given me its challenges, from sleeping out in the open during a downpour to hiking through the worst snow conditions of the whole year. I loved the state but was excited to keep moving forward. I knew, however, that my experience in Colorado would be different since it would exclusively be road walking to avoid the dangerous snow in the high mountains.

Even though I was walking along the road, the scenery was still outstanding. Everything was covered in tons of white powder, reminiscent of a winter wonderland. If someone had told me that this is what it looked like in January instead of April, I wouldn't have doubted them for a moment. Even though I was on pavement, majestic mountains surrounded me, their peaks seemingly within arm's reach. The sheer magnitude of the snow, not limited to the highest summits, was awe-inspiring. It reaffirmed my contentment with opting for the lower elevation alternate route.

After nearly two rest days, my body felt great, and I was flying with the easy road walking. Apprehensively, I had to walk at night along the road, but I hiked a 44-mile day and camped at a baseball field in Antonito, CO.

Baseball fields are a great place to camp in a town if need be. Granted, I never used them during the summer, when kids were out of school and actually going to the baseball field. It probably wouldn't be great for children to show up and discover a homeless-looking man sleeping on the field. But out of season, baseball fields were great. Most of the time, I wasn't sure if it was allowed, illegal, or just frowned upon, so I usually cowboy camped in a dugout — out of sight.

It was a cold night, still below 20 degrees when I started moving the next morning. I questioned how I did it on the AT when it was much colder. I felt like I might be getting softer as the year went on, when the reality was that I had better gear in winter. Nonetheless, it was at least a chance to tell myself that I was soft and needed to toughen up if I wanted to accomplish my goal. A little bit of self-deprecation can help in the pursuit of a goal.

I did a small resupply at the store in town and grabbed a Dr. Pepper to motivate me for the day. As I exited the store in shorts, an old man accosted me and told me I was going to freeze to death if I didn't put on some long pants. I smiled, said, "Yeah, maybe," and continued on my merry way down Route 285. It was a short and easy 30-mile day on the road into Alamosa, CO, where I treated myself to a motel.

The next two days were not as short and easy. I covered a staggering 77 miles in two days, which was easier on the road than it would be on the trail, but still taxing on the body. My legs grew increasingly stiff from doing the same motion repeatedly, rather than climbing up and down mountains. The repetitiveness of the flat road wears them out in a different manner than the varying motions of climbing and descending. Anytime I stopped, they would immediately lock up. This led to me not stopping often, a good practice for covering big miles.

The first night after Alamosa, I had to camp near the road. I tried to find a secluded spot, but there wasn't much to choose from. Nobody stopped by or said anything, but I felt out of place that close to a busy road.

The next day, I reached Salida, CO, where I got a motel for the night with a hot tub. It felt like much-needed physical therapy after the cold weather and stiff muscles I had been dealing with. Other than the hot tub, the only redeeming quality of these road days was that I had cell reception the whole time, and I didn't need to worry about my phone's battery. With these two factors culminating, I was on the phone catching up with friends and family the whole time. The road walking wasn't the best, but it did go by a little faster, passing the time with people I love.

The day leaving Salida would be my last on this section of the CDT. It was a short 22-mile jaunt to Monarch Pass where the official CDT crossed the road. I arrived there in the late afternoon and went inside the gift shop at the pass with a few hours to kill before a friend would pick me up. I was certainly the first CDT hiker to be there for the year, and I celebrated by downing five breakfast sandwiches.

All in all, it was a quick 180 miles, and I had to do it in a day less than I planned. But I made it. I loved this southern section of the CDT, but I was more than ready to leave the CDT and head to the heat of southern California, especially with the recent nights in the teens. I was ready to finally begin the last trail of my journey, the trail where it was all supposed to begin, before the idea of the Calendar Year Triple Crown ever entered my mind.

Phase III:

Pacific Crest Trail

Mexico to Canada

April 26th–July 25th

Fun in the Sun

After spending three days resting up with a friend in Orange County, swimming in the Pacific Ocean for the first time, and going to a nightclub where I felt extremely out of place, I started on the Pacific Crest Trail at the Mexican border on April 26th. Uncharacteristically, I commenced this leg of the journey with two other hikers I met at the border, already a departure from my near 2,500 miles of solitary hiking thus far.

I hadn't seen anybody on the trail since that couple gave me water in southern New Mexico. This was an unfamiliar world for me. We hiked together for a few hours, which flew by with ceaseless conversation. It was a pleasant change from the hiking I had been doing previously, and one of the things I was eagerly looking forward to about the PCT. April 26th was near the latter end of the popular window in which thru-hikers start the PCT. That, combined with the fact that I would be hiking fast, meant that I would see people all the time. I was fine with being alone like I had been, but life is simply more fun and interesting with other people around. The downside of my swift pace was that I likely wouldn't spend a lot of time with any one person, so I wouldn't form a long-lasting relationship that typical hikers enjoy and hold on to for the rest of their lives. Nonetheless, I made the most of the limited time I had with each individual, cherishing each encounter.

The shock of the first day was that it was raining at the Mexican border and kept raining until I set up camp for the night. *I can't escape poor weather!* I didn't expect to have wet feet on my inaugural day on the PCT. However, the optimistic side of me thought it was a good thing to get the rain out of the way. Now I was pretty well set on not getting rained on, at least the rest of my time in the desert, statistically speaking. That didn't prove to be exactly true in New Mexico, but a man can dream.

Having started at the border after 5 p.m., it was a measly 11 miles for my first day on the PCT, but I was eager to get after it the next day. The morning entailed carefully maneuvering through dew-drenched overgrowth in the faint hope that I could keep my shorts and shoes dry. Arriving at Lake Morena with a soggy lower-half, I replenished my water supply, and was joined by the two people I had started with the previous day.

Because I hit the ground running and was moving faster than most people, when I said goodbye to someone, it was usually for good. And when I bid farewell to the two people I started with, I realized that they were the first of many that I would come to know for a short time, and then never see again.

Upon leaving, I felt an unusual tingling sensation in my hands. It was odd since I didn't feel dehydrated or experience any other issues. Like any rational man would do, I ignored it until it went away and hoped it wouldn't come back. Meanwhile, I was starting to feel the scorching heat of the southern California desert. Many hikers take siesta breaks in the desert section to avoid the hottest part of the day, roughly somewhere between noon and 4 p.m. I passed a few hikers taking siestas in the shade, but wasting that much time wasn't in the cards for me. I had a schedule to keep.

After I reached Interstate 8, I started a 3,000-foot climb. It was a generous reminder that the PCT was graded for pack animals, and the trail would be much more forgiving than the Appalachian Trail. It didn't feel like a climb. However, during this climb, my ego took a substantial blow. I thought I was this pretty fast hiker, doing the Calendar Year Triple Crown and all. Yet, a girl swiftly caught up with me and was on my heels, prompting me to step aside and let her pass. She flew on by and I never saw her again. I rarely got passed, and the handful of times it did happen, I caught up to the person later. But that wasn't the case here. It was good to be humbled, but I was still astounded. She was moving so fast that it didn't seem real. *Was I hallucinating along with my tingling hands?*

It rained again for a few minutes in the afternoon, not even long enough for anything to get wet, just long enough for me to get out my rain jacket, and then immediately take it off because it stopped raining. Nonetheless, the sight of the billowing clouds over the desert made the short-lived rain worthwhile.

I ended up calling it a day after 28 miles. It looked like there would be limited camping ahead, and I didn't want to arrive exhausted at a campsite, only to find it fully occupied. This concern plagued me throughout the desert section since I hiked later into the day than most. Hikers who just started their PCT journey were still adjusting to the demands of hiking, limiting the distance they could cover in a day. Meanwhile, I wanted to hike until I had to stop from exhaustion. I was disappointed with 28 miles. On the PCT and CDT, I was hoping to average 30 miles per day to be able to finish the trails in the timeframe that I needed to. I wanted to consistently beat my average in the desert section, given its easier terrain. With this being my first full day and only hitting 28 miles, I felt behind schedule.

One factor that contributed to the disappointing mileage was my chafing. The New Mexico desert was still transitioning from winter to summer when I was there, so this was my first time dealing with intense heat, and the first time I had to deal with chafing. I forgot to bring Body Glide or any other remedy to help with it, so I had to endure the discomfort until my body adjusted to the heat and associated sweat.

That night, I had a restless sleep due to my lazy choice of setting up my tent in an unfavorable location. The relentless wind battered my tent, creating loud flapping sounds that frequently jolted me awake. Despite the less-than-ideal start, the following day turned out to be quite pleasant. It was only a couple of miles to the Mount Laguna campground where I got some clean water and used a porcelain throne. When I was outside the bathroom, a dad was going into the ladies' room with his two young daughters and one of them stopped, looked him dead in the eye, and said, "You can't go in there." After some convincing, she reluctantly allowed him entry. I got a good laugh out of the ordeal.

It was a beautiful and easy day of hiking. Most of the day was walking on a ledge over a grand desert valley. However, an encounter with my first rattlesnake on the ledge posed a slight dilemma. I threw a rock to the top side of the ledge, thinking the snake would go the opposite way. Instead, it lunged at the rock and curled up in a bush right alongside the trail. Gathering my courage, I sprinted by it and carried on with my day. My more favorable encounter with a snake was later seeing a bird flying with one in its beak. I hate snakes with my entire being.

Because of chafing and limited camping ahead, I stopped early in the evening again after 32 miles. The mathematical part of my brain was satisfied that my average was back to 30, excluding the first day which was only four hours of hiking. Although the spot I chose for camping was too rocky to set up my tent, I embraced the idea of cowboy camping since it was still as windy as the previous night. I didn't want to listen to a tent flapping in the wind again all night, and drifted off to sleep lying flat on the ground.

I woke up at 3 a.m. on the dot, with the wind completely gone, only to be greeted by the persistent buzz of mosquitoes. Knowing I wouldn't fall back asleep, I took it as a sign to get moving. I made good progress until the sun rose, but as the day heated up, I noticed a significant decrease in my pace. I even took an hour lunch break, which wasn't part of my usual routine. Throughout the day, I consumed over three gallons of water without experiencing the sickness I had endured on the CDT. Now my body truly needed the hydration in this scorching desert heat.

Since starting the PCT, where timing was more important, I had been paying more attention to my mileage and pace. On the AT and CDT, my mindset was basically to make it as far as possible in the time that I had. But now that I was on the PCT and reaching the ideal hiking season, I had to average 30 miles per day to make my plans for the year work out. After waking up at 3 a.m., I had surpassed 20 miles by noon, and 30 miles by 5:15 p.m. I contemplated calling it a day at that point, even though it was unusual for me to stop so early. Eagle Rock, an iconic rock in the shape of an eagle, was five miles away. I wasn't sure if I'd be able to make it before sunset since I had been moving slowly in the heat of the afternoon. After a few minutes of rest and getting pumped up listening to Pop Smoke, I cantered at 4 mph to get there well before dark. After struggling through the afternoon, I had a new surge of energy after the temperature cooled down a bit.

Despite my desire to continue, I had to end my day after covering 38 miles. I felt good physically and mentally, but I had to stop because I had a food package a half mile further up the trail in Warner Springs. As much as I wanted to continue on, doing so without food would've been tough. I fell asleep to a chorus of frogs singing their hallmark tune.

I unintentionally overslept by an hour but managed to arrive at the post office just as it opened. While charging my phone outside a gas station next to the post office, I was chatted up by an attractive biker lady. She was the kind of scary-pretty that is unique to goth girls, bikers, heavy metal fangirls, and women of that sort. After exchanging jabs of flirtation, I floated down the trail, carried by the weightlessness of my elevated ego.

Even in my blissful state, it just didn't feel right for it to be over 80 degrees by 10 a.m. Most of my days in New Mexico hovered in the 70s. Around 11:15 a.m., I found some shade and took a four-hour break as the temperature soared above 90 degrees. This felt strange because I was programmed to try to take full advantage of daylight, but it was getting to the point in the year where daylight wasn't a concern anymore. I took this break because I wanted to give the midday siesta a try. I confirmed it wasn't for me. Other than constantly thinking to myself that I should be moving, I didn't sleep at all during this time and mostly spent the time swatting away bugs. Even when I did get moving again, it was still dreadfully hot and my shirt felt like a dirty bar rag. Whenever I took off my pack, there was salt residue outline covering the pack from my gnarly back sweat.

As I turned a corner later in the day, I heard a loud hissing sound that caught my attention in a primal manner. I like to call rattlesnakes the gentlemen of snakes because they at least warn you before they try to kill you, and this one was courteously making me aware of its presence from ten feet away. We entered a tense standoff, staring each other down for a seemingly endless 15 minutes. Eventually, the snake slithered off the trail, but again to my dismay, it went to the top side of the trail rather than the lower side, like I would have preferred. Patiently, I waited until it was at a safe distance, and then made a run for it.

To compensate for the time lost during my midday break, I pushed myself to hike well into the night, arriving at my campsite to find numerous tents already there. Trying to be as least intrusive as possible, I cowboy camped right by the trail but slept poorly because it turned out to be on a slope. Choosing good campsites after dark was always a challenge. I woke up several times during the night after my inflatable sleeping pad completely slid off of my ground sheet below me. Any sort of slope while cowboy camping with an inflatable pad was a recipe for problems.

Despite my efforts to be quiet, I unintentionally became the rooster for other hikers in the morning. After chatting for a bit, I resumed my journey. My objective was to make it to Mary's Oasis before the midday heat. This was a dry and open section of trail, but at the oasis, there was allegedly a water tank and shade.

While on my way there, I had to stop and answer the call of nature. Doing this with other hikers around was something I had not dealt with all year. This area wasn't great for it either. All of the brush was short, and there was nowhere to hide. I went a good distance off trail and started my business. While doing so, I looked up and saw a person descending a ridge who could easily see me. I was watching him and could tell the exact moment he saw me, because his demeanor shifted abruptly. His body jolted with shock, and he then avoided eye contact at all costs and looked around in the sky like, "Hmm, I have a very serious thought that I need to ponder, and I should look up in the sky to think about it." Later in the day, I met someone who I thought was that same guy, so I apologized. It turned out it wasn't him, so I only made the situation worse for myself, now having to explain the story to a stranger.

When I made it to the oasis, I was mystified. Not only was there water and shade, but trail angel Mary was there, selflessly cooking up food for the hikers. It turned out she did this two days every year, and I got lucky with my timing! I savored the taste of real food, indulging in a refreshing soda pop and a delicious chicken taco in the middle of the desert. The only thing that satisfies better than a Dr. Pepper is an ice-cold Dr. Pepper when you're spending all day in the fierce desert sun.

Unable to pull myself away from the lively conversations with other hikers, I lingered at the oasis longer than planned, relishing the camaraderie. While they intended to halt their journey at the next road and hitch a ride into Idyllwild the following morning, I aimed to hike all the way into town. They joked that we would get there at the same time with my brisk pace.

After crossing Highway 74, the day was filled with gorgeous views of the San Jacinto Mountains. It was a long day of hiking and a short night of rest. While I rationally did want to get into town as early as possible, the competitive part of me wanted to beat the hikers who were hitching a ride to town — not to prove anything to them, but just for my own personal challenge. To do this, I hiked until midnight and was moving by 4 a.m. to try to make it into town right when the grocery store opened.

Sure enough, right as I was walking out of the grocery store after my resupply, I saw the hikers from the oasis. They were both unsurprised and delighted that I had beaten them there, truly eager for me to move as fast as possible and achieve my goal.

The positive reinforcement in the thru-hiking community is something to aspire to for any group of people. People were encouraging me to go fast and succeed at my endeavor. I was encouraging other people to go as slow as they wanted and make their experience last as long as possible. And everyone is encouraging of everyone else for simply being out there, doing this crazy thing, and loving it along the way.

After my resupply, I was joined by a fellow hiker from that group at a nearby pizza place, where I shamelessly devoured a 16-inch meat lover's pizza and breadsticks. It turned out to be one of the best pizzas I had ever tasted. As we prepared to leave, my pizza buddy informed me that he had booked a hotel room in town and kindly offered me the chance to shower before resuming on the trail. I gratefully accepted the opportunity for a refreshing shower in hopes of it relieving my chafing. After days of sweating in the intense desert heat, it was a luxury I couldn't pass up, even if I had only been on the trail for a week.

Regrettably, I hadn't paid much attention to the map prior to leaving town. It was during my departure that I discovered the daunting truth — a steep 5,000-foot climb up to San Jacinto awaited me. *Maybe I shouldn't have eaten that whole pizza.* For the next four hours, I tediously plodded up the mountain. Not a second passed by without me trying to burp to relieve the gas in my stomach. At the same time, I was struggling to not throw up because I was so bloated. I was doing all this while trying to not completely disgust the day hikers in this busy area. While I tried to hide most of my burps under my breath, I had to check and make sure nobody was around before I ripped a big one that might frighten small children.

Eventually, I reached the junction for the summit with 60 minutes until sunset. The official PCT skirts around the summit. To get to the peak, it was an extra 2.5 miles up and 2.5 miles down. With as bad as I was feeling, and as slow as I was moving, I wasn't sure if I could make it there in under an hour. But I was going to try — the peak calling my name like a siren.

Pushing through the bloated discomfort, I triumphantly arrived at the summit just before sunset. There was another hiker there relishing in the breathtaking view. All the clouds were below the mountain, and the sun was setting over them as if Hollywood had produced it. None of the pictures on my phone turned out because of the lighting, but that was the beautiful reminder from moments like these — you had to be there to truly experience them. *Anything else was poor translation.*

The other hiker talked me into camping in the hut near the top of the summit. The hut was more of an emergency shelter so you weren't really supposed to stay there, but all the campsites on the ascent were still buried under snow and looked unusable. It would've been a considerable distance before the next campsite, so I opted for the hut, but maybe I wouldn't have if I knew it would be a terrible night of sleep.

There were wooden bunks in the hut, but there were several problems with them. The main one was that they felt like they were going to collapse if I so much as inhaled too deeply. I was actually worried they wouldn't be able to handle my body weight, and the wood would just snap in the middle of the night. Other than that, they were extremely uncomfortable. They sagged in the middle and really hurt my back. Lastly, they were just too small. It couldn't fit my sleeping pad or me comfortably. I only got a few hours of sleep, vowing to never return to that hut.

To avoid a scolding from a ranger, I left early the next morning. Although I didn't think it was illegal, I thought sleeping there was frowned upon. Stepping outside above 10,000 feet, I was met with a chilling reminder of my elevation with the temperature around 20 degrees. My fingers were going numb while filtering water in the morning. I wasn't even remotely thirsty, but it was 20 miles until my next water source. Shortly after doing so, I looked at the elevation profile for the day and noticed it was unlike anything I had ever seen — a continuous 9,600-foot descent stretched out over 24 miles! *Awesome!*

I hate inclines and love descents because they're easier. I've heard other hikers say they hate descents because of the painful impact on their knees. When I get to that point, I'll just hate all of hiking since I already hate ascents, and there's really no such thing as a flat landscape in reality.

My love for the long descent waned as the day progressed — it was effortless. But as the day went on, the absence of shade on the descent from San Jacinto began to take its toll. I hadn't expected a 9,600-foot descent to drain me so thoroughly, but it did. As I was nearing the end of the decline and looking forward to a break, I started to hear a buzzing, and then realized there was a massive beehive in the side of the mountain right on the trail. Without hesitation, I broke into a sprint, narrowly escaping a potential sting. I'm sure that spot claimed its fair share of victims during the 2021 season.

By the time I reached the bottom, I was utterly depleted. I replenished my water supply, rested briefly, and decided to cover just seven more miles before setting up camp.

Later, I arrived at a highway underpass with a water cache and shade. I always seemed to get to these underpasses early in the morning or at night, never in the heat of the day. While there, I met a couple that was hiking together, which reminded me of how content I was to be hiking solo and not reliant on anyone else. The husband displayed unwavering kindness and tolerance, repeatedly asking his wife what she wanted to do, but she kept giving non-answers. "Do you want to camp here or keep going?" *Grunt.* "If we do keep going, how much farther do you want to go?" *Silence.* "Do you want us to cook dinner here?" *Ehh.* "How much water do you want me to carry for you?" *I don't know.* "We can stop here if you want. What do you want to do?" *No response.*

I wanted to shout, "Just answer the man!" But I didn't. I ensured that they'd be okay, and hiked on, later cowboy camping in a dry creek bed.

I was hiking by 5:15 the next morning, but the heat also started early. The morning featured a series of short climbs and descents leading into a valley, but once I reached Mission Creek, it was a steady uphill climb the rest of the day. Much of the trail was along a creek. For once, I had consistent access to water. Being around water also made it slightly cooler, and there were trees that provided precious shade — a true luxury.

The bad part about this particular section of the trail was that it suffered from frequent washouts, rendering it difficult to navigate for extended periods. Coupled with the scorching heat and the relentless uphill trek, my progress was slower than desired. As the day neared its end, exhaustion crept in, and I spotted a cluster of tents slightly off the trail. I ventured closer and discovered a friendly gathering of fellow hikers to chat with before passing out. The best aspect of that campsite was the immediate availability of water in the morning, which was a blessing since the next water source lay 20 miles ahead. On the downside, I once again found myself cowboy camping on a slope, battling gravity for a decent night's rest.

On the bright side, my inability to sleep led to an early start, and it turned out to be an excellent day of hiking. Although the trail wasn't consistently uphill, the high elevation kept the temperature slightly cooler, and the presence of trees offered refreshing patches of shade. In the afternoon, I got a hitch into Big Bear, CA by a Spanish-speaking mother and daughter, the latter of which was practicing for her driving test. I don't know what it is, but whenever people are talking in a language you don't understand, you just always assume they're talking bad about you. Maybe I've just seen too many movies. Although, they very well could've been talking about how putrid I smelled.

After my resupply and pizza, I ended the day hiking the last few miles with three other people and making camp with them to cap off a 42-mile day. This was the first night that I had ended around a massive camp of PCT thru-hikers, and it was exhilarating. I kept my goal for the year a secret for a while, before it finally came out due to questions from others.

Typically, I refrained from immediately sharing my pursuit of the Calendar Year Triple Crown with others. Doing so often led to the same predictable conversations which I enjoyed having with people, but not while I was hiking during the day or getting ready for bed. I didn't want to stop and burn time. However, when I found myself spending significant time with fellow hikers and not in a hurry, I relished talking about it. Witnessing the realization dawn on people's faces when they grasped the enormity of my endeavor always brought a smile to my face. The only thing I didn't like was that people would immediately downplay their own thru-hike. "I'm only hiking the PCT." I never found a good way to remind someone that they were still a badass without sounding corny, but every single person that I met out there was kicking ass. Some people just did it at a different pace.

That particular night turned out to be incredibly enjoyable. I became acquainted with a tramily (trail family) and discovered their peculiar tradition or joke — I couldn't quite discern which it was. Whenever one of them arrived at camp, they would loudly declare, "My trail name is motherfucker!" to let everyone know they had arrived. It was beyond stupid, but I loved it.

The night was so fun that, for once, I actually enjoyed sitting down and not moving, rather than thinking about the miles I should be covering. I met people from all over the country and heard their captivating stories and amusing mishaps from the trail so far. People were freely sharing the alcohol they carried out of town — a luxury I never really enjoyed due to time and weight concerns. People were also looking to me for tips and tricks, but I didn't have much to offer. Even though I was almost 3,000 miles in by this point, I still felt like a newbie. Each trail was so different that I felt like I was right there with them, learning the ways of the PCT. The only real difference was that my body had become more acclimated from spending such a prolonged time on the trail.

I drifted to sleep with a pleasant buzz, only to be awakened a few hours later by alarmed voices saying, "What's going on? What is that?" I thought a bear stumbled into our camp, so I was mentally preparing to throw fists. But when I looked up, a mesmerizing light show greeted my eyes. Lights streaked across the sky in a perfect and unnatural manner, entrancing me for a solid 30 seconds. In that moment, I found myself mentally preparing for an alien invasion. *Okay, we're not in an urban area, so we have plenty of time to prepare. There's a town nearby where we can stock up on food. I'm surrounded by people that are okay with living in the mountains, which will be the safest area. Although, I am okay going it alone if I have to. If they do find us right now, I don't have any weapons.* My mind was all over the place.

Finally someone shouted out that it was Starlink, an initiative by Elon Musk to launch satellites in order to bring Wi-Fi to remotes areas. I could put my alien invasion concerns to rest for the time being.

The Calm Before the Storm

The morning passed by with the swiftness of a rejuvenated spirit. My body was filled with momentum, and my soul, a desire to keep going, passing by several water sources to maintain my inertia.

As I was foolishly walking while trying to select an audiobook on my phone, I carelessly ran into a branch that was exactly at head level, jolting me back to reality. Potent at first, the pain quickly subsided — no concussion protocol needed.

The day unfolded along the rim of Deep Creek Canyon, reminiscent of the awe-inspiring Gila but with a slightly diminished allure. By 1 p.m., exhaustion and thirst set in, prompting me to lie down on the trail for a quick five-minute break. Like a grain of sand on a beach standing up to a wave, slumber swept me away, and it was the arrival of two friends from the previous night that woke me from my unintended nap. They informed me a water source was a mere 30 yards away. Irritation mingled with amusement as I scolded myself for stopping just shy of the much-needed hydration.

I passed Mile 300 on trail and made it over 20 miles to Deep Creek Hot Springs around 2 p.m. Twenty miles by 2 p.m. was a good indicator that I was going to have a strong mileage day. Briefly, but appreciatively, I soaked my feet for ten blissful minutes before hiking again. Soon after, I came across a baseball-sized hole in the ground. I was about to step right beside it when a triangular head peeked out of the hole. It was like whack-a-mole but with a venomous snake. I panicked a little, backed up, and made a loop around the perilous pothole. Throughout the year, I came across countless similar holes, always fearing a snakehead might pop out. Previously, I tried to dismiss the fear as irrational, but this incident proved that fear valid.

With limited camping options ahead, I stopped to camp early with a tramily after a 33-mile day. Most tramilies that I saw were a combination of men and women, but this one was all men. Unbeknownst to them, I called them "The Dude Crew" in my head. It was a cool group of dudes from college-aged to post-retirement. We talked for over an hour, covering topics ranging from curiously deep to incredibly stupid, before I decided it was time to return to my cowboy camp and get some sleep.

The morning greeted me with dew-laden surroundings — the nearby stream causing the dampness that enveloped everything. Still nursing the remnants of chafing caused by the unyielding heat, I hesitated to put on my wet shorts. Opting for an unconventional approach, I embarked on the first five hours of the day wearing only my underwear. It was both liberating and nerve-wracking, as I strongly hoped to avoid encountering any unsuspecting day hikers. Thru-hikers genuinely wouldn't care, or might not even notice, but with normal societal folks, you never know. Thankfully, those initial hours remained devoid of fellow wanderers, and after some time of drying while hanging on the outside of my pack, my shorts were wearable.

It was a hot and cumbersome day of hiking, but I only had one thing on my mind — McDonald's. Cajun Pass beckoned with the promise of a McDonald's located just half a mile off the trail, an irresistible oasis for every hiker seeking respite in the heart of the desert. By 3 p.m., I covered the 24 miles to McDonald's and was eager to get some greasy fast food. Knowing I had more hiking for the day, I exercised restraint in my order despite how famished I felt. Humbly, I ordered six double cheeseburgers, two large fries, and a McFlurry.

Joining the ranks of 50 other haggard thru-hikers, I sat down in the shade outside the revered sanctuary that was McDonald's, ready to feast. I was talking with some people when I saw "The Dude Crew" roll up. This was shocking because whenever I said goodbye to people, I expected to never see them again because of the speed at which I was moving. I was happy I stopped here and could see them one more time. They even pitched me their bold plan. Eat McDonald's now and later tonight, sleep in the parking lot, and then get Taco Bell in the morning. It was one of the trashiest things I had heard lately, and I loved it. Unfortunately, I had to press on, called by the constant voice of my time constraints for the year.

I arrived at a water cache where I chose to camp, relishing the luxury of being in close proximity to a water source for the second consecutive night. McDonald's had brought together a multitude of hikers, many of whom I encountered at the campsite. I reveled in the joy of connecting with fellow thru-hikers, only a recent opportunity for me.

While the solitude of my solo hikes along the AT and CDT had its merits, the company of others amplified the enjoyment exponentially. In the last weeks of his solitary life, the enigmatic Chris McCandless, better known as Alexander Supertramp, penned the words, "Happiness only real when shared." I've thought about that quote a lot, especially while hiking alone for weeks on end. While I don't fully subscribe to it, I do personally believe, "Happiness MOST real when shared."

What is this life if only a lonesome existence, speaking only to one's own conscience and God? Humans are inherently sociable creatures. Man is meant to exchange ideas. Man is meant to share. Man is meant to love.

And I felt the love on the PCT. Whether it be talking to other hikers while pounding six double cheeseburgers, or just chatting with people before going to bed, I felt genuine love all around. It wasn't the "You complete me" *Jerry Maguire* kind of love, or the unwavering, unconditional love of family evident throughout *The Pursuit of Happyness*.

Instead, it was a — "I love your passion"; "I love your open-mindedness"; "I love how you are choosing to live your life" — kind of love. Outside of thru-hiking, I have never felt this much respect, community, and love while sitting around a group of strangers.

Yet, a bittersweet reality accompanied all of these encounters for me. I knew they would all be short-lived, impermanent, fleeting like a leaf in the wind — destined to fade as we all traversed the ensuing 2,000 miles. While my journey propelled me ahead at a brisk pace, these newfound friends would forge lasting bonds through continued companionship while traveling at roughly the same pace the whole trail. But after our initial meeting, the chances of our paths crossing again were minimal.

And maybe that's what made it truly beautiful — the ephemeral nature of these connections. Much like our mortal lives, these encounters were finite. We would never be the same people as we were in that moment, doing the same insane endeavor, living for today instead of tomorrow, and reaching euphoric states of nirvana most days of the week. All things come to an end, but it was the awareness of the thru-hike's ultimate conclusion, mirroring my encounters with these extraordinary individuals, that bestowed upon them a special aura.

Everything was more beautiful because it couldn't last.

Although sacrificing valuable time for camaraderie detracted from the opportunity to achieve greater daily mileage, I wholeheartedly embraced the trade-off. As long as I maintained an average of over 30 miles per day, I remained content. The desert terrain called for considerably higher daily distances, given its relatively easier hiking conditions. However, I yearned for a taste of the authentic thru-hiking experience. Concluding my days around 6:30 p.m. with 30+ miles under my belt and savoring a few hours of companionship at the campsite was the closest I was going to get.

Rising at 4 a.m. with the intention of reaching Wrightwood before the all-consuming heat descended upon me, I moved faster than usual uphill because another person was accompanying me. I was pulling him up the mountain and he was pushing me, so we moved at a good clip.

In town, I got a pizza from Mile High Pizza. As usual, I got a large meat lover's. This pizza was overloaded with meat, which I loved, but it was a lot. I wasn't going to make the same mistake that I did leaving Idyllwild, so I only ate 60% of it and packed the rest in Ziploc bags. Leaving town was when I left the densest concentration of hikers. I saw many hikers after, but not at the consistency and intensity that I had the past few days.

Later in the day, the area allegedly had a decent amount of poodle dog bush, which is basically the California version of poison ivy or poison oak. The overgrown trail demanded nimble maneuvering as I delicately wiggled past the encroaching plants, hopeful to avoid any unwanted encounters. Upon reaching my campsite, shared with a couple of fellow hikers, I basked in the awe-inspiring sunset that bathed the surrounding mountains in majestic hues of pink.

The next morning, I made it to a water spigot just as the day was starting to heat up. The trail immediately after the spigot was allegedly filled with poodle dog brush, so I opted to walk a forest road that ran parallel to the trail. Even when I got back on trail, it was overgrown, and I just had to hope for the best. I knew what poodle dog bush looked like, but I was at the point where everything started to look like it, so I wasn't sure.

The day unfolded as a magnificent journey, featuring remarkable views from high ridges. There were a lot of times where I would turn a corner and audibly say "damn" because the view was so incredible. But the fantastic day had a taste of near-tragedy as I was listening to a podcast in the afternoon that made me laugh so hard my eyes started to water. Hiking along with blurry vision, I inadvertently stepped a bit off of a ledge, teetering on the edge with a catastrophic fall below. I managed to regain my balance, but it was a scarily close call from laughing too hard at *This Is Important*.

I ran into some trail magic late in the day. Trail magic is any sort of good surprise along the trail. It could be as complex as someone at a road crossing with a big grilling setup or as little as a beer hidden in a creek. This time, there was a big jug of water and coolers of pop for sale. I grabbed two pops for two bucks and sat by a few other thru-hikers. We talked shop for a while before I said I had to go, but one of them insisted on buying me another pop to persuade me to stick around. Their friendly gesture beat out the constant voice in the back of my head telling me to keep going.

By the end of the day, I made it down to a parking lot with a KOA campground nearby. I didn't want to pay to stay at the campground. It just felt absurd to pay for a campsite when I had been setting up my tent for free so often. I was hoping to sleep in the pit toilet in the parking lot, but it was so repulsive I couldn't even do it. I ended up cowboy camping on concrete by a nearby bench. It was noisy with people stopping in the parking lot for Lord-knows-what reasons, but I did get a few hours of decent sleep.

Awakened by a train repeatedly blasting its horn before sunrise, I got going and made it to Agua Dulce around 9:30 a.m., but not before passing through Vasquez Rocks — an area renowned for its use as a filming location in numerous movies and TV shows. I passed a sign with some of the movies and was a little confused how *Over the Hedge* was filmed there since it was an animated movie.

Later, when responsibly chowing down at Big Mouth Pizza in town, I remembered my lesson and only consumed a 14-inch pizza, instead of 16. I had planned on doing a two-day resupply in town, but that proved impossible. The only place to buy any groceries was a liquor store. What little was there was already picked over by the horde of PCT hikers.

I got a few candy bars and thought I would have to get off trail tomorrow to do another resupply. However, just as I was preparing to leave town, a hiker I had met earlier happened to receive a food box with an excess amount of food. He gave me his extras, which turned out to be the perfect amount. The trail provides!

Leaving shortly after noon, I perfectly timed the uphill climb to be in the hottest part of the day. It wasn't too terribly taxing though, being a gently-graded PCT climb as opposed to a steep AT climb. When I got to camp that night, tired from the heat of the day, a girl had just gotten into her tent. Being the suave gentleman I am, I offered a friendly greeting of "Howdy." But my polite gesture didn't stick the landing. I inadvertently startled her, prompting an initial shriek followed by laughter of embarrassment. I must move more stealthily than I thought.

The next day, I arrived at Hikertown. I didn't know what to expect, but I was pleasantly surprised. The story goes that it started out as a water spigot on private land that the owners allowed hikers to use after a few stumbled onto their property. Now it turned into a cool and established hiker hangout spot before they tackled the infamous aqueduct. The trail follows the LA Aqueduct for 20 miles, a notorious section because there is no shade and it's swelteringly hot across the open desert. This leads most people to hike it at night, me included.

My plan was to sleep at Hikertown until 1 a.m. before setting off on the aqueduct, ensuring I had sufficient rest and the advantage of hiking during the cooler nighttime hours. That plan did not come to fruition. I had so much fun talking and drinking beer with the other hikers that I didn't sleep at all. Caught up in the excitement of a big group of hikers leaving, I left around 7 p.m. with no sleep.

The sun began to set shortly after I started on the aqueduct. Less than an hour later, the Four Loko that I bought for the aqueduct was gone. It was only a single can, but with it being the equivalent of five beers, it packed a punch. I was buzzing and feeling fantastic, feeling so fantastic that I found myself running, which I normally didn't do. I covered five miles in the first hour as my buzz was crescendoing. This had me considering that I should drunk-hike all the time. I was ready to go all night, but then I had the four worst words in the English language enter my mind: "I need more beer." Disappointed by my foolishness to only bring a single drink, I soldiered on, lamenting the lack of additional refreshments.

After a considerable stretch of hiking alone, I eventually caught up to a group ahead. The Roxanne Gang — they exuded a wild energy and had a fun aura. They were acting goofy, and I assumed they were probably drunk too. They were party people, an activity which I missed desperately while on this journey of pushing myself to my physical limits.

It was an entertaining night with lively conversation. Then they played the song "Roxanne" something like 180 times in a row. I wanted to stay in their company, but I had to escape for a bit. I couldn't hear that song one more time without losing what little was left of my mind.

I decided to forge ahead, seeking some respite from The Police. Growing increasingly tired and yearning for sleep, I veered off the aqueduct and laid down in the dirt. I would allow myself 30 minutes of sleep, so I didn't want to get anything out of my pack to make it comfortable enough to where I'd want to stay. After 15 minutes, there was an onslaught of bugs crawling on me, making sleep an impossibility.

Without a choice to stay, I caught up to The Roxanne Gang, who was surprised to see me. Without listening to Roxanne another time, we hiked together through the night until we reached the next water source around 6:30 a.m. Amidst the nocturnal journey, the combined effects of sleep deprivation and the onset of a hangover began to take their toll, resulting in an uncomfortable state of exhaustion.

At that point, my priority shifted to satiating my voracious hunger, which had become painful. It was also high time to catch up on sleep. I wearily laid on the dirt near the others and passed out for two hours. However, as the sun began to beam down, I awakened in a sticky layer of sweat and embarked on a quest to find a suitable spot to evade the scorching rays. I found a shaded spot, albeit slanted and infested with ants, but at least somewhere sheltered from the sun.

My attempts to sleep were largely futile as I spent the day warding off the persistent ants while battling the slippery slope. It was an arduous and unpleasant experience. Nonetheless, spending the day bonding with The Roxanne Gang helped pass the time because sleep obviously wasn't. Around midday, I learned they had been tripping on acid the previous night. The night made a lot more sense in context now.

Remaining under the shade of the ant-infested tree until 4 p.m., I bid farewell to the Roxanne gang and resumed my journey. The hiking proved challenging, not because of the trail, but rather the toll the sleep deprivation had taken on my body. I covered a mere nine miles, ending the night early in the hopes of getting back on a normal sleep schedule where I could consistently wake up at 4 a.m.

I woke up the next day, still feeling hungover worse than after a week-long bender. *Damn, going a night without sleep really messed up my body.* The morning then greeted me with a refreshing breeze as I strolled through wind farms, catching sight of a group of majestic horses along the way, but I couldn't stay there too long. It was too much horsepower in one place.

After hitching into Tehachapi, I resupplied, making sure to replace my water bottle tainted with the lingering, nauseating taste of Four Loko.

As I was packing up my food outside the grocery store, an old man approached and started talking about the PCT. I should say preaching more than talking. He asked where my group was. After telling him I didn't really have one, he said I better get one, or I wasn't going to finish. Part of me wanted to go into a Walter White monologue of, "Clearly you don't know who you're talking to, so let me clue you in…" But instead I said, "Yeah, maybe," and let him stroke his own ego, preaching his self-righteousness.

Feeling my usual town-food hunger, I ventured to Burger King. The inside was closed, but the workers let me charge my phone while I was outside, eating my four double cheeseburgers, 30 chicken nuggets, and two large fries. When it was time to return to the trail, it took me an hour to get a ride. Finally, a nice police officer stopped and offered to help. As he pulled up, I wasn't sure if it was going to be a good encounter, or a bad one. I wasn't sure if I was going to get a ride, or a ticket. Some places outlawed hitchhiking, but it was pretty much impossible to know whether it's actually enforced or not until you got caught. Relieved, I rode shotgun in the cruiser back to the trail.

The next morning, I woke up over two hours late, my body still out of whack and recovering from that all-nighter. I then wasted an hour filtering four liters of water. The source was a tiny dribble coming out of a pipe. There was also a line of six hikers trying to fill up because the next water source had a connection with a recent norovirus outbreak. It would be 26 miles to the next risk-free consumable water. It was a tedious process of getting water, filtering it, and then waiting in line, but the ordeal at least gave me the opportunity to get to engage with other hikers since lately I hadn't been seeing as many at camps.

While hiking in the afternoon, I gave a tree a strong shoulder as I was passing by clumsily, tearing a sizeable hole in my shirt. My sewing skills leave much to be desired, so I resigned myself to the fact that the hole would remain taped until I found the time and motivation to deal with it. But the tape also never held, so it was an area that I accepted would get terribly sunburnt.

Towards the end of the day, I was feeling poorly, wanting to stop after 25 miles, but then I turned on *Tha Carter IV* album in my earbuds and zoomed the last three miles to camp. This was the second night in a row that I was at a large community campsite, but all alone. It was an eerie feeling. *Where did everybody go?*

The next morning, I awakened with renewed determination. My body was finally starting to get back on track, and I was feeling better. Then, several miles into the day, I realized that Kennedy Meadows, CA, my next resupply point, was a daunting 30 miles farther than anticipated. This revelation of my miscalculation meant that I had to cover 97 miles in the next 2.5 days to reach my destination before 5 p.m. Failure to do so would force me to waste an additional day waiting for the store to reopen to pick up my package. While completing 97 miles in three days wasn't implausible, the deadline added an extra layer of difficulty.

I embraced the challenge with excitement. Occasionally breaking into a run, my engine was fueled by a mixture of adrenaline from the impending deadline and inspiration from listening to interviews with David Goggins. The day's greatest obstacle came in the form of relentless winds gusting at 50 mph, reminiscent of the wind I encountered back in New Mexico. But it didn't matter. The tailwinds of my determination were stronger than any possible gust of these headwinds.

Surprisingly, the water situation turned out to be favorable on this day. A couple of water caches dotted the trail, providing relief in the absence of natural water sources. Although the morning initially hinted at leaving the desert behind, because of a brief encounter with a forested area, the majority of the day was spent traversing the exposed desert landscape. It wasn't until the day drew to a close that I witnessed the landscape transition from desert sands to the distant allure of granite formations and trees.

That same afternoon, I was walking up behind a person, following him closely for a while before I finally said hello. I assumed he had heard me behind him, but I guess not because he jumped and let out a small screech. Unintentionally, it was the second time in a few days that I had inadvertently scared someone. Ironically, later on, I had my own scare when a guy flew a drone dangerously close to the trail at an alarming speed. Worried about the possibility of getting decapitated, I picked up my pace, eager to distance myself from the situation.

I capped off a 36-mile day by 8:30 p.m. and went to bed, excited to go just as hard tomorrow. The wind kept me from getting a perfect night's sleep, but I still woke up raring to go. I crossed over Walker Pass in the morning, which many would consider the end of the desert section of the PCT and the beginning of the High Sierra. To me, everything from Walker Pass to Bighorn Plateau was an odd middle ground — not fully desert, nor fully High Sierra. That section was the awkward teenage phase of the PCT.

Early in the afternoon, the sky was clear, until I went through a mountain pass and on the other side it looked like all hell could break loose. The impending storm waited 20 minutes, and then rain started pouring down. *And I had just gotten used to being dry in the desert.*

Not wanting to get drenched, I took shelter under a tree, wedging myself between it and the steep hillside. Sitting there for 30 minutes until the rain stopped, I felt like a genius when I started hiking again, proud that I had avoided the rain. My intellect proved short-lived as it soon started raining again — and continued for hours. It was my second encounter with rain on the PCT, and it ironically happened on my first day "out of the desert."

Even though I was still pushing for my goal, I didn't feel great. I noticed myself going into a trance-like state a few times. I was definitely a little dehydrated and had not been consuming enough food for the mileage I was pulling. My ankle had also been bothering me for a few days. However, it seemed particularly worse on this day. But it didn't matter. I refused to let any of these challenges become excuses. I was going to reach Kennedy Meadows by 5 p.m. the following day, so I hiked past 10 p.m., only to wake up at 3 a.m. and continue hiking.

When my alarm went off, I was not in a good mood. I was still tired as hell, and all of my gear was soaked from condensation. This would be my last night of cowboy camping for a while, after doing so for every night but three in the desert. I loved its simplicity, but it wasn't worth waking up wet.

With extreme fatigue and determination, I trudged the 26 miles and made it to Kennedy Meadows around 2:30 p.m. with plenty of time to take care of logistics. The sending and receiving of packages actually took a long time. At first, they couldn't locate my package, which worried me, even though I knew it had to be there. Once I finally got it, with all my extra gear I had sent to me for the Sierra, I had to decide what I would keep for the 200+ mile stretch to the next town of Mammoth Lakes, CA, and what I would ship back home.

The Sierra is an extremely remote area in California at a high elevation that can get extreme weather. With no road crossings for over 240 miles, hikers need to be self-sufficient and well-prepared. There are some evacuation points along the way, but they are all a half-day's journey off trail. Snow lingers in the Sierra well into the summer, and the hiking can be dangerous if not properly prepared. Because of this, hikers need to bring extra gear to be able to handle the snow and ice. They also need to be able to handle dangerous river fords during melt season. Luckily, it was a low snow year, and I was passing through before most of the snow melted, so the fords wouldn't be a serious concern for me.

Another hiker at the store mentioned the weather was looking good for the Sierra. I had no cell service and didn't want to pay for the Wi-Fi there, so I took that as good enough, sending home my ice axe, winter sleeping bag, crampons, mittens, and extra warmth layers that I had sent to this outpost. I switched out my backpack for one that could carry a heavier load with a long food carry of six days. The only additional items I kept were my microspikes and Under Armour leggings. I would later find out that I forgot to mail home my rain pants and found them hidden in my pack.

After I got my logistics taken care of, the day was kind of a crapshoot. I weighed myself for the first time in a long time, and I was 185. Yikes! I was down 30 pounds from when I started. I was hoping to end the whole year around 185, and I still had 5,000 miles to cover.

As I was charging my phone and portable charger at Kennedy Meadows, they turned off the power when they closed the store. My phone wasn't fully charged, and I did not want to enter the Sierra like that. I got a ride to Grumpy's, a bar a few miles away, in hopes that I would be able to charge my phone fully. As soon as I got there, I realized that my sleeping bag was still drying out at Kennedy Meadows. *Stupid!*

I got a ride back to Kennedy Meadows to retrieve my sleeping bag. Grumpy's was supposed to send a shuttle to pick me up, but never did. I was resigned to enter the Sierra with half of my charging capacity, something that would have been pretty dangerous. Thankfully, Legend, the trail angel that gave me a ride earlier in the day, let me charge my phone and portable charger in his truck overnight. The trail provides!

If it wasn't for that, I would've been in big trouble because I was in too much of a hurry to sit around and wait hours for a charge the next morning after the store opened. It turned out to be a blessing in disguise.

In addition to letting me charge my phone, Legend also cooked a big spaghetti dinner for the hikers camping at the store. I had a fun night talking with the other hikers. I even met a hiker named Snowflake who mentioned he may be doing roughly the same daily miles as me. He was going for the Great Western Loop, a 7,000-mile loop with the PCT and CDT that connects in the north and the south. I was elated at the prospect of having someone that could hike the same miles as me. Almost more impressive than Snowflake going for the Great Western Loop was his friend that joined him on the PCT only a week earlier and was doing 25- and 30-mile days right off the bat. I was overjoyed to have met them and was hoping we would be hiking together for a while.

Into the Eye of the Storm

After a delicious pancake breakfast made by Legend the following morning, I set off with Snowflake and his friend Sam. Leaving Kennedy Meadows, I had my summer hiking gear, microspikes, leggings, a bear canister, six days of food, and a pack that weighed well over 40 pounds. I felt the strain immediately. My shoulders, back, and neck were aching all day, unaccustomed to carrying such a heavy load.

Aside from the physical discomfort, I was glad to have the comfort of companionship. Obviously, it was nice to talk to people during the day, but they could also act as bait...

As we were hiking along, I was between them. A couple of feet ahead, I heard the undeniable and spine-chilling sound that was a rattlesnake. Sam had nearly stepped on its head, and it was not pleased. In that split second, Sam swiftly retreated, screaming in terror, which in turn startled me into silence, paralyzed by fear. Snowflake, right behind me, also let out a scream as the rattlesnake lunged out, not necessarily targeting us, but clearly agitated and ready to strike at the slightest provocation. The snake continued rattling intimidatingly for the next ten minutes, so we cautiously made a wide detour to bypass the irate creature. The Sierra almost claimed its first victim before we even entered its realm.

Before we left Kennedy Meadows, I had spent a lot of time trying to perfectly pack everything to be as comfortable as possible with the heavy load. A few miles into the day, we were stopped by rangers and had to show our permits. Of course, mine was buried at the bottom of my pack, so I had to unload everything and then hurriedly pack it back up because the other two were waiting on me. The pack was not as comfortable the second time around. For the remainder of the day, I had a series of missteps and falls.

From one of the falls, I obtained a decent-sized cut on my leg. It got covered up with dirt quickly, so based on my vast medical knowledge, I figured it would be okay. I had fallen a lot while hiking in the snow, but not much since then, and it hurt considerably more on solid ground.

The day took a turn for the worst when I realized I lost my Oakley sunglasses. I was extremely upset because they were gifted to me by a friend. I knew I would never have a pair of sunglasses that nice again because I would never allow myself to splurge on expensive sunglasses. This was an especially unfortunate place to be without sunglasses, given the merciless sun at high altitude and the snow's blinding reflection. Fortunately, luck was on my side, and I stumbled upon a cheap pair of sunglasses along the trail the next day, providing some relief. The trail provides.

In the afternoon, I became concerned about another hiker I encountered. I noticed a girl walking back and forth, taking ten steps forward, then turning around and repeating the pattern several times. Worried that she might be experiencing heat stroke or altitude sickness, I approached her and asked if she was alright. She didn't speak much, but indicated she'd be okay. I made sure she was going in the right direction and continued on. Soon after, I learned she was just high.

Around 4:30 p.m., I began feeling increasingly sick. My stomach was hurting; waves of nausea washed over me, and hiking became a strenuous task. The weight of my pack compounded my discomfort, and the constant strain on my back and neck intensified the pain.

Unable to bear it any longer, I reluctantly asked Snowflake and Sam to continue ahead while I took a much-needed break. I ended up taking two long breaks and didn't catch up with them by the end of the day. I hoped to catch up to them soon. As I settled into bed that night, fear plagued my mind. Was my physical distress a result of pushing myself too hard with the heavy pack — something that would improve with time — or was it a sign of a more serious underlying issue?

I didn't manage to get up and start moving until around 7 a.m. the next day due to the chilly weather. To add to my concerns, my sleeping pad had been slowly deflating and I had to re-inflate it four times throughout the night. Clearly, it had a hole somewhere. It was deserved, though. I was telling someone a few days prior about how surprised I was with its durability, especially with some of the rough surfaces on which I camped.

As I resumed hiking, I still struggled with the weight of my pack. Despite having my mom mail me six days' worth of food, she had packed more than necessary based on an overly cautious pre-departure list I left for her. Throughout the day, my pace was slow, and I took consistent breaks to alleviate the strain on my back and shoulders. Towards the end of the day, however, I began to feel a glimmer of improvement and picked up my speed. It was a relief to start feeling like myself again.

The official entrance to Sequoia and Kings Canyon National Parks held a special significance for me. These parks sparked my love for hiking just three years prior. Never in my wildest dreams did I imagine that I would be entering these parks as part of this unbelievable adventure. I was incredibly excited for the next few days.

In the park, I crossed paths with a hiker that warned of incoming bad weather. There was a chance of snow for a couple of days and the temperature would get down into the single digits with the wind chill. He said everyone he talked to was getting off trail.

Externally, I said I would think about it. Internally, I knew there was no way I was getting off trail. I had a schedule to maintain. I didn't have time to be cold. Even though I essentially had only my summer gear, I was hoping that my compounded misery on the AT had trained me well enough to get me through the harsh weather.

The following day, I truly felt like I had entered the heart of the Sierra. The "aha" moment was when I reached Bighorn Plateau, a vast flat expanse surrounded by majestic, jagged mountain peaks. I found myself involuntarily smiling at the natural beauty. I had arrived.

It was in this area that I began to encounter marmots. The adorable high-altitude groundhogs are a brave bunch. They can be the most mischievous food thieves and aren't too afraid of people. The bear cannisters required in these two parks are much more beneficial in safeguarding against marmots than they ever are against bears.

When I crossed over Forester Pass, the highest point on the PCT, the snow on the pass had recently melted. Although there was still a substantial amount of snow on the descent, I was grateful for the tracks left by winter and early-season hikers who had blazed the trail before me.

As I was ascending, the high elevation began to take its toll, leaving me breathless during the last half mile of the climb. I was unsure if my quickened fatigue was due more to the elevation or the continuous climbing.

Finally reaching the pass around 5:30 p.m., I immediately began a swift descent to escape the biting cold. Typically, the temperature drops 3–5 degrees with every 1,000 feet of altitude, and standing at approximately 13,200 feet, I yearned to descend a few thousand feet. The journey down into the valley was nothing short of spectacular. As the sun was setting, rays were partially blocked by a mountain ridge, and it looked like light was magically radiating out of the valley.

The sad part about that day was that I wisely but woefully chose to bypass the side trail to summit Mount Whitney, the highest peak in the lower

48 states. I was planning on doing it, but the inclement weather changed my plans. I could have summited late in the day, but if I did, it would have been zero degrees when I was tackling Forester Pass the next day. Since I didn't have adequate cold-weather gear, I wanted to get the highest elevation sections out of the way before it really cooled down. With as cold as it was supposed to be, I had to climb the high elevations in the daytime, and then sleep as low as possible to stay as warm as I could.

When I woke up the next morning, I apologized to the other campers around. I rolled into camp well after everyone was asleep, and while I tried to be as quiet as possible, I couldn't help but make a ruckus as I tiredly stumbled around, tripping and fumbling with my tent stakes. Feeling like a nuisance in the late night was a recurring issue, but fellow thru-hikers never seemed to mind. They knew the daily struggle and never got mad at someone for pushing a long day. Or maybe they were too exhausted to even notice. Either way, it was never a problem, but I always felt guilty about it.

During our morning conversation, I learned they were all getting off trail because of the storm. They planned to exit at the last reasonable evacuation point a few miles ahead — Kearsarge Pass. Beyond Kearsarge Pass on the PCT, the side trails to evacuate were unmaintained and likely not tracked out in the winter. I leapfrogged with some of them up the climb to the final junction where they would depart.

On our way, a girl fell into a stream while trying to rock-hop across — fully submerging both feet in the spine-chilling water. With a glow of fear in her eyes, she told me her feet were numb and asked me what she should do. I could tell she was scared because it was dangerously cold.

It felt strange at first. I had earlier mentioned my ambitious journey to this group, so they viewed me as an expert. However, when she sought my help, I felt like I hadn't yet earned the right to be giving advice like that. Even though I was over 3,000 miles into the journey, I couldn't shake the feeling of being a beginner for some inexplicable reason. I had already hiked a longer distance than any common trail but felt like a neophyte not permitted to give advice.

Whether it was midwestern humility or my insecurities demeaning me, my imposter syndrome was not based in reality. The reality was that I was a veteran by this point. I had forgotten that I was capable of anything and had been working on becoming uncommon among the uncommon since January. Not only had I earned the right to give advice to others, I had the obligation to help this person with my knowledge gained from lived hardship. Having spent months on the Appalachian Trail in winter, I knew exactly what she should do.

I told her to take off her wet socks, let her feet air out for a few minutes even though the air felt alarmingly cold, and put on new, dry socks. She did this, and, within a few minutes, was feeling much better. *I was the shadow in her storm.* I bid farewell to them. While calling me crazy, they wished me luck on my journey.

Shortly after I said goodbye, the snowfall began. I wasn't worried. From what I heard, it was just going to be snow showers. The cold temperatures were the bigger concern. As I was approaching Glen Pass, the snow intensified. I glanced back at the mountain ridge behind me, hoping to see a patch of blue sky taking over, but it was not to be. The snowfall only got worse and worse. Initially, there were tracks to follow on the ascent, but once near the pass, I found myself in a whiteout with the blustering snow and high winds. All the previous tracks had vanished into the snow.

Upon reaching the crest of the pass, my face began to numb as unobstructed gusts of wind ripped through me. Slight worry began to build as I could sense my usual feeling of safety and control deteriorating. The conditions were becoming more perilous by the minute. Although I desperately wanted to put on my microspikes to improve traction for the descent, it was too cold at the pass. Fearing another bout of frostbitten fingers, I had to drop in elevation for slightly warmer temperatures and less wind before I stopped moving or took out my bare hands.

With no added traction, I began the challenging descent in the whiteout. The route was tough to discern as the snow covered the previous tracks and I couldn't see more than ten feet in any direction. I would have to find my own way down the mountain.

In the chaotic snow, I managed to spot a rock protruding from the snowy mountainside nearby, providing a momentary respite. I sat down to put on my microspikes, deeming it safe enough as some feeling had returned to my face. However, as soon as I took three steps — WHOOSH!

I slipped and fell.

When you are sliding down a mountain on snowpack, it seems harmless at first. You start off slowly, with no apparent risk of injury. It even feels a bit exhilarating, like a roller coaster ride. But as you keep sliding, you begin to pick up speed without even realizing it. Before you know it, you're hurtling down the mountain, wondering what will stop you, and how much it's going to hurt.

As I was sliding down the mountain at a worrisome pace, I saw a big pile of rocks below me. Panic mounted, and all I could think was, "Oh, fuck. This is gonna hurt! This is gonna hurt! This is gonna hurt!"

I now knew *what* was going to stop me, but I also knew it was going to come with *a tremendous amount of pain*. Without thinking, a few feet before I hit the rocks, I stuck out my right foot with microspikes on it. My heel jutted into a small rock sticking out of the snowpack, jolting my body to a stop.

While sitting there for a minute and catching my breath, I tried to comprehend what had just happened. Then it hit me. *I was really in the shit.* If I wanted to stay alive, healthy, and keep my goal intact for the year, I had to approach the next few days with utmost seriousness.

Once I regained my composure and descended more in elevation, I started to regain feeling in my fingers. I couldn't help but laugh at how absurd the situation was. It was late in May, and I was in a genuine blizzard in one of the most remote areas in the lower 48 states. My gear was essentially the same as when I hiked through the scorching and arid desert of southern California. Despite being advised to leave the trail due to the treacherous conditions, I stubbornly ignored the recommendation in my commitment to adhere to my schedule. If something were to go wrong, search and rescue wouldn't risk their lives during a storm like this. I was still over 110 miles from my next food resupply. And just moments ago, I had inadvertently glissaded down a mountain at a speed no person should experience when out of control. This was crazy! And I loved it.

As the day progressed, I started feeling reasonably warm again from tirelessly trudging through snow. The fatiguing experience in the heavy powder became oddly enjoyable. I may have started to lose my mind a little as I started talking to marmots, yelling at them to take shelter from the storm like a concerned parent.

Mentally, it was a tough day, trying to reassure myself that everything would be alright when deep down, I wasn't entirely certain. One thing that helped me through was shouting, "My trail name is motherfucker!" at the top of my lungs, knowing that nobody was around to hear me through the hellacious storm. It cheered me up and brought a smile to my face every single time, reminding me of the tramily I met in the desert.

The Rae Lakes area is stunningly beautiful, or so I've been told. I couldn't see anything except the outer edges of a body of water. Everything was hidden by the falling snow. I was planning to stop at a campsite after hiking 14 miles because it was in a valley with the lowest elevation in the area — around 8,500 feet. Therefore, it would be the warmest. But I looked at the map and noticed there was a stream ford coming up soon. I figured, since I was already wet and cold, I might as well do it now rather than early in the morning and start the day on a depressing note.

If you think it'd be cold walking barefoot across a stream of snowmelt water while it's snowing and below freezing, you'd be right. When I initially stepped in, the shock wasn't too severe, but after three seconds, it was literally breathtaking. Thankfully, right on the other side of the stream were some fellow Ohioans, recovering after their crossing, who gave me a towel to dry my feet.

Right before I crossed, one of them motivated me by yelling over the rushing stream, "Don't worry! It's not as cold as it looks... It's colder!"

The first few seconds after stepping out of the water were the worst. While the water was excruciatingly cold, the real pain came when my soaked feet were exposed to the frigid mountain air. The pain subsided once my feet went completely numb. Only insulated by my thin trail runners, my feet gradually regained feeling over the span of an hour as I plodded through multiple inches of freshly fallen snow.

After pushing on for a few more miles after the ford, I ultimately set up camp in a flat area around 9,800 feet. In my tent, I had to confront some harsh realities. My initial logistical plan was no longer feasible. I had brought six days' worth of food, and I was counting on a friend to hike in through Bishop Pass and bring me a couple of days' supply. This would help me reach Mammoth Lakes without having to waste a day hiking out and back in on a long side trail. However, given the fresh snow and treacherous conditions, I couldn't allow my friend to put himself at risk for my sake. Thus, I decided to stretch my six days of food for however long it would take me to reach Mammoth Lakes. Good thing I brought too much.

I realized that the next day would be more of the same. I would hike over a high mountain pass in the late morning, but then by the time I got down, it would be too late in the day to climb over another with the cold temperatures. If only I had kept my mittens to protect my hands, I would be able to push through. I cursed the guy at Kennedy Meadows who told me the weather looked promising.

After removing my socks in my tent, I realized my feet were in rough shape. They were soaking wet all day, and very much looked like it. A lot of skin was peeling off, and I began to worry about the possibility of trench foot. Nevertheless, I convinced myself they would be fine. I dealt with the same thing every day on the AT. However, it didn't help that I tossed my Vermont Bag Balm while in the desert section because the heat caused it to leak everywhere. That stuff was magical.

Attempting to fall asleep that night proved to be an insufferable experience. The temperature plummeted to the single digits, and my low-quality 20-degree sleeping bag, which felt more like a 40-degree sleeping bag, offered little comfort. I wore every layer I had, yet I still felt cold. I spent the entire night shivering, to the point where my back ached the next day from the constant tensing up of my muscles.

Moreover, my sleeping pad deflated faster than ever, leaving me lying on the cold, snowy surface every 45 minutes, forcing me to re-inflate the pad repeatedly. Though I set up my tent as taut as possible, the heavy snowfall accumulated on the edges, causing the tent to sag and inevitably touch me. I tried my best to brush off the snow, but it would quickly freeze my hands, and within minutes, it would accumulate once again. I slept for a total of 30 minutes. It felt like the night would never end. All I wanted was for the sun to come out and the snow to stop. But it didn't. And it wouldn't.

It was snowing when I got to camp around 4 p.m. It snowed as I laid awake all night. And it was snowing when I left camp in the morning. I had to wait until 8 a.m. to get up because it felt scarily cold. I then didn't leave camp for over two hours because of the arctic chill. I would pack up for a few minutes, and then would have to take a break and shove my hands in my crotch before the pain dulled enough to where I could use them. I was again at the point where my hands hurt so bad that I was nauseous.

Once I finally left, I started to get a feeling that I especially didn't want to deal with at the time. I had to go to the bathroom. With as cold as I felt, I was actually scared that it would be dangerous. But I didn't have much of a choice, so I took care of business as quickly as possible, having to wipe with a hand so numb that it felt like it was injected with Novocain.

With the recent snowfall (8–18+ inches depending on the area and elevation), there was no inkling of where the trail was. Thankfully, the

Ohioans I met yesterday left before me, so I followed their footsteps. They diverted from the trail substantially at times, but at least it was something to follow rather than wandering across the massive white landscape.

Progress was excruciatingly slow as I trudged through 12 inches of snow with fresh snow falling intensely. Pinchot Pass, still a demanding route under normal circumstances, became even more difficult with the added layer of snow and cold. But upon reaching the top, it was a similar feeling to Glen Pass. I basked in the madness surrounding me and laughed at the preposterous whiteout conditions that enveloped me in some of the most remote mountains in the lower 48.

On the descent, I caught up to the Ohioans, and another young hiker named Tas. They asked if I'd seen a Frenchman. I hadn't, but they had. On the way up Pinchot Pass, a Frenchman approached them from an area off trail. His English wasn't great, but they deduced that his phone was dead and he had no maps. He asked them where the PCT was, and they explained that they were going over Pinchot Pass and he could join them. He nodded and asked where it was. They pointed to it. He then proceeded to walk 30 degrees left of where they pointed, disappearing into oblivion. We couldn't do much more than hope he was okay.

I hiked a few more miles with Tas and we made camp before the ascent to Mather Pass. We were at 10,026 feet, but this was the lowest altitude around, and that was the goal since it was too late in the day to go up and over Mather Pass. Just beyond our campsite, the South Fork Kings River was flowing fast and high since it was later in the day. Rivers tend to grow stronger as the day goes on because more snowmelt enters the stream with the higher daytime temperatures. Knowing this, we scouted a route of rocks and logs to cross the river with dry feet the next morning, when the river was at its lowest. Some of the rocks we needed to cross were under a couple of inches of water, but we hoped they would be exposed in the morning, allowing us to keep our feet dry.

Upon returning to the campsite, we faced a moral dilemma. Park regulations prohibited fires above 10,000 feet, a rule we were well aware of. But after a few minutes of talking it out, we convinced ourselves that it was okay since it was in the middle of a multi-day blizzard and was almost a necessity for safety, given the conditions. Standing 26 feet above the no-fire zone, we sparked up a fire with as much appreciation as the early Neanderthals. The source of warmth in this frozen wilderness raised our spirits insurmountably, even if it didn't raise our core body temperature.

In addition to feeling a faint touch of warmth, the fire was also made in a futile attempt to dry out some of our gear. After we set up our tents and were collecting more wood, the Ohioans showed up. They, too, stopped to set up camp. Later, as we sat around the fire, two more hikers rolled in, then another, and then a couple more. Every time another person rolled up, we exclaimed, "Hell yeah! Another crazy motherfucker!" Or, "Hell yeah! Another dumbass that was too stubborn to get off trail!" Both statements were true.

We ended up having ten people huddled around the campfire, holding socks near it while the snow continued to fall. It was such an outlandish scene, and one of my favorite memories of the year. As there was a lull in the conversation, we sat there in silence for a short time before someone looked around and said, "What a fuckin hobby."

We all burst into laughter, acknowledging the truth of it. This was ridiculous. I didn't know why we loved it, or why we were doing it, but we did, and we were.

After another night in the single digits and less than an hour of sleep, the morning brought a welcome change as the temperature quickly began to rise. The snow had finally stopped, and it was 25 degrees. I felt WARM as I was the first person to pack up and continue onward.

When I got to the river, I was pleased to see that the necessary rocks for a dry crossing were now jutting out of the water by an inch. However, now that it came down to it, the jump seemed riskier. The rock was four feet below from where I would be jumping off, and five feet away. A reasonable leap, but I couldn't help but think of its potential slipperiness. It would be an extremely unenjoyable — and more so, dangerous — incident if I were to slip and fall violently into the river.

After a few minutes of searching for an alternative crossing spot with no luck, I built up the courage, said, "Fuck it," and jumped.

I stuck the landing, and with a few more risky hops, I stood triumphant on the other side, still dry. Looking back, I saw the others behind me taking off their shoes and socks, preparing to ford the river because they didn't want to take that same risk. I felt sorry for them.

Following nearly two days of constant snow, more than 18 inches of fresh powder blanketed the area south of Mather Pass. All tracks from previous hikers were gone, so I was trail blazing for those behind me. The basin on the south side of Mather Pass was stunning, adorned in a pristine coat of fresh snow. Despite knowing that others were a few miles behind, it felt like I had it all to myself since there was no trail and no tracks to follow.

It felt truly wild.

The ascent to the pass was also wild in the craziest sense of the word. From a distance, a mountain pass normally looks intimidating. *How am I going to get up and over that?*

With Mather Pass being covered in fresh snow, it was even more daunting on the approach. With no tracks to follow, I tried my best to straight-line the ascent to the pass, and it actually wasn't as challenging as I anticipated. It felt adventurous making my own route, yet completely safe.

The real adventure began at the pass itself. First, I took in a view so stunning that it made me stop in my tracks. Only a handful of other humans would get to see it before it drastically changed from the melting snow. The sight was truly epic — witnessing all the surrounding mountains covered in a fresh blanket of white with a wide-open snowy basin stretching out below me. Everything appeared immaculate. But I quickly learned that forging my own route on the descent would be twice as difficult as going up.

The initial stretch was a steep snowfield that had me treading cautiously. If I had one misstep, I would go flying down the mountain faster than a newly licensed teenage boy on The Autobahn. Each step required careful placement, sinking my foot as deep as possible into the fresh powder. Sometimes my foot sank four inches, other times a foot, and occasionally not at all. I had to get violent with my trekking poles, driving them into the snow as deeply as I could. I placed as much of my body weight on them as possible to reduce stress on my feet and minimize the risk of slipping.

Although there were a few brief slips and heart-stopping moments, nothing catastrophic happened. However, the strain on my right arm grew, as I relied heavily on my trekking pole on the higher side to maintain stability. Every step became a calculation of confidence along with the likelihood of slipping, but every step was also a full-body workout. It was utterly exhausting. It felt like a half day's journey, even though it was only 75 steps. After that first snowfield, subsequent challenges proved slightly less dangerous. It was still tough to find a safe route, but the snowfields were slightly less steep and hazardous the rest of the way down.

Finally reaching the basin on the north side, I had the exhilarating experience of walking on dry ground for the first time in days. It was hard to believe that just on the other side of the pass, everything remained buried under 18 inches of snow. It seemed the worst of the storm had zeroed in on my exact location — just my luck.

The day presented a beautiful dichotomy. The morning was an amazing macro-environment with the vast landscape on the south side of the pass. In the afternoon, I enjoyed the enchanting micro-environment of a gorgeous valley. Water was flowing everywhere, and lush green covered everything. The crystal-clear water carried a hint of emerald, complimenting the surrounding verdant scenery. It was delightful having visibility for the first time in a few days after walking through a snowstorm.

It was warm in the middle of the day, so I took an hour-long break to dry out my still-wet sleeping bag and tent. I reflected on how lucky I was to stay non-hypothermic over the last couple of days. Sleeping with a wet, summer sleeping bag, in single digit temperatures in a wet tent, and with a deflated sleeping pad that usually had me on the cold ground, put me at a high risk. It was quite a deadly combination given the circumstances, but there was no other way. The only way was thru.

I camped several miles before Muir Pass, around 9,300 feet, fearing that if I went much farther, everything would be covered in snow. By the end of the day, I started to calculate if my phone battery would last all the way to Mammoth. It lost 40% in a single day with me hardly even using it. The cold drained the battery rapidly. I hadn't been listening to music in the Sierra because I knew it would be a long stretch. Even with that, it was going to be close due to the slower progress in the snow. My phone battery wasn't life or death, though. The Sierra was the only area all year where I brought paper maps as a backup. This area carried the highest potential of shit hitting the fan — and it sure did.

The next morning greeted me with a familiar chill, which didn't necessarily surprise me. I camped near water, and water holds pockets of cold air. But there was no escaping the water in this area. It was everywhere.

With a later start, I crested Muir Pass around 10 a.m. The ascent wasn't overly difficult, although the last 1.5 miles involved emphatically marching through deep snow. It was slow and tiring progress but lacked the danger of the previous days.

I took a quick peek inside the emergency hut at Muir Pass and was glad I didn't camp in there. The musty odor permeating the space was less than inviting. The descent from Muir Pass was gradual and manageable, but a solid snowfield extended for five miles. My pace was slow and my feet were soaked, but the worst part of it was that I was getting fried by the sun. The reflection off of the snow amplified the UV rays. Even with the pair of sunglasses I found, my eyes felt like they were burning. I couldn't help but wonder how much damage I did to my eyes on the AT without sunglasses.

On the descent, I got frisky with another stream crossing. I didn't think there was even supposed to be a stream under normal conditions, but there was so much snow melt going on that it was flowing fast and wide. Determined to not completely submerge my feet, I looked for a dry spot to cross. The only thing I could find was fairly precarious. There was a skinny rock five feet into the stream, only a couple of inches wide, with a few small rocks after it to complete the crossing. I figured, since I got lucky with jumping the day before, I might as well try it again.

After hyping myself up, I took the leap. I landed with the skinny rock jutting into the arch of my foot while I wobbled to keep my balance. With intense concentration, I was able to keep from falling and made it across without getting wet. Shortly after, I came upon an actual stream that fed Evolution Lake. This one had a perfect walkway of stepping stones so hikers could stay dry. *This was more like it.*

Later in the day, I barefoot forded Evolution Creek. Normally, it is said to be one of the toughest fords in the Sierra, but thankfully, the water only went up to my mid-calf. That was the benefit of being 6'2" tall and going through early, before most of the snow melted.

Since I left the AT, my legs had been consistently coated in sand and dirt. It was so noticeable that another hiker once asked me if I rubbed dirt on my legs because they were so dark. While I didn't smother my legs with grime on purpose, having my legs coated in layers of dirt actually provided a certain level of protection. Near Evolution Creek, I slipped going down a steep area and my knee scraped a rock. It definitely should've been bleeding, but it just took off a few layers of dirt. *It felt good to be dirty.*

The worst part of the day was an injury I inflicted upon myself. Earlier that day, I had my first scare with a tick. I wasn't sure if that's what it actually was because I had never dealt with one, and I didn't know if they were in the area. Nevertheless, it scared me, so I was extra cautious about any sensation I felt on my legs. When I later felt something on my leg, I instinctively went to brush it off with my hand while still holding my trekking pole. The bottom of the pole jammed into a rock on the side of the trail, and the other side jammed into my babymaker. I collapsed in pain and skinned up my wrist. I laid there in agony for a bit, reflecting on how idiotic the last 30 seconds were.

Realizing that both my food supply and phone battery were running low, I knew I had to push myself the following day if I wanted to reach town comfortably. My food was getting thin since I had to make six days of food last nine days. I finally tackled two passes in a day, which I had planned to do every day in this stretch to keep my pace, but with the extremely difficult weather and my summer gear, that became an impossibility.

I went over Selden Pass early in the morning, and it was child's play. The descent started out easy, but soon increased in difficulty when the trail became covered in a thin sheet of ice. It added a touch of danger, but more than anything, it slowed me down. Around midday, I decided I had enough battery to listen to some music for the first time in four days, and I began to float down the trail like a sweet melody.

In the evening, I crossed Silver Pass, which lacked any threat of a challenge after the previous days. As I sat down to take in an epic view with the sun dropping on the horizon, I ate my first calories all day — a few bars and nuts. After I ate, I changed into my Under Armour leggings, knowing the temperature would drop along with the sun. Less than two minutes after I was buck-naked, a hiker rolled up to the pass and almost got a free show. I was in one of the most remote areas in the entire U.S. and felt completely alone, yet someone nearly walked up on me while I was changing.

The near full moon (not a reference to me changing) cast a majestic glow on the mountains, creating a surreal nighttime atmosphere. Filled with vigor, the miles unnoticeably passed by until I hit Lake Virginia. There, I encountered a challenging section where I had to navigate a narrow strip of land near the lake, while trying to avoid becoming a soggy mess.

There were a few rocks above water, but not enough to get across safely. With as much luck as I had recently, I went for it again. But this time, it didn't work out as planned. I made a long jump onto a skinny rock, but wavered when I landed. Teetering like a man with a weak core at his first yoga session, I lost my balance and dipped my left foot in the water. Feeling like I might tip over if my momentum continued, I dropped both trekking poles while trying to regain my balance, so I didn't completely fall in.

After regaining my balance, I was happy to learn that my trekking poles floated, and they were still within reach. I knew my luck with risky river crossings had to end sometime. I just wished it wasn't at night. With one soaked foot and feeling the midnight chill, I kept moving.

My morale waned after this mishap, and the trail became harder to navigate. Frequent snow patches obscured the trail, forcing me to clamber over them and then struggle to find the trail afterward. Around 1 a.m., feeling exhausted, I decided to set up camp at the first flat and snow-free spot I stumbled upon. It was yet another cold night, and to add to my woes, my sleeping pad had completely deflated within ten minutes of inflating it. For as much time as I had spent in my tent the last few days with the cold and the storm, I hadn't gotten much sleep.

I began hiking around 8:15 the next morning, but I was glad I hiked late because it was cold again. It was a quick morning to get to the side trail into Mammoth Lakes, CA. It was a few extra miles on the side trail and then a road walk before I got a ride into town.

The driver and I discussed hiking from the moment he picked me up to the moment he dropped me off. I thanked him while standing outside the truck and was about to shut the door, but then asked, "What is your name by the way?" which I normally didn't ask and wasn't sure why I did.

He responded with, "Johnny Muir." My hand on the door refused to move, and I stood there in shock. He smiled and said they weren't related, but still, what a name to have in that area.

Arriving in town, I had a mere 20% battery left on my phone and only half a bag of peanuts for sustenance. I collected a resupply package containing food and some replacement gear before getting a motel room. I had an old sleeping pad sent to me. Unfortunately, there was some miscommunication and the wrong one was sent. This one was older and uncomfortable. The optimistic side of me thought it would at least force me to sleep less and push bigger miles if I wasn't going to sleep well anyway. I also acquired a replacement shirt since mine had sported a large hole for the last 250 miles. The exposed area of my shoulder, constantly sunburned and in pain, would finally have shelter again. Additionally, I obtained two fresh pairs of socks, which I usually needed to replace every three weeks, but my current pairs had been wrecked after only nine days in the Sierra.

I was extremely excited to get into Mammoth. The High Sierra wiped me out. I was exhausted and ready for some hardcore rest. After a short day in town, I ended up taking a rest day the following day. I was hoping to go through the PCT with no rest days, but I was beat up, and my feet were in bad shape after that last stretch. With the rest day and the recent low mileage days, I was falling behind schedule. I knew I had to pick up the pace to stay on track for my goal.

Foot Fungus

I departed Mammoth Lakes still tired, my perpetual state of being, but I felt much better than I had upon entering. Taking advantage of the luxury of a real bed, I allowed myself to sleep in, knowing that the coming days would entail resting on nothing more than a thin layer of foam.

Once back on the trail, everything seemed to fall back into the familiar rhythm. I encountered numerous hikers embarking on weekend or multi-day trips, and it always brought a smile to my face when they asked me how far I was going, only for me to reply, "Canada." Little did they know that my journey for the year extended far beyond that. Canada was merely a fraction of the ultimate goal.

After only a few hours, I noticed a sunburn developing on my arms from wearing a short-sleeve shirt. It was nice to have a new shirt, but it did leave me vulnerable. With more exposed skin, I also began to encounter swarms of mosquitoes, constantly swatting them away in annoyance. I hoped it was just temporary and wouldn't linger.

As I packed my things the following morning, I discovered a critter had feasted on my toilet paper. After some traumatic flashbacks to mice on the AT, I climbed over Donahue Pass and entered Yosemite National Park. Progress was slow with postholing and no discernible trail because of the four feet of snow, but my excitement for Yosemite carried me forward.

I hadn't covered much ground by midday, but I rejoiced when I came upon a long, snow-free valley, where I encountered hordes of people embarking on backpacking trips from the accessible entry point of Tuolumne Meadows. I was feeling worn-out from snow-hiking all morning and must've looked like I needed a morale boost, because one of them kindly gave me a beer. He didn't even ask if I wanted one. He simply placed it in my hand before I finished saying hello. Even for an IPA, it went down smoothly and revived my spirits.

After receiving the beer, I endured a steady rain shower. Although it wasn't a torrential downpour, it didn't improve the situation either. The valley I was trekking through was already waterlogged from the abundant snow melting at higher elevations. The trail and surrounding areas were submerged under several inches of water. My feet were already soaked, and the rain was just adding to the problem. To add to the mix, a thunderstorm rolled in, which can be one of the scariest challenges hikers have to face. Fortunately, I was in the valley and didn't really care, as the lightning was striking the surrounding high mountains. Instead of being afraid, I found myself listening to Lil Wayne and shouting along at the top of my lungs as thunder boomed overhead and reverberated off the walls of granite.

Even after finishing a disappointing 29-mile day on flat terrain in the valley, the following day wasn't any better. Lingering snow was a constant hindrance. It hid the trail, and I would often find myself on the side of a mountain, far off trail, and have to backtrack. I wasted a lot of time going nowhere. It was also warm, resulting in constant postholing, further slowing my pace. When not battling snow, I was playing hopscotch attempting to avoid water, which seemed to be omnipresent on and around the trail. Frequently, I had to take extensive detours to bypass massive puddles and small ponds that inundated the path. This was Yosemite for me. Despite my excitement, and unlike most people, I hated my time in the park.

Amidst the persistent snow, I encountered a multitude of stream crossings, adding to the challenges of the day. There were seven serious stream crossings, but I managed to avoid fording all but two. Those two were bitingly cold from the snowmelt, but regardless, if I forded them or not, they slowed me down. I spent valuable time trying to find any way to cross without having to get my feet wet. Oftentimes, there were logs that lay across the stream, some a bit sketchy, but they saved me from getting wet.

The two streams I did ford took a lot of time. I would stop, take my shoes and socks off, wade across the frigid stream, find a good spot on land to dry my feet, and sit there for a few minutes before I felt my feet were sufficiently dry to put on my shoes and socks. If I didn't care about having wet feet, this wouldn't have been a problem, as I would've marched through with my shoes on. But with the shape my feet were in, I was concerned.

The worst crossing was in the evening at Piute Creek. I didn't want to ford it. It was flowing strong and deep, but mostly I just hated fording near the end of the day because I was so close to being done. I found a log to cross one part of the river, and then another, and another, and another. It turned out, there were numerous channels and islands in the area. I ended up wasting over 30 minutes crossing logs onto different pieces of land before I got to where the trail actually was. *I wished I'd simply forded the river.*

To make matters worse: it was a mosquito hell. Along with rain, the tiny bloodsuckers were something that peaked my irritability level. Now, any little thing infuriated me. I wasn't expecting mosquitoes to be a problem this early on, but I'd killed hundreds in the last couple of days.

My disdain for my time in Yosemite turned into full-on hatred the following day. I had to ford six streams, always taking the time to look for a dry crossing, usually to no avail. One of the fords turned into a disastrous series of missteps. The river was wide, and by the time I made it across, my feet were numbed by the bone-chilling water. You know the ford isn't going well when halfway across, you are lifting your leg to your chin, seeking just a brief second of warm air outside of the numbing water.

Walking through this river of chilling snowmelt was the inverse of fording the river when the air was colder and the pain didn't start until I got out. Although I successfully made it to the other side, I had to climb a steep and slippery rock face to get onto dry ground. As I attempted to hoist myself up, I accidentally dropped a trekking pole. I defeatedly watched it float away for a second with the instant reaction of, *Ah, fuck it, I'll get another one.* But then reality struck me: *I need that to set up my tent!*

As I started wading through the water to retrieve to it, I realized I wouldn't catch it with how fast the current was pulling it downstream. I got on land and began running barefoot on what would probably have been a painful surface of gravel and rocks, but my feet were still numb from the cold water, so I didn't feel a thing. As I jumped back into the water to try to grab it, it slid into a fast channel of water and slingshotted down the river. I immediately got out of the water, took off my pack, put on my shoes and socks, and sprinted 200 yards downstream before jumping into the water again to successfully retrieve it.

This whole ordeal all happened while getting swarmed by a legion of mosquitoes. There was a lot of yelling and cursing. It was not fun, and I was soaked up to my belly button. Being wet only enhanced the aggression of the mosquitoes, which were already unbearable. I could not stop for more than three seconds without being covered in the tiny blood-sucking monsters. The task of putting on my shoes and socks when I got out of the water, as I noticed my feet were bleeding from running barefoot, became impossible. It was difficult to get my hands free for a single second to put anything on. They were constantly in use swiping over my arms and legs as hundreds of the tiny fiends flocked to me at once.

Near the end of the day, I approached another formidable river and realized I would have to ford it. I yelled angrily for a few minutes while prepping to do so. When I got to the other side, there were people camping close by, so they just casually heard me losing my mind. We waved at each other, but I continued on, not wanting to discuss what just happened.

I arrived at another stream ten minutes later, with no dry crossing available. At that point, I felt defeated. I didn't get mad. No emotion even stirred in me. I just sorrowfully took off my shoes and socks, and waded across the river without uttering a single word.

The next day, I learned that hungry dogs do not, in fact, run faster. Since I had been covering fewer miles than expected the last few days because of the snow, river fords, and mosquitoes, I was nearly out of food. When I woke up, I had a single 180-calorie tuna packet to fuel me for the next 18 miles before I stepped foot on the road at Sonora Pass. Ten calories per mile was not an ideal ratio, especially after rationing food the previous day and going to bed hungry.

Several miles into the day, I passed the 1,000-mile marker on the PCT while brushing my teeth. Feeling depleted and moving slowly, it didn't feel as nearly as important as the 1,000 mile-marker on the AT. The conditions made the PCT hard for the last week or so, but overall, 1,000 miles on the AT was substantially more difficult.

The suffering made it feel more gratifying.

A few miles after the anticlimactic achievement, I ran into two thru-hikers from South Dakota that gifted me some snacks. One of them was an ex-NFL player, and I was grateful the big guy was kind enough to part ways with some of his food. It was all I needed to push me the rest of the way.

The trail provides!

Aside from that act of kindness, the day did not go smoothly. There was a significant amount of snow near Sonora Pass, making my footing precarious, and for most of the day, the trail was non-navigable. There was a lot of "make your own adventure," trying to find some way down to Sonora Pass without perilously sliding down the mountain. I'd frequently do a big loop up, down, or around a huge pack of snow to avoid the treacherous steps on the steep surface. Other times, I'd try to follow the mostly melted footsteps of somebody that traversed the area a few days before. When I did that, I usually wished I hadn't. The snow was soft and deep, making each step a struggle, and the constant fear of slipping and tumbling hundreds of feet down a precipice added to the exhaustion.

Even though it was a tough day, I was happy to go over the last 11,000-foot mountain of the PCT. I relished the prospect of descending to lower elevations, hoping that the snow would become less of an obstacle. After completing the 18-mile stretch to the resupply point, I decided to call it a day and spent the night at a hostel. My feet had been perpetually saturated over the past few days, and the odor emanating from my socks, due to the combination of dirty snowmelt and river water, was unbearable. A chance to clean up sounded like a welcome respite. The water in Yosemite was not like that in Sequoia and Kings Canyon. There was a lot of stagnant water from the overwhelming snowmelt, and it smelled rather unpleasant.

When I got to the hostel, I bought my resupply, along with a 12-pack of Dr. Pepper for the day. I then started laundry for the first time in 1,000 miles and 37 days. With only one pair of shorts while hiking in the summer, I normally lacked an alternative garment for my lower-half to wear during laundry. But here, another thru hiker at the hostel graciously let me borrow his rain pants to wear while I tended to my laundry.

As I was hanging out with two other thru-hikers, one more showed up — it was the crazy Frenchman from the Sierra! As soon as I heard his accent, I had to confirm it was him, and it was. I heard all about his misadventure of being lost in the snowstorm in the Sierra without a phone or maps. I missed a lot of the details of the story because of the language barrier, which was the reason he got lost in the first place. When he was asking the other two thru-hikers I met in the Sierra about directions, he couldn't understand what they were saying, so he just took off. He was a jovial and interesting character, and I was just relieved he was okay.

The next morning, I shipped home my bear canister, consumed a hearty breakfast, and sucked down a few delightful Dr. Peppers before getting a ride back to the trail around 11 a.m., joined by the Frenchman.

When we got to the trailhead, I started heading down the trail. The Frenchman said goodbye and took off in a totally different direction, leaving me bewildered. Several miles later, while I stood atop a ridge, I glanced down and spotted him below! He was climbing an extremely steep side of the mountain, rather than taking the gently graded PCT, and all I could do was laugh. I couldn't resist asking him what he was doing, to which he replied, "I wanted to go my own way." This man was full of surprises.

I enjoyed dry feet, for all of two hours, when I was hiking on a ridge void of snow. As I rounded the other side of the mountain and descended into a valley, snow blanketed the landscape. The trail disappeared under the snowy terrain, forcing me to carefully glide downhill and find the trail's intended location at a lower elevation, where the snow had melted more. It was slow going with frequent postholing and constant wet feet.

Just as I neared the bottom, within the last 200 yards, both feet plunged through the snow and into a frigid stream. My feet went from wet to soaked, and I went from irritated to full-on pissed off. It could have been worse, though. When I saw the Frenchman again, he had fallen and one of his entire legs was bleeding, but he just laughed about it and kept limping on.

Later in the day, I veered off trail for a while before I realized it. As I was bushwhacking my way to reconnect farther up the trail, I stumbled upon a naked guy squatting near a fire. *He probably fell in a creek and needed to dry his clothes. That's reasonable. A normal person would do that.*

His back was to me, so I obnoxiously made as much noise as possible — banging my trekking poles on rocks, tripping loudly, grunting — so he would know I was there and wouldn't think I was sneaking up on him. He never moved a muscle to even look what was behind him.

That's not normal.

I didn't say anything; I expected him to apologize first, or at least say something in regards as to why he was naked, but he didn't utter a word. As undeterred as he was unapologetic, I strolled on by — 20 feet away from a naked, feral man, so disinterested in anything else that he never spoke a word, let alone even look away from the fire. I was glad to escape that weirdo and get back to my usual kind of hikertrash weirdos.

As I settled into bed that night, the pungent smell radiating from my feet and socks was more putrid than usual. Originally, I thought it was just the water in Yosemite that made them smell bad, but this was after washing them and only one day of hiking. The next morning, I regretfully realized what was happening. The small areas underneath my toes were excruciatingly painful, tender, and had taken on a reddish-purple hue. At first, I thought my feet had little cuts underneath the toes from rocks in my shoes, or from rough, dried-out socks. But after getting one bar of cell service, I learned that it was likely athlete's foot or some other foot fungus.

This condition was unlike any I had experienced before. Previous bouts of athlete's foot had been itchy and uncomfortable, but this was exponentially worse. It felt like shards of glass were stabbing into the area underneath my toes with every step I took. The agony was relentless, making every footfall a visceral exercise of the outer reaches of my pain tolerance as a piercing pain shot into all of my toes.

It was one of the hardest days of hiking all year. All I could think about was how bad it hurt, but that was all I was trying not to think about.

Every time my foot hit the ground, it was an instant reminder that there was no avoiding this pain. Although small in area, it was immense in agony.

Pushing through the pain, I hiked until midnight and resumed my journey at 5 a.m. the following day, *needing* to reach the nearest town and find relief for my feet. Occasionally, I had to get down on my hands and knees, just to give my feet a short break. They still hurt while crawling on my hands and knees, but walking was physically unbearable at times. I knew that if I didn't get this problem taken care of soon, my mileage would suffer, and I would fall behind pace for the year.

Luckily, South Lake Tahoe, CA was one of the largest towns along any of the Triple Crown trails. It had a pharmacy where I procured Lotramin Ultra and peroxide to soak my feet in. If it was like 90% of the towns I went through during the year, there wouldn't have been a store with athlete's foot cream. So, on the bright side, at least the timing of my foot fungus was lucky. It just didn't feel lucky in the moment. I felt nothing but pain.

I also seized the opportunity to utilize the post office, acquiring a smaller and lighter backpack since I was through the Sierra with longer food carries, a new pair of shorts since the ones I had been wearing had a large hole in the undercarriage area, a replacement inflatable sleeping pad, and a much-needed set of new socks. In a few days, I would acquire new shoes as well, a welcomed prospect. I hoped that these changes would expedite the healing process of my feet. Upon removing my shoes at the motel, I made the disheartening discovery that fungus had taken hold inside my shoes, specifically on the bottom of the shoe insert. Though I aired them out during my stay, the fungus remained.

Wanting to let my feet air out as long as possible, I slept in and left the hotel as late as I could. After getting back on trail around noon, I had a better day. My feet were feeling markedly better, and the pain with each step diminished. It was a rather nice feeling.

The next morning, I put on Deet insect repellant for the first time to fend off the relentless mosquitoes buzzing around camp. Fortunately, they were blissfully absent for the rest of the day. Most of the day was spent hiking on ridges with strong winds, far away from water sources — an effective recipe to avoid mosquitoes. Still adjusting to my new pack, I had initially packed it poorly, resulting in tightness and discomfort in my back. But after rearranging the contents ten miles into the day, I was pleasantly surprised by the comfort and freedom afforded by the smaller pack.

Although my feet felt relatively good early on, a burning sensation surfaced on the bottom and side of my right foot, soon followed by the left. The pain intensified throughout the day as the fungus continued to spread. My fear of it enveloping my entire foot was now becoming a painful reality.

I went to bed satisfied with a 29-mile day. I knew, however, that tomorrow was probably going to be much more challenging with my continually increasing foot pain. My anticipation was justified when I woke up to searing pain in my feet while just lying in my sleeping bag. Previously, the sharp pain only occurred upon contact, such as taking a step, but now, the burning torment persisted even in moments of rest.

Since my feet were hurting from simply touching air, the pain was significantly worse while walking. Gritting my teeth with each agonizing step, I made my way up to Donner Pass until I reached a 30-foot wall of snow with a steep slope and a vertical drop-off on the low side. Not wanting to die, I opted to veer left, do extra climbing, and summit Mount Lincoln nearby to avoid the worst of the snow. There were few things I hated more than extra climbing, but falling to my death would definitely be one of them.

After the summit, I walked down on service roads from the ski lift. Through intense, ever-present pain, I made it nine miles to Donner Ski Ranch and enjoyed a pizza and a free beer they gave to all PCT hikers. I even managed to get a couple more beers from hikers that didn't want theirs. They were 40-ounce Steel Reserves, so they added up quickly. But that was good — anything to numb the pain.

I succumbed to my foot pain and got a bunk in the hostel for the night. With as bad as my feet were hurting, I wouldn't have covered much ground the rest of the day. Rather than hiking slowly in dreadful pain, I really just needed them to heal because the pain was too poignant to be able to cover any decent mileage. I aired them out all day, and applied Lotramin Ultra every 30 minutes, hoping and praying that the pain would subside.

Picking Up a Hammer

I left the hostel at 4 a.m. to get back on the trail, low on food because I couldn't hitchhike into a town nearby. There was a road closure making the nearest store 90 minutes in the opposite direction. Hoping that the massive pizza I had devoured the previous day, along with my dwindling food supplies, would sustain me, I pressed on.

To my relief, I immediately noticed my feet felt better than the day before. They still hurt, but every step wasn't unbearable like it had been. With manageable pain, I accomplished a 40-mile day and set myself up to get a package of goodies when the post office opened the next morning.

When the morning came, it greeted me with a slight chill, but it didn't hinder my elevated spirits — uplifted at the prospect of getting new non-fungal shoes, along with my repaired shirt that had fallen victim to a tree's merciless tear. My arms had already gone through the sunburnt phase and were now just tan, but I was happy to get the protection of sleeves again. I felt like a kid on the first day of school with my new outfit. Additionally, my craving for Fudge Rounds was satiated after over a month of longing. I hadn't come across any since venturing west of the Mississippi.

My feet continued to improve throughout the day, and the miles passed by significantly faster than they seemed to a few days prior. Although they weren't healed, the progress was remarkable. I received an unexpected surge of energy when I encountered a few day hikers and stopped to chat over a Modelo beer. Finally, someone had given me a regular beer instead of an IPA! I always appreciated the hiking community's generosity when it came to sharing beverages, though I couldn't fathom why nearly everyone seemed to prefer IPAs that tasted like acidic backwash.

The weather exhibited some peculiar behavior, with foreboding clouds looming overhead. The winds persisted, prompting me to don my coat for most of the day. I alternated between feeling chilly and then being warm and sweaty, mostly depending on the strength of the wind in a given area. Towards the end of the day, I was surprised by snow flurries in June. As I struggled to find a suitable campsite, the snowfall intensified. The flakes were enormous, and it took only a few of them to dampen my belongings.

When I stepped outside the next morning, I discovered a solid slab of ice, measuring three by twelve inches, on top of my tent. The snow had melted and then frozen solid overnight. I allowed my tent to dry for a while before starting my day. Nearly the entire day involved hiking through a vast burn area, requiring me to maneuver past numerous massive, fallen trees. Instead of taking a longer detour around them, I often resorted to climbing over the fallen giants. I would ascend, and then leap eight feet down, hoping my knees wouldn't buckle under the strain. Some jumps were questionable, because of the immense size of the trees and the steepness of the terrain they occupied, but I lived to tell the tale.

Amidst the fallen jungle, I encountered two men engaged in trail maintenance. We all resembled coal miners, our bodies covered in ash. I expressed my gratitude to them, though in my mind, I couldn't help but feel sorry for them and their daunting task. I couldn't fathom how two individuals could possibly clear all the fallen trees that obstructed the trail in this area. The sheer number was overwhelming.

The next morning was a short 1,000 feet up, and then 4,000 feet down into Belden. As I was descending, I saw my first bear of the year. It was a black bear and stood 20 feet below me on a switchback. We locked eyes for three seconds, and after it analyzed my imposing figure, it took off down the mountain. I couldn't understand how it ran down the slope instead of doing somersaults because the pitch was awfully steep. Yet, it barreled down the mountain at a pace that made me jealous.

It was exciting seeing my first bear of the year, and I wanted to see as many as possible, just all before I entered grizzly country. Then, I didn't really want to see any. Black bears are basically big puppy dogs. Grizzly bears are more like irritable killing machines.

When I arrived at the road, I hitched a ride to Caribou Crossings to retrieve my food package. I didn't like sending food packages because it was another variable that I couldn't control. However, at some places, there either wasn't a food selection, or it was so small, it wouldn't be reasonable to do a resupply. Caribou Crossings fell into the latter category, prompting me to send a food package.

While there, relishing a good burger and a world-famous milkshake, a few other thru-hikers walked in. They attempted to persuade me to spend the night and enjoy the company. It was a tempting proposition, and as we conversed, I contemplated whether to continue hiking or stay and socialize.

While I was deliberating in my head, "Kickstart My Heart" came on the radio, and my choice was made for me. That song was my go-to anthem anytime I needed to get amped up, motivate myself, and get my adrenaline pumping. I took it as a sign to stay hard and head back out to the wilderness.

Before I set foot on trail, I faced one final test. As I was dropped off at the trailhead, the booming sounds of EDM music emanated from the campground across the street. It sounded like a good time, but I needed to hike miles, not get drunk with Kyles.

I embarked on the grueling 5,000+ foot climb out of Belden, and was glad I did. I only made it seven miles before I set up camp, but it was good to knock out a chunk of the big climb. Once inside my tent, I carefully rolled up the Lotramin tube and squeezed it tight to get the last of the remaining cream to apply to my feet.

The following morning started on a lively note with a massive spider crawling on the inside of my tent fly. I ruffled the tent so it would fall off, but instead of fluttering onto the ground, it veered six inches to the right and plummeted into my pack. I had to carefully caress it out before climbing the remaining 3,000 feet. After that, it was a mellow day into the evening. Not feeling great, but not feeling terrible, I contemplated calling it a day early.

Then, my thoughts drifted back to all of my training from the previous year. I thought about all the time I put in: running seven days and over 60 miles a week, lifting five days a week and refusing to lose muscle mass, daily stretching, daily core exercises, daily ankle exercises, barefoot walking and running to toughen the skin on my feet, and so much more.

I reminisced on running 100 laps around a track two consecutive days when it was 90 degrees. I recalled the night when I got off work and then hiked 40 miles through the night to simulate sleep deprivation. Above all else, I thought about my favorite training technique. I'd purposefully do my long runs of the week on Saturday or Sunday mornings when I was hungover and felt my absolute worst to prepare myself for the physical misery of the trail. If I could get through those torturous runs, I could get through any rough day on trail.

My favorite training memory was when I partied until 5 a.m., woke up at 9 a.m. on a friend's couch, ate a banana, walked out the front door, and ran 15 miles. Just reminiscing on the amount of work I put in, and some of the unorthodox training methods I used, gave me the spark to hit a 30-mile day and pass the halfway marker on the PCT.

This day also birthed another piece of motivation. One of my favorite things of all time was the Kanye West Grammy acceptance speech where he said, "Everybody wanted to know what I would do if I didn't win... I guess we'll never know."

For some reason, this popped into my head, and the thought of being able to apply that to myself at the end of the year motivated me and made me hike faster. I wouldn't be ending the year at a trail terminus, so I knew I would have to make the finish special on my own.

The next day presented the choice between a short or long day — nothing in between. The boundary to Lassen National Park lay 23 miles down the trail from my camp, but staying overnight there required a bear canister, which I didn't have on me. Therefore, I couldn't camp within the 19-mile stretch of trail that ran through the park.

Before entering the park, I met another thru-hiker named Boom, who, within two minutes of conversation, offered to help me when I got back on the AT. I was once again reminded of how kind and genuinely helpful this community was, even with people they just met. We hiked together for a while, both pushing each other to move faster, until he stopped to get water while I kept trucking.

I ended up getting to the park boundary around 4 p.m., far too early to end the day, so I pushed all the way through the park and a few miles beyond, before calling it a night around 1 a.m. By that time, I was exhausted. It was a long day of hiking, but more notably, it was way after my bedtime, especially since I had been hiking less and resting more lately due to my feet problems. Forty-mile days weren't overly challenging with an early start to the day, but I didn't start early. Days this long, with a late start, made it tough to have a good following day.

During my nighttime hike, I saw 50 sets of eyes over several hours. Initially, I fixated on the one pair I saw, hoping it wasn't a mountain lion. But as more pairs of eyes emerged, my apprehension eased, realizing that only deer gathered in groups like that. Toward the end of the night, I encountered a couple of snakes, their presence puzzling, considering they are cold-blooded animals. There was also a bat circling around my head for five minutes. It was starting to get annoyingly close and about made me go into Manu Ginóbili mode and smack it out of the air.

The next morning, around 9 a.m., the sun's rays began to fry me inside my tent, forcing me to leave. I had a brief six-mile hike into town, as the trail delineated a boundary line of a past fire. Everything to the left was charred and blackened, while the right side remained untouched — a striking contrast made possible by the presence of the trail.

When I made it into Old Station, CA, I mistakenly thought I sent a food box there. Since I didn't, I visited JJ's Café to feast on some food while I could, and I was extremely glad I did as I savored every bite. It was some of the best food I had all year.

After leaving town, I began the hike along the Hat Creek Rim. In the past, this stretch presented a considerable challenge due to a 40-mile section without water. However, a water tank had been installed halfway through, alleviating the difficulty. I managed with only my 1.5 L water bottle. And it was the perfect kind of hiking — flat and easy, but also with constant views overlooking the valley to the west.

I camped near the water tank and was greeted by cows as I prepared for bed — then waking up to the same "Moos" in the morning. Prior to this, I had only encountered cows in a single spot along the PCT, whereas they were essentially a daily occurrence on the CDT. The — not highlight — but memorable event of the day occurred when two cows decided to run down the trail, just barely ahead of me, for a quarter of a mile. Eventually, they veered off the trail. As one of them turned its head back, it began projectile defecating while maintaining eye contact with me — its hind end positioned just ten feet away. My appetite quickly dissipated.

Even on a queasy stomach, it was easy hiking down to Burney Guest Ranch, which used to be a hostel but had been sold recently. The new owner, Bob, was letting hikers pick up packages if they had previously sent it there like I did, so I went to get my package from Bob. The man wasn't a big talker, but he was interesting. After talking to him for about five sentences, he inexplicably took off in his truck and left me alone at his place, doors unlocked and me confused.

Several minutes later, another man pulled up in a truck. He eagerly approached, greeted me, and said he was ready to talk business. He then started to spout off a bunch of ideas, of which I had no idea what he was talking about. After rambling for about two minutes, he stopped and asked, "Wait, are you Bob?"

I responded, "No."

Then he asked, "Are you related to Bob?"

Again, I responded, "No."

Finally, he asked, "Do you know Bob?"

I said, "Not really."

He sat in a puzzled state for a minute on the tailgate of his pickup truck, and then asked, "So, what are you doing here?"

Gesturing to my food sorted out in front of me, "I just came to pick up this stuff."

Looking more confused than ever, the man cautiously got into his truck and drove away. While it was enjoyable messing with this guy, I couldn't help but think it would've been even funnier if I had pretended to be Bob during the conversation.

Before he left me alone, I had asked Bob if there was a faucet where I could get water. I filled up. However, it tasted like battery acid. Since it was hot, and there wouldn't be water for a while, I hitched into the town of Burney to get some consumable water. Since I was already there, I indulged myself by devouring four double cheeseburgers and two large fries, justifying the treat by telling myself that the food package I picked up might not last three days. In reality, that was a lie. I just wanted McDonald's. Once again, I got a hitch from a cop, but this time I had to sit in the back.

Upon reaching the campsite that night, I noticed a few tents but didn't think much of it. I greeted the other campers briefly, but quickly sought out my own spot due to the relentless mosquitoes. The next morning, I overslept. Since it was later in the morning, I was surprised to see one of the other tents still standing when I peered outside my tent.

With mosquitoes still present, I packed up my belongings, and just as I was about to leave, the occupant of the other tent was also ready to go. His trail name was Hammer Grease, and he asked me about the daily mileage I typically hiked. I said, "Around 30," assuming that it would be too much for him. Instead, he said that the two people he had been hiking with, Ground Score and Berk, were finishing their thru-hike and getting off the trail in a couple of days. Wanting to continue hiking with someone, Hammer Grease said he would try to keep up with me.

Outwardly, I expressed excitement and confidence, agreeably assuring Hammer Grease that he'd be able to keep up with me. Inwardly, I couldn't help but be realistically skeptical, thinking to myself, "Sure, buddy, I've heard this before. You're not going to keep up with me." Little did I know, we would end up hiking over 1,000 miles together, and he would become one of my best friends.

Around midday, Hammer Grease and I took a short break in the shade for a snack, slightly dehydrated from spread-out water sources, and tired from the extra hiking off trail to get to them. As we were venting and commiserating about any extra hiking off trail, we heard a ruckus near us. A black bear was bumbling down the trail at a leisurely pace. Once it noticed we were there, it panicked and took off straight up the hill. This was a pretty relaxed bear encounter, considering we remained seated the whole time.

In the afternoon, Mount Shasta came into view, a significant mountain that remains visible for 300 miles along the trail because of its prominence. After an astounding sunset, painting the sky a fluorescent pink, with wisps of clouds for the final touch, we hiked in the twilight, refusing to put on our headlamps out of stubbornness, and tripping frequently as a result. Ground Score and Berk, who were both early risers, greeted us when we clumsily strolled into camp.

The next day brought scorching heat, reaching a staggering 97 degrees. Fortunately, shade covered the trail for most of the day, which was unexpected but welcomed. Though there weren't many scenic views, I was willing to trade them for respite from the searing heat. In the morning, I heard rustling in a tree to my left and spotted two bear cubs. As I made noise to alert them, a couple of seconds later, I locked eyes with their mother, who was about 20 feet below me, giving me a stern gaze. I kept walking and went on my merry way. Later in the day, we encountered three more bears, another mother with two cubs. Again, I strolled on by, admiring their beauty while keeping my distance.

Around midday, we reached McCloud River and took a pleasant break. I rinsed out one pair of socks and cleaned my feet, providing some relief for my lingering athlete's foot. Additionally, my arms and legs felt a burning sensation, likely from brushing against some skin-irritating plant. For the third consecutive night, I camped near Hammer Grease, Ground Score, and Berk, and joyously recapped the day with the group. This was an unusual experience for me. *Was this what hiking in a group felt like?*

We all woke up around 4:30 a.m. to hike the quick 12 miles into Dunsmuir, CA. Hammer Grease and I waited for a hitch at the road crossing for all of five minutes before calling and overpaying for a shuttle. Two cars stopped and offered us a ride while we were waiting for the shuttle to arrive. The cheapskate inside me was outraged.

We resupplied at Dollar General before getting a small breakfast at a restaurant. Really, we were just killing time until the pizza place in town opened. We were both craving it. While there, Ground Score and Berk showed up, and we congratulated them on finishing their thru-hike. They had hiked the trail north of Dunsmuir the previous year but had to cut it short due to fires. Now they finished the whole thing. Part of me felt bad for them having to finish at an anticlimactic spot. Then I remembered I would be doing the exact same thing on the other two Triple Crown trails.

When the pizza place finally opened, we eagerly migrated there and were more delighted by the air conditioning than the quality of the pizza. Nonetheless, the cool air provided much-needed relief.

While Ground Score and Berk were finished and awaiting transportation, Hammer Grease and I had to head back out. We initially told ourselves we would leave by 1 p.m., but the hours ticked by, and we delayed our departure until 2 p.m., and then 4 p.m. The outside temperature had soared to 102 degrees, and we couldn't muster the courage to start the 5,000-foot climb in such sweltering conditions. We lingered in town until 6 p.m., hoping the heat would subside slightly. It took us an hour to hitch a ride out of town, and we didn't get back on the trail until after 7 p.m.

Even at that late hour, the heat persisted, exacerbated by the lack of a cooling breeze. Both of us were drenched in sweat as we continued climbing past midnight. Around 1 a.m., we set up camp and set our alarms for 4:30 a.m., hoping to beat the intense heat. According to the weather report we saw in town, the daily highs would surpass 100 degrees for the next two weeks straight.

Unsurprisingly, being up for 21 hours straight, and then planning on getting up after three hours of sleep, didn't go as planned. I awoke around 6:15 a.m. Hammer Grease slept a little longer before getting up and around. The morning was warm but tolerable. We reached Porcupine Lake around 2 p.m. and took a break, attempting to catch up on sleep and wait out the hottest part of the day. We resumed hiking around 5:30 p.m. Although it was still hot, the heat was starting to break for the day.

We were hoping to do 21 more miles after leaving the lake. I arrived at a bathroom a few miles later. Even with 1,000 flies swarming about in it, I still opted for the comforting luxury of the porcelain throne. We felt good until midnight when we hit a wall, suddenly feeling exhausted, moving sluggishly, and tripping constantly. Ready to pass out, we found some flat spots to cowboy camp three miles short of where we aimed for. The mosquitoes were out and on the prowl, so I slept with my head net on. They were still annoying — buzzing near my ear — but I was too tired to set up my tent. We went to bed after 1 a.m. and set the alarm for 5 a.m.

I woke up at 7:30 a.m., already toasty, and kicked Hammer as I was leaving to wake him up. Since he and I were essentially the only person each other saw, I started calling him Hammer for simplicity's sake. Since I overslept, I hiked through the scorching heat of the day, and it was tough. To make matters worse, my athlete's foot had returned with a vengeance. The only redeeming quality of the day was that I saw a comically fat bear, like a super obese "This guy really needs to start taking care of himself or he's going to die" kind of fat bear. It struggled to run away when it saw me. It was more like a frightful waddle.

Taking a side trail to use a pit toilet, I got separated from Hammer. Feeling tired, I camped a few miles behind where I estimated he'd be. I was hopeful it wouldn't be the last time I saw him, but I wasn't sure. I didn't know where he was, and we didn't make an agreement to stay together, other than our initial meeting of him saying he would try to keep up. Now the tables had turned. Truthfully, I never expected him to keep up, much less be a faster hiker and get ahead of me. When we first met, I thought I would pass him by like everyone else, but after spending five days with him, I was really enjoying our time together. Now I didn't want to lose him.

Happiness most real when shared.

I woke up punctually at 3:30 a.m., determined to catch up to Hammer. Sure enough, within a few miles, I was strolling by his tent as he was waking up. Together, we hiked 23 miles down to a road to resupply in Etna. For a while, we thought we brought enough food to skip this resupply, but we reluctantly accepted that we needed just a little more to make it to the next town. We got a ride into town from a generous trail angel. She did our laundry while we shopped, and then got a burger and plenty of Dr. Peppers at a diner. I could only wash my shirt and socks since I had one pair of shorts, but some clean clothes felt better than none.

My athlete's foot was worsening again and hurt with every step. Unfortunately, the store in town only had poison ivy cream, not athlete's foot cream. Despite the beautiful scenery in the morning, I couldn't even appreciate it because my foot pain consumed all my attention. Thankfully, after my socks were cleaned, my feet felt slightly better. The miles after town passed by quickly in a state of moderate pain rather than intense pain, and we reached camp a little after 10 p.m. — an early night by recent standards.

After waking up late, I hiked separately from Hammer all day as a result. My feet were hurting again, although not as severely as when the athlete's foot first appeared, so I managed to fight through the pain relatively well. A thunderstorm began in the middle of the day, and I anticipated it would only last for a short while before stopping. However, the rain persisted on and off for over an hour. Considering how hot it had been, I didn't mind. The rain brought some relief from the heat. As the skies cleared up in the evening, I found myself moving faster with the heat and sky at bay.

I was getting back on schedule until all hell broke loose. I was on the phone with a buddy and the call dropped. I lost service. No big deal. It happened a lot. This time, it was a bad omen.

Immediately after that, I began the descent into Seiad Valley and the trail became a nightmare. I had heard bad things about this area, but it was worse than I imagined. It was unbelievably overgrown. The brush seemed to want to pull me deeper into the thicket and keep me to add to its collection. Twilight approached as I found myself in the midst of it all, and I hadn't thought to get my headlamp out beforehand. The tight surroundings prevented me from removing my backpack to access my headlamp, and for a while, I couldn't see where I was stepping. I was certain I was traipsing through plenty of poison oak, and I stumbled, yelled, and ended up with cuts on my legs. Because of these obstacles, I didn't reach the campsite until after 10:30 p.m. When I arrived, it was pitch black, yet I could still make out Hammer's smug grin since he knew what I had endured in the dark.

The following morning, I continued bushwhacking through an overgrown trail, with the added nuisance of being harassed by a persistent bird. It followed me for over half a mile, emitting a constant annoying screech. I was tempted to use my trekking pole as a javelin to make it stop.

After it decided to leave me alone, I arrived in town around noon and was soon joined by Hammer. The town consisted of a small store and a neighboring diner that only served carry-out food. It was 108 degrees, so we loitered until 5:30 p.m., waiting for the temperature to drop as we charged our phones and forced down thousands of calories. While sitting in a picnic area near the store, we also had to contend with another bothersome bird. The aerial nuisance flew over us throughout the day, searching for food and even defecating on my food bag. I was ready to declare a war on birds.

Another thunderstorm formed as we packed up, but it brought wind and cooler temperatures, which was fine with me. Supposedly, the trail was overgrown on the ascent leaving town. We'd had enough of that, so we hiked out of town on a forest road to reconnect with the trail instead. It was a long and gradual climb, but not terribly taxing. I didn't notice it until we stopped near the top, but my legs felt acutely worn out from doing the exact same motion while ascending thousands of feet on the gentle road.

Both Hammer and I decided to cowboy camp that night. I woke up a few times to find deer sniffing around our camp, but I was too tired to care. Then, one came alarmingly close to my food bag, so I made some noise, hoping to scare it away. It abruptly ran off and headed directly for where Hammer was cowboy camping.

I was frozen, half scared and half curious as to what was about to happen. I continued watching as the deer gracefully hurdled directly over Hammer and disappeared into the night. Still in disbelief, I laughed myself back to sleep, but first laughed even harder when Hammer said he woke up as the deer was airborne over him. That must've been quite the alarm.

When we started hiking after our actual alarm, we met a guy that said he flip-flopped from farther south on the trail. He said he was excited to start hiking with some people. Hammer and I exchanged a glance and both read each other's minds. *This won't last long.*

We were polite on the outside, but without saying a word, we both knew he wasn't going to match our pace. We were on a different journey than most. Thru-hiking is hard no matter what, but we were pushing ourselves as much as we could every day. We were simply hiking longer and faster than most people out there. I wanted to finish as soon as possible to stay on track for my goal, and for some reason I still don't understand, Hammer wanted to tag along for the madness.

After chatting with the guy for a bit, we continued hiking. He stayed with us for ten minutes before he said he was going to stop and take a break.

In the afternoon, I finally experienced the spiritual release I waited 1,700 miles for — I crossed the border into Oregon. As I took my final steps in California, I could feel the dopamine rushing through my body.

I was still sweating due to it being 103 degrees. My legs and feet still hurt from hiking 30 miles a day. My pack still weighed its normal amount on my aching back and shoulders.

But none of it mattered. All I could do was smile. It was bliss.

Stressed About a Stress Fracture

We celebrated being in Oregon by sleeping for a full 9.5 hours, hoping it would do a little bit to make up for getting six hours or less for nearly two weeks. We were sleeping less because we were rising early and hiking late to maintain our mileage in the blistering heat, which was expected to persist for a few more days.

After swiftly covering 15 miles to reach the road leading to Ashland, OR, we were picked up by an amazing trail angel named Charley. Hammer disappointedly learned that his gear replacement package hadn't arrived at the post office yet. Without hesitation, Charley offered us a place to stay at his house until the package arrived the next day. We resupplied, took refreshing showers, and did laundry. Charley kindly lent me some clothes, marking my second time doing a thorough laundry session on the PCT. Initially, I considered heading back on the trail in the evening to gain a small lead on Hammer, but I ended up staying at Charley's place, enjoying some brews with the boys while watching Bo Burnham's *Inside*.

I left the next morning while Hammer had to wait for the post office to open. It was tough heading back out into the 100+ degree heat after spending a day in air conditioning, but I was thrilled to get back on trail, just not for the normal reasons. One of my favorite artists, Tyler the Creator, had released a new album on the same day, and I was eager to have uninterrupted hours to listen to it straight through.

As I resumed hiking, I realized I had run out of toilet paper and forgot to get more while I was in town. Optimistically, I continued hiking, hoping Hammer would catch up with me before nature called. But that evening, the choice was taken from me. I was in an area that had only pine needles, which I decided wouldn't be a great option. Without going into too much detail, I made use of a Little Debbie wrapper and the cardboard roll from my old toilet paper.

Right before dusk, I came across two people hanging out by a van at a road crossing. They had been there for hours to reward hikers with trail magic, but I was the first person they saw. I let them know that I was towards the front of the pack, and most hikers were probably 500 miles behind. I sat down and had a nice chat with them while sucking down a few beers. They had hiked the PCT in 2008, so I liked hearing their stories. I told them what I was doing for the year and they loved hearing my stories.

Even though thru-hiking costs money, and it's nearly impossible to have a real income while doing it, the stories amassed during the journey are valuable currency for the rest of a lifetime, especially when other hikertrash are around. I stopped and talked for longer than I should have, but it was fun, and of course, I couldn't turn down free beer. I assured them Hammer would be the only other hiker coming through the area, so they left a beer with a note for him in the middle of the trail as we both prepared to depart.

I hiked a few more miles before going to bed after 11 p.m. I was tired, and there wasn't a hint of rain, so I decided to cowboy camp.

Maybe it wasn't the best choice.

Less than two hours later, I was rudely awoken by a gigantic forest rat rummaging around my campsite. It smelled my alleged "odor proof" food bag and was looking for dinner. After shooing it away, I attempted to fall back asleep, only to be awakened two more times. After the third time, I was fed up. I laid out a piece of food as a trap, willingly sacrificing a Clif Bar, since I now retched at the sight of them after having so many.

The rat approached in a zigzag pattern, as if it was blind and only moved based off of smell, or as if it was trying to run away from an alligator. Shoe in hand, I was ready to strike. When it was finally in position, my shoe came crashing down on its grotesque body. I hit it, and it was hurt, but it was still moving. I hit it again... and again... and again. I had to hit it 13 times before it finally stopped moving.

After bludgeoning this beast of a rat to death, there was rat blood on my shoes and some of my gear. I was disgusted and shocked at the savage situation that had just occurred, but more importantly, I was tired. I went back to bed but woke up a few minutes later, only to find out he must've called for reinforcements in his dying breath. There were three more rats coming out of a hole in the ground and trying to go for my pack.

That was it. I was done. After less than two hours of rest, I packed up all my gear and headed out for the day.

I was still juiced up for a while, after killing a small animal and all, so I didn't feel too tired, but by 9 a.m., exhaustion engulfed my being. I was falling asleep while walking. It would feel like I blinked my eyes, and all of a sudden, I was stumbling five steps to the right of the trail, about to faceplant into a rock. Laying down on a log to try to take a quick nap, I only slept for five minutes before waking up to "Wild Side" by Motley Crue in my headphones. *That was all I needed.*

Energy surging high after that, I covered 21 miles by 1 p.m., but was basically crawling the last few miles because the insufferable heat took the life out of me. I then stopped and took an extended break at a water source. While taking my long break, I was profusely sweating and atrociously tired, just lying down in the shade. *It was exhausting — just existing.* I later learned it was a historically hot day, with a temperature of 111 degrees where I was.

I didn't have much of a plan, other than lie down and try to catch up on sleep until Hammer caught up to me. Even that plan didn't go well. The area was shaded, but with the sun moving all day, it was ever-changing. Every hour or so, I found myself drenched in unbearable sweat as the sunlight reached me. The oppressive heat made it nearly impossible to fall asleep, no matter how fatigued I felt.

Hammer showed up around 6 p.m. I knew he was close before I even saw him when I heard a, "Sheeeeeesh!" off in the distance. I'm not sure if all hiking partners have a call signal, but that was ours.

I let him know that I was not happy to see him. I was glad that he caught up, but I did not want to resume hiking. I knew that when he showed up, we had to. We had 11 miles to get to the next water source where we planned on camping. I felt slightly better once we got moving, but not much. We both struggled immensely during the final miles to camp, so we started a cappella singing every Kanye West song we could think of. It was horrible singing, but a great distraction from how awful we both felt.

When we got to camp around 11 p.m., all the decent campsites were taken, so we had to camp cluttered in between trees, right by the water. The mosquitoes were unyielding, tormenting every inch of exposed skin, and even attacking through layers of shirts or shorts. It was my worst and most precarious tent setup of the entire year because of the trees and my inability to think straight amidst the relentless mosquito assault.

As I was packing up the next morning, they were equally vicious. It was going to be 15 miles to the next water source, so I wanted to chug several liters and bring plenty with me. I didn't do that, however. The mosquitoes were so overwhelming, I couldn't stand it anymore. I filtered two liters of water and had to run because it was unbearable to sit there a single second longer.

The heat had died down a little but was still far from comfortable. As the morning was full of exposed sections, I could feel the intense rays of the sun boiling the water out of my body minute by minute. Dehydration began to set in. After struggling through the last few miles, I slugged down a bunch of water at the first source we hit. After that, there would be water 1.7 miles later, and then nothing for 20 miles until Crater Lake National Park.

Frustrated, we realized that we would have to hike all the way to Crater Lake, which we weren't planning on doing. We lingered at the last water source for an hour, dreading the thought of leaving. Even after consuming seven liters of water, I remained dehydrated, not urinating all night. I also didn't have much carrying capacity because I pictured Oregon having water and streams everywhere, not consistent long water carries. Because of this, I only had enough bottles to hold two liters of water. Knowing this wouldn't suffice for the 20-mile stretch, especially when already dehydrated, I filled my bottles, but also my peanut butter jar used for cold soaking. I even went full hikertrash engineer and filled four Ziploc bags. Despite gathering as much water as I could, it was only around three liters.

While we both wanted nothing more than to continue lounging by the water source, Hammer and I left around 5 p.m. We hiked together for a bit, but Hammer soon separated from me since I was moving slower than usual because of my intense foot pain.

By 11:30 p.m., I was exhausted and debated making camp three miles short. Instead, I turned off my headlamp and looked up at the stars with a full blood moon in the sky. *What a sight.* After taking in that majestic nighttime beauty, I was ready to keep rolling, feeling high off the sky.

Arriving at Crater Lake Campground around 1:30 a.m., I found an open campsite near the back and slept there for the night. It was a bit of a walk to get up to the camp store in the morning. As I intersected with the main campground road on my way to the store, Hammer was right there! We hadn't communicated. We hadn't planned on a time. Yet, we ended up perfectly timing each other at an intersection without breaking stride.

We stayed at the camp store until noon, eating, drinking, and charging. I purchased a couple of pints of ice cream, which felt like I was eating little cups of heaven with all the heat we had been dealing with. I may have left the freezer open too long and air-conditioned the whole park, because it was the first day below 100 degrees in two weeks. It still felt hot, but it was slightly less encumbering.

After a few miles back on trail, we reached Crater Lake. It was truly one of the most mesmerizing things I had ever seen. The water didn't look real. I had never seen a body of water that perfect a shade of blue. It was one of those things that you have to see to understand and truly appreciate.

Hammer and I agreed that another late-start, 30-mile day would put us in bad shape for the coming days. We ended the day early at 23 miles to get a decent night of sleep, with the added benefit of sleeping at a water cache so we could load up and hydrate. This was needed since I had essentially been in a perpetual state of dehydration for over two weeks.

After getting a full, eight hours of sleep, something that felt foreign in recent history, I started off the day by getting a bloody nose while doing a farmer's sneeze. This happened quite a bit. My nose was dry from living outside, and a farmer's sneeze was the only way to clear my nose. Combining the two often led to a bloody nose. It didn't bother me much, but I just wanted to keep it off my clothes. Hitchhiking was already hard enough. I didn't want to throw being covered in blood into the equation.

The weather was a welcomed change, with temperatures in the 80s and the occasional cloud in the sky. The cooler temperature made the 22-mile water carry feel easy. But not everything was perfect.

It was the beginning of a long stretch of mosquito hell. The mosquitoes were just as relentless as the ones at the water source I had to hastily retreat from a few days ago. But now they seemed to be everywhere. No matter how fast I walked, they were just as fast. I spent the entire day swatting at the mosquitoes, wearing only shorts and a thin shirt that provided no defense. Although the temperature was cooler than it had been, it was still too warm to throw on more layers for protection. At one point, in a desperate attempt for distraction, I called one of my most talkative friends and simply said, "Talk! I need a distraction!" Much like happiness is enhanced with others around, misery also loves company.

I had planned on getting up at 3 a.m. the following day and making it to Shelter Cove Resort to resupply before they closed. That was a good plan, until I overslept for a whopping five hours — a new personal record. I awoke after 8 a.m., only rising because sleep became an impossibility with the sun roasting me in my tent. The main reason for my reluctance to get up was the presence of over a hundred mosquitoes waiting just outside my tent door. It was intimidating, seeing the enemy so close and always battle-ready. All it would take was for me to unzip my tent door, and the battle was on.

After I unzipped, packed up, and got moving, the day was filled with constant aggression and not one moment of tranquility in the Diamond

Peak Wilderness. It was one of the most frustrating days of hiking I'd experienced. I couldn't stop moving all day because the swarm was ever-present. The only respite came after 15 miles where I collected some water in an area that was slightly better. I seized the opportunity because I was only being swarmed by 30 mosquitoes instead of hundreds. But the small swarm still weighed on my patience. I pushed the remaining 13 miles to camp without breaking stride. After being unable to eat any food all day because I couldn't stop moving, I was unenergized and exhausted. I camped just before the resort, which was closed by the time I got there due to our delayed start. As I laid in my tent, I estimated how many mosquitoes I had killed during the day. *Let's say I killed four mosquitoes every minute, and I did this for 30 minutes out of every hour. I hiked for ten hours. So I killed 1,200 mosquitoes today.* I still felt like that was a conservative estimate.

We did a small resupply at Shelter Cove Resort the next morning, and I made sure to buy Deet. I had been carrying it the whole time, but when I recently pulled it out to use it, I learned it had all leaked out. Thankfully, it wasn't 100% Deet, otherwise it would've melted holes in everything it touched. After downing a few pints of ice cream and chugging as much water as possible, we headed back out to brave the swarm.

The first eight miles after the resort were pleasant. The trail was shaded. A gentle breeze cooled my skin. And miraculously, there were no mosquitoes! That didn't last. They returned with a vengeance, forcing Hammer and me to take a lunch break in a ski shelter to escape their relentless assault. I loaded up on Deet before heading back out, and it actually worked for a while. They were still swarming around, but not landing on me or biting my arms and legs. Combined with my head net, I felt invincible. *My name is Ozymandias, king of kings!*

Oh, how I would be reminded of my mortality!

Seven miles before camp, we encountered a burn area with a flowing breeze and, to my delight, no mosquitoes. I removed my head net, enjoying the freedom from their incessant buzzing. However, as we continued and the wind diminished, the mosquitoes came back for another round. I hastily donned my head net once again, but it proved insufficient.

They were savages, undeterred by my feeble attempts to swat them away. The Deet must have worn off, and I was hesitant to reapply it so close to bedtime. As a result, the last few miles turned into a chaotic spectacle of yelling, frantic swatting, and occasional bursts of running in a futile attempt to outrun the unyielding swarm. During one of my hasty sprints, I tripped over a root and slammed into the ground. Luckily, while falling, I managed to twist to my side, cushioning the impact with my pack. It wasn't too bad, and I brushed myself off.

That fall didn't dissuade me from continuing to try to escape the mass of mosquitoes. While we were running the last bit before camp, literally the last 300 feet, my left foot popped and I felt a sharp pain.

Both of my feet hurt throughout the duration of the journey from the sheer pounding they had to go through, but this pain was different.

Fear instantly consumed my entire body. I'd had six stress fractures in my feet in the past, along with other foot problems that had led to surgery. The pop seemed to occur in the same area where I had previously had problems. I was terrified that it might be another stress fracture, but I refused to acknowledge it. I didn't even mention a word of it to Hammer because I didn't want to give it power. If I spoke it into existence, that would make it real. Instead, I silently set up camp, pretending that nothing had happened, even though I was limping around like a wounded animal. *If I kept it to myself, the pain would subside, and I would forget about it.*

We overslept by three hours the next morning and got over ten hours of sleep. Oregon had become the state where we caught up on sleep after depriving ourselves during the heatwave. We didn't push for excessively long miles in Oregon, but the forgiving terrain allowed us to sleep 10–12 hours most nights while still managing to cover 30 miles.

Before I even went to sleep, I saw the mosquitoes setting up their battle lines on my tent door. I was unhappy but unsurprised to see they were still there in the morning. I assumed they were all whispering, "He's got to come out sometime" or their general was repeatedly yelling, "HOLD!" until I emerged from my walled protection.

When I stepped out of my tent, I didn't notice them for the first five seconds. It was serene.

I foolishly thought, *Wow, this is going to be a glorious day!*

Then they descended upon me with the fury of determined demons. I quickly put on my head net and reapplied Deet. It helped a little bit, but they remained bothersome all day. I reapplied Deet twice later in the day, and I think I overdosed a little on the poison because I got a pounding headache. In a sick kind of way, it was nice to have a different kind of pain — a short-term distraction from my injured foot.

The following day was a big one. We woke up knowing we'd end near to the 2,000-mile marker on the trail. As much as I tried to avoid big-picture thinking to keep me from being overwhelmed, I couldn't ignore this one. This was my first time ever hiking 2,000 miles straight thru on a trail. It felt like a big deal, and if I reached it today, I would be at roughly 4,500 miles on the year. Furthermore, it marked day 180 on the trail — a sobering realization that I had spent half a year out here. This was now my life.

In the morning, we emerged from the dense forest we had been hiking through and entered a stark volcanic landscape. Walking on fields of lava rock felt otherworldly. The constant breeze and absence of mosquitoes was a welcome relief, but the terrain itself was harsh. I stumbled and slipped frequently, and the unforgiving rock aggravated the pain in my already injured foot. Later in the day, a thought crossed my mind: *Wouldn't it be wild if one of these volcanoes erupted right now? I'm not sure how I'd outrun the flowing lava, but that'd be a hell of a way to go out.*

I convinced Hammer, who didn't require much convincing, that we should hit the 2,000-mile marker that night and find a campsite afterwards. We split up, and I hit the marker around 11:00 p.m. It was a moment of affirmation, a significant milestone on my journey. I allowed myself a brief moment of enjoyment, although I didn't want to get too excited because sleep was calling me with a sweet whisper.

When I arrived at our campsite — a small flat area that Hammer had found — my joy multiplied. He had managed to acquire two beers from some campers we passed and saved one for me. I was overjoyed — a celebratory beer to top off reaching the 2,000-mile marker!

I planned on setting up camp first and savoring the drink afterward. However, as I was setting up my tent, a trekking pole accidentally punctured the can, causing it to spray and leak. Obviously, I couldn't let it go to waste, so I had to chug it. It wasn't the relaxing and rewarding beer I was hoping for, but it was a beer, nonetheless.

We knew the next day was going to be a weird one. There was an upcoming fire closure without a feasible alternate, so we had to get into Bend, OR and find a ride around it. We were both looking forward to getting into town since we were still drained from hiking in the heat wave. It was a relaxing morning, devoid of the usual rush to get up and get moving.

However, the sun soon made its presence felt, turning our tents into saunas and prompting us to rise around 8 a.m. We made our way to the road, just a mile away, essentially marking it as a rest day.

Arriving at the road, we patiently awaited a hitch into Sisters, OR, which took over 90 minutes to secure. From Sisters, it only took us a mere five minutes to catch another ride to Bend, OR. While waiting for the first ride, a motorcyclist pulled over and kindly handed each of us a Coors Light. Standing there, trying to get a hitch with my backpack on, dirty as hell, and Coors Light in hand, was one of my finer hikertrash moments, and I relished every second of it.

When in Bend, we opted for a night in a hostel. We were the only hikers staying there amidst a crowd of "normal people," which was strange. We resupplied and then went to a sports bar in town because we were both craving greasy bar food after eating nothing but hiking food lately.

It turned out to be a historically poor dining experience. They were out of chicken wings, only had kid-size pizzas, and we only got one refill in the three hours it took to get our food. I was actually impressed that a restaurant could be that bad.

Maybe I should've stuck with my cold-soaked ramen.

We embarked on the next leg of our journey by catching a bus to circumvent the fire closure. We got back on trail and checked out the Timberline Lodge, a renowned ski resort. Normally, it had a can't-miss buffet, but they weren't offering it because of the pandemic — probably a wise financial choice for them with me showing up.

We met a forest service worker who was shocked to hear we were PCT hikers because of how early we were. There were a few ahead of us, but we were gradually closing the gap.

It was a pleasant day of hiking... until the evening.

We had been reading comments from other hikers, and releases from the PCTA, about how wrecked the trail was in the Mount Hood Wilderness because of a windstorm last year. Despite knowing it would be tough, we had no choice but to press on. It didn't matter that the trail crews hadn't been out yet because we got there so early. The only way is thru. Plus, *people usually over-exaggerate things. It wouldn't be that bad, right?*

Wrong. The scene that unfolded before us was incomprehensible. The trail transformed into a twisted maze of colossal, fallen trees, forcing us to scramble over and under them continuously. There was no discernible path left. It was as though a giant had marched through, toppling every tree in its wake, leaving us with a bewildering obstacle course of logs stacked 10 to 20 feet high, covering every inch of what used to be forest. Progress was excruciatingly slow, and it became a challenge to maintain our sanity amongst the chorus of chaos all around.

With darkness descending, we made the decision not to continue the acrobatics without proper visibility. Instead, we climbed up to a ridge in search of a passable camping spot, but found nothing of the sort. We were at a loss. Rather than retracing our steps to reconnect with the treacherous "trail" buried under fallen trees, I convinced Hammer that we could follow the ridge for a while and rejoin the trail later near a campsite. It seemed like a reasonable plan in theory, but reality had other ideas.

The ensuing hour was an onerous ordeal as we painstakingly covered a mere 0.4 miles. Leading the way, I pushed through chin-high brush — my surroundings obscured from view. My movements were guided solely by instinct, as my legs bore the brunt of the relentless undergrowth. I stumbled frequently, relying on blind faith when stepping off logs, hoping solid ground awaited my foot somewhere below. There were perilous drops of over five feet that I had not seen and rocked my body on impact. Though I endured considerable pain, I managed to avoid any serious falls. Eventually, we emerged from the brush and stumbled directly into the campsite I referenced earlier, scaring some hikers camping there.

Just like I planned — sort of.

I decided to cowboy camp since there were no bugs — another mistake. Around 4 a.m., as a gentle rain began to fall, I laid there, convincing myself that it was a minor inconvenience. I planned to rise with the light in an hour, believing the rain would subside before I resumed walking. But it persisted, drenching all my gear.

Reluctantly, I forced myself to leave at 7 a.m., hoping the rain would relent as I embarked on the day's journey. The initial hours were grueling, battling both rain and a constant hurdle of fallen trees. While the obstruction wasn't as severe as the night before, it remained a persistent nuisance.

Eventually, the rain ceased, the logs disappeared, and the sun emerged. Things were looking up, but everything wasn't exactly perfect. I took the Eagle Creek Alternate, which had recently reopened and had garnered much excitement among hikers. However, the trail proved difficult to follow from the beginning and soon vanished completely.

Hiking through dense underbrush, Hammer and I were joined by Buckle, who we had met at camp the previous night. After some time, we made the collective decision to descend the mountainside and regain the trail, rather than aimlessly wandering around at the top looking for the seemingly nonexistent trail. It was still difficult, but eventually, we discovered the actual trail at a lower elevation, offering a more enjoyable experience. Upon reaching the river, I understood the hype. Following Eagle Creek, I was treated to breathtaking views of numerous waterfalls.

When I got into Cascade Locks, the town on the Columbia River which separates Oregon and Washington, I met up with some relatives and got some grub. One of them was a chiropractor, so I had the luxury of getting adjusted on some pallets in the back parking lot of a grocery store.

Cascade Locks was a weird place. Hammer and I were sitting outside the grocery store, drinking a beer after I got adjusted in the parking lot, and that was one of the more normal things going on. Hammer was asked by a random woman where to buy heroine. We watched a person seemingly from the 1970s trying to recycle bottles in a machine for 20 minutes straight with little success. And there was a shirtless guy on drugs scaring people away from the public restrooms in town. It's a rare thing when thru-hikers are one of the more normal things in a town.

Leaving town was tough, both physically and mentally. Physically, I struggled with the discomfort of carrying over five days' worth of food in my ill-fitting 36-liter pack. I had to get a little creative and carry a peanut butter jar in my chest pocket. Mentally, it was tempting to stay in town, especially when I saw Buckle and his hiking partner heading to a bar instead of hitting the trail with heavy packs. The allure of fun and relaxation was strong, but I knew I had to push forward.

One of the main reasons staying in town would have been appealing was to deal with the post office in the morning. I was expecting a package with new shoes and socks, but they hadn't arrived when I checked. I was frustrated because my current shoes were going on 800 miles. There was a chance the package might've arrived the next morning, but I decided to bounce it ahead on trail. If I stayed and it didn't show up the next day, I would've been infuriated. I tried to look at the bright side. I would get almost 1,000 miles out of one pair of shoes. Budget-wise that was a good thing, just not so much for the health of my feet, especially since my one foot was in debilitating pain, all day, every day since popping it.

We left Cascade Locks that evening, ready to be done with mosquito-infested Oregon. As we crossed the Columbia River on the Bridge of the Gods, the sun was directly ahead, as if it was a beacon of hope that Washington would be better than Oregon. We hiked a few miles out of town before setting up camp for the night. There were a lot of weekend campers out, so we made do with some awful campsites. I slept on a rocky slope. It was the best thing I could find, but still horrible. I completely wasted my chiropractic adjustment. When I woke up the next morning, my back and neck were so tight that every movement hurt. This, combined with my heavy pack, made the whole day a struggle.

I tried to alleviate some weight by eating as much food as possible before setting off. Even after doing so, my pack still felt extremely uncomfortable and burdensome. As I continued hiking, the weight seemed to bear down on me even more, and I realized it was probably closer to six or seven days' worth of food, rather than the intended five.

Despite the difficulties, I tried to maintain relentless optimism, hoping the extra food would allow me to bulk up and provide me surplus energy. But I couldn't ignore the fact that my pack's weight certainly exceeded its recommended limit of 20 pounds, and without a doubt surpassed the absolute maximum of 25 pounds.

Washington didn't exactly have the best welcome party. The trail was difficult, and there weren't many views on the first day. It was still easier and more beautiful than the Appalachian Trail, but relative to what I had been doing, it was a poor ratio of work to reward. A 3,000-foot climb would be rewarded with an immediate 3,000-foot decline, then a 1,500-foot climb and decline. That cycle just seemed to repeat itself.

The next morning, I came across a campground where I was eager to dump some trash to lighten my load, even a fraction of an ounce. I continued to eat as much as possible, taking advantage of the opportunity to discard trash. This campground also had a water pump, but I think it required black magic to work properly. After a tutorial from the camp host, I still struggled with it for ten minutes. I got it to work a little and some water trickled out, but the process was frustrating and made me feel like an idiot. Thankfully, I was also able to acquire (steal) some toilet paper. Otherwise, I would've run out again, an experience I never wanted to repeat.

Leaving the campground, I knew Hammer had a head start on me since he went farther yesterday. I took a forest road parallel to the trail to do a gradual climb to the top, instead of a PUD (pointless up and down climb), which takes more time. I met Hammer again at the top, and we pushed on for a while, before he ended up going farther for the day. The more time went on, the more I ate out of my pack, and the better my neck and back felt. I knew, like anything else, only time would help, but I just wanted to feel normal again. It was coming, slowly but surely.

On a short night's sleep, I woke up early once again to catch up with Hammer. After four miles, I passed him as he was getting out of bed for the day. We encountered another thru-hiker who informed us that there likely weren't any hikers ahead of us at the moment. Her group had flipped up to Washington from farther back and hadn't heard of anyone ahead. Although we had heard that a couple of people had recently finished, we weren't aware of anyone ahead of us. It was a remarkable feeling to realize that, to the best of our knowledge, we were now at the front of the pack. After starting towards the back of the pack on April 26th, it was a gratifying sense of accomplishment. All it takes is consistency.

Later in the day, we met some weekend campers who were astonished to hear that we were already this far north by July 10th. One of them, with a deadpan expression, repeatedly exclaimed, "You're not supposed to be here," as if we were intruding ghosts.

So far in Washington, the mosquitoes rotated back and forth from being a real pain in the ass to being absent. In the Indian Heaven Wilderness, I had to dig a cat-hole, and they were a literal pain in the ass! They smelled my vulnerability and attacked with all their might, rushing me in one of the activities man least likes to be rushed.

The following day started on an agitating note, with the mosquitoes being horrendous for the first 15 miles. When I encountered a day-hiking couple on the trail, they asked if it was the worst mosquito experience I've had. Comparatively, it didn't even come close to the mosquito plague in Oregon. Although there was a lot of climbing up and down throughout the day, the mosquitoes finally disappeared in the afternoon when I reached a more exposed area with some wind.

Aside from the mosquito ordeal, it was a great day for wildlife sightings. While hiking alone, I came across a magnificent elk with antlers that stretched out over five feet. It was an awe-inspiring sight, and it took me by surprise as I was walking along, singing to myself. It darted ten feet ahead of me on my right, then began running to my left. Later in the day, a marmot posed like a Vogue model on an outcropping rock. It was a perfect sight with the sun dropping in the sky behind it, but it was also charmingly funny how much this marmot was trying to look good for me.

Reaching Cispus Pass in the late afternoon, Hammer still hadn't caught me. He always slept in a little longer and caught up with me since he was faster. Today was the one day I actually wanted him to catch me. I knew once we climbed high in the Goat Rocks Wilderness, it would be beautiful, and I wanted some pictures of myself in that stunning landscape.

After that pass, there was a short, flat stretch where I was moving a little slower because my foot was hurting terribly. Thankfully, Hammer caught up right as we were about to embark on the final ascent up to Knife's Edge, a majestic part of the trail that rides a skinny ridge. Despite the slow progress over the steep and uneven loose shale rock, it felt surreal — hiking the ridge at sunset added another layer of indescribable beauty.

Ethereal beauty stretched in every direction as far as the eye could see, enhanced by the thought that if you fell on either side, death would come swiftly. The trail lacked the added difficulty of snow, which was unusual for this time of the year. I was grateful at least one good thing came out of the seemingly endless heat wave.

The following day, we woke up early and sauntered 15 miles to get to White Pass, our next resupply point. I picked up my food box, which was sent a while ago. My package with my shoes and socks was also supposed to be there. But it was not. Again. I walked 150 miles faster than that package could get there in a vehicle. I remained calm on the outside, but internally, I was ready to lead a revolution against the United States Postal Service.

As I walked back outside, I saw Hammer sitting on a bench, chatting with another hiker named Gary. I went over and explained what happened. I felt like I had to vent to somebody. Gary had just finished up a section hike and was waiting on a ride from his mom. He told me that she could pick me up a pair of shoes and socks on her way, even though, I really don't think it was on the way.

I was stunned by the kindness. I was excited to get new shoes, but really, I was touched that someone could possibly be that nice, to go out of her way to pick up a new pair of shoes for a person she had never met.

Hammer and I loitered and talked with Gary for seven hours until his mom showed up. I wasn't in any hurry. I was desperately excited for new shoes. Nothing else mattered. I didn't want to start hiking. I was enjoying the air conditioning, Mountain Dew Voltage, and simply sitting. *I was loving not hiking.* When she did arrive, I repeatedly thanked her, reimbursed her, and we headed back into the woods to press forward to Canada.

Foot Rot

It was not a warm welcome. The mosquitoes were a hundred times worse north of White Pass than they were south of it. To add to the misery, Hammer lost his phone. I anxiously stood there for a half minute, hoping he would find it, so I wouldn't have to turn around and help. The last thing I wanted to do, while being swarmed by a scourge of mosquitoes, was stand still and look for a small phone in the dark.

Just as I was ready to yell at him for being an idiot of the highest degree, he found it, and we started running to get away from the mosquitos.

As we were running in the dark, my foot still throbbing from a previous run, we struggled to locate the campsite marked on our map. We thought the location might be incorrect, so we hiked an additional quarter mile before giving up and turning back. Eventually, we did find it, only to be devastated that it was right beside a stagnant pool of water — an ideal breeding ground for mosquitoes.

It was perhaps the single, worst spot that I dealt with mosquitoes all year. I couldn't set up my tent for more than a few seconds before having to drop everything to vigorously wipe my arms and legs, attempting to rid myself of the hundreds of relentless insects. *It was madness.* When I opened my tent door for a split second, jumped inside, and hastily closed it, over 50 mosquitoes snuck inside with me. The next few minutes were spent clapping and swatting dozens of mosquitoes to death. My hands were covered in mosquito blood and carcasses, leaving me with no choice but to wipe the mess on my legs. Unfortunately, the future looked equally bleak, with hundreds of mosquitoes already preparing for battle outside my tent walls.

While there had been nights when I heard the faint hum of mosquitoes just beyond my tent, this night was different. The hum was constant — a persistent reminder of their presence. I listened to their buzz as I drifted off to sleep, as I woke up throughout the night, and even when I awoke in the morning. As I prepared to sleep, I noticed that my watch had become loose, prompting me to tighten it by a notch. I hadn't weighed myself in a while, but that slight change was not a promising sign.

In the morning, I was jolted awake by Hammer's voice. Glancing at my watch, I groaned, realizing it was already 7 a.m. "Fuck!"

"I know," said Hammer in a calm but defeated voice.

We overslept an hour and a half again. This was a bit of a tradition Hammer and I had. After waking up late, I had to lie there for 15 minutes of meditation, trying to tell my body it wasn't allowed to go to the bathroom for many hours to come. The mosquitoes were so bad in that area, it would've been a death sentence. I was in discomfort and moving slowly all day, until I came across a parking lot with an enclosed toilet in the evening.

The trail provides.

Near that parking lot, I enjoyed the closest and most awe-inspiring view of Mount Rainier thus far. We had been admiring the massive peak for a while. It was a breathtaking mountain, jutting out of the landscape like Shasta and so many others in the Cascade range.

After waking up late and moving slowly, it wasn't a great day for distance, ending at 27 miles. I stopped early because campsites were scarce. I ended up cowboy camping right on the trail in a semi-flat area. It wasn't a great spot, but the map made it look like it would be a while before there was a viable campsite, or even a flat area that wasn't on a ledge. I couldn't set up my tent because the area wasn't big enough, but the mosquitoes were still vicious. It wasn't a great night of sleep, hearing their incessant buzzing on my head net which was sticking to my skin with sweat. Other than getting a view of Rainier, seeing two herds of elk, and crossing paths with a fat marmot that squared up for a fight, it was a rough day overall.

I woke up at 5:30 a.m., determined to catch Hammer, and was greeted by a vibrant, glowing morning sky. It was easier to wake up like this, rather than cowering in my tent from a mosquito battalion. Around midday, I arrived at a cabin on trail and found a cooler of beer for hikers — a much-needed trail magic surprise. One major benefit of losing over 40 pounds on trail, and being dehydrated most of the time, was that I could start buzzing after a beer or two. Being a lightweight has its perks.

Needless to say, the next few miles rolled on by, but as dusk approached, my legs tightened up, and Hammer wasn't feeling great either. We stopped a few miles short of our planned destination, but it was still a formidable 36-mile day through tough Washington terrain.

I actually got up on time at 4:30 a.m. with the help of blasting some tunes to get me going. Hammer, on the other hand, followed his usual routine of waking up and then promptly going back to sleep. The day was filled with continuous short, steep ascents and descents.

Around 6:30 p.m., I finally reached Snoqualmie, and indulged in a massive 21-inch pizza with Hammer. We ended up staying longer than anticipated as we got caught up in conversation with some spirited southbound hikers. I loved talking to southbounders. They were so young and full of vigor. I had been getting the shit beat out of me every day by the trail for a half year, and was eternally exhausted, but they hadn't reached that point yet. They would soon enough.

While we were sitting in the store and talking, another hiker busted through the door and yelled out, "Is one of you Hammer!?"

Hammer skeptically said "Yes," indicating that he was either afraid he was in trouble, or that something was wrong with this crazy guy.

The crazy man said he had been seeing Hammer's name in the trail log books for over a thousand miles. He was always just a few days behind. Hammer was much better at signing trail registers than I was. Usually, I would pass them and tell myself that it wasn't worth stopping for 30 seconds to sign it, as if that would limit my mileage for the day.

The hiker said his name was Terminator. He had to wait there to pick up a box the next day, but he assured us he would catch us afterward. Hammer and I exchanged glances and said in unison, "Sure you will, buddy," fully confident we'd never see him again.

We got back on trail around 9:00 p.m. and knocked out four miles of steep climbing before setting up camp. We were both still wired from too many Dr. Peppers, but we didn't want to push it and ruin tomorrow by hiking too late into the night.

When we were less than 100 yards from camp, I tripped on a root sticking out of the ground, and it was a rough fall. My body was propelled forward with the momentum, but my feet remained caught by the root, so my body slammed into the ground with a violent crash. The impact was so forceful that even my jaw hurt a little. The next morning, both Hammer and I were jolted awake by a large branch that crashed down between us as we cowboy camped only a few yards apart. *These trees were out to get me.*

Although our sleeping bags were slightly damp from the wet, foggy night, it was still warm enough that a wet sleeping bag wasn't as detrimental as it would have been in the Sierra. While it wasn't raining heavily, the mountain was engulfed in a cloud, and the air held a substantial amount of moisture. The cooler morning was a welcome change, but consequently, this area, known for its remarkable beauty, remained concealed within the fog.

Progress was also sluggish due to the steep hiking over large, loose rocks. After two hours, I checked my phone and discovered I had only covered 3.6 miles. Initially, I suspected a malfunction, but the truth was, I was simply moving at an unusually slow pace.

Around noon, I climbed over a ridge, and the other side revealed a clearer, lively landscape. Later in the day, we began another arduous 2,000+ foot climb, with Hammer forging ahead to get to camp earlier. The pain in my foot was more intense than usual, and I didn't get to camp until 11 p.m.

On the way, my throat started to hurt out of nowhere. I wasn't sure if I was getting sick or what was happening. Then I felt something in it, like a chunk of Luna Bar. I tried to spit it out but didn't have much luck. A few minutes later, it must've gotten stuck on my uvula, because I started gagging and threw up — my first puke of the year. It felt good to clean the pipes.

The next day was brutal, and I knew it would be. I had to do 30 miles with nearly 8,000 feet of elevation gain. The morning proved painstakingly slow with a long and gradual ascent. By midday, I reached a roaring river, fed by melting snow, that I had to ford. There was a potential five-foot jump across, but it came with deadly consequences — a ten-foot drop into a raging waterfall if anything went wrong. I stood there, contemplating for ten minutes before deciding that I valued my life slightly more than dry feet — but not by much. I walked 30 yards downstream, where the crossing was slightly less treacherous, and made it across without incident. However, my shoes and socks were saturated for the next few hours, causing extreme discomfort for my feet.

After moving slowly all day, I finally reached the last big climb. At Piper Pass, my mood went from sad and soggy to happy — and still soggy. The sun was setting, but the vibes were rising. Dramatic music enhanced my mood. I felt better and my pace quickened, arriving at camp by 10:30 p.m.

There was an outhouse, which I was looking forward to all day. It was a toilet, but it forgot the house part. It was just a hole in the ground with a wooden seat. I was always happy to have a seat while relieving myself since my legs were always dead tired, but once again, I was eaten alive by ferocious mosquitoes in my exposed state.

As I entered my tent and took off my socks, a fearful chill went down my spine as terror gripped my body. I didn't know what to do when I saw the state of my right foot. It looked atrocious, with raised white skin covered in black spots on the ball of my foot. This oddity had been around for a while, but after spending hours walking in wet shoes that day, the skin appeared significantly more raised, and the black spots looked dangerous. Everything was much more swollen and unhealthy-looking now. Strangely, it wasn't painful, which provided some small comfort. Nevertheless, it was definitely uncomfortable. The skin felt slightly irritated, and scratching it provided such a satisfying relief that once I started, I couldn't stop. When I was scrubbing my feet with wet wipes to clean them off, the satisfaction from the itching was the most pleasure I had felt in a long time.

Cell service was practically non-existent in this remote area of Washington, and I had heard that it only got worse further north. I knew the trail would become even more remote in that direction, making it nearly impossible to see a doctor without taking a major detour and spending a lot of time and money to do so. There was no way I was going to get off trail. I vowed to myself that I would endure the discomfort for the remainder of the PCT, and then try to see a doctor before starting the CDT, if necessary. Although my foot wasn't hurting yet from the sickening anomaly, I expected the pain would come soon, given its grotesque appearance. Without a doubt, my foot was the most repulsive thing I had encountered all year and one of the most revolting sights in my entire life. It looked like it was rotting.

When I got to Steven's Pass the next day — the last place with dependable cell service on trail — I called a few of my friends in medical school. I knew it was a futile endeavor. It was like my friends asking me legal questions because I wanted to go to law school. I had no idea. I hadn't learned it yet, and neither had they. They certainly were not experts on feet, but I was just looking for someone to tell me it would be okay.

After a few discussions, and a lot of Google searching by them, they determined it wasn't a bacterial tissue infection, like they first feared, which terrified me when they explained its seriousness. They didn't know what it was exactly, but they reassured me that if it wasn't hurting, and it wasn't red, I should be alright. That was enough for me. I also sent a picture to my parents and asked them to contact our doctor to get a professional opinion.

While at Steven's Pass, I picked up a food box from the ski lodge. The place was closed, but they had one worker there to help out the hikers. I appreciated their generosity, but I was a little disappointed because I was craving some ice-cold Dr. Peppers. I had to kill time for a few hours, waiting on Hammer. He didn't send a box to the lodge, so he had to hitch into a town nearby, which was a bit of a challenge in this area. He hiked ahead the previous day, so he'd have enough time for his side quest. While waiting on him, I talked with a few southbounders, and a mother and daughter that knew nothing about the trail. Describing what I was doing, and answering questions about thru-hiking to a child, was amusing.

I ended up staying there longer than expected and didn't leave until 2 p.m. After doing a few miles, Hammer caught up with me with plenty to talk about. This was the longest time we had spent apart since meeting each other. It was fun catching up on all that happened in the last day and a half and how rough the prior day was.

At one point, I made a *Pulp Fiction* reference and Hammer looked at me, perplexed. It turned out he had never seen the movie. Subsequently, I learned that he had never seen *Talladega Nights*, or *The Big Lebowski*, or so many other great and common movies. I wondered how many obscure references I made since we met, where he had no idea what I was talking about. We ended up camping a little short of where we planned. Allegedly, the mosquitoes were extra ravenous there. It was a resupply day, so we weren't too disappointed with a 25-mile day.

The next morning, I overslept again, but Hammer played some music, rousing me from my slumber. The mosquitoes weren't bad initially. But of course, as soon as I went to answer the call of nature, they smelled my vulnerability and swarmed. That wasn't my only mistake.

I made a boneheaded move that I had gone the whole trip without doing so far. I had come close a few times, but today was the first time I actually did it. First, I swallowed a fly. I wheezed for a few minutes before I spit it up. After this unpleasant experience, I put on my head net to avoid repeating the incident since bugs were everywhere. A few minutes later, I let out a wad of spit, not thinking that I had my head net on. There are few things in the world that made me feel dumber than this, and now I had to look at the spit caught in my head net, because of my own idiocy.

Lifting my downtrodden spirits, we entered Glacier Peak Wilderness, which I had been hearing about for a long time. To my amazement, I got a bar of cell service, and a message arrived, delivering some comforting news from my doctor — my foot ailment was nothing serious, merely plantar warts and athlete's foot.

The sheer joy I felt was immeasurable! I quickly caught up with Hammer, who had paused to chat with another hiker. Bursting with excitement to share the news that it wasn't a rare foot bacteria or fungi, I eagerly told both Hammer and the other hiker. The latter gave me an odd look before continuing on his way, but I didn't care.

I felt elated that it wasn't a rare or severe foot condition, and the discomfort wasn't expected to escalate. It did surprise me, though, that the athlete's foot had persisted for almost two months since its onset. I got some prescribed treatments, but I wouldn't be able to pick them up until I finished the trail. That didn't matter. I had been dealing with intense, underlying, foot pain since my foot popped in Oregon roughly 500 miles back. I had learned to deal with it. My only fear was something coming along and making it exceptionally worse, and now that fear was alleviated.

Nothing could stop me.

The Final Push

Five miles before camp, there was a stream crossing, and I didn't see an easy way to get to the other side. With the condition my feet were in, I wanted to avoid getting them wet at all costs. I opted to get a running start and jump across to a rock on the other side.

While I successfully made it across, I misjudged the landing, and the pointed edge of the rock dug into the arch of my foot. The pain overtook my body, and I collapsed onto the ground. Hammer found me sitting there 15 minutes later, my foot still throbbing. With his assistance, I managed to get back on my feet, but it hurt so much that I was moving at a useless pace. We soon set up camp because it didn't seem worthwhile to continue at that turtle-like pace. I took two Ibuprofen to reduce the swelling. This was only the third time I used Ibuprofen all year. Pain relievers were something I used sparingly because it's easy to become dependent on them while enduring a thru-hike, and pain is an unavoidable part of the journey. After popping my pills, I retired to bed, hoping my foot would feel better in the morning.

And it did. It still hurt, but it was significantly better than it was the night before. I commenced the day's hike with a 2,000-foot climb — feeling better than expected. As anticipated, the scene from the top of Fire Creek Pass reaffirmed my belief that while the climbs in Glacier Peaks were challenging, they were rewarded with wide-spanning, lush, epic views. While traversing one section of snow, I postholed straight through to a cavern below and did a face plant into the snow. I learned my lesson and tried to walk around snow patches after that.

After Fire Creek Pass, we descended 2,500 feet, only to go 2,500 feet back up. Before we began the climb, I needed to gather some water because my bottles were empty, and I was thirsty.

This proved to be the most difficult-to-get water I'd ever seen. It was a raging river with large rocks lining the banks. I contorted my body to narrowly avoid falling in, while leaning over a rock on my stomach, in order to just barely get the tip of my water bottle into the spray zone of the water. It was a solid abdominal workout, just holding there long enough to get the bottle filled with the splashing water.

After my acrobatics exercise, we took a short break on the bridge, and Tim Olson rolled up. He was an ultrarunner that was going for the Fastest Known Time, or speed record, on the PCT. He was doing it supported, which meant he had a crew and often didn't carry much more than water and a few snacks, but he still had to average over 50 miles a day. I didn't realize it was him, until we started hiking again, and Hammer pointed it out to me. Tim caught up to us once we reached the top of the climb. Hammer and I were then proud to keep up with him for a half mile before we decided that was enough.

Shortly after our running stint, we stopped to get more water. While we were sitting and filtering, we saw another figure approaching in a systemized and unrelenting manner — it was Terminator. After a lot of sarcastic joking about our frustration that we'd been caught, Hammer broke out his used car salesman techniques and convinced Terminator to finish with us, rather than pass us and leave us in his dust.

I was thrilled to add a third member to the crew. Other than just being able to meet someone new, it was good to have a third. I loved Hammer like a brother, but by this point, we were like a middle-aged married couple after spending so much time together. I don't think either of us could say anything without the other one mocking him or having some sort of smartass rebuke. It was good to add new blood.

When we got to camp, I went down to the creek to fill up on water, but it was a total waste of time. The water had so much rock dust in it from glacial melting that it looked like milk and would've clogged my filter. I had to dump it. On the way back to camp, my leg started to burn and felt like something was stabbing it. I touched some stinging nettle — a pernicious and painful plant that hurts for hours after touching it. I went to bed with another new pain, but luckily, it had subsided by the morning.

Terminator proved to be an excellent rooster and an invaluable motivator, ensuring we rose earlier than usual, and adhered to our planned schedule. However, I soon found myself separated from both Hammer and Terminator, as we embarked on a challenging 3,500-foot climb at the start of the day. Their speed on inclines surpassed mine, leading to the initial distance between us.

Around 1:30 p.m., a southbound hiker said she had a message for me. They were going to take the bus into Stehekin at 6:15 p.m. Initially, I was a little upset, because if I had known that originally, I would've gotten up earlier to be there on time. But that anger and self-pity lasted about three seconds. I decided that I was going to get to the road, get lucky with a hitch, and surprise them in town.

I had to average just above 3 mph to get there by 7:30 p.m., which I felt would give me a good chance at a hitch before sunset. With ten miles remaining, my left foot started intensely hurting again. My pace slowed, and I began to get drowsy. I laid down on a log for a minute, resigning to give up and take a catnap, but then snapped. *You're being a bitch. You have to get moving!*

After turning on a Slipknot-heavy playlist, I began zooming down the trail with newfound energy. I was still on pace to get there before 8 p.m. with plenty of daylight. But with five miles left, I stepped on a pointed rock, precisely on the arch of my foot. It was the exact same spot that I injured a few days prior when jumping across the stream and jamming it into a rock.

I screeched like a wounded dog and collapsed. After whimpering in self-pity for 20 seconds, I rose anew, now vowing to get into town to spite the trail that had been trying its hardest to stop me. Limping and embarrassingly slow, I pushed forward for another half mile, before finally succumbing. I resorted to my fourth dose of Ibuprofen for the year, numbing the pain slightly.

Arriving at the road by 8:30 p.m., my hopes dwindled as I encountered an absence of cars. Resigned to setting up camp, I decided to visit the restroom first. As I was in the privy, the sound of an approaching vehicle reached my ears. Hurriedly, I sprinted back to the road, only to witness a truck driving in the opposite direction. Crestfallen, I sulked back toward the flat area to camp.

Just as I began setting up my camp, both a car and the same truck returned. Seizing the opportunity, I dashed back to the road and got a ride in the truck. It turned out that he owned a rental property and had to help a tenant who had inadvertently locked her keys inside her car. I was extremely thankful for that lady's misfortune, otherwise, I wouldn't have gotten a ride until morning. Remote wouldn't even be an appropriate word to describe this road. It was literally only traveled by the bus from town, and maybe a few cars every day that people ferried over from the mainland.

Stehekin was one of the most postcard-like towns I had ever seen. Nestled along the shores of Lake Chelan, this picturesque enclave could only be reached by ferry. I arrived just as the sun was setting, casting a radiant glow over the surroundings. Filled with excitement, I eagerly sought out Hammer and Terminator, scouring both campgrounds to no avail. Ultimately, I settled for my own campsite, reveling in the breathtaking view of the lake, as dusk quietly transformed into night.

I woke up around 9:30 a.m. to pick up my food box at the post office, and then stumbled upon Hammer and Terminator eating breakfast. There was no cell service in town, so it was fun not knowing where they'd be and having to find them. It made me think about how rare it was in my life that I couldn't rely on cell phones to find people. I'd had a cell phone since I was 14, and even before that, my parents had cell phones. There was always that ease of communication to find someone. Without cell service, I had to find people the old school way — with common sense. I had been doing it with Hammer, but we were always following the same pre-set line that was the trail, so it wasn't anything special. It was fun to live the "pre-cell phone" life while in town, where there were more places people could be.

The bus didn't leave town until 2 p.m., so we hung out, talking to people and rangers about the upcoming, growing fire, several miles east of the trail. We weren't hearing good news. So much so, that I was actually leaning towards stopping 60 miles short of the border at Rainey Pass, because there weren't any easy evacuation points after that.

After pondering for a few hours while hiking alone once I got back on trail, I decided I was going to hike on. The trail organizations were justifiably cautious, so if they didn't close the trail, it should be safe. It might not have been the best reasoning, but it was enough for me.

On the bus back to the trailhead, we stopped at the renowned Stehekin Bakery. After hearing rave reviews for months, the brief ten-minute stop felt like a primal discovery of sustenance, as we hurriedly devoured the delectable treats in a barbaric manner. Nonetheless, I was grateful for the opportunity to indulge. When we returned to the trailhead, a momentary hesitation gripped us, as none of us relished the idea of embarking on a 20-mile trek starting after 3 p.m. Eventually, we mustered the energy and reached our campsite around 10:30 p.m.

It was a grueling day of hiking, not necessarily because of the terrain, although it was tough, but because my pack felt uncomfortably heavy. Once again, I over-packed for four days of food, but I was also carrying nearly four pounds of alcohol to celebrate at the Canadian border. I felt so rough that I had to break down and drink one of my Natural Lights to cut some weight. I was truly testing the weight limits of this pack and came to understand why they recommended keeping it under 20 lbs.

Arriving at camp late, we opted to cowboy camp to save some time. Earlier in the day, Hammer gave me his ground sheet because mine was torn in four pieces, and he said he didn't need his. I told him that he better not come crawling back asking for it. In his defense, he didn't ask for it back, even though he really needed it to cowboy camp. I got a good laugh out of it while I was laying comfortably on the ground with his sheet below me.

We woke up knowing it had to be a big day. We had to cover 90 miles in two days. It was 60 miles to the border, and then 30 miles back to the nearest road in the U.S., since the Canadian border was legally closed. Hammer was Canadian and couldn't even walk into his home country.

The terrain didn't assist us on our already challenging journey. We started out with a 2,000-foot climb, and then had another 2,500-foot climb later. The constant rocky terrain aggravated my already-injured foot. Whenever I would step on a rock wrong, a sharp pain shot through me, and I would let out a yelp like a dog that was just stepped on.

Reaching Hart's Pass, the last road in the U.S., late in the day, I left my extra food in a hiker box for others, since my pack was still too heavy for 1.5 days. While we were there, Tim Olson and his crew drove by in a car. He had just gotten back from finishing the PCT and setting the record, finishing in less than 52 days. Seeing him fresh off his accomplishment served as a motivating reminder for us to keep pushing forward.

We woke up the next day as men on a mission. We had to do 25 miles to the Canadian border, and then turn around and do 30 miles back to Hart's Pass. Gary — the hiker that Hammer and I met at White Pass in Washington — was a saint and offered to pick us up the following day, but it had to be by 10 a.m. that day because he was busy later.

All I could think about all day was that it had to be a 55-mile day in less than 30 hours. We simply had to do it. The task was both thrilling and daunting. I knew I would have to hike continuously to meet the mileage. Hammer and Terminator might be able to take short breaks and snatch a few hours of sleep. But given my slow pace due to my foot injury, it seemed likely that I would have to forgo sleep altogether.

Again, the terrain didn't do me any favors. It was rocky all day, which limited my ability to go fast and intensified the foot pain I already had. There was also some tough climbing early on, but I was justifying it by telling myself we would get to do it downhill on the way back.

After 2,653 miles, we reached the Canadian Border around 4:30 p.m. I felt relief, but not really joy. I had been thinking about this day since I started at the Mexican border, but all I could think about now was going 30 miles back and staying on schedule. It was a crazy, momentous achievement, but my mind didn't want to celebrate. It only wanted to focus on what was next — and that was getting back to the road before we missed our ride, while a wildfire kept approaching.

I managed to push that out of my mind after the initial resistance. I had just walked from Mexico to Canada in 90 days! Just three years prior, I would've thought that to be an impossible venture, much less something I would ever do — much less something I would do in only three months!

So, we sat there, enjoying having reached the U.S.–Canadian border. Even though it was completely arbitrary, man-made, and really had no importance in the wild mountains, it had immense meaning for us. It was the end of the line.

After soaking in the scene for a bit, I turned on my satellite phone to let my parents know I finished. I discovered I had some messages from our man, Gary. He informed me that they closed the road 30 miles back, so we would either have to go back 60 miles to the next available road, or take some side trails for roughly 45 miles to a road that was still open. This was a historic vibe check. The side trails weren't the PCT, so we knew they would be a little rougher, but we decided to go with that option since it was shorter.

Our moment of victory was instantly shattered. It was now going to be significantly harder to make it back to civilization. Regardless, we put our packs back on and got to work. I hid a Smirnoff Ice in the container with the logbook for the next lucky finisher, and we began our hike backwards.

Thankfully, Gary assured us that he would be able to pick us up late the next day because there was no way we would complete our new route by 10 a.m. Part of me was relieved that we didn't have to hike a 55-mile day, covering 30 miles after 5:30 p.m., but I also felt a tinge of disappointment. I was thinking about it all day, and I was excited for the challenge. I even told Hammer and Terminator that I was prepared to try coffee for the first time in my life that night when I needed the energy!

I was mainly relieved that I would now be able to sleep. I knew it would still be a late night. Hammer and I both dropped extra gear, like our sleeping bags, sleeping pads, tents, etc., 15 miles before the border to cut some weight on the last stretch. We thought we were going back to Hart's Pass the same night, so we just planned on picking it up on our way.

Since plans changed, we had to make it back there to get our sleeping gear to camp. That gear played a significant role in our decision to take the side trails to a road. I would be lying if I said we didn't think about just illegally hiking into Canada when we heard they closed Hart's Pass because of the fire. Hammer was even explaining places along the border where we might be able sneak back into the U.S. We were all liking the idea more and more because it involved less hiking, until I remembered that Hammer and I had hundreds of dollars' worth of gear sitting by a tree 15 miles back. We had no choice but to turn around.

For some reason, my reassurance from the morning — that it would all feel downhill on the way back since it all felt uphill then — did not come to fruition. Around 10 p.m., extreme fatigue began to set in. Drowsiness began to spread like a virus. Our conversations dwindled, and we found ourselves slipping on rocks frequently. Hammer took a nasty fall near a ledge, but thankfully managed to avoid sliding down the mountainside. A few miles before reaching camp, while climbing a 1,000-foot ascent, we decided to take a "two-minute break." However, what was meant to be a short rest turned into ten minutes of sitting on the trail, fighting the urge to doze off. We could have all slept right there, regardless of the fact that we were on a ledge with a lethal fall directly below.

Sensing that nobody wanted to move, I started playing some tunes from my phone to inject some energy into the group. It worked, and we pushed forward, arriving at camp around midnight. Despite our weariness, our spirits revived as we jammed out to Katy Perry's "Last Friday Night." Terminator was taken aback by how Hammer and I knew every word perfectly. It was an unforgettable end to the day.

We treated ourselves to some well-deserved rest, relishing in seven glorious hours of sleep — a luxury, considering we had been getting six or less hours during most of our time in Washington. Staying true to ourselves, Hammer and I slept past our planned wake-up time. We didn't want to break tradition on the last day on trail.

We hiked a couple of miles back to Holman Pass, and then hopped off the PCT, and onto the PNT (Pacific Northwest Trail). We knew it was going to be less maintained and more rugged, and our expectations were immediately confirmed.

There was a downed tree within the first three feet, and the first six miles were littered with blowdowns, which brought our progress to a crawl. The climbing was tough. It wasn't graded like the PCT — it was actually steep. Washington felt pretty tough, but I was worried that I'd had it too good for too long with the generously graded trail. I feared that going back to the AT, which was uncomfortably steep, was going to be a shock when I did. These side trails enhanced that fear.

Late in the day, I noticed a cut, high up on a nearby mountain, and joked that it was our trail. I figured that it was actually a water-made cut, so it would be a funny joke because it wasn't accurate. We all got a good laugh out of it. As we kept hiking, we kept getting closer to it. We all kept getting quieter, until it was silent, and we realized that it actually was our trail.

Then Hammer aptly declared, "This is such a stupid fucking trail."

It was absurdly steep, climbing straight up the side of the mountain on loose rock, which cascaded down with every step. I laughed most of the way up because it was incomparably steep in relation to the PCT.

Around 10:30 p.m., I spotted a big sign with trail information — the kind that is normally right by parking lots.

I rejoiced, anticipating the imminent arrival of a parking lot. However, as soon as we passed the sign, the trail abruptly disappeared. We were faced with two options: either descend and ford the wide, swiftly flowing river (an extremely undesirable choice), or clamber over a massive fallen tree and try to find the trail after it. We opted for the latter.

While maneuvering over the tree, I absentmindedly placed my hand on a branch for support. I heard a faint hum and looked down to find myself inches away from a hole in the tree teeming with hundreds of bees.

In a panic akin to Chris Farley in Tommy Boy, I started yelling, "BEES! BEES!" while hastily descending. In the process, I unintentionally shook the branch, further agitating the bees. Poor Hammer was still behind me, and he had to rush through the swarm to avoid getting stung. Miraculously, we both emerged unscathed.

We pressed on for half a mile before reluctantly admitting defeat and turning back. Deep down, we knew we should have taken the river crossing, even though we vehemently wanted to avoid it. Returning near the fallen tree, we finally resolved to ford the river. I had planned on hugging the bank, scouting for an ideal crossing spot, and playing it smart.

Then Hammer spontaneously plunged into the water, exclaiming, "We gotta go!" Terminator and I followed suit. Stepping into the river, I could feel the plantar warts on my foot swelling up like water balloons on a faucet. The water wasn't deep, but it was fast flowing. Thankfully, we were all strong hikers, so it wasn't a big deal.

Once we got across the river, we got lost for 15 minutes before we found the parking lot. We couldn't find any trail, so we were just aimlessly wandering through the woods. It also didn't help that we had no maps for this section and didn't even know which direction the parking lot was.

It was a high-stress situation, to say the least. I was pretty angry, and Hammer was ready to explode. But all turned out well. After enough wandering, we came upon a bridge that led to a parking lot where we reunited with Gary. He greeted us with Dr. Pepper and Little Caesars.

What more could you ask for?

I felt like I was finally done with the PCT. There wouldn't be any more closures, side trails, or extra hiking. I was on my way back to civilization, and I was ready to enjoy it for a few days. After lounging around Gary's house like freeloaders, and a lot of persuading on my part, to try to get Hammer and Terminator to hike the CDT with me, we said goodbye, and I hopped on a train to East Glacier, Montana.

It was time to finish off the CDT.

Phase IV:

Continental Divide Trail

Canada to Monarch Pass

July 30th–September 28th

Southbound

In East Glacier, MT, I took some much-needed rest, allowing my worn-out body to recover from the challenges of the Pacific Crest Trail. From the Sierra onwards, the trail exacted a heavy toll on me — a blizzard, an approaching fire, scorching heat, decaying feet, an army of mosquitoes, and the fear of a stress fracture. I was ready for some hardcore rest.

It was tough to get a motel room in the busy summer season. After four full motels, I found one with a vacancy. I was even lucky enough to be joined by my friend Evan, who was road tripping out west and stopped in Glacier to spend a couple of days with me on his way home. I got the sense he wanted to explore the beautiful park. All I wanted to do was lie around in the motel room with my feet airing out, while moving as little as possible, and eating and drinking as much as possible. After a couple of days of putting weight back on my emaciated frame, it was time to get back on trail.

I had to start a day later than I wanted to. The permitting system in Glacier National Park wasn't ideal for thru-hikers because you had to reserve campsites, and there was limited availability at each site. Normally, when I started a day of hiking, I didn't know where I'd end up. Realistically, I could cover anywhere from 25 to 45 miles.

On the day I wanted to start, there were no permits available for the northern campsites. I went back the next day and was able to secure one for the following day. It took some convincing for the rangers to give me permits to hike 30–35 miles a day, but eventually they gave in. I didn't know how to say, "Don't worry about me. I've already hiked over 5,000 miles this year. I can handle it," without sounding like an asshole.

On July 30th, after four days of rest following the completion of the PCT, I headed to the Canadian border to commence my southbound journey along the Continental Divide Trail. I was incredibly fortunate that my friend agreed to meet me there and provide transportation to the starting point. Without him, the logistics would have been a nightmare. Due to the pandemic, the U.S.–Canadian border was closed, resulting in a deserted road. During our entire 80-minute drive, we didn't encounter a single car.

After pounding a Coors Light at the border, and saying goodbye to Evan, I began hiking southbound on the CDT. It felt good, but strange. So much was the same — tall mountains, lush grass, and big trees. Yet, everything felt different. The air had a distinct quality; the surroundings felt more pristine; and the trail was more rugged right from the start. However, the primary difference was that I immediately sensed the danger of being in grizzly bear country. I didn't see any, but I was more on edge than usual. I couldn't go a few minutes without the thought of the large beast entering my mind. This was the first time all year that I felt a strong sense of danger.

There were a lot of rattlesnakes in southern California, which I actually feared more than bears, but this felt different. Maybe the idea of being mauled to death was bothering me more than slowly dying of venom. Or maybe, it was the idea that I might actually have to get into a fight with a grizzly bear. The bear scene from *The Revenant* played on repeat in my head.

Or maybe it was just the fact that I was well over halfway done with the year, and was undeniably on pace to achieve my goal. Maybe I was scared because things were going so well. I had just under 2,000 miles left on the CDT and 500 left on the AT. That was plenty of time for something to go wrong and spoil my aspirations. Maybe getting attacked by a bear and ending up in the hospital would be that trip-ender. Whatever it was, I felt different immediately upon stepping on the Continental Divide Trail.

Even amidst my uneasiness, it would've been hard to ignore the beauty of Glacier National Park. From Red Gap Pass to Poia Lake, every passing glance was breathtaking. This undeniable beauty had a therapeutic effect, allowing me to escape the hamster wheel of self-doubt that plagues one's mind when thinking about an intimidatingly ambitious goal.

There were wildfires in Montana and Idaho reportedly making the area smoky, but it wasn't bad on my first day. Though a faint haze lingered in the distance, visibility remained relatively clear. I anticipated the situation to change, considering I wasn't even close to a fire yet. I wanted to relish the mostly unobstructed skies while I still had the chance. A northbound hiker I encountered mentioned that Montana had been smoky throughout his entire journey. Although disheartening to hear, it was cool to witness someone on the final day of their trail while I embarked on my own beginning.

I was surprised when I got to my camp for the night at Many Glacier. The rangers got permission to "overbook" me for the night. Yet, when I showed up, it didn't look overbooked. At my campsite alone, there was room for at least eight tents. I couldn't help but feel frustrated at the delay in starting my hike, assuming the situation was similar the previous night. The rangers did their best to assist me, but the park's system simply wasn't designed with thru-hikers in mind. Thru-hikers will sleep in a ditch to hike the mileage they want. I would, at least.

The following morning, my dislike for people grew stronger as I had to wait 20 minutes to use the bathroom. I then proceeded to hike amidst a pseudo-parade along Swiftcurrent Lake, constantly asking people to let me pass. As I ventured farther from the parking lot, the crowd thinned out. Beyond the initial picturesque view, many people would turn back and return to their cars. After half a mile, the majority would consider their trip completed, deeming a mile to be their limit. Once I walked a mile away from the parking lot, solitude returned. *Why should I do all this walking when I can drive my car on neatly paved roads, take in views from overlook parking spots, and pump exhaust into this clean mountain air?*

In the afternoon, I stopped to chat with a cute day hiker and asked how she was doing. She jokingly said she was dying, but I assured her she was close to the parking lot and offered her some water. She declined, but after I moved on, I chided myself. *What a fool! You didn't know when your next water was, and you were going to give it away to someone that is nearly back at their car!* It's astounding how stupid a man can get when he sees a pretty girl.

It was a warm and exposed climb going up to Piegan Pass. I was sweating like a greased hog and couldn't wear sunglasses because they quickly became coated in sweat, and I couldn't see. After I got back down in elevation, the terrain was mostly flat, but it wasn't easy. For ten straight miles, I trudged through dense overgrowth, which I was surprised to see in a national park. I figured no day hikers used this trail because it wasn't scenic and was far from a parking lot.

Before getting to camp, I came upon a blind chipmunk in the middle of the trail, frozen like a statue. He refused to budge, and I nearly stepped on him before lightly tapping him with my trekking pole. When I arrived at the backcountry camp, I met a few fellow campers out for the night. One was named Kim. She lived in the northeast and offered to help me on the AT. We talked for 20 minutes while they shared some wine, and I shared some stories. The soothing buzz from the wine began to rock me to sleep as my bedtime approached.

Before retiring to bed, I went down to Red Eagle Lake to fetch some water, and it was the most serene experience all day. It was a calming natural beauty — the pristine tranquil lake, surrounded by pines on some parts while others were burnt to a crisp; life and death around this body of water which fuels life. In the lake, I saw a perfect reflection of the glowing red mountain behind it that was illuminated by the setting sun. I saw six elk on the other side of the lake, interchanging between staring at me and drinking the same water I was. An eagle landed on a dead tree near me, and scouted for several minutes before swooping down to the water and shattering the perfect mirror world.

It felt like I had lived a lifetime in a few minutes. Nothing happened, yet I felt so much. Life was beautiful. Life was simple.

After enduring a restless night, constantly awakened by the abrasive gusts of wind flinging sand into my face, I reluctantly made my way to the privy. The stench that assailed my senses was undeniably one of the most repulsive odors I had encountered throughout the entire year. Eager to escape the unpleasantness, I started my hike, fully aware that it was going to be a demanding day. I had set my sights on conquering at least two passes, possibly three, and faced a decision on whether to stay at Two Medicine Campground and secure a walk-up spot or press on to exit the park and find a free camping spot beyond the third pass.

There were a few oddities during the day. Surprisingly, I was moving faster on the steep climbs than on the flat ground I had covered beforehand. There was a lot of overgrowth on the flats, but on the uphill, not as much foliage could grow over the trail. Another oddity was that I noticed the smoke must have been more prevalent than I thought. My arms were black and grimy with ash moistened by sweat. The last was that I ran into an old man who said he was hiking north on the CDT, yet, he didn't know where he was or how far he had to go. He didn't even know he was in Glacier. When I told him the way, he asked where "the one really beautiful spot" was. From what I saw, that was the whole park.

When I got to the second pass of the day, I paused for ten minutes to decide if I should take the Dawson Pass Alternate or stay on the official CDT. While the alternate was more scenic, it would add miles and was said to be tougher hiking than the official trail. With the timing and miles I had to do, I stuck with the CDT and rode it down into the valley. One benefit of the CDT was having options like that because there were so many alternates that you could make your own adventure along the way. The CDT was different from the AT and PCT in many regards, but the availability of alternates was one of the key differences — along with grizzly bears.

At Two Medicine Campground, it started to get dark. Since I didn't want to pay for a campsite there, I opted to push over the third pass of the day and exit the park to camp for free. I didn't see much after dark, except a few stars though the black clouds of smoke.

In the morning, I picked up my food box in East Glacier and got a 16-inch pizza at 9 a.m. to start off the day. I was pleasantly surprised when I asked the guy behind the counter if they served pizza, and he said he could make one. After an existential first day leaving the border, similar to the AT, I felt much better now, sitting down, and eating pizza with clarity. All I had to do was just keep doing what I was doing: ignore this monumental endeavor and only focus on the next resupply.

Leaving town, I brought food for a six-day carry, but was thinking about rationing it to last eight days to avoid wasting time with a tough hitch. My pack felt heavy getting back on trail, but my mind felt light, unburdened by the fears I had been allowing to creep in recently.

Cloudy skies provided some respite from the heat as I embarked on the day's hike. The sky teased rain all day but only sprinkled a little. The terrain was predominantly flat, occasionally punctuated by pockets of overgrowth that made for challenging progress with my heavy pack. Most of the day either smelled like dirty feet (from some plant that smelled weird) or horse feces (from horse feces).

Along the way, I encountered ten stream crossings, having to ford four of them barefoot and skillfully rock-hop across the rest. Although the water levels were not high or swift, and the temperature not as bone-chilling as the fords in the Sierra, the barefoot crossings proved painful with every step on the uneven rocks covering the bottom of the streams. On a positive note, keeping my shoes and socks dry spared my feet from getting saturated, which was particularly beneficial for the plantar warts I was still nursing. During one crossing, I spent ten minutes painstakingly arranging rocks to bridge a gap that was too wide. Regretfully, I inadvertently dipped my toe in the water when the rock I stood on gave way under my weight. My foolish idea of outfoxing nature was ineffective.

The next day marked the beginning of my hatred for the Bob Marshall Wilderness. The whole day seemed to be hiking in burnt valleys, and the only life in the forest was all the annoying overgrowth that ensconced the trail. Copious amount of vegetation made each step feel like a resistance training exercise. I didn't even remember passing any sort of open area all day where setting up camp would be possible, so I had to stop early when I found an acceptable spot on an island nestled between two streams. Despite its rocky terrain and less-than-ideal location, it stood as the only spot not engulfed in thick brush.

Given that I was traversing grizzly country, I had been diligently hanging my food in trees each night. It was a real pain, and there were few things I hated more than extra work at the end of a long day, but I was doing it. It was a half hour endeavor every night, but tonight was the first night where I didn't hang my food — but not by choice. All the trees in the vicinity lacked branches, reduced to mere charred matchsticks by previous wildfires. Faced with the prospect of sleeping in close proximity to my food, I devised a new strategy for times when hanging my food wasn't a possibility. I would hide my "odor-proof" food sacks in the brush about 20 feet away from my tent. I wanted to be far enough away, so that if a bear came, he wouldn't be snooping around for the food *inside* my tent. But I would also be close enough where I could hear animals and scare them away, so they wouldn't eat my food. Being five days away from a town, with no food, and unlikely to see anyone, might be just as bad as getting attacked by a bear. However, this system was far from foolproof. Every time I woke up during the night and heard something moving, my first thought was that some animal was feasting on my food.

I awoke the next morning to find everything inside my tent saturated. While I had anticipated some dampness due to camping near water, I hadn't expected it to practically rain inside my tent. The day started off chilly and damp, but my spirits were lifted when I ran into a couple of northbound hikers. As the sun illuminated the gray sky, I began shedding layers and enjoying the warmth.

It was another day of laborious hiking through overgrowth, except this time, I faced the added challenge of climbing over fallen trees. I was expecting them to be much worse based on reports from other hikers, but like many times during the year, the reality wasn't as bad as the hype. Right at the end of the day, it started thundering overhead, and there were some sprinkles that made me consider stopping at a poor but serviceable campsite. Without much thought, as usual, I pushed on to the next legitimate campsite a few miles down the trail.

After hiking for a little longer, the rain grew heavier. The wind picked up, and then it started to hail. The hail was the size of whoppers (the candy, not the sandwich). It hurt! Being in a burn area, I sprinted 100 yards until I found a tree with branches that offered some semblance of shelter. I stood there for ten minutes, but the hail only intensified. Even under the tree, I was getting thumped with painful pellets. I tried to protect myself by covering my head with my hands, but the impact was hurting my hands, forcing me to take breaks and alternate where I'd let the pain strike.

The hail eventually transitioned to a heavy downpour, and the hailstones did a dreadfully fantastic job of holding the water in pools to make the whole trail a river. The last two miles to camp were utterly miserable. I was trying to avoid stepping in the deep puddles, but still trying to walk at a decent pace, sidestepping constantly, and having wet feet regardless. Unsurprisingly, when I took my socks off, the plantar warts had swelled up with fury. They had been slowly disappearing, but this setback seemed to have revived them.

I naively slept in, hoping that my gear would be drier if I laid there longer and let the sun come out. That hope was futile. Everything was still drenched, and I was moving especially slowly because I was grimacing with every step, weaving through overgrowth on the trail soaked with ice-cold water. After a few minutes, my shoes had puddles in them again, and my shorts looked like they had just been through the washer.

When I escaped the dousing overgrowth, I took a long break and strew out my gear to dry in the sunlight, albeit my shoes and socks remained soggy all day from those few miles in the dewy morning. The plantar warts had now spread to both feet. I was lucky they weren't painful with as long as they lingered and as bad as they looked.

Most of the day was hiking along the Chinese Wall, a mountainous slab of rock that runs over 20 miles of the divide. It was an impressive phenomenon to see, but I felt like I couldn't escape it. All day, I'd look to my right, and there it was. It felt like I was hardly moving. I camped by a stream and slept by a lovely bubbling brook that sounded extensively more soothing than my noise machine at home with the same sound. As I went to bed, I heard an animal rustling around in the brush nearby, and just hoped it was a deer, because I didn't want to deal with it.

Waking up dry for the first time in several days, I rejoiced. I forgot how much I took it for granted until there were a few consecutive wet days, and then I realized how simple a blessing it was to be dry. It's like never appreciating being healthy until you get sick.

After a few barefoot fords and again hiking in a burn area all day, I ended the day early after 27 miles. Despite being plagued by campsite anxiety, due to the overgrowth and remnants of the burn area, I took solace in the fact that I was officially out of the Bob Marshall Wilderness and hoped things would improve soon.

I made a vow to come back to Montana some other time. With as remote as it was, I expected crisp views of everything. But with the smoke from the fires, the skies went from a black to a light gray in the morning, remained hazy all day, and then gradually shifted to dark gray in the evening.

The following day got off to a rough start. I overslept by 90 minutes. Once I got moving, I took a wrong turn, but rather than just turn around, I thought I'd bushwhack back to the trail to save time. After 30 minutes of forging my own path, I realized I did so in the wrong direction. My brain was so used to hiking northward all year, I instinctively went there. I felt like an idiot.

Even after this debacle, it ended up being one of my favorite days of the entire year. I climbed to a ridge, leaving behind the burnt valleys I had been hiking, and I finally got to do what I came to the CDT to do — ridge walk on the divide of the country. After a little climbing early in the day, the views were constantly stunning. The smoke seemed to ease back solely for my personal enjoyment. It was funny how pretty scenery could make up for everything else. That day was around 7,000 feet of climbing, which I'd normally hate, but I was enamored all day and didn't realize how much climbing I'd done until the end of the day.

The only minor downside to the day was the overwhelming presence of crickets, making me feel as if I had stepped into ancient Egypt. The area was teeming with them, and the strong wind caused them to leap into the air, and be propelled 30 feet. I found myself constantly pelted by these resilient insects, and they had a knack for sticking to my clothes and hair. It was an unexpected nuisance, but I couldn't help but find it amusing to see how far they would fly, carried by the force of the wind.

Physically, I felt remarkably better. It was the first time since early Oregon that I didn't endure excruciating foot pain throughout the entire day. Feeling an improvement in my condition, I even managed to run for a short while. It may not have been much, but it was a promising sign, like a traffic light changing from red to green right as you approach it. I could only hope that this positive trend would continue.

A mile before camp, I saw something off in the distance. There was a group of eight brawny creatures standing on the trail where I would be hiking in the morning. I couldn't see in sharp detail from that far away. The only thing I knew for sure was that they were brown and looked big, but I didn't think grizzly bears typically gathered in groups on a grassy mountainside. It might've been cows or elk. I wasn't sure.

I set up camp a half mile away and hoped it wasn't a gang of grizzly bears. It was so windy, I assured myself they wouldn't even be able to smell me since the wind was whipping fiercely in every direction. I camped at Lewis and Clark Pass, where the wind exceeded 70 mph. It was the first time I had to use all the extra lines and cinches on my tent to stake it down. It didn't seem to matter. The wind was so strong, it still flapped incessantly. It was difficult to fall asleep with thunderous flapping every few seconds.

After being all high and mighty about the ridge walk yesterday, I was soon reminded of its drawbacks. Around 11 a.m., I got down to Rogers Pass as the sky looked scary and it was starting to storm. I checked the weather forecast, and it looked pretty bad — over an 80% chance of thunderstorms the rest of the day. Since the upcoming trail was still ridge walking, I decided to avoid that in an all-day thunderstorm. I road walked at a lower elevation to preferably avoid getting struck by lightning. It was a few extra miles, but I felt much safer than being at the highest elevation in the surrounding area with lightning striking all around me.

Most of the day was uninspiring and uncomfortable. I was able to get back on the official trail later in the day after hanging out in a pit toilet to wait out the worst of the storm. When I got going again, the sky still didn't look encouraging, but at least it wasn't booming anymore. It rained off and on, which wasn't ideal, but it was preferable to the painful hail of a few days ago. It was also chilly with the biting wind. My hands were numb most of the day. I realized I would probably need gloves soon, even though it was August. The divide was unpredictable and unforgiving.

I also lost my pack cover again. This was the second time I had carelessly lost it. Of course, I didn't realize it until I needed it. Thankfully, I had a garbage bag lining the inside of my pack to provide a layer of water protection and keep my things from getting thoroughly soaked.

It was a good thing I got ahead on sleep at the beginning of this trail. Despite hiking late into the night, I still pushed myself to rise early the following morning. I felt a heightened sense of urgency, as I had been misled by my power bank falsely indicating a remaining charge when it was dead. My priority was to reach town as soon as possible to recharge my electronics. It was the most cautious I had ever been with my phone usage.

On other trails, a dead battery would have been an inconvenience, but navigating was usually relatively straightforward, aside from the snow-covered challenges of the Sierra. The CDT presented a different scenario — navigational checks became more frequent, and the seemingly obvious path often turned out to be incorrect.

On that day, I limited my phone usage to junctions, ensuring I followed the correct route. Serendipitously, I arrived at the road leading to Elliston and managed to secure a hitch just before sunset. I had the opportunity to charge my phone and power bank overnight, ensuring they would be topped off by morning.

After picking up my food box, which also contained a pair of shoes, I felt like a new man. The shoes I had been wearing had endured over 1,000 miles, so I was ready to get fresh kicks. After buying a new pair of sunglasses at the store because I lost mine again, I got a hitch back to the trail in the bed of a rusty 2000s pickup truck zooming 80 mph down the highway. As we approached the trail crossing, I gave a few strong taps on the side of the truck to let them know it was time to stop.

When they dropped me off, they repeatedly offered to bring me into Helena. "There ain't nothin for ya out there." They thought I was homeless and had no idea what I was doing here in the middle of nowhere. Rather than try to explain to them again what the CDT was, I thanked them and assured them I'd be alright.

It was another day full of dirt road walking, a recurring feature of the trail as of late. Some thru hikers aren't fans of road walking, but I loved it as long as it was on dirt roads. I knew it wouldn't ever become excessively steep or pose any serious climbs. The dirt road would nearly always be void of fallen trees, and oftentimes, it had more constant open views. I liked dirt roads. With the smooth terrain, I was flying most of the day compared to my normal speed. Having fresh food and being blessed with good weather again also helped. Ever since that storm, the weather had turned a corner. Nights were refreshingly cool, while daytime temperatures pleasantly remained in the 70s, accompanied by a gentle breeze. It was a stark contrast to the perpetually scorching conditions I had experienced for much of the summer.

As the day drew to a close, I found myself in a forested area as the vibrant colors of the sky radiated through the trees, presenting a breathtaking display of at least seven different shades of color, ranging from pink to orange. I hiked past dusk until I found a serviceable campsite. When

I did stop, the site turned out to be a bit more narrow than I had preferred. My tent jutted right up against two trees like an obese person trying to squeeze through a turnstile gate.

I awoke in the middle of the night to something rustling near my tent. Instinctively, I began making noise, causing the intruder to run away. The rumbling, stumbling, and bumbling sounds indicated a weighty presence — possibly a bear, a moose, or an extraordinarily large elk. Although still half-asleep, I found solace in the fact that my "not too close, not too far" system for storing my food bag without trees had proved effective.

The next day was a boring day, but in the best of ways — it was unremarkably pleasant. The terrain was trouble-free, and the weather was benign. There was a 20-mile stretch without water, and it wasn't even challenging with the mild temperature. Before the dry stretch, the last water source was a cow trough. It had been a while since I had to pull from one of those, but thankfully there was cold, clear, and clean water flowing into the trough. The delightful water made loading up for the long carry easy. I even filled up an old Dr. Pepper bottle I brought. It still had a residual taste of the sweet nectar which was satiating in every sense of the word.

After coming across a mountain biker who was lost, I helped him figure out where he was, so he could get back to his truck. It always amused me when day hikers, bikers, or other people asked thru-hikers for directions, advice, or information on the area. In reality, thru-hikers are often the least informed people about the surrounding area. We know which direction we're going and the line to follow on our map. We might occasionally know about a side trail to a scenic view or a water source, but usually not. Thru-hikers are singularly set on their goal of "hike this trail," and that is it. Yet, because of the incredible feat they are attempting, they're looked to as knowledgeable experts by many people.

Using Guthook and my backup Ley Maps, I was able to study the biker's description and help him locate his truck, which felt rewarding. It was a chance to pay back a fraction of the kindness that strangers had shown me throughout the year. Later, I was rewarded when other bikers insisted I take some water from them because they had too much. *Karma works quickly.*

In the evening, some dirt bikers stopped to talk to me and were shocked about my thru-hiking of the CDT. They knew about the trail, but just kept saying, "That's crazy you're going the whole way." They said it at least seven times. I never knew what to say when people said something like that, other than, "Yup." Little did they know, I was going the whole way three times. If I said that, their heads might've exploded, much like mine only three years earlier when I learned of the AT and PCT, and, more so, that people actually hiked them.

Much like it had been lately, the next day was filled with a lot of cows. I never liked it when they were in a large group, staring at me in unison, seemingly discussing amongst themselves. It felt like they were formulating some sort of master plan to ruin my day, and maybe they were. On this day, they did a good job of making me lose the trail repeatedly. I frequently followed their tracks to nowhere, which looked like a trail because the CDT was exceedingly faint, unlike the AT and most of the PCT.

On the PCT in Oregon, I began to notice that there were a few tiny holes in my tent. I must've accidentally packed it up with some small rocks which created the holes. It hadn't been a problem until now, even though I was clinically paranoid about it in mosquito country. The Montana ants were getting smart and finding the holes. Recently, I kept waking up to dozens crawling on me. This happened a few times as I was camping near the road to go into Butte, MT. The major downside of camping near a road was the traffic noise, but it was funny to think back to the AT, where in some of the "backcountry" shelters I could still hear traffic nearby.

I made a conscious effort not to dwell on my AT experience for a few reasons. First, it was slightly traumatic. Second, I wanted to use this time to cultivate new thoughts rather than reminisce. But most importantly, I wanted to try to avoid comparing trails, places, and experiences constantly. We live in a time where everything has a rating; everything has a ranking; and everything is judged. I wanted to try my best to appreciate things as they were and appreciate them in the moment. But I am human, so I was not perfect at this desire. I couldn't help but compare things to other parts of the journey at times — notably, the start of this northern CDT section with the start of the AT. Both presented new concerns:

For the AT, winter hiking, and thru-hiking in general, posed a steep learning curve. For the CDT, both hiking in grizzly bear country, and the beginning of the end-of-the-year clock starting to tick, weighed on my mind. On the AT, everything seemed new, and on the CDT, everything seemed new again. Before I started hiking in Montana, I never feared bears because they were only dopey black bears, and I didn't really have to worry about my pace because the journey was too absurdly long to warrant thinking about mileages on a daily basis. Now I was in the heart of grizzly bear country, and summer was winding to an end.

It all seemed overwhelming at first. My mind ran rampant. But it all went back to the early days of the AT — stay the course. Break down the fear-inducing goal into manageable goals. *I've just got to make it to the next town. I've just got to make it to camp tonight. I've just got to take this next step.* After a couple of weeks on the AT, all that anxiety washed away, and I was only focused on getting through each day. The CDT was the same way. Early on, I was fretting over all the new perceived stresses, but after a few weeks, I was back to living in the moment and living my dream.

Summer would fade, and winter would come as it may, but that didn't mean I had to preemptively live with the eventual, and inevitable, season-changing storm looming over my head. I could still make hay while the sun was shining.

After resupplying in Butte the next day, I began a different journey. Since the border of Idaho and Montana, where the trail was supposed to go, was on fire, I had to take an alternate. I started hearing about the Big Sky Alternate back in Glacier because of the fires. Luckily, I was a late hiker, so somebody else took the time to make a massive GPX file of all the different routes on the Big Sky Alternate — of which there were many.

Given my poor experience mapping it out, I cannot imagine how long it took him. I tried doing it for five minutes before I got frustrated and quit. I downloaded Gaia, a navigation app, which would be my only source of navigation for this alternate. While I usually preferred to have two navigation sources on the CDT, such as Guthook and Ley Maps, this alternate was less traveled, and I had to make do with a single source.

Other than the excellent reviews of the alternate I was hearing and reading about, I was also enticed by its cool name. You could put "Big Sky" in front of anything, and I'd do it.

After having a small meal of four double cheeseburgers and a large fry, I left town and began the alternate. The day was mostly paved road walking after starting the alternate, and I was getting cooked, walking on the blacktop under the blazing sun, even with smoky skies.

Pleased to come across a small creek that ran under the road, I eagerly ran to it and collected water. I sat there for over 20 minutes, filtering, drinking, and filtering, and drinking. As I started to climb back up to the road, my heart dropped into my stomach — and then my stomach started churning. There was a decaying deer carcass less than ten feet above the creek I had just drank from. I felt sickened and disgusted, but it was too late to do anything now. *It'll be alright.*

Walking along dirt roads surrounded by picturesque ranch country, I questioned why my family's farm had to be in Ohio. If my ancestors had continued moving west and established a ranch in this captivating landscape, life would have been far more intriguing.

Although I doubted that the ranchers in the area desired to raise deer, I often spotted these graceful creatures grazing in their irrigated fields. As beads of sweat trickled down my face, dampening my clothes, I was tempted to emulate Alexander Supertramp and take a shower under the irrigation systems spraying tantalizing water in the fields. But I resisted the urge, fearing that trespassing may lead to getting shot.

After hiking step-for-step with a few cows for a quarter of a mile, I set up camp shortly after reentering a national forest. Right after I threw all of my stuff in my tent and was about to crawl in, I noticed a massive wasp with the biggest stinger I'd ever seen trapped inside my tent. This guy was an idiot. I spent 20 minutes banging the walls of my tent with the door ajar, and he still wouldn't fly out. He eventually landed on my sleeping bag, and I yanked it out into the open air to liberate the intruder. After disposing of the unwanted guest, I settled in to go to sleep.

The strain of pushing for big mileage days was starting to take its toll. The next morning, I recalled waking up to my alarm but immediately turning it off, lacking even the slightest intention of getting up. I began my day an hour later than planned, feeling lazy from my delay.

Shortly after setting off, I encountered a herd of cattle, and whether it was their presence or the area itself, an unbearable stench overwhelmed me, causing me to gag and nearly vomit. Not much later, I stumbled upon the carcass of a dead animal, possibly a badger. I didn't dare approach too closely due to the putrid smell and the swarm of 10,000 flies buzzing around it. The lifeless creature was sprawled over a rock in a peculiar and unnatural manner, like some sort of sacrifice. I was confused about what happened, but primarily wanted to escape the foul stench.

After regaining my composure, I encountered the Bennett family, who was hiking northbound. This inspiring family of six, accompanied by their dog, had already conquered the Pacific Crest Trail and the Pacific Northwest Trail before tackling the CDT. This wasn't their first rodeo. Few families in the world share the bond and level of connectedness that they had with each other after hiking thousands of miles together and overcoming continual hardships as a family.

As an individual, I later struggled to overcome some of the challenging climbs. After the first one, I descended into a valley and trespassed aggressively. I came to a junction where there were two trails. One looked like it meandered off to the left of where I was supposed to go, and one looked like a straight shot down. I took the straight shot, of course, but when I reached the bottom, I was in somebody's backyard. I prayed they weren't home, and quickly ran and jumped over the fence to get on the dirt road in front of their house. It probably saved some time, but I was waiting for someone to come out with a shotgun and ask what the hell I was doing.

Challenges mounted throughout the day. I thought the worst climb of the day was 2,000 feet, but on the way up, I realized I had miscounted topographic lines. It was over 3,000 feet. It was rocky all day, so it was slow moving. The terrain also intensified my foot pain, which had been manageable as of late. To compound matters, I missed a turn and only realized my error after hiking an additional half mile before retracing my steps. There were few things I hated more than extra miles, especially because of my own negligence.

When I was dead-tired and ready to be done for the night, I encountered another setback. As my tent was halfway set up, I realized there were shards of glass from a beer bottle on the ground, so I had to move. I'd held the belief for years that drinking beer out of a can is superior to a bottle, for the main reason that you can't shotgun a bottle, but another valid reason is that you can't shatter a can. There were numerous times, when I was in a more accessible area, that there was shattered glass in the campsites. Glass in camping areas might've even upset me more than extra miles.

To compound my troubles, I discovered that I had lost one of my tent stakes. It must have slipped out of my pack when I was packing up in the morning. Left with no other options, I resorted to using a twig as a makeshift stake, which was far from ideal. I knew it wouldn't hold on harder ground. Usually, I would opt for cowboy camping, but my ground sheet had been torn to shreds. It seemed that camping would continue to be a challenge until I could obtain a replacement stake.

It was an effortless 16 miles down to McAllister, MT, a "town" that consisted of a post office and a restaurant. Since I got there on a Sunday, I knew I wouldn't be able to get my food box from the post office. Planning ahead, I called the restaurant on Friday. The worker was kind enough to pick up my box from the post office and hold it at the restaurant, so that I could get it when I rolled into town. The restaurant was remarkably friendly, letting me charge up and sort my food, even though they were closed.

Leaving there was tough, primarily due to the scorching heat and the absence of any breeze. As I walked along Ennis Lake, I envied the people leisurely enjoying their day on jet skis while I struggled to make progress in the sweltering heat. Carrying an excess of food — enough for four days when I only needed 1.5 days' worth — added unnecessary weight to my pack, making it feel even heavier on my shoulders. It was my own fault for getting too much sent and being too stubborn to throw anything away. I was also carrying extra gear that I hadn't been able to send home for a while because I hadn't been to a post office. I got my usual hiking shirt back after getting its eight holes repaired. So now, I was carrying my old shirt along with six pairs of socks, of which I normally carried two. Those little bits of extra weight add up fast.

Seeking respite from the scorching sun, I paused at a pit toilet along the shores of Ennis Lake. I didn't even care about the smell. Every step had become a daunting task, and I longed for even a momentary reprieve, even if it meant lying on a concrete slab beside a toilet in over 90-degree weather. I attributed my worsening condition to the combination of extreme heat and the smoke from the wildfires, but it felt far worse than usual fatigue.

After a grueling climb back into the high mountains of the Spanish Peaks, I unintentionally veered off the trail for a while, bushwhacking through the wilderness. With numerous cow paths crisscrossing the area, I found myself uncertain of what constituted the actual trail. The trail was my home, and now my home had vanished, leaving me disoriented.

When I began to set up camp in the middle of nowhere, something felt off. It might've been the fact that I wasn't near a trail, but my sixth sense was tingling. Even though I didn't hear or see any indications, an unshakable intuition told me that a grizzly bear lurked nearby. I should have heeded the warning and pressed on, but fatigue consumed me, and I couldn't muster the strength to continue. Despite hanging my food bag 30 yards away, I spent the night on high alert, straining my ears for any signs of danger. I was so tired, I might've slept through it if anything came near my tent.

The next morning, I awoke with a deep sense of unease, realizing something was seriously wrong. The persistent discomfort I felt couldn't be solely attributed to the heat or dehydration. I was plagued by dizziness, bloating, and nausea. Desperately attempting to burp in hopes of finding relief for my upset stomach, I struggled to find an ounce of respite. Every part of my body ached and felt tight, while overwhelming fatigue had taken hold even before I began hiking. It seemed that I had contracted an illness from drinking the water near that decaying deer carcass a few days prior.

To begin the day, I ventured into half an hour of bushwhacking before eventually rejoining the trail — a brief moment of triumph amidst the ongoing hardships. Throughout the morning, I frequently lost the trail, necessitating bouts of bushwhacking until I stumbled upon it again. The sun was already blazing by 7 a.m., exacerbating my deteriorating condition. By late morning, I felt like a mere shadow of myself; my movements reduced to half-speed. Each step became a grueling battle against gravity, and the large rocks alongside the trail beckoned me to sit and rest. I had to be extra cautious with every step, as dizziness made it difficult to discern the actual trail from its phantom duplicates, and I had to concentrate on keeping my food down, fearing I might vomit at any moment.

Struggling to maintain a reasonable pace, I set up camp early in the evening to get some rest. I was delightfully surprised to see no return of the plantar warts when I removed my socks after it had rained all afternoon. Previously, they had reappeared whenever my feet were water-logged.

I wasn't delighted most of the night, however. It was hard to sleep with as sick as I felt. I still felt like I could puke at any moment. All night, I was ready to pull open my tent door in case of an emergency. Whenever I managed to fall asleep, I would wake up shivering in my sleeping bag, even though it wasn't cold. After resting, not necessarily a lot of sleeping, I got moving again at 10 a.m. I felt even worse.

It took every ounce of strength I had to make it to the town of Big Sky, MT, which I was supposed to reach the previous afternoon. I felt the same symptoms as the prior day, except everything was 25% worse. After I exited the national forest, I tried following the line on my GPS track to head into town, but ended up walking right down someone's long driveway. By the time I realized it wasn't a road, it was too late to turn around. I hurried down the hill on the side of their property to quickly make it down to the highway and walk into town.

When I got into town, I ordered a pizza. I hadn't been able to eat anything all day, and very little the day before. I knew if I couldn't eat pizza, I was in real trouble. While not close to my normal consumption amount, I managed to get some calories in me. The silver lining of me carrying way too much food and my lack of appetite was that I didn't have to buy groceries in town. Relaxing at the pizza place for hours, I recovered a little, more so mentally than physically. Leaving town, I felt slightly improved — still physically awful — but I left town with clarity.

I felt mentally strong because I felt like I had weathered the storm. I couldn't imagine feeling much worse than I did, unless I was dying or had some sort of serious condition. After leaving town, I felt like things were trending up. Much like I told myself that *tomorrow would be better because it had to be* when I had a tough day on trail, I knew that *things would get better because they couldn't get worse*. It's easy to thrive when things are going well, and you've got the wind at your back. When you're sick, aching, disoriented, hungry but can't eat, tired but can't sleep, and it just hurts to exist, that's when you truly test yourself on a thru-hike. That's when you see if you can still cover the needed distance when things aren't going in your favor. If you're stubborn enough to continue covering miles and stay on pace when the winds of fate are gusting against you, that's when you know you'll be successful on a thru-hike, but more so, in any endeavor or challenge life can throw at you.

Overcoming physical hardship is the truest test of character.

After camping early again and sleeping for 12 hours, I felt closer to my usual self the next morning. Not even the pouring rain could dampen my mood. It had been a while since I dealt with a heavy, all-day, steady rain, so before leaving, I looked back at some old pictures from the AT to remind me what true pain was. True pain was rain below 35 degrees. True pain was getting up every day with the temperature below ten — or even ten below. True pain was frostbite. It was summer now. *This was nothing.*

Other than leaving the smoky clouds of Montana and entering the rainy clouds of Wyoming, it was an uneventful day with zero visibility and wet feet. The bad weather forced me to skip the supposedly epic Sky Rim Trail, but I was perfectly content with the lower elevation route since I felt healthy again. In an odd way, it felt good to be moving in poor conditions with nobody else around, reminiscent of my time on the AT. The poor conditions were my biggest concern. It made me appreciate the simple blessing of being healthy. And it was a good thing I was feeling better because I couldn't drink water all day. I was in Yellowstone National Park, and some workers were poisoning streams to kill some fish for population control, which seemed odd but presumably served the park's ecosystem.

I rolled into the town of Mammoth, WY around 10:30 p.m. and slept in a bathroom for the night. It had been a while since I had done a privy bivy. While it was a much more desirable shelter when it was freezing cold, it lost most of its appeal in the summer. This was also one of my worst nights of sleep all year. The LED lights in the bathroom couldn't be turned off, and when I rarely managed to fall asleep, I would soon wake up from the manufactured sun in my eyes. After laying there for a few hours, I got up to make sure I was out of there before anybody else arrived.

Before heading to a lodge, the only open establishment in town, I explored the area. I learned that the sole restaurant in town was only open for supper, so I ended up overpaying for a bagel at the lodge and lingered there until the ranger station opened. After a lot of frustration, two wrong phone numbers, and being transferred after 30 minutes on hold, I got my camping permit for Yellowstone National Park.

When I left, it was raining and foggy again, with no visibility. I road walked nearly all day, and the only redeeming aspect of the day was that I saw my first bison. My simple appreciation for being healthy was starting to wane and be overtaken by a feeling of malice toward the weather. I made camp in the rain that evening and broke camp in the rain the next morning.

There was still hardly any visibility, but I decided to take a side quest to see Old Faithful since I was so close. It wasn't directly on the route I was taking on the Big Sky Alternate, so I had to hitch from a trailhead. Hundreds of cars passed, offering nothing more than bewildered looks. Until finally, a couple stopped to pick me up. They turned out to be interesting people: one from Estonia and the other, Thailand. I got numerous rides during the year with people from other countries. Hitchhiking doesn't have the stigma, or perceived danger, in other places like it does in the United States, so I was grateful whenever I saw a person from another country behind the wheel. It's also impossible to have a boring conversation with people from a different part of the world while hitchhiking.

When I got to Old Faithful, I had to wait an hour before it was scheduled to erupt. So I waited, sitting there in the rain, getting progressively wetter and colder while not moving. The scheduled eruption time came and went, and nothing happened. Growing impatient after ten more minutes of wasting time sitting in the rain, I decided to leave, giving up the front-row seat I had maintained for over an hour. As I was 100 yards from the geyser, I heard people yelling. I turned around and saw Old Faithful erupting. My impatience and stubbornness to keep moving had gotten the best of me.

I posted up at the parking lot exit to get a ride back to the trailhead from which I had come. It was pouring, so I was hopeful I would get a ride quickly out of pity. After 15 minutes, a truck stopped. As I was climbing in, I noticed the driver was holding a large knife by his leg. It appeared to be in a defensive manner, rather than threatening, so I didn't make a big deal of it. I must've passed his ocular pat down because he set it down and started driving. Other than an unpleasant conversation with ramblings of unsolicited life advice from an old man, it was a perfectly fine and safe ride.

When I arrived at the park campground later, I was displeased to find that my campsite was in the farthest possible spot a half mile away, and it was surrounded by bulky RV's with loud generators.

It was a rough night. Everything was soaking wet; I was cold; and there were noisy generators kicking on and off constantly. The saving grace was that there was a heated bathroom nearby, so I woke up at 4 a.m. to dry out my gear before people started waking up. It took a couple of hours, and by the end, people were walking in as I was sitting there with my things strewn all over the place. Most either acted like it was normal, or like I wasn't there and didn't say anything. Only a few asked what I was doing. None of them knew about the CDT and were all surprised to learn about it. They looked at me as an expert and asked what they should do around the park. I couldn't offer any knowledge other than the boring route I had taken with no visibility to rejoin with the official CDT sooner rather than later.

After picking up a food box at Grant's Village and a short road walk, my time on the Big Sky Alternate had come to an end. I was back on the official CDT. I was glad to be back on the official trail, where I'd feel more comfortable, and now had three sources of navigation since adding Gaia for the alternate. I wasn't sure if it was just my comfort level, or the fact that it only drizzled instead of rained all day, but I was in a significantly better mood. Having dried out my gear also helped.

My feet were sopping from hiking in wet grass all day. There were also numerous barefoot fords, but they were all calm, so I was able to prevent my shoes and socks from having to get fully soaked in the water. As I was crossing one stream on a pile of logs, they started to shift below me. I wavered. I flailed. I balanced. I was about to fall into the stream and get everything wet, but I caught myself at the last second. Even still, when I pulled off my shoes at the end of the day, my feet were in rough shape from having been soggy for so many consecutive days. It would take some consistent dry hiking for them to recover.

In the evening, I was in an open meadow when my bear sense started tingling. Earlier in the day, I saw a large brown body through the trees and quickly pulled out my bear spray, only to discover it was a group of horses and mules. This time felt different.

I looked around but saw nothing immediately. Within the next minute, I saw bear scat on the trail, and then proceeded to sing loudly for the next 20 minutes. I didn't end up seeing the apex predator, but shortly before I arrived at camp, I saw a different level of the food chain. The two-toned body with a dark brown head and light coat caught my eye. This majestic elk, 100 yards ahead, was one of the most beautiful creatures I'd ever seen. As I approached, it turned to look back at me. Our eyes locked for 30 seconds as I stared into its soul. I took a single step, hoping to get closer, but instead, prompted the elk to gracefully gallop away into the evening glow. I camped right outside the national park boundary with another CDT hiker and chatted a little bit before bed.

For as good as that day was, the pendulum swung back hard the next day. It dropped slightly below freezing, causing me to start my day late, despite a restless night. I realized I might need to acquire cold weather gear soon, which felt odd considering it was August. As I began walking, I reached for my toothbrush but couldn't find it. Lacking any real choice, I resigned to going without brushing my teeth for a while.

I encountered more barefoot fords in the morning, but my feet were already soggy from walking through wet grass again. My feet were perpetually wet. While it was rare for me to notice any unpleasant odors from myself or my gear, I had been constantly noticing the putrid smell of my soggy socks lately, so I knew they had to be extraordinarily bad.

Around 2 p.m., I took a lunch break and changed into a pair of dry socks. I felt like a new man… for a few hours. My optimism waned as I approached a section of trail heavily frequented by horses, turning the path into a muddy disaster with their deep hoof prints. To hope for continually dry socks was a waste of energy.

By 4:30 p.m., the rain started pouring again. I sought shelter under some trees, hoping the rain would pass or at least ease up. Resistance was futile. Frustrated that I had wasted an hour, I decided to resume hiking. In this beaten-down state, I realized that if a bear ever wanted a free meal, all it had to do was attack me while it was raining. My motivation to fight back was nonexistent, so I would just want my demise to be quick.

Setting up camp early, I hoped to warm up inside my sleeping bag before the temperature dropped again. Everything around me was soaked, and the temperature hovered around freezing. There were also small puddles in my tent as soon as I got in from the water on my body. With the combination of me being soaked to the bone, all my gear being sodden, and it being near freezing, I hardly slept. I spent the whole night shivering, eagerly waiting for the sun to come out. When it did rise in the sky, my back was tight from shivering all night.

I laid my gear out in the sunlight to dry before I got moving. My head was in a better space. It wasn't raining for the first time in a week. I was jubilant! The trail was still a mud pit because of horse traffic, but I didn't care. I had wet feet, but at least everything on me wasn't wet. I accepted the fact that even though I was a person who tried to avoid being controlled by my emotions, bad weather could absolutely wreck me for a few days.

When I made it to the highway, I got a hitch to Lava Mountain Lodge a few miles off trail. I had a food box sent there to keep me from having to go farther off trail into town. However, I learned the hard way that the postal service didn't always work well out there. The lodge said my package was likely at the post office in town, which was already closed. I got a room for the night and would have to go into Dubois, WY in the morning. Although my plan hadn't worked out, I was excited at the prospect of my first shower since starting at the Canadian border nearly a month ago.

Early at the lodge, I met a person biking the Great Divide Mountain Bike Route from Canada to Mexico who mentioned there was another hiker, named Chezwick, staying there the same night. I made my way over to the restaurant to get a large meat lover's pizza and meet this fellow crazy man.

I'd heard about Chezwick while on the PCT. He was attempting the Great Western Loop, and it turned out he had the same problem with his food box at the lodge, but he opted to spend a lot of money resupplying at the little gift shop at the lodge, rather than go into town in the morning. We talked about our journeys and commiserated before catching up on some sleep for the night. He was truly a fascinating character. He was more than ten years older than me, hiking more daily miles than me because he was on a condensed time frame, was sleeping less than five hours a night, and was smoking a pack of cigarettes a day — often shocking people when he passed them on ascents with a cigarette in his mouth. I was glad I met him. It was a humbling reminder — no matter how great we think we are, or how crazy we think what we're doing is, there's always somebody out there going harder and doing something even crazier.

I said goodbye to him and the several bikers I met the next morning when I went to hitch into town. By the time I got to town, retrieved my package, and got back to the trail, I had wasted well over three hours. A large part of that was spent walking over two miles out of town because hitchhiking was illegal and actually enforced, which was unusual. Once on the outskirts of town, I still struggled to catch a hitch, until an Amazon driver picked me up. The only redeeming aspect of the whole venture was that I got a 2-liter of Dr. Pepper and pounded it on my way out of town. When I completed my side quest around noon, I was ready to start moving forward on the trail again. The first half of the day was walking on dirt roads that were mud pits, but I got back on actual single-track trail later in the day.

To my surprise, I started encountering other southbound hikers. I met five or six of them, and they all mentioned that they hadn't seen many others until that day. It seemed to be a convergence point for southbounders. I passed the last of them around dusk and assumed I wouldn't see them again. Just after that, I caught sight of my first fox of the trip. It ran parallel to me and the trail for a while before stopping to stare at me. There was something mischievous in its gaze that made me uneasy.

By nightfall, I was beat. I was carrying six days of food, which was definitely more than the max load of 25 pounds for my pack. Whenever I carried that much weight, it was tough on my body because the pack wasn't designed for it. My upper back was exceptionally tight, and no matter how much I tried to crack it or relieve some pressure, nothing would budge. It felt like there was enough pressure in my back to air up four truck tires.

After following a river for a half mile and finding a place where I could jump across and stay dry, I made camp for the night. I had to hang my food close to my tent because it was the only tree around. It wasn't an ideal tree for hanging. I spent over 30 minutes hanging the bag, sounding like Yosemite Sam while doing so, before getting it to stick and going to bed exhausted. I woke up around 3 a.m. to the sound of wolves howling nearby. They were loud, so it was hard to go back to sleep. It was even harder to go back to sleep because I realized they kept getting closer. They kept coming. It got to the point where they couldn't have been more than 200 yards away. I was shoving my shoes on my feet, and had my bear spray ready to roll, trying to visualize how this fight would go.

It was definitely a wolf pack, so they'll likely fight in a unified manner. If they surround me, what's my game plan? If I spray one of them and he retreats, will they all retreat? Or is it just "next man up" mentality? Maybe that will just make them angrier. If they do surround me, I might have to spray all of my bear spray while spinning around like a ballerina. That will likely get in my own eyes. Oh, well. That's better than getting torn apart by a pack of wolves. But will my bear spray even have enough juice for me to continuously spray in a circle to get all of them? And what if it runs out and they're still unaffected? And now angry. And now I'm having trouble seeing. I should probably grab a rock too. You never know. That might come in handy. I can't remember exactly, but I think wolves are like a prison gang. If you take out their alpha, they'll retreat out of fear or respect. Maybe I'll do that, just try to go for the biggest one. Well, it's almost game time. I hope they tap out before I do. Here we go.

When the pack was less than 50 yards away, they must've realized there was a human by the food they smelled and decided to retreat. I let out a sigh of relief, holstered the bear spray, got back inside my tent, took my shoes off, and went to bed satisfied, remembering — *I'm the true alpha.*

Waking up to the sound of chipmunks squeaking outside my tent, just like I had nearly every morning in the past month on the CDT, I was ready to lead a war on the chipmunks. I rarely took advantage of the early wake up and got moving. I was always so tired that I'd just lay there and get sub-par sleep until I built up the will-power to get up for the day.

Once up, the trail led me through a vast, exposed area, offering stunning views of the surrounding landscape and the Wind River Range — my destination. The only drawback was the lack of privacy for going to the bathroom with no vegetation in sight. Unable to hold it any longer, I ventured off the trail, but still within view, and relieved myself. I told myself that it was the CDT, and I hardly ever saw anybody, so it would be okay.

Just as I was finishing up, I heard two voices approaching. I completed my task less than 20 seconds before they spotted me, and I informed them that they had narrowly avoided witnessing a rather graphic start to their day. We hiked together for a while before eventually separating and leapfrogging throughout the day. Later, I realized I had lost a water bottle, but thankfully, one of the hikers caught up to me and returned it, saving me from relying on a single liter for hydration.

I had a peculiar "first" of the year. I walked into a herd of cattle, and it was the first time they approached me rather than ran away. I did become a little wary when they formed a battle line. Again, I felt like they were plotting something. Then, two of them unexpectedly started to try to make a cow baby, and I realized I didn't want to be there to witness that. I hiked a little faster past the herd.

Later in the day, I came across two hikers that warned me about "incomprehensible blowdowns" ahead, and I couldn't help but chuckle. If I had learned anything all year, it was to <u>not</u> trust most people when they hyped up how bad something was. This was never more evident than with southbounders on the PCT, but I figured it would apply here too, and it did.

The blowdowns weren't fun and slowed me down a bit, but I was glad I dealt with life-altering blowdowns in the Mount Hood Wilderness on the PCT. Now, most scenarios seemed benign by comparison. *Bad turned into okay simply because it wasn't terrible.*

The truth also was that I was just doing something harder than what a lot of other people were doing. Everybody's level of acceptable misery is different, and mine had to be extraordinarily high for the year. If the weather was bad, I had to keep going. If my feet hurt, I couldn't stop for long. If I was sick, I had to keep moving. If there were "incomprehensible blowdowns," I had to plow through. I was on a mission with a singular goal where the only way was thru. Nothing was going to stop me.

Near Death in the Winds

After camping high on the banks of the Green River engulfed in the magnificent Wind River Range, I awoke to a morning covered in dew. As I stepped outside my tent, I saw something off in the distance.

With my vision still a little blurry, I squinted to get a better look. I could make out a large brown figure. I was slightly worried, but more intrigued. It was on the other side of the river, which alleviated most concern. When my eyes adjusted, I realized it was a moose, and it was the first moose I ever saw! Then I noticed there was another one eating bushes 30 yards to his left. They were massive beasts that made me question my previous perception of the size of a moose. It was a true joy watching them while I was packing up my gear. Part of me just wanted to sit down and watch them all day, but I had miles to cover through tough terrain, so reluctantly, I had to leave the elegant giants behind.

After a few miles on the CDT, I hopped on the Knapsack Col Alternate. It was a high route that received a lot of high praise, so I wasn't going to miss it. I was quickly surprised with how different it was. After a few miles, it became a total boulder scramble. It was the first time I had ever done anything like that, hopping from car-sized rocks to truck-sized rocks, with deep and dark pits between, and no real trail to follow.

It was slow-going, and while I never fell, I constantly questioned my footing. It also was not ideal to be carrying a heavy pack. There were a number of times where I stepped on a rock, it wobbled, and I panicked and had to jump off quickly. There were some interesting paths and tough jumps, but I made it up to Peaks Lake, a truly picturesque location of pristine water surrounded by radiant granite mountains.

After getting there at 3 p.m., I opted to stop for the day. The next possible campsite was six miles ahead, and I thought it would take a while to get there. From my location, it was 2.5 miles and over 2,000 feet of vertical gain to make it to Knapsack Col, followed by a demanding descent of nearly four miles. I assumed it would be mostly boulder scrambling, so I would be moving around 1 mph again. I didn't want to play around with any scrambling after dark since I still felt uneasy doing it during the day. The bright side with being done early was that I was excited to catch up on sleep.

When the sun came out the next morning, I began hiking. It was a slow ascent because I was right — it was indeed a boulder scramble up to Knapsack Col. Taking my time, I navigated the rocks carefully and reached the top without incident. The view from the summit was unlike anything I had ever witnessed. It possessed a beauty similar to the Sierra, yet was distinct in its own way. Even at an elevation of nearly 13,000 feet, the landscape offered no glimpse of green, only gray and white rock. There was no life, but it was undeniably beautiful.

I had read comments on Guthook from other hikers that said you could save a mile or two by cutting across the glacier. There wasn't a trail in this area. There was somewhat of a general route to follow, but frankly, I just needed to descend into the basin near the lakes where a trail would exist. I looked at the flat basin below me but determined that the obvious route must be the longer one. That would be too easy.

I must have to climb the ridge and hike over the glacier to the other side of the mountain. Then I would see where I was supposed to go for the shortcut. There were currently large rocks in the way obstructing the view, but once I got over those, I would be able to see this shortcut.

After hiking up the ridge for a bit, I arrived at a challenging point. There were two, 70-degree avalanche chutes, but on the other side of them was the big view-obstructing rock. *Once I get on top of that, I'll be fine.* I started to climb across the avalanche chutes of loose dirt, vertically on all fours, trying to do it as safely as possible. Every time I moved a hand or a foot, I slid down three feet in the loose dirt. It was as if Spiderman was trying to climb something, except he only had 20% of his grip power.

With a lot of white knuckling and bated breath, I made it over the two chutes and on top of the rock. That was a scary experience, and I was ready for my moment of salvation. What I got instead was a view that made my heart sink into my stomach, cause an ulcer, fill up with stomach acid, and then shoot back up into my chest — pounding 200 beats per minute.

Even with all the incredible, natural beauty around me, I forgot any of it existed. All I felt was growing fear and overwhelming anxiety. All I could see was two more avalanche chutes in front of me, and then a vertical wall of ice. It was too late to turn around, because it would be just as dangerous. There was nowhere to go, nowhere to run, nowhere to hide. I wanted to scream. I wanted to cry. I wanted to call for help. All I wanted to do was to be anywhere in the world except right here. But none of that would've made a difference.

I got myself into this mess; now I had to get myself out of it. *There are no shadows in the storm.*

I began to crawl across the next avalanche chutes, again sliding with every movement, but it was a little different this time. I felt even less stable. The fear of tumbling backward and falling hundreds of feet down the mountain consumed my thoughts. I tried to tell myself to not think about it, but it was all I could think about.

Just move your hand. Now move your foot. Whoa, slow down! Breathe.

Just Breathe.

After taking what felt like a half hour to move 30 feet across the next two chutes, I reached an inevitable decision point. There was a decent-sized rock protruding out of the side of the mountain, and then a four-foot gap of vertical loose dirt that would have been impossible to even stand on because it was so steep. After sitting there for a bit and weighing my options, I decided that the best course of action would be to hang from this rock. From there, my feet would be able to reach the pile of rocks lining the vertical wall of ice that was close by. Once I got on those rocks, I would find my way down somehow.

Still with my heavy pack on, I maneuvered my way down to the sizeable rock, so that I was hanging from it. Once I was fully outstretched, with only my two hands holding onto the rock, preventing me from a 600-foot drop straight below, I realized that my feet wouldn't be able to reach the pile of rocks. They were dangling in the air, only able to graze the loose dirt below the rock from which I was hanging.

At this moment, I questioned every choice I had ever made in my life that brought me to this point. *Is this the culmination of all my life's decisions? I did so much just so that I could fall to my death in the Wyoming wilderness and probably never be found.*

As those thoughts were starting to pile up, I noticed that the rock I was hanging from had a lot of small chunks of rock on its outer edges. Many small parts of the rock had broken off. *Now how long would the part that was currently supporting all my weight last?* Unless I wanted to fall to my death 600 feet below when my handholds naturally broke off, I had to get up. Summoning every ounce of my strength, I pulled myself up, action-movie-style, back onto the rock.

Whew! That was something, but there's still nowhere to go!

I was in the same position I was before I decided to dangle from the outcropping rock — still trapped.

After pondering every possible move from my current position, I concluded the only feasible option was to lie down on my stomach, on the vertical loose dirt with my feet below me, and start to slide down the mountain until I could grab onto the pile of rocks lining the wall of ice. So, I did. I started out slow but was unable to reach the rocks. Then I began to pick up speed. I was starting to get worried. Panic gripped me as I frantically reached out, desperately trying to grab a lifeline, but kept falling short of reaching a rock. With one last effort before I started flying down the mountain at an uncontrollably dangerous rate, I lunged out a final time and grabbed onto a rock, using all of my remaining upper body strength to stop my momentum and pull myself up to the rocks lining the wall of ice.

I felt all-powerful… for a grand total of one second. Then I realized again; there was still nowhere to go!

Well, this is it. This is gonna hurt.

I tightened my pack to my body, made sure my trekking pole straps were secure around my wrists, sat down on the vertical dirt next to me, and began to slide down the mountain on my butt. Again, it started out slow. It hurt a little, but it didn't feel too dangerous.

Then I started sliding on rocks. Once again, I began picking up speed. Pretty soon, I was sliding down the mountain at a terrifying pace. I wanted to scream, but I was so petrified, nothing would come out. Rocks were flying all around. I didn't just cause a massive rockslide — I was IN a massive rockslide. I felt them hit my pack or my arm. Luckily, none hit my head. I heard my shorts tearing and could feel the rocks cutting into my butt. I tried putting my hands out to slow me down, but all that did was cut them, and it hurt so badly that I couldn't do it for long. I then had the brilliant idea to have my pack take the brunt of the pain. I arched my back and leaned far back, so my butt was no longer touching the ground, just the pack. I kept sliding for a few more seconds before coming to a halt in a jumble of rocks with projectiles still flying around me.

Not moving, just panting, I sat there for 30 seconds before yelling at the top of my lungs in a fury of anger and self-recrimination: "FUCK!!! YOU'RE SUCH A DUMBASS!!!"

I put myself in a terrible situation, which could have easily turned out differently with a tragic result. I was lucky to be alive. I was irate at myself for making a series of such poor decisions. I felt like I had passed a point of no return early in my detour, but that was more pride at wanting to avoid backtracking than anything else. In everything in life, there is always a choice, and the choices I made could have easily led to my death if I didn't have a little luck on my side and God looking over my shoulder.

There is no time a man feels closer to God than when he feels he narrowly escaped death.

I wasn't at the bottom yet, but the unbelievably difficult and absurdly idiotic part was over. Before reaching normal terrain, I had to do one more stupid thing. By that point, it seemed like nothing. After sliding down 500 feet on my butt, there was still a slab of ice below me before reaching the bottom. However, to my right there was a patch of powdery snow, and then a field of rocks, which I could use to make my way down.

After broad jumping into the snow, I slid down 12 feet before I slammed into a boulder which stopped me. I then climbed down on rocks the rest of the way into the basin. I looked at my phone. It had been over 2.5 hours, and I moved a quarter of a mile. I was still pissed off. My hands were bleeding. My arms were bleeding. My butt was exposed and bleeding. And I was mentally and emotionally depleted. I turned on a playlist of all Rage Against the Machine songs, and hiked on, trying to release my anger.

Covering Distance With Pain and Persistence

It was several hours later, and I was still seething with fury until I ran into a hiker going in the opposite direction. He looked awful, even for a thru-hiker. I was planning on saying hi, and just hiking by, still lost in my anger. When we reached each other, he smiled and said, "I wasn't sure if we were ever going to meet."

Then it clicked in my head. I had seen pictures of this guy. This was Buzz, another person going for the Calendar Year Triple Crown in the same year. My mood instantly changed. We had been near each other a lot of the year, but flipped trails at different times, so I wasn't sure if I would see him, or his hiking partner Woody. When our paths crossed, I was elated.

We sat and traded war stories from the year. I learned that he was getting over Giardia and E. Coli, which explained his haggard appearance and why I hardly recognized him. I shared my own experience with sickness in Montana from drinking the deer carcass water, but his sounded much worse. We talked for over 30 minutes before he suggested we should probably keep moving. I knew he was right, but I didn't want to.

Happiness most real when shared.

Several minutes later, I ran into his hiking partner, Woody. I knew this would happen. As I was speaking to Buzz, I was hoping Woody would catch-up, so I could talk to both at once and kill two birds with one stone. Regardless, I was still overjoyed to meet Woody, who looked considerably healthier than Buzz. We talked for 30 minutes, too. I mentioned my near-death experience earlier in the day, and he said they had a similar harrowing experience the same day.

It was incredibly rewarding to talk to the only two other people that could truly relate to me all year. The three of us knew the specific hardships each other had to go through for the Calendar Year Triple Crown in 2021, and we knew how insanely difficult it really was. We could tell other people our stories and experiences, but we three were the only people in the world to live those harsh realities. After our brief encounter, we said our goodbyes and continued on in our separate directions.

Shortly before the sun began to set, I took the wrong trail for a half mile before I realized it and bushwhacked back to the main trail. When I got back, there was a stream crossing that was supposed to be simple — but nothing ever was. With the recent rain, the water level had risen, and now was flowing much faster and higher. I was determined to avoid wet feet at all costs, so I meticulously surveyed the crossing for 20 minutes before I found the only potential spot to get across without getting wet. There were a few high-risk jumps on rocks that were less than a quarter of an inch out of the water, and a few jumps on unstable logs, but I made it across with dry feet.

After a poor night of sleep on a slanted campsite and being awoken by several animals, I was delighted to look outside my tent in the morning and be greeted by pink skies. I was joyously appreciative to see colorful skies again after all of Montana was hazy with smoke, and my first week in Wyoming was filled with dark skies of bleak rain clouds.

Unlike the previous day, which was filled with the highest of highs and lowest of lows, the sole objective of this day was to reach the Cirque of the Towers Alternate. It was another scenic high route I refused to miss. I reached it towards the end of an uneventfully pleasant day, and camped by an alpine lake before dusk settled.

There were some weekenders camping at Shadow Lake. I finished early for the day because it was too late to start the climb up Texas Pass, which would be a boulder scramble. I was becoming more comfortable with scrambling, but not comfortable enough to do it in the dark.

After chatting with other campers for a bit, they gave me a beer, which acted quickly at 10,000 feet. I was happy we could break liquid bread after our initial meeting. We introduced ourselves, and they said they were from Michigan, and me from Ohio. We looked at each other in a suspicious manner, wondering, "Are we about to duel?" before laughing about the rivalry that is infinitely bigger than a single college football game once a year. I truly do hate Michigan, though.

I started off the next morning by getting lost on the myriad of faint trails around the lake. It was a popular spot for weekenders, so the area was wrecked, making it difficult to discern the actual trail. While bushwhacking, I caught sight of a pair of tall and skinny, black-looking, animal legs beneath a bush, less than 30 feet away.

My initial thought was that it was be a horse, but that was strange. *Why would a wild horse be up at this elevation?* As I moved closer, I realized it was a moose. Excitement coursed through me at the sight of a moose so close, but I also felt a tinge of fear due to the unpredictability of these massive creatures. I cautiously grabbed my bear spray and took a few more steps to gain a clear view. For five minutes, I watched the mild-mannered moose as it chewed on leaves and curiously stared back at me with its own look of intrigue, before it turned and walked away.

After my glorious standoff, I scrambled to the top of Texas Pass, from which I had the first jaw-dropping view of the Cirque of the Towers. The majestic wall of peaks, stretching 11,000 feet, looked like they belonged on a postcard. After dipping back down in elevation a little, I ascended over Jackass Pass and continued on the alternate through awe-inspiring landscape. As I neared the end, things changed drastically.

I found myself entangled in a labyrinth of downed trees, which was expected. I had heard and read a lot about them, and this was the first time in a long time, that something truly lived up to the hype of its difficulty. There had been a historic windstorm in September, the previous year, and it wreaked havoc on the area, leaving countless fallen trees. The forest floor was completely obscured, making it impossible to locate the trail.

After wandering in circles for 20 minutes, I gave up on finding the designated trail and decided to bushwhack my way towards the official CDT, beyond the point where the junction was to reconnect. I set my sights on a lake that appeared on my map, thinking it would be easier to skirt around its edge, rather than navigate the chaotic mess I found myself in.

Upon reaching the lake, I realized I was partially correct. I could avoid the fallen trees by walking the lake's banks, but I was faced with massive boulders surrounding the water. With caution, I maneuvered over the boulders, careful not to fall into the water as some of them wobbled beneath my weight. When I finally reached the other side, remaining dry, a wave of relief washed over me. However, the struggle was not yet over. I still had a considerable distance to cover before rejoining the actual CDT. I was still in the middle of nowhere, so I had to make my way back.

After a lot of wrong turns, cussing, and following animal tracks, I stumbled upon the CDT once again. Seeing a clear trail ahead, free from cumbersome fallen trees, was an immense relief. Just before darkness descended enough to necessitate using my headlamp, I noticed something to my left. It was difficult to discern in the dim light, but as my eyes adjusted, I realized it was yet another moose, and its calf was right next to it! Incredibly, this marked my fifth moose sighting in just three days. Considering I had never encountered one before, it seemed I was making up for lost time.

I went to bed that night, filled with gratitude for my time in the Wind River Range, but ready to get back to some easier hiking. And I got what I asked for. The next day was the beginning of the Great Divide Basin, an endorheic basin, which means that no water flows out of it. Every particle of precipitation that falls in the basin stays there until it eventually evaporates. However, that didn't mean the basin had plentiful water. It was a flat, arid, and barren desert valley, surrounded on all sides by the high mountains that formed the basin. It was quite the shock to arrive at a mass void of life after the vibrant environments of Wyoming that I had just recently seen, but I was excited for it. It was by far the flattest and easiest part of the trail. I wanted to cover big miles and go for a 50-mile day.

The following morning, I got a late start because there was frost on my tent, and I waited for it to melt. By this point, my summer sleeping bag was so poor that I was uncomfortably cold most nights. This frost was a further sign that it was cooling down, and I would need warmer gear soon.

As I hiked my last miles into South Pass City to pick up my food box, I felt rough. I had run out of food. I was tired, thirsty, and just wanted to be there already. Like a mirage, two ATV's pulled up and asked if I wanted a beer. I eagerly accepted and was handed a Coors Banquet. All beer is good, but this was the best beer I'd ever tasted. It was at that moment, my belief that all Coors beers taste better out west, was formed. They also gave me water, which was much needed. I kept passing on water sources because they were gross, and I was being a prima donna.

I talked with them for a while and Yogi'd some food off of them to push me through the last bit. When hikers "Yogi" something, that means that they chat with people while casually bringing up that they need food, are out of water, or need help of some sort. It's not explicitly asking for help, but it's trying to get the other person to offer help in the first place — a skill I improved on throughout the year.

When I arrived at South Pass City, I was surprised. I expected it to be small, but it was legitimately a gift shop that accepted hiker boxes with a small public restroom outside. I desperately looked around the gift shop in the faint hope of seeing a toothbrush and toothpaste. It had been over eight days since I brushed my teeth and they were aching in agony. I was foolish and forgot to buy one when I went into town in Dubois, and now I was paying the price in pain. I was beginning to consider using my finger and spit to possibly wash them, but my hands were always so dirty I figured that was a surefire way to get sick. I'd never considered having a toothbrush to be such a luxury, until I didn't have one.

After failing to find a toothbrush in the gift shop of frontier town knick-knacks, I picked up my box and went around back to charge my phone and power bank. After that long stretch of trail, my charger was completely dead, and my phone didn't have much juice left. I had to wait a few hours before I got a decent charge, so I got all my food sorted and tried to catch up on as much as I could, planning and otherwise.

Joyously and relievedly, I was out of grizzly territory, so I parted ways with all of my bear-related gear. I mailed home my rope and food hanging bag, and I left my bear spray at the store for other hikers heading in the opposite direction — entering grizzly bear country. I also mailed out a woman's ID I had found on the trail in The Wind River Range — a small good deed for all the many I had received during the year.

Just as I was preparing to leave, I discovered that the new Kanye West album, *Donda*, had just been released. There was no way I was going to miss out on that when I had hours of hiking to listen to it. So I sat there for 40 minutes, with one bar of terribly slow Wi-Fi, until the album downloaded, leaving just before sunset.

I woke up the next morning, determined to crush a 50-mile day. Well, I think I was determined. I overslept and didn't want to get up, but once I physically got up and started moving, I was excited.

Foolishly, in my excitement, I was careless with my water consumption. It wasn't scorching hot, like the two straight weeks of 100+ degrees in Northern California and Oregon, but it was warm, and there wasn't a lick of shade. I passed only two water sources all day, and I should've carried more water bottles. My carrying capacity was only 2.5 liters, which wasn't enough given the constant exposure to the blazing sun.

The first source I encountered was a spring that was dry on the surface, but had a manhole with water below the ground. Later on, I passed a creek that was allegedly "good water." But as I was walking up, I saw a bunch of cows, so I knew it wasn't going to be great quality. The surface was covered with algae and surrounded by cow pies. The simpleminded bovine creatures were even drinking out of it the same time I was. However, for as much as they mucked it up, it wasn't the worst tasting water I'd ever had.

In the afternoon, I felt a new pain in between my two small toes on my right foot. It was my first painful blister of the year. With trail running shoes, I never had problems with blisters, but I guess after 6,000 miles, it was deserved. I stopped to take a look at it, but it was in the perfect wrong spot. No matter what I did, I couldn't see it. All I knew was that it hurt.

As I hiked late into the night, I passed an RV and heard some barking, immediately knowing some tomfoolery was about to ensue. Two dogs came barreling at me in a full sprint, and we battled it out for a few minutes. I slowly backed away, with them still pursuing me, lunging forward and backward at my legs, before they agreed I was far enough away and turned around to run home. The owners must've been having a restful night of sleep, because they made no effort to come out and control their dogs.

By the end of the night, it was physically difficult to walk. I was severely dehydrated. My entire legs, from my quads to my calves, were so tight that it felt like I wasn't walking, but instead was being incessantly hit with the blunt force of a ball-peen hammer on every square inch of my upper leg. My hips felt like they lost the ability to rotate. They were continually caving more inward. I was like a robot that had never been greased up, and was walking straight-legged, awkwardly and uncomfortably. Every step was exhausting, every movement painful, but I was going to hit 50 miles or die trying.

When I did reach 50 miles after more than 17 hours of hiking, I was not triumphantly proud of my grand achievement, only relieved. But it wasn't over. This basin was unbelievably flat, yet, there was nowhere to camp because everything was covered in sharp plants. I had to walk an extra three miles before I came across a spot that was solely dirt. The only reason it was devoid of plants was because it was a dirt road that branched off of the main dirt road I was hiking. I pitched my tent and hoped that nobody would drive on this side road before I resumed hiking in the morning.

Falling asleep proved to be an impossible task. My legs were so tight that they hurt while laying down. They were spasming along with my back. I wasn't scared, but I was overfatigued. All I wanted to do was sleep, but I laid in discomfort for two hours before I was able to ignore the pain and succumb to pure exhaustion. I slept in the next morning because I expected to feel rough, and I did.

This was one of the few times I broke my own rule of, "Don't let what you're doing today ruin tomorrow." To be successful at my goal, the biggest factor was consistency. Peak and comfort mileages are different for everyone. For me, 30 miles was in the middle of my comfort mileage range. It's what I'd consider pushing myself hard, but not too hard and causing issues. The edge of my comfort mileage was around 35 miles. After any day with more than 35 miles, I'd usually feel at least some hampering effects the next day, and that wasn't what I wanted. I'd rather be consistent. I'd heard about people on the PCT going for a 50-mile day and then taking four rest days to recover. It's cool to cover that many miles in a day, but that drastically ruins your daily average. With my estimates for the year, I knew I'd have to average right around 30 miles per day on the PCT and CDT. I wanted to do that by consistency, rather than big mileage days that could lead to injury or necessary rest. Even with all my discipline, I couldn't resist the urge to go for 50 miles at least once.

I was dying of thirst as I got moving, counting on an upcoming water source after not hitting one for 27 miles. When I got there, it was bone dry. I was disappointed, but I didn't panic. I was too exhausted to panic. I didn't sweat it, because I didn't want to waste any sweat. I just kept hiking, even though it was going to be 20 miles before my next water source.

After another couple of hours of walking in my dehydrated stupor, a truck drove by on the dirt road I was hiking on. Even though I had been walking on predominantly dirt roads throughout the whole basin, it was the first vehicle I saw. Like a guardian angel, he stopped and asked if I needed any water. I couldn't even express how thankful I was when he gave me a gallon jug. I filled up my water bottles and then sat on the basin floor and chugged the rest before I started moving again. *The trail provides.*

Even after the water, my legs still felt rough. My hips remained so tight that I had to consciously extend my legs to try to stride out to a healthy length. My quads were so tight that every step felt like I had just finished a marathon and somebody was stabbing ice picks into them. This was the worst my legs had felt in ages, and I had to take much longer breaks than usual to give them some rest. Maybe pushing for 50 miles wasn't the smartest thing to do, but neither was hiking the AT in winter, or trying to hike all three triple crown trails in one year.

As I was lying down for one of my many breaks, baking in the sun because there was no shade, I learned that there were fire ants in the basin. I began to feel some irritation on my legs, and then I felt their pinching bites. Alarmed, I got up, brushed everything off my body in a spastic manner, and kept hiking to get away from them. That was one way to get me moving again. The painful bites lingered for over 30 minutes.

In the evening, I had cell service and plenty of phone battery. I began calling friends to catch up. Whenever I was able to do this, the time flew by. It also did a great job distracting me from the pain in my feet, legs, hips, back, and neck. The pain was still there, but I wasn't thinking about it with every passing moment. After dark, I realized that while hiking in the basin, it was impossible to not hate moths. They were everywhere after dark, and they all wanted to go on Kamikaze missions toward my headlamp. They would usually miss their target and end up in my eyes or mouth, of which the latter was still aching from not brushing my teeth.

After having to move cow pies to clear an open spot to camp, I awoke the next morning, ready to get into Rawlins, WY and be done with this mini desert. I came upon my first person in a few days that appeared to be a thru-hiker. She was headed in the opposite direction, and I was excited to talk to someone.

I said hello two times with no verbal response. In return, she started doing sign language. I then realized that I knew absolutely nothing in sign language. I tried to make some sort of a gesture that I was a fool and didn't know anything, and we just went our separate ways. She had a few dogs with her, which I assumed were to help alert her in case of danger, but it was still impressive to see a deaf person hiking the trail.

It started to rain. I was surprised to see precipitation with the arid desert landscape, but it came at a price. The dirt beneath my feet transformed into thick mud that was constantly stuck to the bottom of my shoes. I had to frequently stop and knock off the big chunks that had engulfed my feet. I never thought I would be so disappointed to see rain in the desert, but I opted to road walk the last miles into town on the highway that ran parallel to the trail, to avoid the desert mud.

Tiredly arriving in Rawlins, I got a room at the Econolodge in town. I was ready to put my feet up, binge eat, drink a gallon of Dr. Pepper, enjoy being comfortable for the first time in a long time, and buy a new toothbrush and toothpaste since I hadn't brushed my teeth for two weeks.

The next morning, I woke up feeling awful and still suffering the effects of a 53-mile day while dehydrated. I took an impromptu rest day. It ended up being a terrific decision because it rained in the afternoon, and I watched it from the comfort of my motel room.

After a day of exceptional rest, incredibly little physical movement, and a monstrous number of calories consumed, I left Rawlins heading south.

I was ecstatic to see a tree for the first time in a week! It was the first semblance of shade in 200 miles and much appreciated.

As I was going to bed, I realized there was a fire closure coming up. That was something I should've realized and planned for, while in town, but I was enjoying my leisure time too much. Fortunately, my lack of planning didn't have costly consequences. All it meant was that I would have to do a road walk detour, and I was carrying way too much food for this stretch.

The next day was a little rough. I wasn't enjoying it, and my back was hurting from my heavy pack. In the evening, Andrew, a guy I had met a week prior, caught up to me and brightened my day. He was a fast hiker, faster than me, and he forced me to pick up my pace. I could've let him pass on by, but I wanted company for a while. Due to the combined factors of me starting late, and there being dozens of different alternate routes with the wildfires along the Idaho border, I had seen a total of maybe 30 thru-hikers on the CDT, so I had to appreciate them when I could.

After dark, we were walking on a dirt road, still without headlamps because the moonlight offered some visibility, when a car came roaring up on us. We hopped off the road quickly, and then the driver stopped to ask if we were okay. In hindsight, two guys walking on the road after dark with no lights might have looked strange.

It was getting late, and we were tired. I had hiked 38 miles, and Andrew had gone even farther. We were looking for a campsite on the side of the dirt road, and I saw a sign for the Routt National Forest. Then Andrew said, "Oh, wow, look!"

I didn't notice anything. Then, he said it again. I was alarmed something was wrong. *Did he see a bear?* Then, I realized he was pointing out that we were entering Colorado. Wyoming was one of my favorite states all year, but I was ready to enter Colorado and finish my last state on the CDT. After the sign, we immediately hopped in a ditch on the side of the road, and moved tree branches and rocks to make some egregiously poor campsites.

The next day was a road walk into Steamboat Springs, CO because of the fire closure. I was told it was 42 miles into town. The truth, however, was that it was closer to 50 miles. I was also led to believe it was all downhill. It, in fact, was not.

On the dirt road in the morning, it felt like I was going gradually uphill the whole time, like a creaky old rollercoaster. When I hit the paved road, it was actually downhill. Within a few minutes of me stepping foot on the paved road, a friendly lady stopped her car and gave me a beer and a seltzer. Power walking downhill, while drinking a beer and listening to "Way 2 Sexy" in my headphones, made me feel like I was on top of the world.

While walking and drinking my beer, two sheriffs drove by. I was curious to learn if drinking a beer while walking on the side of the road was illegal. They didn't stop, so there must not be a law that specific yet. Or maybe they just liked to party.

It was a monotonous day of road walking, and my hips tightened up again late in the day from the repetitive movement. I was not moving as fast as I should've been, but I made it to Steamboat Springs, and went to the thru-hikers' unofficial meeting spot: McDonald's. I devoured six double cheeseburgers and two large fries. Then Andrew showed up! We hadn't mentioned it to each other. It was just the right place to be.

Andrew got a motel room for the night, but I was feeling cheap. I walked along the train tracks to the baseball field in town and slept in the dugout. Waking up at 3 a.m. to the sound of sprinklers, I was instantly terrified. I anxiously sat there for a couple of seconds, waiting to see if all my belongings were about to be soaked. My entire world rested on the spray radius of these sprinklers. When the water ominously reached my area in rotation, it fell short by about eight feet. Relief washed over me, and it did so much more pleasantly than the water would have.

It was a cold night and a cold morning. I started the day with some breakfast from McDonald's. Then, it was a long and arduous road walk out of town with a lot of traffic. It felt unendingly uphill, which was worse on pavement because I couldn't use my trekking poles to leverage myself on the incline. When I made it back to dirt roads, I was grateful to be off the highway and away from traffic.

I met another thru-hiker named Clouds, and it was refreshing to talk hard rock with someone. It had been a minute since I intellectually discussed the intricacies of Slipknot compared to Killswitch Engage. We hiked together for a while, and he offered to let me take a rest day at his house since he lived in Colorado. As appealing as it sounded, I had to decline. I was on track to beat winter, and I wanted to stay ahead of it, in both Colorado and the Northeast back on the AT.

At dusk, I called my brother. I was talking and walking on a slope of loose dirt, when my foot completely slid out from under me, with all the weight of my body landing right on my hip. I laid there for 30 seconds, groaning and getting mad at the dirt. Then my brother, who had been quiet the whole time, said in a totally monotone and disinterested voice, "What's wrong?" I angrily yelled back, "Nothing! Keep telling me what happened in the NFL!" — just wanting to continue on as if nothing had happened. *Maybe if I ignored it, it wouldn't hurt.*

That hope was futile. My hip was bruised and acutely painful when I started hiking the next morning. On the bright side, this new pain was distracting me from the back pain I had been dealing with from constantly carrying too much food and a heavy pack.

All the suffering was proven worthwhile when I reached Parkview Mountain. It was a brutally steep climb, with an elevation grade around 20%. I reached the summit just before sunset, and it was one of the most spectacular scenes I had ever witnessed. Even though the sky was a little hazy from wildfire smoke further west, it was an unbelievable fiery orange, with silhouettes of mountains as far as the eye could see. I sat up there for 30 minutes, eating some cold-soaked ramen and heaps of peanut butter, simply appreciating being alive. After the sun had dropped to the horizon, and it was beginning to get dark, I hustled down to get off the ridge before it got pitch black. I made camp once I got back down below the tree line.

I took the wrong dirt road the next morning and ended up a couple of miles off trail. Thankfully, I downloaded the surrounding area on Gaia, and was able to find some connector trails, so I didn't have to backtrack. It might've been longer than just backtracking, but my brain wouldn't allow me to go backwards at all. After reconnecting with the trail, I climbed over Bowen Pass, which felt like nothing after Parkview Mountain.

From there, it was all downhill to Grand Lake, CO, which was a welcomed change from the constant up and down as of late. I did a small resupply in Grand Lake, and got a pizza at a sports bar, arriving at the perfect time to watch the first NFL game of the season. I was pleased with the accidental convenience, but one thing I wasn't pleased with was the price I paid for the pizza. I heard Grand Lake would be expensive, but paying $45 for a pizza hurt me to my core.

One of the tasks I had planned to take care of in Grand Lake was to pick up my cold weather gear at the post office. However, the nights had been warmer lately, and I was no longer waking up shivering. To lighten my load, I decided to bounce my package farther down the trail. It puzzled me that despite Colorado's higher elevation compared to Montana and Wyoming, it felt noticeably warmer.

After leaving the sports bar late, I had to find a spot to camp. I walked outside of town and was delighted to find a bathroom at a trailhead that was unlocked. Inside the four-walled shelter, I actually woke up in the middle of the night and was too warm! *That was rare.*

I had a pleasant start to the next day, packing up in the comfort of the warmth. I spent the morning dipping in and out of Rocky Mountain National Park, and then doing the same thing later in the day with Indian Peaks Wilderness. Between the two were some quality campgrounds, and I took advantage of the bathrooms and water spigots. My happiness level rose significantly when I got water that I didn't have to filter. Anytime I made it far into a trail, my Sawyer filter would clog from not being cleaned regularly, and it would take ten minutes to filter a single liter of water.

Shortly before I got to camp for the night, blood began running from my nose. The altitude was getting to me. Nearly the whole trail in Colorado was above 10,000 feet. I had been doing okay, but certainly was not completely unaffected. I felt more fatigued than normal and became out of breath much faster than usual.

On this day specifically, I was dizzy, and also dealt with a throbbing headache and neck-ache. The bloody nose was just another symptom of the altitude, but I didn't have time to bleed. I walked hunched-over until it stopped. I didn't want to get blood splotches on my clothes. I was already a sight when I walked into towns. I didn't need to add blood-stained clothes to the mix. But I also didn't want to stop hiking. Walking hunched over and letting the blood drip in front of me was my compromise.

When I arrived at my campsite, it was not what I was hoping for. It was an area void of fallen trees, a rarity in the area, but it was incredibly slanted. I was too tired to move on, so I accepted the nuisance and set up my tent. It was like a slide inside, with everything shooting towards the bottom of the tent, thanks to the unavoidable annoyance of gravity.

After sleeping on an extreme slope, I somehow woke up feeling better than I had the night before. My headache had vanished, and my neck and upper back didn't hurt for the time being. In the morning and early afternoon, I was high on a ridge and had cell service — a wonderful surprise. I listened to a live broadcast of the Ohio State football game, and I could feel the energy from Columbus out there in the middle of nowhere. I was so amped; I was ready to run up the mountain. As the game neared its end, I took a break for an hour on the summit of James Peak, over 13,000 feet, to listen to it before I would lose signal. The Buckeyes lost, and I shouldn't have wasted my time. I was doubly mad.

Late in the day was another 3,000 foot climb up to Mount Flora, the second 13,000-foot mountain of the day. I was hoping to get there right at sunset, like Parkview Mountain. It turned out to be a tough climb, so it was dark by the time I reached the top. It was a rocky climb, but there were beautiful big rocks aligned all the way up like a puzzle, which made it easier than precarious rock-hopping. Whoever took the time to do that is a true trail saint. I couldn't even imagine the amount of work it took.

From atop Mount Flora, I could see all the lights of sprawled-out Denver. It was a weird feeling. It felt like I was so alone out there. It was only my headlamp and me. However, just a short distance away, there were a million people going to bed like any other day. I camped above 11,000 feet that night, and the nighttime chill reminded me of the changing seasons.

The next morning, I took the Silverthorne Alternate. I *needed* to get into town. I was feeling dreadfully fatigued. My back was in constant pain and felt awfully tight. The heavy pack I had been carrying combined with sleeping on slopes did not help. My neck was also increasingly tight from the same things. I was just tired. I wasn't feeling sick from the altitude, but it was wearing me down in a new kind of way. I struggled to push myself through one more tough day and camped outside Silverthorne.

The next day, I entered town early, but since I still had plenty of food, I only bought a few snacks from a gas station. In need of rest, I checked into the cheapest motel. They said my room wouldn't be ready for a few hours. I said that was fine, but I had nowhere else to go, so I sat down on the couch in the lobby and began working on my plans for the coming days. After sitting there for only ten minutes, the front desk clerk informed me that my room was ready. It wasn't my intention, but I guess having a smelly and dirty hiker sit in their main lobby was a good way to strong-arm them into giving me a room immediately.

As soon as the room to my door closed, I collapsed on the floor and took a nap. I knew I should shower first, so I could nap in the bed like a normal person, but I was so physically exhausted, the immediate sleep on the floor sounded more satisfying. I had only walked a mile into town that morning, but I was drained. It was a struggle to just stand up at the hotel counter earlier, when the front desk clerk was entering my information.

The extreme exhaustion wasn't a surprise. Lately, it had been tougher hiking because of the high elevations in Colorado sapping my energy. I was definitely moving slower, but I was still determined to hike over 30 miles a day, which also cut back on my sleep. My body was also still suffering from the lingering effects from breaking my rule about consistency and pushing my limits on a 53-mile day without drinking enough water. And there might've been some mental fatigue from nearly dying in the Wind River Range. A reminder of the relative ease and closeness of death from one simple mistake can wear on a man.

I was tired, and I knew I was tired. But I was so close. Now was not the time to get soft. One rest day here and there was fine, but to an extent, I had to suck it up. I was so close to being done with the CDT and didn't have much left on the AT. I wasn't going to lose sight of the ultimate goal. I could rest for a day, then I had to get back to being a consistent hiking machine. I had to get back to being Horsepower.

Run Through the Finish Line

Colorado had been beautiful the whole time thus far, but leaving that motel was the first time I realized I was hitting it at its most scenic time of the year. The aspens were turning for the fall, and everything had a beautiful contrast: the tall golden grass, entrancing yellow aspens, and still lush green vegetation. Everything was vibrant, and I got my first taste of true Colorado weather with the beauty. Later in the day, the sky alternated a few times between blue and clear to dark and scary before starting to drop hail. They were good-sized chunks, and I didn't feel like getting pelted, so I took shelter under a tree and sat down for ten minutes while it passed.

It was also the first time I stepped foot on the generous and welcoming Colorado Trail, and it was noticeable. The Colorado Trail overlaps the CDT for a good portion of the state, but the conditions of the trails were much different. The CDT was rugged, wild, and seemingly not taken care. Meanwhile, the Colorado Trail was in excellent condition and much more pleasant to hike on. I also never feared I was off trail on the Colorado Trail. It was incredibly well-marked and easy to follow. I was seeing more people too — catching up to more southbound CDT hikers and also seeing Colorado Trail thru-hikers. It was unusual to see hikers at camp for the night by 4 p.m. because CDT hikers would never do that. Seeing these people on their sub-500 mile journey of the Colorado Trail was a good reminder of how far I had come, but also, how far I still had to go. I had to keep pushing. There would be no early days for me anymore.

After sleeping cozily in a pit toilet at Tennessee Pass, I woke up at 5:30 a.m., raring to go. There was a cooler outside with drinks for hikers. I opened it up and heartily kicked off the day with a beer at 6 a.m. It felt like two years prior, on a college football gameday, except now I had to walk 30 miles after that first beer.

Most of the day was in wooded areas, including the early morning. I was walking in the woods before the sun came out. It was reminiscent of the AT, except that it was warm. I passed a guy that was bundled up in multiple layers, while I was rocking shorts, a shirt, and a jacket. He said he couldn't believe how cold it was. Internally I thought, *Aw, how cute, you don't know real cold*, but out loud, I just agreed and kept moving.

In the afternoon, my stomach started to hurt after I consumed a lot of Sour Patch Kids, peanut butter, and Cheez-its, all at one time — apparently not a great combo. My back was also hurting, so I laid down to take a break for five minutes. I ended up falling asleep for a half hour. I was upset, but my body must have needed it.

Thirty-two miles into the day, I felt rejuvenated and wanted to hike on. However, I had to camp before I passed Twin Lakes because I had to pick up a food box and the gear I had bounced there. With hindsight, I wished I didn't send anything there. I didn't even buy food in the last town, and I still had plenty to keep going. If I didn't have to pick up my cold weather gear, I could've hiked past Twin Lakes, but I wasn't going to leave it stranded there all by its lonesome, like Tom Hanks in *Castaway*.

The next morning, I met a few other hikers and talked shop while waiting for the store to open. After it opened, I picked up my box, and of course, some Dr. Pepper. I traded out some of my summer gear for colder gear and got ready to send my unneeded stuff home. The worker said they didn't usually send out packages, but he was benevolent and helped me out. I was immensely thankful he did, otherwise I would've been carrying two backpacks and two sleeping bags. The sad part about the day was that I had to throw away my hiking shirt. It had been sewn, stitched, and repaired a number of times, but it had reached the end of its line after 5,000 miles of wearing it. I counted 22 sizeable holes and tears when I threw it away.

The new gear I picked up was as follows: a winter sleeping bag, a heavier-duty backpack, two warm base layers, and winter mittens. I was determined to stay warm if an early winter came to Colorado. With my new gear, it was definitely heavier, but the new pack also carried the weight better. It had an internal frame to support more weight, unlike the frameless packs I had been using for over 4,000 miles in the summer. It was the same pack I was using in the winter on the AT for my heavy gear. My back felt a little better today with the new pack, and I hoped the frame taking the brunt of the weight would allow it to gradually heal.

Leaving Twin Lakes, I thought the trail posed a meager 1,500-foot climb, but it turned out to be over 3,000 feet up to Hope Pass. After an abominably steep ascent to, and descent from, the crest of Hope Pass, where every person hiking in the opposite direction complained how ridiculous it was, I still had another 2,000-foot climb over Lake Ann Pass. By the time I crested that, it was well after dark. As I settled into my new sleeping bag, I was giddy with excitement like a kid on Christmas. This sleeping bag was significantly warmer than my summer one, and it was definitely overkill for the current temperature, but I would rather have it early than late.

I enjoyed how warm my sleeping bag was a little too much, and overslept until 7:30 a.m. Unlike a few months ago, when the days stretched long, I actually needed to try to be conscious of when I got up because daylight was dwindling every day. I ran into a hiker that said he saw frozen puddles on the trail when he started hiking at 4:30 a.m that morning.

Another reminder — *Winter is coming.*

Entering the Collegiate Peaks Wilderness slightly skeptical because it had been hyped up so much, it surpassed my expectations. It was truly remarkable. After the initial climb out of the valley, sweeping landscapes adorned with vast golden grass and autumnal aspens unfolded before me.

At the sole road crossing of the day, there were a lot of people and cars, but two RVs provided the only source of shade in the area. I was warm, so I sat down beside one to take a break. Within 30 seconds, the driver got in and drove away. I moved to the next one, and the same thing happened. I suspiciously looked around and wondered if I was on a hidden camera show.

For two consecutive nights, I found myself cresting a pass after sunset. Having done less night hiking in the summer, compared to early in the trip, I was again becoming accustomed to it being a daily occurrence. I didn't get to enjoy the spanning views after the sun took its leave of absence, but with some good tunes, I could get in my zone and simply go, without paying attention to how much time passed. The only real negative to the exceptional day, was that I felt a twinge in my foot again. It didn't hurt as bad as some of the odd, frightening pangs I had experienced in the past, but it was something that worried me when I was so close to finishing.

I woke up the next morning, knowing it would be the day I finished the CDT. I had less than 30 miles to Monarch Pass, the spot where I got off the CDT in April. The whole day flew by, and before I knew it, I was taking my final steps to Monarch Pass.

It felt sensational to have completed the CDT, but I was following a mantra of David Goggins. "I don't stop when I'm tired. I stop when I'm done." And I wasn't done with the CDT yet. I had been working on my logistical plans for a while, and determined I was going to do some extra hiking in Colorado for a couple of reasons. The first was to make up for the mileage that I cut off due to taking the Big Sky Alternate, because of the fires, and my road walk in April, because of snow. My plan was to do ten more days and 300 miles in Colorado to make up for those. The second reason for my extra hiking in the state was because I had the time. I was well on pace to finish the Calendar Year Triple Crown before winter hit in the Northeast. It would be a little colder and more challenging with me delaying it ten days, but it would still be doable. As long as I summited Katahadin by October 15th, normally its last legal day to summit, I would achieve my goal.

When I went into the little store at the pass, I was disappointed that they no longer had the logbook from the last time I was there. I guess I was there too early, and it was still from the previous year. The earliest entries in the new book were dated a month after I went through. I was keenly curious to see what I had written back in April. Part of me thought that I called my shot and vowed that I would be back there by the end of September, but I couldn't remember exactly. I charged up in the store, did a small resupply because I thought I was still carrying too much food, and ate three breakfast sandwiches. After a few hours, I headed back out and continued south from Monarch Pass. It was time to pound out some bonus miles.

I slept in a small shelter, similar to one on the AT, at 11,500 feet. There was an uneven dirt floor, so it wasn't ideal for my back, but I took advantage of every opportunity I could to avoid setting up my tent. I woke up in the middle of the night and heard something approaching the shelter. I sat up, then heard it run off. Shortly after I left in the morning, I saw a few deer close by and assumed one of them was the culprit.

The morning greeted me with cold temperatures, as clouds hugged the 11,000-foot ridges I was hiking, enveloping me in their damp chill. The rocky trail took a toll on my eternally pain-ridden feet, causing me to slow down. There were also a lot of dirt bikers, so I was frequently stepping off of the trail to let them fly by. I felt bad all day, and late in the day, my foot had a twinge and felt weird again. I unexpectedly got overwhelmingly dizzy. My legs became wobbly, and I was stumbling along like a drunkard for a few minutes. I could tell something was wrong, but my determination to keep moving clouded my judgment. My mind felt foggy, struggling to discern the exact location of the trail, yet my instinct pushed me forward. I weaved back and forth over the trail shakily, continuing my forward progress until regaining my composure after several minutes of disorientation.

Despite the challenges, I capped off a 30-mile day by 8 p.m. and set up camp for the night. As I was packing up the next morning, I looked at my watch to see it said September 20th. *It was my birthday.* I was now 24. There were no gifts, no party, no celebration to look forward to. All I had was another day to live my dream and hike 30 miles.

It was a boring day of hiking through the Cochetopa Hills. The hiking was easy, but there weren't awe-inspiring mountains around. I was having a pretty unenjoyable birthday — bored from the lack of scenery, lack of cell service to call anyone, and lack of food.

Shortly before sunset, my dismal mood and poor attitude shifted. A herd of elk appeared to the left of the trail. The herd stood still, except for the one big bull literally running circles around the others while they grazed. As soon as they noticed me, they stared for 45 seconds before gracefully retreating. Less than five minutes later, I came across three moose. Standing less than 40 yards away, I watched in awe. Two smaller moose, measuring under five feet at the shoulders, were accompanied by a colossal third moose, towering over six feet tall at the shoulders with a massive rack of antlers. I wasn't sure if they saw me or not. They didn't show any sign they did, but they were lucky I wasn't a hunter. It was moose season, and they were only 40 yards away from a dirt road — not their best move. After a few minutes, they gracefully trotted off into the trees. This encounter completely redeemed my day, leaving me utterly satisfied with my birthday experience.

Already riding high, my excitement rose even more several minutes later when I passed a stream with a beaver frolicking in the water. *Nature was smiling at me.* With blithe appreciation, I cruised through the rest of the night. There were two stream crossings, which I opted to do that night, so I would end with wet feet, rather than start the next day with them.

I was stubborn enough and made it across both water ways with dry feet. I was planning on camping after the second one but looked at my map and saw a parking lot three miles ahead with bathrooms. The prospect of sleeping inside a bathroom was strongly motivating now that it was cold again. I turned on my hard rock playlist, led by "Kickstart My Heart," and glided through the last three miles to cap off a 37-mile day.

As I emerged from the cozy confines of the bathroom the next morning, I was greeted by bone-chilling cold. This was the first time in months that my nose and cheeks felt numb. I talked to a guy later in the day that camped at a lower elevation, and his truck said 21 degrees when he woke up. Winter was coming, and I had to readjust to its icy embrace.

I was feeling particularly rough, having made a mistake during my last resupply; I thought I had more leftover food in my pack, and didn't check before leaving Monarch Pass. I only bought a modicum of food, and it wasn't enough. The prior day, I consumed a mere 2,500 calories, and now I had only 600 left — quite a change from my normal 5,000 calories per day.

This hungry dog did not run faster. My lack of energy was palpable on a 2,000-foot climb, having to stop frequently, becoming short of breath quickly, and lacking my usual vigor. I was at 12,500 feet, but still, I didn't normally get winded after 20 steps and feel like I needed another break. It was a grueling and seemingly unending morning.

After that climb, it was at least downhill. I took the Creede Cutoff Alternate to keep my schedule. I made it down to a dirt road and saw a man returning to his truck. Even though I was struggling, I was still foolishly prideful, and felt ashamed to ask if he had extra food. But I mustered the courage, and he did. He was more than welcoming, and I downed the food and a Coke while chatting with him. He was amused that I devoured all the chocolate first, before going to the trail mix and banana crisps. After thanking him for helping me much more than he knew, I arrived in Creede, CO feeling much better. I was still hungry, but I wasn't starving.

Creede greeted me with an abundance of kindness. I went to the grocery store to resupply, and while I was waiting in line to checkout, sticking out like a sore thumb, a wonderful woman said she would pay for my groceries. She asked my start date, and then went on her way after paying — a random act of kindness with absolutely no expectation of anything in return. People rock. The cheerful cashier then asked if I had any trash she could take for me, which was helpful. I went outside the store and sat on a bench, and as I was rearranging my pack, some people stopped by to ask some questions. They were thrilled to hear about my goal, and said they'd pray for my safety. It was constant kindness after constant kindness. The town of Creede exuded an unwavering benevolence that felt almost surreal.

The following day was a pleasantly undemanding day of flat road walking into South Fork, CO. I got to town around 4 p.m. and spent the night there to rest a bit. The place I stayed had this neat little trick. The room's price was lower than all the other places in town, but when I showed up to pay in person, there was a $75 cleaning fee added at the last second. I was fuming on the inside, but I stifled my anger with a large meat lovers pizza and a couple of 2-liters of Dr. Pepper. Somehow, I lost my toothbrush and toothpaste again, so I had to buy new ones in town. Thankfully, I didn't have to go two weeks before doing so this time.

When I reached Wolf Creek Pass the next day, I hopped back onto the official CDT. At the pass, I met a young couple who said they had a bottle of cheap rum that they both didn't want. From the way I looked, they must've assumed I'd be willing to drink anything — and they were right. I took a healthy swig, and after a few seconds of chugging, I didn't want it either, but it gave me a sharp jolt to get started back on the dirt trail. It was a good day of hiking on actual trail again.

The following day wasn't so pleasant in the regal but rough South San Juan Wilderness. It quickly became apparent that I was back solely on the Continental Divide Trail, not the Colorado Trail. The trail was wildly uneven, hard to follow, overgrown, and looked like it hadn't been taken care of. In a weird, masochistic way, it felt good to be back on the cold-hearted CDT, but it did hamper my speed.

I was moving slowly all day, but around 5 p.m., I came across the first person on this stretch. He was lying down on the other side of the creek. I went up to say hello, and he muttered a little, so softly that I had to get closer to hear him. After struggling to comprehend him, I realized he said something about "Emergency SOS."

He had just hit the SOS button on his Garmin because he had been having trouble breathing. Between short, struggling gasps, he assured me I didn't have to stick around. He said he'd had trouble breathing for a couple of days, but it had gotten much worse now. I was certainly not an expert, but he appeared to also be having a panic attack.

There was no way I could leave him like that. I awarded myself some rest and sat down, waiting for the helicopter to arrive. Since he was having trouble breathing, I assumed he didn't want to talk much, so I just rested and ate some food. He kept freaking out and muttering things that didn't make sense. In response, I offered the best medical advice I could, occasionally saying, "Don't worry, you're going to be alright." That was where my medical expertise maxed out. Eventually, he calmed down, and we started to chat a little. By the time the helicopter showed up, he was in much better spirits and seemed to be breathing fine.

It was unbelievable how much of a calming effect I had on him, just being there — knowing that he wasn't alone. *I was the shadow in his storm.*

When the chopper showed up, I wanted to ask if they'd drop me off a few miles up the trail, but I figured they weren't the type to joke around. I hiked a few more miles before ending the day early, after only 24 miles.

The following morning, I inadvertently strayed over a mile off the trail before realizing my mistake. Rather than go backwards, I spotted a pass in the mountain and made my own way up to it, hoping to find a route to reconnect with the trail. This detour took me through a marshy area, leaving my feet wet and my temper hot. After some rock-hopping and climbing, I made it up to the pass, and after a few miles of hiking overland, reconnected with the trail. Even though I was walking in the middle of nowhere, it didn't feel much different than the actual "trail" because it was so rugged as of late.

In the afternoon, I smelled something burning. Shortly thereafter, I saw a campfire still smoking. This really pissed me off. Selfishly, I was mad that I had to use all my water to put it out. Unselfishly, I was mad that someone could be so ignorant, as to leave a fire going with as bad as wildfires had been lately. Fueled by anger, I hiked aggressively.

As I exited the unforgettable and unforgiving South San Juan Wilderness, I saw signs that read, "Warning Dangerous Trail," which I thought was inaccurate. They should've said "Warning Nonexistent Trail." Shortly before I made it down to Cumbres Pass near the New Mexican border, I excitedly collected water. Having used much of mine to put out the fire, I had only consumed a liter throughout the day.

The next day, I turned north, and walked the same road I did back in April. Everything looked strikingly different now. Then, everything was covered in multiple feet of snow. Now it was a vibrant collage of contrasting autumn colors. After walking that road for a bit, I took a turn that I didn't take back in April, and continued on the Great Divide Alternate — the bike route from Mexico to Canada along the divide — for the rest of the day.

When I woke up to a glowing orange sky, with a chorus of songbirds, and a breeze that seemed to whisper to me, I knew it was my last day on the Continental Divide Trail. It had been ten days since reaching Monarch Pass, and it was time to head back to the AT.

It was a peaceful and simple last day — the opposite of my final day on the PCT, which was filled with stress, challenging terrain, a tight timeline, and an approaching fire. This final day was effortless hiking with perfect weather, and I didn't even have an endpoint. After 30 miles, my foot started to have some problems. I went a little farther, and called it a day. I didn't want to risk a more serious injury that would put my AT finish in jeopardy. So I just stopped on the side of the dirt road.

No terminus. No endpoint. Just me.

Phase V:

Appalachian Trail

Katahdin to Stratton Mountain

October 2nd–October 25th

Conquering Katahdin and Continuing

After resting for a couple of days with a friend in Denver, I flew into Bangor, ME. Getting to the northern terminus posed a challenge because it was so remote. Thankfully, I got some help! Kim, who I had met in Glacier, offered to get me to the terminus. Words couldn't express how grateful I was, considering she drove over 14 hours round-trip. Her kindness and willingness to help seemed incomprehensible after only meeting for 20 minutes a few months earlier. In life, people often say things they don't really mean. "If you need anything, let me know." "We have to get together soon." "I'd love to help you with that." "Yeah, your baby is cute."

But I've found that in the world of backpacking, and more specifically thru-hiking, people genuinely mean what they say. If someone wishes you luck, they sincerely mean it. If an old friend reaches out and wants to grab a beer when you're nearby, they'll follow through. And if someone you briefly met offers to help you out months from now when you're around their stomping grounds, they actually will. The spirit and community of humanity seem to be more open-minded, open-hearted, and sincere, when people are more vulnerable and at the will of nature.

I had been worrying about my permit to summit Katahdin for a while. *What if they're maxed out for the year? What if I can't get one? What if I hiked this whole year, but can't hike the last five northern miles of the AT?*

Like all worrying, it was a waste of energy. Everything went fine, and I commenced my ascent of Katahdin around 9 a.m. The trail was the same-old, same-old for a while. It was going uphill, but it wasn't crazy. I was confused why people said this climb was so difficult. Then I found out. When the trail went above tree line, it became an all-out scramble to the top.

It all came to a head when I reached a point where there was a tall rock slab in front of me, with an iron bar sticking out of the side of the mountain. To continue, I had to pull myself up on the iron bar, and climb over it to the ledge above. I went up to it, grabbed it, began to pull myself up, but then retreated out of fear.

All I could think about was the massive fall behind me. *I had to pull myself up on this bar, and doing so would put all my momentum leaning backwards. If something went wrong, I would go flying hundreds of feet.* It was freaking me out. Then I reminded myself that *this was nothing.* I had depended on rocks all year for hand and foot holds. This bar was man-made and steady. I had pulled myself up over a ledge, after nearly falling in New Mexico, using precarious rocks, and was fine. I went through a traumatic ordeal dangling off a rock in Wyoming, slid down a mountain, was in a major rockslide, and was fine. I made it here. This bar was nothing.

I grabbed onto it, pulled myself up, and even dangled there for a few seconds, leaning completely backwards with a fall of hundreds of vertical feet below me, just to stomp on its grave. I felt free.

After I conquered that, the rest of the climb seemed elementary. As I stood atop the prominent summit, an odd mixture of emotions welled within me. In my head, I always envisioned reaching that point to be an overwhelming flood of emotions for an epic achievement. It was such an iconic spot and the ultimate way to end a trail, but it didn't mark the end of the trail for me. Since I had to flip-flop, it only marked the beginning of my southbound hike. All I felt was the same feeling I had at the end of the PCT and at Monarch Pass on the CDT — relief. I was relieved that this part was over, but I was focused on the work yet to come. I had 500 miles left to make it back to where I succumbed to the cruelty of winter and got off the AT. I wasn't going to let any preemptive celebrating get in the way of accomplishing my ultimate goal.

Following the descent, I came upon trail magic at The Birches campsite, where a group of northbound hikers, set to finish their journey the next day, had gathered. Initially, I wasn't going to stop. Then, I was just going to stop for a beer, and then a burger and two beers, and then I decided that if I was going stay there for a bit, I needed to get a good buzz, so I could hike for a while in the dark. Before I knew it, I found myself immersed in lively conversations around the campfire, slugging beers, and thoroughly enjoying the camaraderie. It was the first time since the Sierra snowstorm in May that I had been in the company of such a large group.

When I did leave, my plan worked like a charm. I had a good buzz going, and I was having an amusing time hiking by myself. After five miles, I sat down on a rock to take a break, turned off my headlamp, looked up at the night sky covered in glittering stars, and felt pure ecstasy. I was so happy.

Still behind on sleep from my travel day, I overslept the next morning by four hours and wasn't walking on the trail until 10 a.m. in the 100 Mile Wilderness. While I had built up a considerable hatred for the AT during the year, mostly due to hiking it in the cruel and unforgiving winter, I was grateful to be back in the green tunnel. I didn't have to worry about sunburns because of the constant tree cover. Water was abundant — no longer a constant worry as it had been in most western sections of the trails. Most of all, I reveled in the availability of shelters and privies — a luxury I had sorely missed. Even for hiking 8,000 miles in a year, I was a lazy person. I loved using privies so I wouldn't have to dig a cat-hole, and I loved camping in shelters to refrain from setting up my tent. The shelters were also more hospitable this time of year. Unlike in winter, I no longer had to wage war against starving, savage mice every night.

My third day got off to an early start when the other hikers in the shelter awoke at 4 a.m., which I liked because it made me do the same. One of the guys said his family would be doing trail magic a little ways up the trail. After looking forward to it all day, I got there in the afternoon. I was delighted to sit down, have a Coke and a Coors, and chat with some hikers. I was getting a small taste of the normal AT experience.

I rolled up to an empty shelter at 8:30 p.m. and was still feeling good. So I pushed on for four more miles to the next one, and arrived two hours later, discovering a negative aspect of the normal AT experience. The shelter was full and all the decent campsites were taken. I camped on a rocky slope near two other people that got there late. It made me appreciate the simplicity of being alone for most of the year. The only other time limited campsites even entered my mind was in southern California on the PCT. I also realized what a luxury I had in the winter, having the shelters to myself nearly every night. I could air out my soaking wet body naked if I wanted. That was not the case for many AT thru-hikers.

The next day was a big ego check. Oversleeping until 9 a.m., I struggled to cover 17 miles. Even excluding the late start, I was moving painstakingly slow over the unforgiving Whitecap Mountains. It was the first real climbing in the 100 Mile Wilderness, which I entered days earlier. Before today, I was moving a little slower, but that was because the trail was riddled with rocks and roots. Today had the killer combination of rocks, roots, and steep climbing. I knew it would be tough to mentally adjust to the lower mileages I would cover on the AT with the tougher terrain, but 17 miles was simply too low. I was disappointed, especially for how exhausting it was.

Around midday, my back tight and craving relief, I succumbed to the temptation to lie down and try to crack my back. Overwhelmed by contentment and fatigue, all I desired was to drift off to sleep while laying prone. However, fueled by pride, I compelled myself to rise and resume my journey, albeit slowly.

The highlight of the day came when I encountered my first ford in the 100 Mile Wilderness. Fording rivers had been one of the main reasons I had chosen to flip off of the AT earlier in the year, in addition to the treacherous snow conditions. When I was there during the high snow melt season, I had been repeatedly warned about the dangers of fording. Yet, in October, these fears proved unfounded. While it was impossible to cross the rivers with dry feet, they posed no real danger.

To my surprise and delight, I stumbled upon a pair of abandoned boots at one of the fords, left behind by a considerate hiker. Thus, saving other hikers from having to soak their own shoes and socks. As I arrived at the river, some hikers had just brought them over. Otherwise, they would've been on the wrong side of the river for me. *The trail provides.*

Having seen no animals on the AT in winter, other than mice and deer, I had my first real encounter after dark when I saw a set of eyes. As I got closer, I realized the eyes were far above my head. It was a moose!

We had a stare down for a bit. Then, I started telling him how time is a flat circle, and after that bit ran out, I discussed how it might be time to shift his portfolio from growth back to value. He didn't want to hear any of that and took off. Whenever I needed to make noise or talk, because of an animal, I was embarrassingly poor at talking to myself, so I would always go into a long movie quote, song, or start up a conversation with the creature.

I recovered well after my 17-mile day with some easier terrain. Getting to an exposed summit shortly after sunrise, I felt rejuvenated from the radiant sky as dawn signaled a new day. But the real treat of the day was when I reached Barren Mountain. After being immersed in the green tunnel since sunrise, reaching a summit with a ladder was a pleasant surprise. I felt a little more angst with every rung I climbed, but once I reached the top, I was awe-struck by the amazing 360-degree view. I had never seen so many different colored trees and such a majestic display of plentiful, vibrant, autumn beauty. It was at that moment, I realized autumn was in full swing. *I was in Maine at the perfect time of the year.*

Upon reaching Monson, I went to Shaw's Hostel to resupply, still having plenty of food. I didn't have to buy much, so it was an interesting dynamic in the store. I was extremely lax about what little food I was going to buy for the next stretch. Meanwhile, the northbound hikers were stressing out about their resupply for the 100 Mile Wilderness because it was the longest food carry for most on the AT. Some people were asking me for advice, which I found amusing. I hadn't even told them what I was doing all year, so they had no idea how experienced I was. I guess they assumed I was knowledgeable by my lack of concern with what I was buying.

After my resupply, I sat at a picnic table with other hikers, charging my phone and drinking Cokes. Everyone seemed like a tight group that had been hiking together for a while, so I didn't overtly insert myself into the conversation. Eventually, one guy started talking to me. I asked him how his hike had been, and he asked about mine. He then asked me if I hiked the PCT or CDT, and I said yes to both. He asked when I had hiked them, and I said this year. He looked at me puzzledly for ten seconds and then asked again. After confirming it by asking me a few more times, he was astounded.

The cat was now out of the bag. He began telling everyone, and I felt like a zoo animal with the way they looked at me. I didn't mind, though. It was funny seeing all their reactions. I hadn't had the joy of seeing many people's reactions to my incomprehensible goal since southern California. It didn't lose its entertainment value.

Some of them began to bribe me to stay with the offer of beer and a campfire, and I was an easy sell. It ended up being a fantastic night. What was initially meant to be an hour, turned into five, as we shared stories and bonded over our experiences on the trail. They wanted to know all about my year — the stories, logistics, places.

What I loved most was hearing about their experiences on the AT. One guy had to hike past midnight for his first few weeks on trail to catch up to his girlfriend that had started earlier. Another guy quit in the middle of the trail, and, once he got home, wondered why the hell he did that, and came back to finish it. One girl had her house burn down while she was away and had nothing to go back to. All she had was what she carried on her back. It was incredible to hear people's raw stories, especially when they were so close to being finished with the whole trail. Even though I was close to being done myself, it was moving.

After my repeated proclamations of "only one more beer," or "only one more hour," the gang kept saying I would end up spending the night, but I was adamant not to. I didn't want to spend the money, and I knew I should cover a few more miles. When the last person went to bed at 11 p.m., I packed up and got hiking, doing a few more miles before setting up camp.

As I expected, I woke up late and hungover. It was bad at first, but this was where my training came into effect. A key point of my training for the Calendar Year Triple Crown was doing my long runs on Saturday or Sunday mornings, when I was still hungover. If I could handle that, then I could handle feeling awful after big mile days on the trail too. It worked pretty well all year, but it was never as directly correlated as that day.

Around 5:30 p.m., I realized, I was just over two miles away from the summit of Moxie Mountain. I couldn't think of what time the sun was setting lately because I hadn't been paying close attention. I just knew it was getting earlier, and there was no twilight at all this far north. I wanted to make it to the summit for sunset, so I tried to run up the dreadfully steep mountain as fast as I could. In my haste, my toe flap got caught on a root, and my momentum carried me forward as my body slammed into the ground with tremendous force.

There was no time for self-pity. I got up and kept running. Although I arrived at the summit just after sunset, the remaining hues in the sky still painted a beautiful scene. The fading luminescent orange mingling with layers of blue mountain ridges captivated my senses. Attempting to capture it with my camera proved futile, reminding me that some experiences are meant to be cherished in person.

The next day, I faced the biggest logistical concern on the AT, other than the timing for Katahdin. It was something I was thinking about before I even began — crossing the Kennebec River. Known for its width, rapidly changing water levels, and danger, fording the river was strongly discouraged. I was a poor swimmer, and I didn't want to get my gear wet, so I knew I was never going to go against that recommendation.

When I was heading north earlier in the year, the ferry that ran hikers across the river during the summer hadn't begun for the season, and when I reached it now in October, the ferry just finished running for the year. With my out-of-season hike of the AT, this was one of the added logistical challenges. Thankfully, there was a woman who lived on the banks of the river, owned a canoe, and could bring hikers across. After doing a small resupply in Caratunk, ME, I went to her house, and we began rowing across the river. I was quickly reminded of how weak my upper body was now. For a while, we were stuck in the current and pointlessly rowing in place. When we wearily made it up the river and to the other side, I was exhausted. That was one of the hardest tenths of a mile I covered all year.

I woke up the next morning before my 4:30 alarm, raring to go. It was the first time I woke up early and felt energized in a while. After breaking a trekking pole the previous night with poor visibility because my headlamp was dead, I replaced the batteries that morning. I was ready to have a good day, but even I wasn't prepared for how great it would be.

With the sunrise, I began ascending into the Bigelow Mountains. The steep climb tested my endurance, but when I reached the summit, I was rewarded with one of the most majestic views I had ever witnessed. The landscape stretched out before me, showcasing the outstretched arm of autumn in all its glory. The vivid reds, oranges, and yellows of the leaves enveloped the surroundings, and the vast lakes added to the otherworldly beauty. This breathtaking sight surpassed even the awe I had experienced on Barren Mountain. In that moment, I understood why people loved Maine so much — it was a wild and magical place.

After the jaw-dropping views of the ridge, I hustled down the 3,000-foot descent as fast as I could, to get into town to resupply. I reached the road crossing shortly after sunset, and there was precisely eight minutes of twilight before it was pitch black. No cars had stopped, so I accepted defeat and called a nearby hostel. It was only marginally more expensive to stay there for the night, rather than to just get a ride to and from the trail to resupply, so I decided I might as well stay the night.

I did enjoy the luxury of getting a shower and doing laundry after barely a week on trail, which was particularly unusual compared to my lack of cleanliness most of the year — going weeks between showers and months between laundry sessions. Lately, I had been enjoying the benefits of the AT compared to the other trails, and if the AT did anything far better than the other trails, it was definitely the ease of laundry and loaner clothes.

The atmosphere was a little strange at the hostel because it wasn't just hikertrash. There were "normal people" too. I even had a woman nervously say, "Oh, this room isn't women only?" when the host brought me in. Comparatively, I looked much more civilized and harmless at that time than I did most of the year — but I'm not sure if that's saying much. Maybe unintentionally scaring people in hostels was a part of the normal AT hiking experience I was searching for. I would enjoy it while I had it.

Lord, You Know I'm Tired

I hopped back on trail the following morning and climbed into a cloud. It wasn't raining, but it was foggy and misty all day. I had no right to complain, however. The weather had been treating me unusually well lately. In the winter, the unforgiving sky spat rain or snow down on me one out of every three days. Now I'd had more than a week of perfect weather since starting at Katahdin. Things were looking up!

Most of the day was in the woods. There were a few summits and a three-mile exposed section above tree line over the Saddleback Mountains, but I couldn't see anything with the fog. Shortly after the sun had set, I searched my pack for my headlamp. After not being able to find it, I remembered that I knocked it behind a bench at the hostel and went to go do something else before picking it up. Well, I forgot about it and didn't pick it up. I was aggravated at my carelessness.

I spent the next few hours using my phone flashlight, either trying to hold it uncomfortably with one hand, thus rendering that limb useless, or wedging it in my shoulder strap pocket, which pointed most of the light to the left and above of where I was walking. It was not an ideal setup. With less than 12 hours of daylight, and me trying to hike 16–17 hours a day, it was a bad time to lose my headlamp. For something so cheap, its absence was profoundly felt, much like my toothbrush several weeks prior.

Within a half hour of hiking after dark, I couldn't see where I was going and got off trail. The terrain would've been tough with a headlamp. Without one, it was like playing hide-and-seek under a new moon. As I walked on an exposed ledge to reconnect with the trail, I saw a pine branch that I was about to step on, assuming it was on solid ground. It turned out to be hanging over the edge, so I stepped onto thin air and fell off the ledge. Fortunately, it was only a 6-foot fall instead of 600 feet.

When I landed, I heard a snap. It wasn't my arm or leg because I landed painlessly on my pack. It was my other trekking pole. This one didn't break at the bottom section, where it was still slightly usable if I hunched over. This one snapped in the middle, so it was completely useless. After nine days back on the AT, I was down to half of a trekking pole.

The following morning, I arrived in Rangeley, hoping there would be a decent gear store. Luck was on my side. Not only did I get a new headlamp, which was my main point of concern, but I also got a new hat, to replace the one I had lost, and replacement parts for my trekking poles. The store had a box of random pole replacement parts, and after looking through the whole thing, they had only three pieces that fit my model of poles, and they were the exact three that I needed.

The trail provides!

After getting a few burgers and fries at the marina, I got a ride back to the trail with a male version of Uma Thurman in *Pulp Fiction*. I got in the car; we looked at each other with a look of tired respect, said hello, and just sat there in silence for the duration of the ride. It wasn't an uncomfortable silence. It was actually refreshing. We were both perfectly content just sitting there and feeling no pressure to make small talk — comfortably sharing the silence. It was just two dudes hanging out. When we arrived, I said thanks, and went on my way. It was one of my favorite encounters of the year.

With my new trekking poles and a fresh headlamp, I set off feeling invigorated. But that feeling progressively faded throughout the day, along with my energy, as the hiking proved exceptionally tiring. After I trudged through the next morning, I made it into Andover, ME for a small resupply, a short respite, and a pizza. While I sat in a booth in my depleted state, a woman passed by me and plainly said, "You look tired."

She was right.

I felt absolutely exhausted and must've looked the part too, but I was so close to the finish line — less than 250 miles away. I told the woman I'd be alright. No matter how tough this terrain was on my body, it didn't matter. I didn't have time to be tired, and I couldn't afford to get soft now.

My mind went back to all my training, and not the physical training I already mentioned, but the mental training. Before I left, I worked on logistical concerns for the year, but I also worked on toughening my mind. In conjunction with physical training, like practicing sleep deprivation or running while hungover, I prepared myself to be miserable.

I read journals of other hiker's adventures, not to read about the majesty of the trail or how great their day was, but to understand how unbelievably terrible things could be sometimes. Applying this secondhand suffering, I would think about the upcoming journey, section by section, and envision the worst possible things happening. If I could mentally prepare myself for the worst beforehand, whatever happened in reality wouldn't be that bad. I had a true "Prepare for the worst. Pray for the best." mentality.

As a big fan of movies, I also turned to them to mentally prepare myself. Just because something is fiction doesn't mean you can't empathize with the characters and gain something from it, and I used movies to prepare myself for success. Whether it was watching *The Revenant* or *The Grey* to prepare myself for the harsh brutality of winter, *John Wick* to see the unstoppable force of a man with a singular objective, *The Pursuit of Happyness* to see the undeniable resolve of the human spirit, the *Saw* series to witness humanity's unbelievable survival instinct, or *Apocalypse Now* or *1917* to show the relentless pursuit of a goal with a destination no matter what gets in the way — these all played a part in setting me up for success to hike over 8,000 miles in a year. I even re-watched the 2016 NBA Finals to see the power of never giving up, no matter how bleak things look.

Thru-hiking is extremely physically demanding, but the mental game of remaining optimistic and dedicated throughout the duration of a journey of that magnitude is even more challenging. Far more people quit because they wear down mentally rather than physically. I wanted to mentally prepare myself to suffer to increase my likelihood of success. When my only desire in the world was to lie down, slow down, or give up, but I kept moving through the hurt, that was where my mental training was monumental — having an even greater effect than my extensive physical training.

So, as I thought about how tired I was, I reinforced the walls of my mental fortress. I thought about how much more miserable I could be, suffering in solitude in the harshness of winter — I had already made it through that. I thought about the sacrifices and how close I had come to death several times in pursuit of this dream — I survived those. I thought about how my entire year of 2021 was dedicated to one singular thing — succeeding at this. And I thought about how my finish line was mere inches away on my map — *I was so close.*

I left Andover, not with a renewed sense of energy, but with a renewed sense of my vision. *I know I am capable. Now I just have to finish.*

Late that night, I began the 2,500-foot climb to the summit of Old Speck. It was well after dark by the time I started, and I wanted a distraction, so I called friends back home to pass the time. Hours slipped away like years to a youth, and before I knew it, I was at the summit. Eager to camp near the top and witness the sunrise, I found a suitable spot to pitch my tent. Such moments of sitting down, watching a sunrise, and savoring the experience were rare for me, but something inside urged me to embrace it as I neared the end of my journey.

I punctually awoke the next morning, which was a rare occurrence, but I was excited to watch the sunrise from the third tallest mountain in Maine. It was worth the extra time. It was one of the most marvelous sunrises I'd seen all year. The sun was gradually creeping over the rolling mountains, breathing life back into the dark sky, and illuminating the sharp autumn colors all around with faint clouds nestled in the low valleys.

Despite the late start caused by my stationary appreciation of nature, it didn't seem to affect the overall progress of the day, because there couldn't possibly have been much progress. Excluding my snow travel and the areas where the trail was wrecked by downed trees, this was the slowest hiking I'd done all year. There were no extra obstacles. The trail was just insanely challenging through the Mahoosuc Range.

It started with a steep descent on the Mahoosuc Arm, where I constantly questioned if man was meant to walk down something of this steep grade. The answer is likely no. At the bottom, I began to cross the Mahoosuc Notch — often referred to as "The hardest mile of the trail." It really wasn't like a part of the trail. Instead, it was a playground of giant boulders, caves, and crevices that hikers had to gradually make their way through, until they were able to rejoin the actual trail. It wasn't incredibly exhausting. It was just meticulously and frustratingly slow going.

Following the notch, I climbed back up to the Goose Eye Mountains, which drained me more than I ever expected. The whole climb was steep rock faces that required careful but exhausting navigation. Though challenging, I was grateful it wasn't raining. That would've been like climbing up a waterslide. While some sections had ladders to assist hikers, I wished there were more. There were a lot of times where I was less than 50% confident in my footing, fully accepting that my feet might slide out from under me, and I'd go tumbling down the rocky slopes.

As the day progressed towards night, I witnessed the sun setting from the last peak of the Goose Eye Mountains — a silver lining in an otherwise soul-snatching day. In the same day, I was able to enjoy an amazing sunrise and beautiful sunset, even in my state of pure exhaustion. (The cover of this very book is me watching the sunset in my dead-tired and depleted state, wondering how I'm going to get up and keep moving.)

After dark, things got weird. The grade of the trail was similar to what it was all day — nonsensically steep. But for some reason, I started moving even slower. I had been working my hardest to try to stay above 1 mph all day, but after dusk, my snail-like pace dropped even lower. I crossed the border into New Hampshire, but was so tired, I couldn't even mentally celebrate. I'm not even sure I was fully aware.

I swore time stopped working in a linear manner. I had planned on getting to the shelter around 9:30 p.m. After going a while without checking the time, I glanced at my watch. It was midnight., and I still had a mile to go!

Maybe it was daylight savings time and somehow my watch knew that, along with my phone, or maybe I passed out for two hours and didn't realize it, or something else happened. I didn't understand how two hours had passed in what felt like no time. I couldn't fathom that I was moving that slow. By that time of the day, I felt awful and must have been delusional. When I got to the point on trail where the shelter was supposed to be, all I saw was a sign. It said it was .2 miles down a side trail.

Fury briefly overtook my fatigue. I thought it was supposed to be right on trail. I was dead tired, so .2 miles seemed like it was ten miles away. I was so angry, but more so tired. I defeatedly hobbled down the side trail. When I got to the shelter, it was the worst I'd felt in a long time. I actually questioned if I had slept the night before. Surely, it was not possible to be this exhausted after getting seven hours of sleep the previous night, and only hiking 16 miles in 17 hours. Yet, it was my reality.

Needing to recuperate, I allowed myself to get a full eight hours of sleep. When I did wake up, I felt fine — like I was surprisingly not hungover after a night of being intensely drunk. *What the hell happened last night?*

I marveled at the view visible from inside the Genetian Pond Shelter, the best view from inside a shelter that I could remember, since most were in the middle of the woods. When I got into Gorham, NH, I was out of food. I went to Subway, scarfed down two subs, and got one for the road. I studied the weather and map to decide what to do about the upcoming section: The Presidential Range. It was an 11-mile stretch of exposed trail above tree line — precisely where I did not want to be in any sort of bad weather. It wasn't unusual for there to be wind speeds of greater than 100 mph, even up to a staggering 231 mph at one time. I began to work on plans A, B, C, and D over the next few days, depending on the weather.

After my planning session, I ventured to Pinkham Notch to hike north over the Wildcat and Carter Mountains until I reached Highway 2. From there, I would return to Gorham, which was accessible from several road crossings, and then decide my next course of action based on the weather conditions. It was changing from fall to winter before my very eyes, so I didn't want to take unnecessary risks. The White Mountains were notorious for experiencing some of the most extreme weather in the United States, and I had no desire to witness it firsthand.

Returning to the trail was brutal, but I had expected nothing less in the formidable White Mountains. One of the main points of discussion on the AT is how ridiculously challenging the White Mountains are. This was the first day I truly understood the tales of their difficulty. At times, there seemed to be no discernible trail. Instead, enormous rocks with white blazes served as markers, requiring hikers to find a way to clamber over them and continue along the "trail." I often questioned the sanity of whoever had designed this trail and was developing a strong feeling of malice toward Myron Avery, the trail's main builder.

After dark, I arrived at my first hut in The Whites. They said it'd be $40 for a bunk, so I kept hiking and found a slanted spot in the woods. Nothing was better than free. Camping through this section was something I had thought about for a while, with its nuances and complexity because of the terrain and the hut system. During normal thru-hiker season, the huts, which catered more to tourists and casual hikers, allowed a few thru-hikers to stay for free every night in exchange for work. However, with as late as it was in the season, they weren't offering that anymore. In fact, this was the only hut that was still open. All the others were closed by this time of year. Winter was coming. Camping was also tough because so much of this area was above the tree line, and when it wasn't, a lot of it was in protected areas that didn't allow camping. It was a tough situation.

The next day, I woke up before my alarm and decided to get moving. I tackled the Carter Mountains before descending to the highway and making my way into Gorham. Knowing it was too late in the day to complete the entire Presidential Range and with a chance of rain looming, I faced a decision about what to do.

My gut told me to go for it. So, I went up Mount Washington via road and hiked north to cover at least half of the above-tree-line section, considering the forecast for rain the following day.

The hiking in the Presidential Range was easier than I expected. With the way things had been lately, and how notorious this section was, I thought it would be intensely tough hiking, but it wasn't bad compared to most of the unbelievably arduous hiking lately.

Throughout the day, I found myself engulfed in clouds, occasionally catching glimpses of the awe-inspiring views of the Presidential Range, before the mist shrouded them once more. The mountains seemed modest, revealing their beauty only briefly. Furthermore, the temperature swung drastically every 15 minutes, causing me to transition rapidly from sweating to feeling chilled, despite no apparent change in my activity level.

After dark, I made it back down below tree line to a designated campsite. The only challenge was that everything was covered in heaps of leaves, so it was hard to locate a good campsite. Moreover, rain added to the disarray. There were tent platforms that I tried, but couldn't figure out how to set up a trekking pole tent on them. I met someone later that made it sound simple, but I couldn't figure it out in the dark, rainy, leafy mess.

The next morning, I swiftly covered the five waterlogged miles to Pinkham Notch, where I had to make another decision on what to do. My "go for it" alarm was going off again. I just wanted to get the Presidentials done and over with. The weather didn't look agreeable for the day, but it didn't look deadly either. So, I got a ride back to the top of Mount Washington with a nice family from India. I don't think they understood when I explained what I was doing, but they said I could hop in the car. I wasn't sure if the dad temporarily forgot which side of the road to drive on, but he drove completely in the left lane for a bit, and the fog was so thick we couldn't see more than ten feet ahead of us. It was a nerve-racking experience, but we made it to the top, and I again found myself standing on the summit of Mount Washington.

It was game time. I was ready for battle. When I decided to go for it, I knew the weather wasn't going to be cooperative. Consistent 50 mph winds, with gusts up to 70 mph, smacked me in the face. It wasn't ideal, but it wasn't supposed to rain until later in the day, so I thought I could beat it. It was also going to begin snowing in the coming days, which I certainly wanted to avoid. When I was going up to take a picture with the sign on the summit for the second day in a row, my rain cover flew off my pack. I had to go chasing after it like a dog trying to catch a squirrel. Once I left the summit heading south, I was glad I had put on my rain gear. It didn't rain one drop, but it was so misty, I got thoroughly soaked.

The trail itself wasn't overly challenging, but the combination of strong winds and slippery rocks necessitated a slower pace to ensure I didn't lose my footing. Throughout the day, there were numerous moments when I simply gazed at my surroundings and thought, *Yup, this is pretty crazy.*

Visibility rarely extended beyond ten feet. I could only see the immediate trail before me, and occasionally, a towering cairn marking the way.

In the afternoon, I came across three day hikers. Though I refrained from mentioning it, I couldn't help but question their sanity for voluntarily choosing to venture out in such harsh weather. Of course, they could have easily expressed the same sentiment about me. We talked for a while before I offhandedly mentioned I was out of food. It wasn't a deliberate attempt to "Yogi" food, but perhaps subconsciously I was asking for help. They were incredibly kind and eagerly offered me most of what they had.

A simple peanut butter and jelly sandwich never tasted so satisfying. With my plan to go for it again today, I didn't go into town to resupply. Before meeting these generous souls, my only sustenance for the day was a Pop Tart. Their help was truly a godsend.

The trail provides!

I eventually descended to Crawford Notch, and that's when things went off the rails. After my recent exhaustion from pushing myself through the tough terrain, and the poor weather, I wanted to stay indoors for the night. However, another hiker made it sound like the AMC Highland Center, which was located right at the notch, was over $300 a night.

That was ridiculous. So I thought I'd head into town and try to get a cheap motel. As I was walking into the Highland Center, just to see if I would be able to resupply there, I started talking to a couple who were also walking in. They asked what I was doing and were amazed when I told them. After a few minutes inside, I realized I wasn't going to be able to resupply, and would have to go into town. I sprinted out to the parking lot and caught the couple just before they left. I asked if they would be able to give me a ride to a motel, and they were happy to help.

We embarked on a 30-minute journey to the first motel, only to find it fully booked. We repeated the process at the next, and the one after that, with no luck. I pulled out my phone and discovered that only two hotels within an hour radius had vacancies, with the cheapest room priced over $400. The area was teeming with "leaf peepers," as the locals called them, who flocked to witness the autumn foliage in its full glory. The town was gridlocked with traffic, and I couldn't help but feel deeply embarrassed. I was wasting these kind strangers' time, and I had no idea what to do next.

However, the woman mentioned recalling a conversation at the Highland Center about a bunk available for $40. It was my last glimmer of hope. I promptly dialed the number, and indeed, that was the price. I hadn't even considered trying the place due to a fellow hiker's comment on Guthook, and now I felt like a complete fool.

I shouldn't have listened to other people.

In one of the most humbling and pitiful moments of my life, I asked this beneficent couple if they could drive me an hour back to the Highland Center, assuring them they didn't have to. They were true saints and were enthusiastic to help, never even considering not doing so. I got two footlongs and a resupply in North Conway before we turned around and headed back to where we came from. I was embarrassed about having wasted so much of my time — but more so theirs. However, I actually think they enjoyed it. They said it was an adventure for them, even though it only occurred because of my stupidity.

When we made it back to the Highland Center, I thanked them so much that they probably got annoyed. We took a picture and said goodbye, expecting to never see each other again. I was overwhelmed with gratitude and continued to be astonished by the boundless generosity of strangers. They had just wasted two hours driving a smelly and dirty hiker around, who they hadn't known for more than five minutes beforehand. People were unbelievably amazing all year, but it never stopped surprising me. This particular act of compassion stood out as one of the most incredible acts of kindness I was granted all year.

Wanting to get an early start the next morning, I stood by the road with my thumb out just after sunrise. With no luck, I ended up waiting for the shuttle from the Highland Center and didn't start hiking until after 9 a.m. I figured the shuttle would be free since I stayed there, but the driver said it was $20. As I was reaching for my wallet, he said it was his last day, and since I was an AT thru-hiker, I didn't have to worry about it. "What are they going to do, fire me?"

After spending a night indoors, I felt rejuvenated. I did a 1,500-foot climb like it was nothing to start the day. After that, the trail was flat for a while, which was odd on the AT. Given the heavy rainfall the previous night, I spent my time cautiously hopping around, attempting to keep my feet dry, and was partially successful. The day remained cloudy, with occasional clearings, but most importantly, it didn't rain. I had been getting lucky with it looking threatening during the day, but only raining at night.

When it started to get dark, I only had a few more miles to get to Garfield Shelter. I thought I might get there early, but that section of the trail was a swampy mess from the rain. I was moving slowly to try to avoid the worst of the water. The last quarter-mile before the shelter was absurd and slowed me down even more. I found myself climbing vertically on all fours, scaling a waterfall. I kept looking around to make sure the trail didn't go somewhere else. *This was so stupid that there was no way this was the actual "trail."* But, sure enough, it was. That was New Hampshire.

That night marked the first time I had truly felt cold since being back on the AT. I had my zero-degree sleeping bag the whole time because I was expecting it to be much colder in October. Now winter had arrived. As I slept, it snowed, and when I resumed hiking the next morning, the snowfall continued, accompanied by icy conditions. Even before reaching Franconia Ridge and ascending above the tree line, snow and ice covered the trail. Progress became slow and treacherous on the slippery surface.

When I climbed above tree line and atop Franconia Ridge, the situation grew more precarious. Snow and ice were ubiquitous, but there wasn't enough on the ground to get a decent grip. It was just enough to make all of the rocks terribly slippery and impossible for my microspikes to dig into anything. The wind howled fiercely, surpassing the intensity I experienced while hiking through the Presidentials. At times, I resorted to crawling on my hands and knees, feeling too unstable to stand upright on the icy terrain amid the strong gusts. It seemed as though a forceful gust could send me sliding off the mountain.

This combination of factors resulted in a painfully slow pace while icy pellets relentlessly pelted my face. I attempted to shield my face with my buff, but the stinging ice still found its way into my eyes. There wasn't much I could do other than futilely wish I had ski goggles. Fortunately, I managed to avoid any major falls, meticulously navigating the three miles of ice on the ridge, cautiously and deliberately.

I didn't even get to remotely enjoy the beauty of Franconia Ridge. I'd heard a number of people say it was the most beautiful part of the entire trail. For me, it was three painstaking miles of paying extreme attention to every step, and just trying not to fall down amidst a constant onslaught of ice battering my face. It was yet another day that made me laugh at the sheer absurdity and unbelievable unpleasantness of the situation.

As I descended to lower elevations, the falling ice transitioned into rain. Everything on me was either soaked or frozen. I decided to call it a day and opt for an early stop. Although I contemplated pushing forward and camping at a shelter, nothing would have dried with how cold it was. So I made my way into Lincoln and got a motel room for the night to dry out my gear and warm up. At McDonald's, I attempted a record feast of eight double cheeseburgers and two large fries, but I hit the wall at my usual mark of seven double cheeseburgers and two large fries. I could have managed the eighth, but I knew I would feel terrible afterward. With seven, I still felt fine.

After enjoying a cozy night indoors, I set out on the trail once again, albeit not from where I left off. Based on advice from a knowledgeable local, I determined that I would go 16 miles ahead on trail to Kinsman Notch, and then hike backwards to where I ended. This was allegedly safer than going southbound over that stretch with the current icy conditions.

As I was on my way to Kinsman Notch in the morning, I realized I left my hat at the motel. I knew exactly where it was. My driver, who would be picking me up later to bring me back to Kinsman Notch to continue south, said she would go back and get it for me. After I got dropped off at Kinsman Notch, I began hiking north to get back to where I ended.

The low elevations where I began hiking were still a swamp. My dry feet didn't last long, especially when I reached wooden planks that were meant to allow you to walk over a bog, but instead, were all under six inches of water. I gritted my teeth, and tried to run through the bog as fast as I could, but my feet were still soaked to the bone. Once I reached the Kinsman peaks, I was glad I went northbound for this section. Nothing felt dangerous, but there were a few exposed sections, and going northbound made it safer traversing the slabs of ice. Progress was slow at times, but never perilous, which was all I could ask for at that late point in the year. From the summit, I gazed at Franconia Ridge, the path I had ventured along the previous day, now blanketed in fresh snow. I felt a sense of relief that I was done with it, as it appeared even more daunting from a distance.

When I met my driver after dark, I was disappointed to hear what happened with my hat. She went back to the motel, and they said they cleaned the room and didn't find anything. She then stayed there for ten minutes arguing with the worker because I told her I remembered exactly where it was. But it was to no avail. I admired her putting up that much of a fight for me. On the bright side, someone got a hat that was almost brand new since I had only gotten it a few days earlier. Luckily, my driver was the perfect person for this situation because she had several hats that other hikers had left in her car that year, so I picked one and just hoped the previous owner didn't have lice.

After being dropped off at Kinsman Notch, I slept in the privy in the parking lot for the night. I chose this because the shelter a couple of miles ahead allegedly smelled rancid. It wasn't until I was laying down and trying to fall asleep that I realized the irony of avoiding a shelter because it smelled foul — choosing to sleep in an outhouse instead. I was a little out of my element, though. I had slept in a lot of bathrooms, pit toilets, and privies this year, but this one was not regulation size. Normally, there was more than enough room for me to lie down diagonally, but not in this one. It was a snug fit and I couldn't extend my body fully, but I still got a decent night's sleep in the fetal position, enclosed by four walls.

The following day commenced with a deliberate and steady 3,000-foot climb up to Mount Moosilauke, which was the last high mountain of The Whites and a huge symbolic victory. After I had finished the two western trails, the only real concern with finishing the AT was making the logistics work. First, I needed to summit Katahdin before it closed down. Second, I needed to find a way to get across the Kennebec River out of season. Last, I needed to make it through the White Mountains before winter came. Standing atop this last summit, I knew the finish was inevitable. In just a few days, I would finish the Appalachian Trail, and become a Calendar Year Triple Crowner. My dream would become reality.

From the summit, I could see the Presidential Range completely draped in snow. I had narrowly escaped the heavy snow by a day or two, and was overwhelmingly thankful, because it looked even more intimidating than seeing Franconia Ridge the day before.

Once I got down to lower elevations on the south side of Moosilauke, the trail was much more enjoyable. In addition to being easier hiking, it was drier. I didn't have to avoid puddles with every step and was able to move much faster as a result.

The elation of leaving the ruthless White Mountains was palpable for innumerous reasons. The end was nigh. Everything was about to get significantly easier. And this was the first day of sunshine since my first day in New Hampshire. I had been living in a perpetual state of gray for days, but now it was over as I was leaving The Whites.

I woke up the next day, ready to finish off New Hampshire. I welcomed an easy day of hiking with open arms. After getting beaten, battered, and torn, both physically and emotionally, from the Mahoosucs and White Mountains, I was glad to embrace any respite that came my way.

In the evening, I arrived in Hanover, and it felt strange to emerge from the woods and find myself immediately on Dartmouth's campus. Prior to my arrival, I had no idea that Dartmouth was located there.

Fortunately, I had a friend at the school named Buckle, with whom I had hiked a few miles on the PCT. He graciously offered me a place to crash in Hanover, and even granted my wish of going to a sports bar, where I indulged on chicken wings for the first time all year. As we caught up on our respective journeys since the PCT, it was fascinating to hear about Buckle's experiences after returning home, while I continued to live in the mountains, drawing closer to the completion of my own adventure. Our worlds had diverged significantly since we had last seen each other.

After a shower and doing some much needed laundry because my socks were ready to start decomposing, I got a good night's sleep before embarking on the final push to finish.

It was a Friday morning, so when I was walking back to the trail to cross the Connecticut River, I passed hordes of college students that looked unhappy and hungover on their way to class. I wondered what I would have thought, just two years prior, if I was walking to class hungover and saw someone looking like me walking by.

Shortly after, I crossed into Vermont — my last state to finish the Calendar Year Triple Crown.

Once I got back in the increasingly bare woods of Appalachia, it was challenging to tell where the trail was. It wasn't as daunting as it had been in March, when I traversed Vermont amidst four feet of untouched snow, rendering it impossible to navigate. Nonetheless, the ground was covered in fallen leaves, making it occasionally difficult to stay on track. Most of the time, I had a good sense of the trail, but there were moments when I needed to pause and decide where I was going.

As the day wore on, I made the decision to push on and camp at The Lookout, a privately owned cabin that welcomed hikers. Although I was indoors for the night, an eerie stillness pervaded the space. In my previous encounters with similar cabins out west, they were infested with squirrels or other critters. I wasn't sure if it was a few mice or just the sounds of my fears scurrying about, but it was hard to fall asleep worrying about another hole being chewed in my sleeping bag.

It was all for naught. I awoke the next morning with no evidence of mice and eagerly ascended to the lookout platform on the roof.

After savoring a superb sunrise in the crisp morning air, the day unfolded magnificently. For a brief moment, it felt like I was living in a movie. I was walking up to a parking lot to go into Rutland, VT for my last resupply on the AT, and just as I stepped foot in the parking lot, the bus to Rutland pulled in. I hopped on and wasted no time. There were few things I loved more in the world than maximum efficiency.

I bought a small resupply and had a feast at Burger King before hopping back on trail. By the time I climbed a few thousand feet, and made it to the junction for Killington Peak, darkness had fallen, so I hiked by the junction to the summit. I was a little disappointed to pass by it because I had heard a lot about it, but I was eager to forge ahead and get this trail finished.

After sleeping for a few hours, I covered the seven miles to Clarendon Gorge the next morning. It didn't even feel like I was hiking.

I was floating.

That was the spot where I got off of the AT in March and flipped to the CDT. That was the spot where I was determined to return to. And on October 24, 2021, that was the spot where I technically completed the Calendar Year Triple Crown.

It was an odd feeling for a few reasons. The first was that it was a strong feeling, and I didn't know what I was expecting. The only marking of note in the area was a little wooden post inscribed with "LT," for the Long Trail, which overlaps with the AT. I never imagined that such a simple marker, one that didn't even bear the letters "AT," would hold such profound significance for me. Yet, when I laid eyes upon it, its power resonated more deeply than any international boundary ever could.

The other reason I felt strange was because I wasn't done with the AT. While this was the spot where I flipped trails, I decided that I would hike an additional 50 miles and end my Appalachian Trail thru-hike at Stratton Mountain. It would serve as a more scenic and special end point than a random road crossing.

After sitting with the wooden post for a while, trying to soak in the gravity of what I had just accomplished, while simultaneously resisting the urge to shut down and reflect too deeply, I resumed hiking, resolute in reaching Stratton Mountain.

Once again — I don't stop when I'm tired. I stop when I'm done.

Having accomplished what I just did, and knowing I was so close to my extended endpoint, it wasn't hard to move fast during the day. I was so buoyant that I found myself running sporadically throughout the day. I knew things were going well because it was rare that I would run throughout the year. When I did, it would last a few seconds, then I would think either, *This is so stupid. I'm going to get hurt.* Or, *Wow. I'm really tired. This was a horrible idea.* But today, it didn't matter. I ran, and it felt so freeing it was intoxicating.

I arrived at my last shelter for the AT and went to bed smiling as rain soothingly pattered on the metal roof. When I woke up, it was still raining, but that didn't matter. This was my last day on the AT, and I wasn't going to let a little rain ruin it.

As I hiked up Stratton Mountain for my final ascent, my mind raced. It started to think about the big picture of what I did this year, and how insane it was. It went to the best days, the best people, the best memories, and it also went to the dark recesses which I didn't want to revisit, at least not yet anyway. But they didn't matter. They were in the past, and now I was going to finish my journey on my own terms.

When I reached the summit, a wave of transcendent serenity washed over me, permeating every fiber of my being, as a profound sense of accomplishment coursed through my veins. In that moment, time stood still, and I was enveloped by a feeling of pure bliss, an exquisite blend of elation, satisfaction, and fulfillment. It was as if the universe conspired to gift me this unique, enchanting experience, leaving me unable to truly comprehend the magnitude of what I had achieved. My body tingled with an electric energy, my heart swelled with pride, and a radiant smile adorned my face, mirroring the immense joy that radiated from within. It was a culmination of countless hours of training and preparation, innumerable sacrifices, laughing in the face of adversity, unrelenting determination of a singular goal, unbreakable mental fortitude, unwavering belief in my capabilities, and a perpetual acceptance of — and triumph over — pain.

In that sublime instant, I stood at the zenith of my existence, basking in the unparalleled beauty of accomplishment and savoring the indescribable sweetness of triumph. *I won.*

Proudly, I inscribed the logbook, "Just finished the Calendar Year Triple Crown" and wondered what future hikers would think when they read that. This was the most monumental achievement of my life, but *would they even know what that meant?*

I soaked in the scene for a few minutes before I did something I had been envisioning for months. I reenacted the Kanye West Grammy video, declaring for an audience of none: "Everybody wanted to know what I would do if I didn't finish... I guess we'll never know." It was funny how quick and insignificant it was, but the thought of just being able to utter those words had pushed me to go to my limits and beyond, on countless days throughout the year.

While I was soaking in the moment, I was also literally getting soaked. It was raining, cold, and foggy, with absolutely no visibility. It was the *perfect way to finish the Appalachian Trail.* I didn't care what the weather was. I had done it: 7,473 miles and 293 days after starting at Springer Mountain in Georgia, I was done. It wasn't the usual ending of the Appalachian Trail, but it was mine. It was my finish, my terminus — my personal Katahdin.

Intermission

When I started at Springer Mountain in January, I never imagined that I would find myself contemplating an even more audacious goal than the Calendar Year Triple Crown. However, my mind started to wander when I was in Southern California. I was crushing big miles consistently and felt good while doing it. Barring serious injury, I was certain that I would finish all three trails. As the miles unfolded beneath my feet, my confidence grew, and I began to have the two most dangerous but exhilarating words enter my mind, fueling my imagination and pushing the boundaries of what I believed was possible — *What if?*

What if I finished in October, and still felt good, and wanted to keep going? What if I could set an even higher goal? Hell, what if I went for 10,000 miles in a year?

On a hot and sweaty afternoon in the desert of Southern California, the bonus goal of 10,000 miles in a year was born. With plenty of time to think throughout the year, I contemplated all the possible ways to get there. I wanted to hike new trails, rather than repeat easy sections like Southern California or New Mexico. I also had to choose ones that would be easier to do, or at least possible to do, in winter. After a lot of thinking, I concluded that I would thru-hike the Arizona Trail and Buckeye Trail, and that would put me around 10,000 miles.

It wasn't until two weeks before I finished the AT, that I fully committed to going for my bonus goal. Immediately after I finished atop Stratton Mountain, my mind wanted to race ahead, envisioning the next steps to set myself up for success. I tried to enjoy the moment, but I think that was why I didn't have a full emotional breakdown in my moment of ultimate triumph. Because of my unyielding focus, I was already thinking of how I was going to succeed on the next leg of my extraordinary journey.

Immediately after descending from Stratton, I got a ride to the airport, where I fruitlessly tried to sleep for a couple of hours before my 6 a.m. flight. I flew into Phoenix, walked the two miles to the bus station just like I had earlier in the year, and hopped on a Greyhound to Flagstaff. I hadn't eaten anything in 24 hours, nor slept because I couldn't get comfortable at the airport or on the plane. It was possibly the most tired and hungry I had felt all year, and I wasn't even on trail. The Greyhound stopped at a McDonald's for a ten-minute bathroom break, and I downed six double cheeseburgers and two large fries in that time frame.

I took a rest day in Flagstaff at a mice-infested hotel. The day proved productive — picking up a new Sawyer water filter, getting a much-needed haircut and shave, and thoroughly enjoying my rest time, even with the rodent-riddled room. My journey had seemingly come full circle from cohabitating with the critters on the AT in winter, to now having a reunion in my low-end motel in civilized society. There was no escaping them.

Almost exactly 72 hours after finishing the Calendar Year Triple Crown, I began the Arizona Trail at the Utah border.

As I stood at the terminus of the Arizona Trail, I knew that I was pushing myself beyond what I once believed was only faintly possible. The Calendar Year Triple Crown was already an improbable experiment of excessive ambition. I couldn't help but marvel at the resilience and fortitude that had brought me this far in my journey.

The bonus goal of 10,000 miles in a year was a further exercise of the boundaries of my insatiable thirst for adventure, unyielding commitment to an objective, unrelenting pursuit of self-discovery, and curious search for what is truly possible.

The quest to find my limit had only just begun.

Phase VI:

Arizona Trail

Utah Border to Mexican Border

October 28th–November 21st

Phase VI:

Arizona Trail

Utah Border to Mexican Border

October 28th–November 21st

The Return to Desert Wandering

After hiking less than 100 yards from the Utah Border, an uncontrollable smile spread across my face. Exuberance flowed through me at the prospect of returning to the desert. I loved the callous but captivating landscape; it was one of the main reasons I had chosen the Arizona Trail. The terrain was also generous compared to the AT.

However, my greatest relief was escaping the clutches of winter in the northeast. Had I been just a day or two later, I would have been pummeled by heavy snowfall on the Presidential Range, and Franconia Ridge would have been buried under a much thicker blanket of snow and ice. I was relieved to be someplace where that wasn't a concern anymore. I could just hike, without having to worry about winter descending upon me.

There was also a beautiful simplicity to desert hiking that I was ready to get back to: find water, determine where the next water will be, walk there, repeat. Water was always the driving force.

As I embarked on the Arizona Trail, I couldn't ignore the weight on my back. Carrying cold weather gear, particularly my winter sleeping bag, added extra pounds to my pack. Anticipating nighttime temperatures dropping to the 20s, or even into the teens, I wanted to be adequately prepared for this late-season thru-hike. I also negligently overpacked my food supplies, which led to my pack being painfully heavy, impeding my progress. I only covered 16 miles in the six hours that I hiked, but I didn't care too much. It was only Day One, and I reveled in the joy of being back in the lifeless yet vibrant desert, basking in the glow of a lustrous sunset.

After a brief contemplation, I set up my tent instead of cowboy camping. It was my first night, and I wasn't sure how cold it would feel. Come morning, I was glad I had set up my tent. The whole thing was coated with fresh dew, and my sleeping bag would've been a soggy mess if I had cowboy camped with that much moisture.

I welcomed the milder terrain to start the day that allowed me to easily brush my teeth while walking. I had developed this habit throughout the year to be efficient, but in rougher terrain like the AT, I often stumbled over roots and rocks. Reflecting on my journey, I estimated I had walked 60 miles while brushing my teeth. Each day, it seemed inconsequential, but over time, it added up — the quintessence of thru-hiking.

After passing no water all morning, I arrived at the first water cache to find nothing there. With my late start to the AZT (most hikers started about a month earlier), I realistically expected all the caches to be empty, but I still naively held out hope. Luckily, there were some hunters nearby. I went over to their camp, and they were astounded to learn that I was hiking from Utah to Mexico, unaware of the full extent of my year-long journey. Enthusiastically, they gave me plenty of water, along with eggs and sausage from breakfast. Despite carrying an excessive amount of food, I couldn't resist real sustenance. I was beyond sick of my usual hiking food.

In the afternoon, I walked through a burn area, so I could see all around me, which had been rare lately. Apart from the first few miles of the trail in open desert, I had been engulfed in a sea of ponderosa pines for the whole trail. In this scorched openness, I was fortunate enough to see three massive California Condors perched atop charred trees.

The days when I didn't feel the need to check Guthook, or obsess over my mileage, were always the most enjoyable. Before I even had the thought of checking my mileage, dusk had descended, and I was 41 miles further without hiking into the night. There was around 5,000 feet of elevation gain, but it was so gradual, I hardly noticed. After southern Maine and New Hampshire, this felt like I was hiking on an airport's accelerated walkways. Even though my pack was heavy and my back was hurting, I cruised through the day without hesitation, fueled by the power of unencumbered ambition and manageable trail.

The next morning greeted me with a thick layer of frost on the Kaibab Plateau. Once the sun rose, I alternated between walking on snow and ice, to sloppy mud pits. Still early in the morning, I had a thoroughly anticlimactic welcome to Grand Canyon National Park at a remote entrance. There was only a little sign in front of a gate, surrounded by a fence that had fallen over, rendering the gate useless. Even after stepping over the fallen fence, the grandeur of the canyon was not immediately revealed. I yearned to descend into the mighty chasm and witness its beauty.

When I arrived at the park entrance for cars, I was relieved to see a blue jug of water that the workers left for AZT thru-hikers. I was thirsty, as I hadn't passed any water all morning, and the temperatures were starting to heat up. I eagerly gulped down several liters and then hiked on toward the visitor center, where I got my permit for the park. It turned out to be the first place all year that had a functional pack scale, so I weighed mine out of curiosity. It was 31 pounds without any water. *Yikes!* Although some of it was attributable to my cold weather gear, it was evident that I was still carrying far too much food and would only lighten my load as I kept eating.

Once I left there, I began the mind-boggling descent into the canyon. It was the first true beauty I had seen since the inaugural miles on trail. Besides the natural beauty, there was an added enjoyment in witnessing the misery of all the hikers going the opposite direction — uphill out of the canyon. It was a 5,000+ foot climb from the bottom, so I understood their pain, but it was still entertaining.

It is a wise man that can joyfully appreciate the comedic struggles of others in the present, knowing he will face the exact same hardship in his own time.

Wanting to savor my time in the Canyon, I resolved to not hike after dark, so I chose the first campsite in the Canyon for my permit. When I arrived at Bright Angel Campground, I was disappointed to find it teeming with mice. They were aggressive — but they weren't at the AT winter, starving, savage level of mice. I fearfully stored my food in the bear box, even though I had seen the irksome pests wiggle their way into those allegedly impregnable boxes before. I went to bed unsure if my food would all be intact in the morning, or if I would have new holes in my tent, yet I still slept like a baby because I was dog-tired.

To my immense relief, I awoke to find everything exactly as I left it. While the Grand Canyon was beautiful the previous day as I was descending it in the evening, this morning was different. It was enchanting. The place truly felt special, radiating a spiritual energy that resonated within me. I had experienced similar sensations before in places like Zion and Kings Canyon. As I hiked while the sun rose in the sky, the way its rays illuminated the surrounding rocks made it feel like God was beaming it down himself. It was a blessed start to the day.

Additionally, the hiking within the canyon itself was a blessing. Walking alongside the river was a refreshing reminder that natural water sources still existed. In the morning, I encountered a few trail runners wearing costumes, which struck me as odd, but I didn't dwell on it. Trail runners are a weird breed of people anyway.

As I continued to see more people in costumes, my curiosity continued to grow. It didn't click until I reached the Colorado River and met a lady dressed as Wonder Woman that offered me candy — it was Halloween. Normally, I loved Halloween. In fact, my general timeline for the

Calendar Year Triple Crown was to be done by late October, mostly to beat winter, but also to be home and be able to party for Halloween. Yet here I was, spending my Halloween alone, and the only costume I was sporting was pretending to be a guy that enjoys a 5,000-foot climb.

The real fun began once I crossed the Colorado River and started the everlasting climb out of the canyon. With the grueling ascent, I wasn't flying uphill, but made progress slowly and methodically. Just like those people yesterday, I was the one looking miserable going uphill, and now the descenders could get amusement from me.

My motivation to move consistently was to get higher to get cooler. It was getting hot in the canyon, especially in the sun. I told myself that if I just kept climbing, it would cool down at the higher elevations. Even if it was only partially true, it was a good motivation tactic.

Reaching the top brought a moment of exaltation. I sat down, took a moment to check the score of the Buckeye victory from the night before, and then glided into Grand Canyon Village. Despite having an abundance of leftover food, I couldn't resist treating myself to a pizza. By this point in my journey, if a town stop didn't involve pizza or real food, it felt like a waste. It was genuinely the only thing I looked forward to eating anymore.

I started off the next day by hiking to a lookout tower just after sunrise, which was a luminous disappointment because the sun was just high enough in the sky to be completely blinding. Soon after, I arrived at my sole water source for the day. It was good for a wildlife tank — fairly clear with floaters and only a bit of algae. I filled up three liters for 34 miles. With November bringing cooler temperatures, I didn't have to drink or carry as much water. My new Sawyer water filter also proved beneficial and significantly reduced the time required to filter. In Washington, filtering three liters would have taken over 30 minutes. Now, it was more like six minutes.

The majority of the day was spent walking on dirt roads, passing by empty hunting camps. Coolers were scattered about, and I couldn't help but imagine the cold beer and sodas they held. *They wouldn't even notice if a few went missing.* Tempting as it was, my morality endured.

I thoroughly enjoyed this section of the trail, despite its dirt roads. Excluding the Grand Canyon, it was the first time the desert opened up to expansive views. I was no longer engulfed by trees, allowing me to appreciate the beauty of the vast desert landscape. Throughout the day, I steadily approached Humphrey's Peak, the highest point in Arizona, knowing I would skirt by it the following day. I also encountered a team of wild horses roaming the terrain. At the sight of me, they initially panicked and fled, only to return in circles, repeating the cycle several times. The leader seemed to square up with me. I thought we might have a competition to see who had more horsepower, but he backed off, and they all followed suit.

The ironic part of the desert being more open was that I had trouble finding a campsite. All around me were huge, flat areas with no trees, but everywhere was covered with prickly plants or rocks. It was the same predicament I faced on my 53-mile day in Wyoming.

I was ready to be done — exhausted — but I couldn't find a campsite in the barren, flat wasteland. My legs were, again, so stiff that they hurt to move. My hips felt like they had 20% of their usual range of motion. My quads were throbbing with every pace. Once again, I failed to drink enough water on a high-mileage day. *I should've learned my lesson.*

It ended up being a 46-mile day before I camped on the side of a dirt road intersection. It certainly wasn't a good spot, and I hoped that nobody would drive by during the night or early in the morning, because there was a decent chance they'd hit me. But I was so inconceivably tired, that was a chance I was willing to take.

Wearily, I woke up after sunrise only because the sun began to cook me in my tent. I also heard a passing truck, so I thought I should get moving, rather than sit and wait to get hit by a moving car.

After a few miles, I made it to a ranch that let hikers use their water. It was my first water in 34 miles, and I desperately needed it. At first, I only saw a grotesque black pond for the cows and assumed there had to be something better. There was a metal box sticking out of the ground, so I opened it up, and there was glorious, clear water inside. There were large creatures, that didn't look like fish, swimming around inside, but the water tasted fine. Several miles later, I ran into my first fellow AZT thru-traveler: Randy. Except, he was a thru-biker instead of a thru-hiker. The AZT was open to both forms of travel, although, with as rocky as it was, I imagined biking it would be frustratingly cumbersome. I was already struggling to walk efficiently at times because of the rocky terrain. I couldn't imagine how irritating it would be as a thru-biker.

In the afternoon, I enjoyed an innocent game of peek-a-boo with a deer. It walked step for step with me until a tree blocked our line of sight. Then, it peeked around the front of the tree when I peeked around the back, and then I peeked around the front of the tree when it peeked around the back, and on and on. We repeated this five times. Smiling, I realized that this probably meant I'd lost my mind by this point, but I didn't care. Teasing this harebrained animal brought me a disproportionate amount of joy.

After dark, I passed the first other thru-hikers I had seen in Arizona. Well, I didn't actually see them, but some trail runners said they were up ahead, and I passed their tents later. With my late start, I didn't expect to see thru-hikers until I got to the southern part of the trail, after having more time to catch up to them.

Fatigued, I once again struggled to find a suitable campsite at the end of the day. Everywhere I looked, the ground was sloped or covered in prickly objects. Eventually, I settled for a spot on a less-frequented, side, dirt road. The next day, I had to bushwhack back to the trail from where I had camped. I wasn't sure if it saved any time, but my brain simply couldn't fathom going backward — a trait that was a detriment at times, like it was in Wyoming. It turned out to be an easy day of hiking around Flagstaff, where I encountered numerous day hikers and trail runners. It was the first time I had seen more than a couple of people on the AZT, excluding the tourist-riddled Grand Canyon.

The day concluded with a shower and a bed at a college friend's house in Flagstaff. It felt undeserved, getting a shower and clean laundry after less than a week on trail. Previously, I had gone over 30 days without a shower, and 60 days without doing laundry. While I knew I could be more rugged, admittedly, it did feel nice after only a week!

While in town, I built up the courage to throw away my cold soak jar. After using the same one for six months, I just couldn't take it anymore. The repulsive smell had begun to make me sick while eating food from it. Doing the rest of the trail and only eating dry food would be a much smaller sacrifice than continuing to eat soggy ramen noodles out of that putrid jar.

I awoke to a glorious breakfast of eggs, sausage, and toast — a substantial improvement over my usual breakfast of Oreos or Chips Ahoy cookies. As I picked up the trail in the morning, I came across a dozen deer. They stared at me for a moment, and then one of them must've said the code word, because they all took off in different directions. It was like kids getting caught doing something they weren't supposed to, and taking off.

Along the trail, I encountered numerous tarantulas, which were less than enjoyable, and reinforced my decision to set up my tent every night instead of cowboy camping. The highlight of the day was reaching a water cache that wasn't empty. This meant I was catching up to hikers who hadn't completely depleted the caches yet, giving me hope that I might soon encounter more people on the trail. I was happy that I could start to at least faintly consider there would be water at caches.

The next morning started off on the wrong foot. I began the day by fully convincing myself I had a stress fracture. My foot felt strange, and the pain seemed more intense than usual. My first metatarsal felt like it was ready to snap, and my third felt like something was seriously wrong. Having experienced foot problems in the past, stress fractures lingered in the back of my mind throughout the year. This wasn't the first time I suspected I had one, but it was the most serious scare since my foot popped while running with Hammer to escape mosquitoes in Oregon.

Initially, I succumbed to the pain. My mind spiraled into a cycle of negative thoughts, contemplating how it would only worsen, how this hike was over, and how I was going to get home. I let the pain rule me... for 15 minutes. After a quarter-hour of hiking with heightened pain, I accepted it. Yes, it hurt more than usual, but it wasn't getting worse with every step, and it wasn't unbearable. *I'd been pushing through pain all year. Why should I stop now?*

Tests of physical endurance are the truest test of character because they largely hinge on one's ability to push through pain. And pain is the most universal human experience. It's possible for someone to live a full life and never experience love, but no one escapes this life without feeling pain.

I had been doing it all year — pushing myself beyond what I previously thought I was capable of, and examining the boundaries of my pain tolerance along the way — but this was an even more intense opportunity to prove my willpower and determination. Each step became a sharp reminder of my relentless progress towards my bonus goal. But each step was also a sobering reminder of how much I had put my body through this year, and how much I expected to continue asking of it. Even Achilles was only as strong as his heel.

After the initial fear, I not only accepted the pain — I welcomed it. Pain is the most universal thing connecting all humanity, and I chose to find solace and strength in the face of it. Other animals feel pain and instinctively stop doing whatever is causing the pain. Humans are special in their ability to push through pain in order to achieve something they want outside of attaining food and water. So, I did the most human thing I could do. I reveled in the rawness of the experience, knowing that the pain I felt was a tangible manifestation of my commitment and passion. It reminded me that I was truly alive, fully immersed in the pursuit of my dreams.

Continuing my journey with a 41-mile day, I walked with a newfound appreciation for the pain that surged through my foot. It was a constant companion, a relentless reminder of my endurance and the depths of my spirit. With each step, I embraced the pain as a powerful force driving me forward, propelling me towards the realization of my goal. For in the face of pain, I discovered a strength I never knew existed — a strength in the vulnerability that made me human.

I wasn't invincible, and that was okay. I extended my goal to see how far I could go, not to see if I could go forever.

The Beginning of the End

After skipping several water sources because they were cow ponds that resembled chunky chocolate milk more than water, I began to stumble along in a dehydrated stupor. Now regretting my pickiness, I tried to move as efficiently as possible, refusing to even open my mouth to breathe so I wouldn't let any water vapor escape. Only nose-breathing for me.

Naturally, when I was less than a quarter-mile from a water spigot, a guy drove by on the dirt road and asked if I needed water. *Where were you earlier, buddy?!* But that's the way things usually seemed to go.

After lounging at the water spigot and drinking enough water to hydrate a family for a week, I returned to the trail. But things seemed different. There were some 400-foot climbs, and I thought, *Wow. This is really something.* I'd been spoiled by the flat terrain so much lately, that the more volatile landscape of the southern AZT would soon be a wake-up call. Shortly before sunset, I came across a tent and talked to a fellow AZT thru-hiker — the first one I had seen in my 300 miles of the trail thus far.

As I continued hiking into the night, a glimmer of light appeared as I rounded a corner, instantly putting me on high alert. In that brief moment, I prepared to face whatever was before me: bear, mountain lion, alien that wants to steal my DNA to sell on the backside of the sun — it didn't matter. I was ready for battle. However, I quickly realized it was just the moon's reflection in a cow pond. My whole body was tense, and now I had to consciously calm it down because I would be going to bed soon.

The following day brought a drastic change in terrain as I descended the Mogollon Rim, leaving behind the pine tree canopy that had engulfed me for hundreds of miles. The trail itself transformed into a rocky and cumbersome path. I had been playing leapfrog with Randy, the biker I met, for the past few days, and when he passed me today, his mood had changed from the last time I saw him, as he now had to walk his bike for most of the day because it was too rocky to ride.

As I approached the road to Pine, AZ, it was already dark, making hitchhiking impossible. Deciding to take refuge in a bar a half-mile away, I ordered some food while figuring out my next move. Within minutes, I left my gear at the bar and embarked on a mile-long run to the grocery store, attempting to beat the closing time. Running along the highway at night, with cars turning on their brights to see what the hell was going on and some honking at me, led me to question if this was the best choice. It was another one of those moments where I thought, *What the hell am I doing?* But it was too late. I was already committed.

A twinge in my foot led to a resurgence of the previous day's excruciating pain, and I again worried it might be a stress fracture. Walking the rest of the way to the store, I berated myself for being reckless enough to run with an injured foot on pavement.

As I was ready to exit the store and painfully hobble a mile back to the bar, I swallowed my pride and asked people behind me at checkout for a ride. They were kind enough to oblige, and turned out to be fellow Ohioans.

The bar had a reputation for being welcoming to thru-hikers and graciously allowed me to camp on their beach volleyball courts. However, this unexpected camping spot came with unforeseen challenges. I had dealt with sandy spots before, but this was a full sand pit. After struggling to get my tent set up, but eventually doing so in a precarious manner, I realized the primary problem of the spot. There were dogs barking nearby. *No big deal.* I figured they would stop soon and go to sleep.

They barked incessantly all night long. They were still barking when I left in the morning after getting maybe three hours of sleep between their occasional gasps for breath.

I felt tired.

As I departed just before sunrise, the world lay before me in a dim light of obscurity. I returned to the road with blurry vision because I was still half-asleep wanting to be fully-asleep. In my haze of semi-awareness, I noticed some peculiar brown spots on the road. As my eyes adjusted, I saw six elk calmly standing there without a worry in the world, some sniffing the ground as if they were going to graze on the pavement. A few meandered away, but several remained, continuing to grace me with the entertainment of their company. Being present in the moment is something we should all strive to do more often, but being present and truly enjoying a moment is never easier than when some of the most majestic creatures on earth are mere yards away from you. Every worry in the world and every thought in my head dissipated, as I simply savored the unique experience.

Lost in this tranquil moment, my reverie was interrupted by an unexpected sight — a Cheetos truck hurtling toward the elk at 60 mph from the opposite direction. Normally, these elk try to avoid getting killed by mountain lions — now they were about to be smashed into a million pieces by a cheese-crazed cheetah. Envisioning the mushroom-cloud of orange cheese dust upon impact, I sprinted onto the road, jumping up and down and flailing my arms to get the driver's attention.

My spastic actions pierced through the veil of the dim morning glow, and the driver slowed down, allowing the elk to wander off the road. As the driver slowly passed by, we gave each other a nod of affirmation, acknowledging the teamwork of our efforts. I tried to do the same with the elk, but they just continued to obliviously look around. *Maybe they were dazed because they also didn't get any sleep the prior night because of the dogs.*

After earning my "save-the-lives-of-three-elk" merit badge, I entered the Mazatzal Wilderness and bypassed two water sources because I thought I'd have enough to make it 11 miles to a later one.

However, my journey took a detour when I turned onto an unmarked dirt road, and hiked several miles before I realized it. The road wasn't on my map, but I decided to take an adventure and go uncharted. *It's got to reconnect with the trail, right?*

That was a mistake.

After more than two hours of walking into the unknown, the dirt road ended at a dry cow pond with a 100-foot cliff below. I began bushwhacking in a straight line to a spot further up the trail because my brain didn't want me to go backwards at all costs. But after 30 minutes of getting cut, poked, and prodded by sharp desert plants, I sullenly trudged back to the dirt road and hiked to where I originally got off-route.

This was the angriest I'd been in a while. If I wasn't so stubborn, I would've accepted defeat sooner and saved a lot of time. However, this same stubbornness was also what allowed me to be able to hike 30 miles per day for days on end. It was a double-edged sword of capability and stupidity.

After wasting five hours wandering around the desert, dehydration set in. The warm day offered no shade, and my body began to feel the effects. By late afternoon, dizziness and tight leg muscles plagued me. In the evening, my walking motion had become completely uneven and inefficient because of how tight my legs were, but I had to do anything I could to keep moving. So I hobbled forward, awkward step after awkward step, breathing only through my nose and trying to only focus on my breathing to distract myself from how dehydrated I was.

Finally reaching a water source around 7 p.m., I greedily drank several liters without hesitation, overlooking the algae in the cow tank.

Feeling replenished, I hiked a few more miles to a spring, where the soothing sound of running water and croaking frogs became an unexpected lullaby in the midst of the Arizona desert.

In the morning, I woke up to melodic running water but didn't know the harmony of miseries that awaited me. The previous day sucked because I was dumb. The new day sucked because the trail was dumb.

The route involved a lot of climbing. I could deal with that. The real torment was how outlandishly rocky and overgrown the trail was. My progress slowed to a crawl as I tried to weave between plants that wanted to slice open my legs, and carefully maneuver each foot placement in this torturous obstacle course. The terrain was so rough that I couldn't find a comfortable step all day, and I began to suffer from swollen and stiff ankles. I didn't actually roll my ankle, but every rock littering the trail seemed to be the perfect size for rolling ankles. Each movement had to be controlled and slow to try to protect my feet, which were already killing me. That continual pressure mounted and manifested in two swollen ankles.

In the evening, my brain unconsciously turned on, and I had the realization, "THIS FUCKING SUCKS." After moving slow all day, I started to truly consider how brutal the terrain was. It was just as rocky as the worst parts of the AT, except this had the added agony of unavoidable sharp plants enveloping the trail. With as many sharp plants as there were, it was a struggle to move anywhere, even a few feet; I couldn't turn around, and I couldn't really move forward.

After entering the Mazatzal Wilderness the day prior, I started to question myself. When things went wrong earlier in the year, I was much better at laughing off terrible situations. Now I was succumbing to them more, and allowing myself to feel sorry for how miserable I was.

For the first time all year, *I began to question if I really wanted to be out there anymore*. It was the first time the possibility of quitting entered my mind. I knew it wasn't a good sign. Like my current location stuck between a maze of desert plants, I was trapped.

I'd come so far. I couldn't quit, but realistically, I didn't know if I could keep moving forward. Continuing on out of habit more than desire, I repeated my bad day mantra: *Tomorrow can only be better, because it has to be.*

I exited the Mazatzal Wilderness the next morning and wasn't sad to see it go. A local later told me its nickname was the "Mad as Hells" because of its irritable effect on hikers like me. But even after I left it behind, I couldn't get the thought of quitting out of my head. Maybe it wasn't necessarily the thought of quitting, but it was a decreasing desire to be out there, and the building of an extreme doubt that I would be able to finish the Buckeye Trail and hit 10,000 miles. The troubling doubt appeared to be more of a planted seed rather than a passing feeling.

After frustratingly taking a half-mile detour off trail to collect water for the first time in 20 hours, I met a thru-hiker heading north, which was unusual for this time of year. We met as I was coming out of the most toilsome part of the rocky area, so naturally, I was complaining about it.

To my dismay, he told me that the rocky trail continued all the way to Mexico. At first, disappointment settled in, but then a valuable lesson I had learned throughout my journey flashed through my mind — never blindly accept what other people say. My motto out here wasn't "trust but verify"; it was "distrust until verified." Everyone's experience on the trail was unique, and their perceptions colored by their own challenges and perspectives. Countless times this year, I had been warned or discouraged by others, only to find that their warnings were greatly exaggerated or outright incorrect. If I had learned anything by now, it was to not get worked up over negative comments other hikers said about upcoming areas — especially those headed in the opposite direction.

That same day, my wildlife encounters took a bit of a turn. Lately, I hadn't experienced much, other than seeing cows and getting eaten alive by tiny no-see-ums, leaving my body covered in itchy, red bites. I finally had a pleasant animal encounter, and even more rare, a new one. In fact, it was so new that I didn't even know what it was. I saw a raccoon-like creature with a long striped tail start to climb a tree alongside the trail. It saw me, and immediately froze halfway up the tree. I froze. We both stood still for 30 seconds. Then I pulled out my phone to start recording and took a few steps closer. It ran across the trail, and disappeared into the beige camouflage of the desert. Of course, I was curious as to what it was.

Once I got cell service, I learned it was a coatimundi, a rare desert creature. I was nearly 8,000 miles of hiking into the year, had lived outside for over 300 days, was on a trail I wasn't even expecting to hike at the beginning of the year, and now, I was seeing animals I didn't even know existed. We live in a big, crazy world, and there's always so much more to learn, see, and do, if we just leave ourselves open to it.

As I stated with my bad day mantra promising a better tomorrow, the next day brought a significant improvement over the challenges I faced the day before. My instincts about the hiker at the water source turned out to be accurate. The miserable, rocky terrain seemed to soften its grip on me. The universe had decided to grant me a reprieve from the unending, hellacious rocks that had plagued me lately.

When the daylight was transitioning to dusk, I was gifted with one of the most awe-inspiring sunsets I had ever witnessed. The desert's vast expanse served as a canvas for a breathtaking display of colors that painted the sky. It was as though nature itself was putting on a glorious show, reminding me of the immense beauty that surrounded me. The desert, with its harshness and unforgiving terrain, had a way of balancing it all out with moments of pure magic like this.

No matter how tough the day was, or how bad things were going, it was always a pleasure to watch the sky transform as I got to witness the physical passing of each day, knowing that the next morning would begin with the same beauty anew. It was a tangible representation of the day's trials coming to an end. Beauty or brutality, it all comes to an end.

Even on my terrible days in the Mazatzal Wilderness, the promise of a better tomorrow was encapsulated in those ethereal sunsets. Each evening brought closure to the day's struggles, paving the way for a fresh start the following morning.

The desert forced me to embrace the beauty of brutality and to find strength in the cyclical nature of life. The sunsets, with their captivating allure over the rugged desert, were a reminder that everything comes to an end. The day has the night. The trail has a terminus. And this journey would eventually end somewhere; but with every ending, there is also a new beginning. Every sunset is paired with a sunrise — we hope, at least.

I cherished these sunsets, not only for their sheer splendor, but for the calmness they instilled in me. It was hard to not feel constant anxiety about the extreme difficulty and improbability of me reaching my bonus goal. I tried to avoid thinking about it, but thoughts of doubt crept in frequently. Those thoughts seemed to dissolve as my eyes soaked in the aura of the setting sun. Now I could just smile upon the sunset, knowing that, more likely than not, I wouldn't finish my bonus goal for the year, but I could still be satisfied that there was a promise of a better tomorrow.

I don't know how far I'll go. Everything hurts. My feet feel like I should be taking Vicodin as vitamins. My back feels like I need OxyContin for breakfast. I'm eternally tired. I can't think of the last time I felt comfortable. I'm perpetually mentally exhausted. But — I'm going to see how far I can go, and I'm going to enjoy it while I can.

The joyousness took a brief pause the next day as I noticed a marble-sized swollen bite on my leg. This wasn't the no-see-ums. It must've been from a spider or something larger. By this point, I had some sizable holes in my tent that I hadn't repaired. The bugs were beginning to find the chinks in the armor — much like the trail was throwing enough agony at me that it was beginning to weaken my previously unflappable resolve.

As I entered the Superstition Wilderness, I saw real saguaro cacti for the first time. During all my time hiking through New Mexico, and doing day hikes in Arizona before this trip, I had never seen one. They were much bigger than I was expecting but also not as intimidating. Most of them didn't even have prickles and many had been scorched by fire.

I later passed the 500-mile marker on trail. I wasn't sure if it was because I already completed the Calendar Year Triple Crown, or because this was a shorter trail, but seeing these numbers had no emotional effect on me. The mileages on the CDT never really mattered because they were always wrong due to alternates, but 1,000 miles on the AT was one of the most gratifying triumphs of the year — the initial major milestone and affirmation of my capabilities. When I hit 2,000 miles on the PCT, it felt unbelievable because a few years earlier, when I heard first about these long trails, I thought walking 2,000 miles was insane and impossible. But when I hit 500 miles on the AZT, there was no satisfaction, no catharsis, nothing.

The next morning presented a less scenic section of the trail, as it kept me distanced from the nearby Gila River, navigating up and down little hills. While it was a far cry from the enchanting experience I had in New Mexico along the Gila, I was grateful for the more temperate conditions.

When I reached a road, there was a water spigot nearby for county workers, and it was spectacular — potable water, a shade tree, picnic table, and lawn chairs. It was the best oasis in the desert that I could've asked for. While I was relaxing for an hour, enjoying shade in the heat of the day, a guy pulled up and talked for a while. It turned out to be a blessing because he offered to take my trash, which unfortunately included my Oreos.

When I sat down for this break, I was hungry, ready to devour some sugar to fuel me for the rest of the day. As I pulled out my Oreos to delve into the delectable snack, I realized that they were infested with ants. *I guess everybody likes Oreos.* It was tough to part ways with my go-to mid-day snack, but I didn't mind the weight savings and ditching the parasitic freeloaders that were bold enough to steal my food while it was on my back.

After dark, I passed four more thru-hikers setting up camp. I didn't say much other than "Hi," but I was happy to be passing, if not meeting, more people. I enjoyed meeting other hikers and talking, but the more hikers I passed also meant the more likely water caches would still be stocked when I reached them — something I had hoped for after being severely dehydrated several times on this trail already.

As the morning array of pink, orange, and blue overtook the sky as the sun rose, I started the day by following buzzing power lines, spanning across the desert, until I took a wrong turn. After following a cow path for several minutes before it faded away, I bushwhacked, much more pleasantly than in the Mazatzals, back to the trail, and didn't waste too much time.

At a trailhead, there was a water cache and a shade shelter constructed of desert brush that was about as useful as an umbrella made of swiss cheese in a hurricane. With the gaps in the roof of the shelter, it provided no shade for most of the day, and only semi-useful shade for a short time in the morning or evening based on the sun's position. If I had burned all the brush used to construct the shelter, the smoke from the fire would have offered more protection from the sun than the nonsensical, objective-failing, aid-lacking, shade shelter.

My frustration with the shelter was amplified because the desert sun had been piling on my mounting miseries lately. In the afternoon, I found a tiny two-foot box of shade, laid down for a quick break, and ended up falling asleep for 20 minutes. Shade was a rare luxury, and I found myself dreaming about winter — something I never thought would happen after living through the wretched winter on the AT. The relentless heat drained my energy, leaving me feeling more exhausted than ever after each long day of hiking. It was a stark contrast to my initial delight with temperatures in the mid-80s — oh, how quickly the body adapts to new norms.

In the heat of the afternoon, I saw my first rattlesnake in Arizona. It was doing the same thing every rattlesnake did. I didn't understand why these idiots would perk up, and be ready to strike at my calf when I was ten feet away, but when I threw a rock right next to the vile serpents, they didn't flinch. We had a ten-minute standoff before I unsympathetically hit him with a rock, and he moved off the trail so I could breeze by. If anything could fuel me to keep moving when I didn't feel like doing so, it was to put as much space between myself and those devil creatures as possible.

While hiking that evening, I was on the phone with my parents, and my dad asked if I was tired — *what a stupid fucking question.* I woke up tired and went to bed exhausted every day. Everything in the middle was working towards the latter. It was an innocent question, but truly nobody else in the world could understand how tired I was. I could tell my family and friends how things were going, stories, and how I was feeling, and maybe they'd even try to imagine themselves in my shoes, but nobody, that hadn't walked 8,000+ miles in a year, could actually know how I felt.

With the recent seed of doubt planted in me, I wasn't even sure how I felt anymore. All year, I had been so singularly focused on success at the Calendar Year Triple Crown, the exhaustion was easier to justify because I knew I was working towards a goal I was going to achieve at all costs. Now with this more unattainable, bonus goal, it was becoming harder to know why I was killing myself every day, for something I would likely not achieve.

During another late night with extreme fatigue, I had my headlamp on and saw a pool of something up ahead. When I got close, I realized it was a pool of fresh cow diarrhea. *I could've gone without that.* I expected to have nightmares about the harrowing sight, but I was too tired to dream. As if this journey hadn't taken enough from me, now it took my dreams too.

When I arrived at camp, I was greeted by the only person that I had seen more than once the whole trail: Randy. Upon seeing my headlamp, he said, "That can only be one person: Horsepower." Bikers can cover ground much easier than hikers, so it was impressive, even to myself, that I was leapfrogging with him for this long.

I woke up promptly the next morning at 4:30 a.m. The benefit of camping near someone else was that it forced me to get up with my alarm, because I felt guilty about waking them up, too. The morning was frustrating, going up and over a hill, to then go back down into a wash, and repeat. There was a circular camp of RVs in one wash with nobody around. I strongly considered going over and taking some water since I was running low. The coolers of beer and soda also called to me, but my righteousness once again won out. My virtue was immediately rewarded with a surprise water cache, which I desperately needed.

The last few miles, before entering Oracle, AZ for a resupply, were brutal. I was getting roasted by the sun, and everything from my clothes to my phone felt hot. I was looking forward to sitting in some air conditioning in town. I couldn't believe how 85 degrees now felt so hot, when I had previously dealt with two straight weeks of 100+. Despite expecting significantly colder temperatures in Arizona in November, I wasn't sure if it had even dropped below freezing yet at night. The weather was supposed to cool down with highs in the 70s soon, and I was looking forward to it.

When I got into town, I bought some food, and spent a few hours recovering at a sports bar, pounding heaps of food and liters of Dr. Pepper. After a half-dozen refills, my waitress began giving me a side-eye and look of disgust with each repeating encounter.

Once I got back on trail, the caffeine was in full swing. I also had a full phone charge, so I was calling a bunch of my friends, and before I knew it, I had climbed over 3,000 feet and was laying down for the night.

The next morning, I climbed the remaining elevation to the top of Mount Lemmon. Reaching the summit, I found myself in the charming ski town of Summerhaven, AZ, where I unexpectedly crossed paths with a fellow hiker I had met back on the PCT in Southern California. Excitedly catching up with an old acquaintance, I ended up waiting for a pizza place in town to open, wasting far too much time.

Leaving town, I was a little chilly which was nice for a change. It was a blessing to have shade again. Mount Lemmon was the first of the unique ecosystems known as "sky islands" that I hiked through. These higher elevations offered a stark contrast to the desert below, boasting abundant vegetation, teeming wildlife, and a sense of life flourishing amidst the arid surroundings of nothingness.

During my descent from Mount Lemmon, an eerie encounter with an unkindness of ravens circling overhead stirred a sense of foreboding.

As I was hiking after dark, I noticed a pair of eyes 30 yards away at my 10 o'clock. At first, I thought it was a cow, like usual, but this time felt different. I stopped to stare at it, and as my eyes adjusted, I had a clearer view. From initially just seeing the eyes, I began to see the long, slender body stretching out behind them. I caught a glimpse of a slightly arched back and four powerful legs outstretched to the ground — not cow's legs.

Fully confident that this was no cow, but a mountain lion, my adrenaline started pumping. I had wanted to see a mountain lion all year, *but not like this*. I wanted to be 100 yards above it, on a steep ridge, and without it seeing me. Instead, it was in a narrow canyon, no more than 50 yards wide, and we both saw each other at the same time.

After I initially saw it and diagnosed what it was, we had a stare down for what felt like forever, but was probably five seconds in reality. All I was thinking was that I didn't have any weapons, so if it came down to it, I had to be ready. I had prepared for bear encounters more than mountain lion encounters, but I figured they'd have the same general guidelines.

First, I'm supposed to make myself big — *well, it's dark, and all it can probably see is my blinding headlamp.*

Second, I'm supposed to give it its space, so it can easily escape — *well, this is a narrow canyon without much room to run.*

Third, I'm supposed to hold my ground — *okay, well, that I can do.*

I got those basics down, but now I need a game plan for if it actually attacks.

Horsepower's Mountain Lion Attack Guide

1. Yell as loud, guttural, and caveman-like as possible

2. Throw trekking poles as it is approaching to deter it

    a. Throw poles separately, as the more objects flying at the animal, the higher likelihood of flight

    b. Do not bend over to pick up more objects to throw, as bending over makes you look smaller and can be seen as a sign of weakness, further making the animal believe you are prey

3. If projectiles fail to deter the mountain lion, and it is in immediate proximity to you, attempt to smash its head, notably its eyes, with a rock

4. If it makes contact with you, you will likely end up in a wrestling match on the ground. First and foremost, protect your head and neck from its powerful jaws

5. Gouge out its eyeballs

    a. If in the chaos of wrestling a mountain lion, you cannot get precise enough to gouge its eyeballs, a secondary option is to punch its nose. Although, it will likely be less effective.

6. Pray

Luckily, I didn't have to use the latter steps of the survival guide. After the five-second stare down, it darted away in a millisecond. I couldn't believe how fast it was with its first step.

Still, my heart pounded in my chest, and I couldn't shake the feeling of being watched. For the next three hours, I hiked cautiously, stopping every 30 seconds to scan my surroundings, fearing any unseen danger. I even talked out loud in a constant voice, not wanting to surprise the elusive predator again. I knew mountain lions were intelligent and skilled stalkers, so I thought it best to let it know where I was, hoping it would avoid me.

Throughout the night, paranoia gripped me, and every rustle of cottonwood leaves or glint of eyes in the darkness set me on edge. A couple of times, I glimpsed pairs of eyes staring back at me, but they disappeared quickly, leaving me uncertain of what lurked in the shadows.

Of course, all I could think about was that if I was writing a movie, being swarmed by ravens earlier in the day would be a sensible foreshadowing tool of some tragedy. After several hours, I hiked by a few different groups of tents, and my anxiety eased, allowing me to set up camp and go to sleep. *If it wanted an easier meal, I had already passed some.*

Early the next morning, I took a little side trip into a campground to appreciate a toilet and yogi some water. I asked the first campers I saw where the water spigot was. They said they didn't think there was one.

Responding "Okay" in a defeated tone, I began to slowly walk away.

Right on cue, they said, "Well, we have some if you need it." I was 99% sure there wasn't a water spigot there when I went in, but I gravely needed water, so I thought I'd try to summon my Yogi powers.

I entered Saguaro National Park, and commenced the 4,000-foot climb up to the sky island of Mount Mica in the afternoon. It looked intimidating on the map, but it was a gentle and steady climb. I was thankful to have a cloudy day and get some rare respite from the sun.

Some other hikers that I met camped on top of Mount Mica, but I pushed on a few more miles. Even in the desert, it was a little chilly up above 8,000 feet near the top of the mountain, so I was eager to descend for camp. Around 11 p.m., I began routinely stumbling and moving exceedingly slow. I knew it was time for bed and began counting sheep at 11:30 p.m.

After exiting the national park the following day, I was running on fumes into Vail, AZ. I knew I was low on food the previous day, but pride kept me from asking the other hikers I had just met for help. I had made it this far. I'd deal with it. Well, I did run out of food and was starting to feel uncomfortable. I wasn't to the point where the giant beetles on the ground looked appetizing, but I was approaching it. On the last half mile before I got to the trailhead, I befriended a group of hikers returning to their cars and got an immediate ride to town, where I inhaled two footlongs at Subway.

While in Vail, I realized I needed to pick up the pace to make the cheapest and most convenient flight after I finished. I ended up hiking until 1 a.m. and thought I would probably have to do about the same for the next couple of nights. I had just mentioned to the other hikers the day prior, that I did a good number of 18- and 20-hour days earlier in the year. I didn't know recalling those memories would foreshadow my immediate future.

After less than four hours of sleep, I was up and rolling again. The ticking clock didn't make it easier to get up when planned, but it made it more necessary. It also helped that with only a few days left, I wasn't too worried about my phone battery. I started bumping music right away to shake off my sleepiness, instead of instantly smashing my alarm and laying there until I fell asleep again.

During the final road walk into Patagonia, AZ, I picked up my pace, eager to get some food before restaurants closed. Luckily, I made it in time to grab some much-needed pizza. After sitting down for a few minutes, the manager approached me, and I knew what she was going to say before she even said it. I could tell she wanted to ask me to move outside because I smelled, but watching her stumble over her words for 60 seconds to try to avoid being rude was entertaining. She ended up going with, "It looks like you've been on the road for a while. Would you mind eating outside?"

I smiled and assured her I didn't mind. One of my goals for the year was to get kicked out of a buffet, so I guess this was a decent compromise.

Although I managed to get a full eight hours of sleep later that night, I still felt exhausted the next morning from pushing myself so hard throughout the entire Arizona Trail — but especially in the recent days. Mornings became increasingly challenging, but some Lil Wayne vocals got me out of my sleeping bag and back on my feet. As the afternoon sun beat down, I took a short break in the shade, only to unintentionally fall asleep for over an hour while lying in the dirt.

It was becoming clear that my body was ready to be done with this trail, and in need of some rest.

Despite the unignorable fatigue, that day turned out to be one of my favorites on the Arizona Trail. The scenery was breathtaking, reminiscent of a setting in a Cormac McCarthy novel, with a classic western landscape stretching out before me. However, it wasn't all sunshine and desert roses. I obliviously took a wrong turn onto an unmaintained jeep track that led me through a gauntlet of brutal plants with tiny barbs that dug into my skin. Removing those barbs was a painful ordeal, and watching my skin stretch like elastic as I pulled them out was sickening.

While hiking around 11 p.m., I nearly had a heart attack. I was walking when a blindingly bright light flashed to my side. A million thoughts went through my head in a second: everything from, somebody is flashing an old Polaroid camera at me, to somebody has Rick Dalton's flamethrower pointed at me. After I considered every feasible and unfeasible explanation, it turned out to just be a trail cam. I put my hands on my knees and panted for 30 seconds before I regained my composure enough to laugh about it.

Pushing forward after midnight, I reached the top of the 3,500-foot climb up to the ridge of Miller Peak. In the dark, I searched for a place to camp but found nothing. I had to hike an extra mile in my fatigued state and settle for a glaringly slanted spot amidst a pile of pine needles. It was my last night on the AZT and my standards were low. I made it work.

It was tough to wake up the next morning after getting four hours of sleep again, but it was the last hurrah. The terrain was overgrown in a lot of places; I was constantly getting scratched and having to move slower to avoid sharp plants.; and the sun seemed to be trying its best to barbecue me on my last day. But none of that really mattered. Plain and simple, that was the AZT, and there was only one thing on my mind: finish.

And finish I did. I arrived at Montezuma Pass in the early afternoon and had to end my hike there. The last two miles of trail were closed due to border wall construction. It wasn't the ideal ending, but I wasn't too upset.

Having already had a couple of touches with the Mexican border this year, I was okay with stopping two miles short of the third. And truth be told, I was ready to be done. I had just averaged over 33 miles per day for 24 straight days, after averaging 30 miles per day on the PCT and CDT, and 24 miles per day on the AT.

I felt tired.

What the hell did I get myself into? Why did I commit to this? It's already miserable, and it's only going to get worse. I don't even want to be out here.

WHY AM I DOING THIS?

The same thought that plagued my mind 11 months earlier on Springer Mountain had returned with reinforcements — bolstered beyond rebuke by that final question.

While thru-hiking, I always hated the question "Why?" Whether it be from non-hikers that asked why I would want to walk thousands of miles or from thru-hikers that asked why I would try to hike three trails and over 7,000 miles in one year, the question pinched the same annoying nerve. People ask this, but they don't want a real answer. They want a simple answer. "I'm doing this because I was born near the Appalachian Trail, and it's been a lifelong dream." "I'm doing this because it was my dad's dream, and he died before he was able to." "I'm doing this because I went through trauma and I'm decompressing." While those all can be reasons, none of them were mine, and I don't believe most people have a simple reason.

I wanted to hike the Calendar Year Triple Crown and more for a million reasons — and for a single reason at the same time. I wanted to see the beauty of nature. I wanted to see how far I could push myself physically. I wanted to meet a wide range of people from all over. I wanted to see how I would fare in some of America's most remote locations. I wanted to try to achieve an epic accomplishment and join an elite class of hikers. There were a million reasons like those. However, it really boiled down to one thing, and I believe it's the reason anybody does anything.

I did it because **I wanted to**.

Now I found myself limping around my home state, caught within its cruel winter grasp, questioning why I was making myself do something that I had no desire to do.

Just a week earlier, I finished the Arizona Trail, another outstanding accomplishment on top of an epic year. Despite my extreme physical fatigue, I was able to finish it in my worn-down state because I did **want** to do it. However, with each pounding step, my normal, inexhaustible drive seemed to wane. By the time I reached the end of the Arizona Trail, I wasn't even sure if it was a real or feigned desire to finish anymore.

I was relieved to have finished the Arizona Trail, but I was utterly exhausted. For as easy as the Arizona Trail should've been, given its elevation profile compared to the AT, and near-perfect weather, it kicked my ass. It wasn't because it was extremely difficult, or that anything went excessively wrong. I was just beaten down, mentally and physically.

My body was in rough shape all year, especially my feet. Those problems only escalated to previously unseen levels in Arizona. I had given up on the idea of my back ever being free of inconceivably tight muscles and pain. The single blister I had developed a few months earlier was only getting worse and was now a constant throb of pain in my foot. And my scares with stress fractures in my metatarsals were becoming more frequent.

More so than all that, my mental strength was wavering. I began to doubt myself for the first time all year in the Mazatzal Wilderness, and once that started, it grew like a cancer inside me. I kept pushing forward, still confident I'd finish the Arizona Trail, but with each passing day, I became less confident that I'd finish the Buckeye Trail and 10,000 miles. There hadn't been a seed of doubt about my Calendar Year Triple Crown goal all year, but once the seed of doubt was planted for the 10,000 miles, it wouldn't stop growing as it was nurtured by self-pity, mounting insecurity, and a lack of energy to fight it.

After finishing the AZT, I got a ride to the airport, but first stopped at a truck stop on the way for a much-needed shower. After I finished the AT, I wasn't able to shower before getting on the plane, but I didn't sweat much on the trail because of the temperature. The AZT was a different story — I thought I should shower for the sake of those around me.

I flew from Phoenix, AZ, to Fort Myers, FL. My family was taking a vacation the week of Thanksgiving with some friends. Finishing the AZT as soon as possible, so I could be with family and relax in Florida, was excellent motivation on trail. As I was struggling in the desert, dying of thirst, all I was thinking was that the faster I moved, the faster I could be sitting on the beach drinking Mai Tai's.

When I landed in Florida, my parents picked me up at the airport. I was still exhausted and groggy from having hardly slept. As I exited the plane, it was impossible to miss them even in the sea of people with faces half-covered in masks. My dad was sporting a Motley Crue shirt, as usual, and my mom was next to him with her bright blonde hair. My mom ran up and hugged me tighter than she ever had. After that long embrace, my dad and I expressed love as most men do towards each other — a single, brief, full embrace with one arm wrapped around the other's back, followed by several strong pats on the back. They were both crying, and I was confused. To me, it felt like any other time we said hello or goodbye. Then my half-functioning brain remembered this was our first time seeing each other in 11 months, since they dropped me off at Springer Mountain.

While the journey was unbelievably challenging for me, it was difficult for them too — not knowing much about thru-hiking, not knowing about the areas I was venturing into, often not knowing where I was, and only hearing from me every few days. I told them not to worry, but of course, they wouldn't listen. I didn't know what it was like to be a parent.

After a lot of catching up, I began to work on my plan for the week. I wanted to ice my feet several times per day. I wanted to scrub off the dead skin on my feet frequently with a pumice stone. I wanted to apply lotion to my feet constantly. And I wanted to be perpetually drunk while on vacation.

It was a good week, and most of my goals were achieved. However, as the week went on, the self-doubt continued to grow, even in the warmth of my family's love. My feet were not recovering as fast as I'd hoped, and after crunching the numbers, I couldn't help but be fearfully mesmerized at the insanity of their attainability.

I would have to average 40 miles a day in the remaining 47 days of my one-year time frame, ending January 13th. *That was alarming.* The Buckeye Trail would be much easier terrain, but averaging 40 miles a day for that long was crazy, even for me.

By the time I got back home to Ohio, the Saturday after Thanksgiving, I was doubting myself immensely. I had a big family Thanksgiving, and everyone was asking me when I was starting the Buckeye Trail and if I was ready. I repeatedly said, "Tomorrow" and "We'll see."

The truth was — I was not ready.

That became evident when I started the Buckeye Trail the next day around noon. My whole time on the AZT, and the week thereafter, when I was doubting myself about the Buckeye Trail, I tried to push it aside. I assured myself that once I got started, my mindset would shift, and I would be driven, just like the rest of the year.

I know this is crazy. I know this is gonna be tough. I know this is gonna hurt. But so has the whole year, and I made it this far. I'll just put my head down, get to work, and before I know it, I'll be done.

After I started, I did feel that potent drive once again… for 20 minutes. I was nervous and excited to start something new. I tried to focus on the positives of the Buckeye Trail. It was going to be inconceivably flat compared to the hiking I had done all year, and I would meet up with a lot of friends along the way. I tried to ignore the fact that the weather would be terrible, and that it would be boring for the most part — hiking on county roads in farm country, looking at rustic barns and barren fields under a perpetually gray sky in winter, just like I had been around all my life.

In my state of nervous excitement, I tried running early on, but my legs were so tight that I couldn't run. This journey had taken my ability to run! My body's revolt against my extreme physical activities had reached new heights. With the combination of the flat terrain and my extremely light pack, I had planned on running most of the Buckeye Trail.

With my whole game plan for success thrown out the window in the first half hour, sub-freezing temperatures cooling my engine, an ominous snow falling, and a blistering 40-mph wind smacking me across the face as it swept over the plains without encumbrance — my mind began to wander.

*What the hell did I get myself into? Why did I commit to this? It's already miserable, and it's only going to get worse. I don't even **want** to be out here.*

WHY AM I DOING THIS?

These negative thoughts played on a loop in my head for the next six hours. There wasn't an ounce of positivity in my body. All I could think about was how badly I wanted to be done, how much I didn't want to be here, how much I would rather be doing anything else.

After hiking in the dark past 6 p.m., I shuffled into the town of Wakeman, OH. It had been less than six hours, and I had gone 18 miles, but it was already pitch black. I realized that the misery and negativity I felt during the day was nothing compared to what it would grow to be. To reach 10,000 miles in my time frame, I was going to have to hike in the dark for eight hours every night on the Buckeye Trail. Hiking that much in the dark would only amplify the borderline unbearable anguish I was already feeling.

The innate implausibility and insane improbability of my bonus goal finally overcame the stubbornness of my bullheaded commitment to its possibility. With the willful acceptance of this, a calmness came over me.

I declared my year of adventure over and walked into a pizza place.

Epilogue

It was an odd feeling.

My mindset was simply "Go" for so long, that it felt weird to finally stop. When I set my bonus goal for 10,000 miles, I chose to do it because it was just crazy enough, just difficult enough, and just impossible enough.

In my research for the Calendar Year Triple Crown, I came across many people who were discouraging those who wanted to attempt the Calendar Year Triple Crown without any previous thru-hiking experience — like me. Many labeled it "impossible."

I thought it then, and I think it now — that is comical.

I love that word "impossible." Perception is reality. *For a person that labels something impossible, it probably is.* For someone that has an open mind and is willing to do anything to transform their goal into an achievement, impossible is nothing.

Without ever thru-hiking before, I did the impossible and earned the title of "Calendar Year Triple Crowner." Although I didn't finish 10,000 miles in a year, one person had done it before, and I'm sure somebody will do it again. Just like when someone on trail said a section was "impassable," it was the same way I view someone saying something is "impossible."

If someone is driven enough, it simply is not.

One of the main reasons I wanted to try for 10,000 miles was because I knew there was a good chance I would probably fail. Failure of a major goal was something I had not felt in a long time. Although I had racked up some good accomplishments in my 24 years of life, I didn't want to keep stringing together wins with no reminders of how much failure hurt. I wanted to be reminded of what it felt like to get punched in the gut by failure. I knew that, regardless of the result, going for 10,000 miles would be empowering. Either I would complete it, and it would be an epic accomplishment, even more so than the already-insane Calendar Year Triple Crown, or I would fail, and it would be a valuable reminder of what that pain felt like. I knew that failure was a real possibility when I set the new goal, and that part of me **wanted** to feel it.

But it still hurt. Even after hiking 8,292 miles in 2021, failing to hit 10,000 miles left a bit of a hollow feeling in my gut. Reaching an agreeable level of emotional comfort with the concept of failure seems to be a vastly unexplored territory of the human condition.

When I quit the Buckeye Trail, it felt strange. I was feeling a little bit of everything. I felt happy. I felt sorrowful. I felt glad to be done. I felt sad that I quit. I felt proud of my incredible achievement. I felt disappointed that I didn't finish my crazier goal. I felt excited to go home and see my friends and family. I felt uneasy because I had to determine what I would do next with my life. I felt smarter than ever because I had learned enough about myself in this single year to cover a lifetime. I felt more clueless than ever because it was the first time in my life that I didn't have a clear path of what I was going to do next. The sun had set on this journey, and for the first time in a long time, I had no idea what tomorrow had in store.

Even with all of these complex, conflicting, and confusing feelings culminating, there was one undeniable feeling that stood out above the rest, and it had been standing out all year.

I felt alive.